Society and Social Science:
A Reader

Editorial Group

James Anderson   *Senior Lecturer in Geography at the Open University and Chair of the Open University's Social Science Foundation Course, D103*
Marilyn Ricci   *Course Manager of D103*
Stuart Hall   *Professor of Sociology at the Open University*
Vivienne Brown   *Lecturer in Economics at the Open University*
Richard Maidment   *Lecturer in Political Science at the Open University*
Margaret Wetherell   *Lecturer in Psychology at the Open University*
John Allen   *Lecturer in Geography at the Open University*
David Coates   *Senior Lecturer in Politics, University of Leeds*
David Wilson   *Editor, Open University Publishing Division*

This Reader was compiled for the Open University's introductory Social Science course (D103: Society and Social Science: A Foundation Course). The Editorial Group is grateful for the assistance of other members of the D103 Course Team who helped to select and prepare extracts from books and articles for inclusion in this Reader. We are also grateful to Linda Clark, D103 Course Team Secretary for helping to prepare the manuscript.

As one part of an Open University course, this Reader is related to other material available to students (which is described in the Appendix at the end of this book). It is designed to evoke the critical understanding of students. Opinions expressed in it are not necessarily those of the Course Team or of the University. If you are interested in extending your studies with any of the D103 course components, you should write, enquiring about availability, to: Open University Educational Enterprises Limited, 12 Cofferidge Close, Stony Stratford, Milton Keynes MK11 1BY, United Kingdom.

Society and Social Science:
A Reader

Edited by
James Anderson and Marilyn Ricci
at the Open University

The Open University (Book Trade Department), Walton Hall, Milton Keynes MK7 6AB

First published 1990, reprinted 1991

British Library Cataloguing in Publication Data
Society and social science: a reader.
1. Social sciences
I. Anderson, James II. Ricci, Marilyn
300

ISBN 0 7492 0061 8
ISBN 0 7492 0046 4 pbk

Designed by the Graphic Design Group of the Open University
Typeset by Medcalf Type Ltd, Bicester, Oxon
Printed and bound in Great Britain by Mackays of Chatham plc, Chatham, Kent

Contents

Acknowledgements

Grateful acknowledgement is made to the following sources for permission to reproduce material in this reader:

Text
P. Raikes, 'Food shortages and famine: how do they occur, where and to whom?' from *Modernizing Hunger*, 1988, James Currey/Catholic Institute of International Relations copyright © Philip Raikes; N. Charles and M. Kerr, 'Just the way it is', an extract taken from *Give and Take in Families*, edited by M.J. Brannen and G. Wilson, copyright © J. Brannen and G. Wilson 1987, reproduced by kind permission of Unwin Hyman Ltd; Extracts from *Inequalities in Health* Penguin Books, 1988, M. Whitehead, 'The health divide', copyright © Margaret Whitehead 1988, reprinted by permission of Penguin Books and 'The Black report', Sir Douglas Black *et al.*, Crown copyright, reproduced by permission of the Controller of HMSO; J. Nicholson, 'Men and women', reprinted from *Men and Women: How Different Are They?* John Nicholson 1984, by permission of Oxford Univesity Press, copyright © John Nicholson 1984; R. Miles, 'Representations of race', in *Racism*, Routledge, 1989; A. Warde, 'The future of work', in *Social Studies Review*, vol. 5, no. 1, September 1989, Philip Allan Publishers Ltd; J.A. Kay, 'Myths and realities', in *1992: Myths and Realities*, Evan Davis *et al.*, Centre for Business Strategy Report Series, London Business School; A. Aganbegyan, 'Plan and Market', in *The Challenge: Economics of Perestroika* Michael Barratt-Brown (ed.), Hutchinson Education, 1988, reproduced by permission of I. B. Taurus and Co. Ltd; N. Crafts, 'The assessment: British economic growth over the long run', in *Oxford Review of Economic Policy*, vol. 4, no. 1, 1988, reprinted by permission of Oxford University Press; B. Stafford, 'Theories of decline', in *The Economic Decline of Modern Britain*, D. Coates and J. Hillard (eds.) Merlin Press, 1983, reprinted by permission of Merlin Press; S. Lukes, *Power: A Radical View*, 1974, extract reprinted by permission of Macmillan, London and Basingstoke/Peters Fraser & Dunlop Group Ltd; A. Carter, *Politics of Women's Rights*, 1988, copyright © Longman Group UK Limited, extracts reprinted with permission; J. Dearlove and P. Saunders, *Introduction to British Politics*, 1988, Polity Press, extract reprinted by permission of Basil Blackwell; Daniel J. Levinson *et al.*, *The Seasons of a Man's Life*, copyright © 1978 by Daniel J. Levinson, reprinted by permission of Alfred A. Knopf Inc/The Sterling Lord Agency; A. Coyle, *Redundant Women*, 1984, The Women's Press Ltd, London; C. Husband (ed.) *Race in Britain: Continuity and Change*,

Figures
Figure 1.1: data from *New Cambridge Modern History*, Atlas, Vol. 14, 1970, Cambridge University Press; *Figure 1.3:* from T. Marsden, *Exploring the Key Dynamics of Capitalist Food Systems*, Urban Change and Conflict Conference 1989, University of Bristol; *Figure 1.6:* from W.W. Rostow, *The World Economy: History and Prospect*, 1978, Macmillan, London and Basingstoke.

General Introduction

James Anderson and Marilyn Ricci

This Reader is an introduction to the study of society and social science. It focuses on society in the United Kingdom together with its wider international and historical context. Part 1 is a collection of readings which cover social divisions, economic and political processes, group and individual identities and the character of different regions of the UK. Part 2 consists of an essay on four traditions of thought in western society – liberalism, marxism, social reformism and conservatism – which have had important, though uneven, influences on social science. Compiled and written for the Open University's introductory social science course (see the Appendix for futher details), the Reader has also been designed to meet the needs of a wider readership. It deals with social issues of relevance to anyone studying different branches of the social sciences and others who take a lively interest in the world around them. It has two main strands – aspects of UK society and the nature of social science.

United Kingdom society

To understand UK society in the 1990s we need to know something of its history and international setting. What are the main processes which have contributed to the making of the modern UK? How has it been affected by its early experience of industrialization and empire and by the subsequent loss both of empire and industrial pre-eminence? How has it been shaped by more recent changes in its European and wider world context or by the rise of multinational corporations? What are the implications of internal conflicts between the different classes, groups and nations which make up UK society? What does it mean to be 'British' in a multicultural society where the 'internationalization' of politics and culture have blurred traditional ideas about national sovereignty and identity? These are just some of the questions which the articles in this Reader address.

Chapter 1 sketches in some preliminary answers. Like the final chapter on traditions of thought, it was written specially for the Reader and gives a broad overview of the UK's historical legacy from pre-industrial times as a basis for better understanding the present (see Section 1 Introduction). It provides a background for the more detailed material in Sections 2 to 6.

These sections build up a more rounded picture of contemporary UK sociey and its wider context. They progress from examining social divisions and the economic processes at work in society (Sections 2 and 3) to addressing questions

1

of political power and how the problems which arise in society are controlled (and sometimes exacerbated) by political institutions and processes (Section 4). The identities and interactions between individuals and groups, and how people's personal and group experiences are influenced by the social, economic and political structures of society are then discussed (Section 5). How these structures and identities shape, and are shaped by, the character of different regions in the UK, their changing relationships to each other and to the international system, is the focus of Section 6. That is the 'logic' or sequence of the approach to UK society.

Introducing the concern with **The Divisions of Society** in Section 2, Chapter 4 follows the material on food by dealing with another (and related) 'real-world' problem – health. Inequalities in people's health in the UK can be explained in terms of their behaviour and cultural environment, but they are crucially related to their socio-economic circumstances, particularly their occupations. Biology is also involved but it cannot account for the significant health differences of different social groups. More controversially, biological factors have often been given as explanations of social differences between men and women and between different ethnic groups. This approach is challenged in Chapters 5 and 6. Chapter 5 discusses biological differences between male and female and argues that they are not as great as is often supposed and cannot explain *social* differences associated with gender. Chapter 6 traces the historical development of the ways in which different 'races' have been represented, particularly by white Europeans and North Americans. In the nineteenth century, some scientists gave credence to the view that there was a hierarchy of superior and inferior races, with white people innately 'superior', though the Irish and Jews were sometimes assigned 'inferior' status through not belonging to the so-called 'Nordic race'. Such views are now scientifically discredited, but they entered popular culture in the UK and surface nowadays in some of the hostility shown towards immigrants and their descendants.

One of the principal concerns of Section 3 – **Work, Markets and the Economy** – is the long-running problem that economic growth rates in the UK have been relatively low compared with those in other western economies. The section focuses on factors influencing economic growth, and also the organization of production and how markets operate. Chapter 7 investigates changes in the way in which work processes are organized and suggests that these changes are due to a variety of causes rather than one common cause (i.e. post-Fordism) as some writers have suggested. Chapter 8 challenges the conventional view that the main advantages of a single European market will be the possibilities of large-scale 'Euro-production'. It will be interesting to see how things actually turn out. The same can be said of *perestroika*; Chapter 9 gives a view, by a supporter of *perestroika*, of the way markets should operate in combination with state planning and regulation in the Soviet Union. Chapter 10 examines factors influencing UK economic performance in the post-war period; and Chapter 11 investigates different marxist explanations of relative decline which concentrate on differences between the financial and industrial sectors or, alternatively, on conflicts between labour and capital.

Social divisions and economic problems lead on to questions of **Politics and**

2

Power, in Section 4. Political institutions, most notably the state, manage social and economic problems and political movements are organized around them. But who rules, who governs, and what is the nature of power? Chapter 12 gives one answer to this question, partly through a criticism of other answers. It argues that power is exercised in various forms in society rather than being confined to political institutions only. Chapter 13 deals with equal opportunities legislation which is designed to counter the discrimination (e.g. in the job market) which is experienced by various social groupings (such as, the disabled, ethnic minorities, and women). It looks at two pieces of legislation in the 1970s which outlawed some forms of gender discrimination (The Equal Pay Act and The Sex Discrimination Act) and examines the different processes and political climates in which these Acts eventually got on to the Statute-book. The third chapter in this section looks at British politics more generally in the context of the tensions between democracy and a capitalist economy. It questions the extent to which the UK really is democratic.

The basic social, economic and political structures of the society in which we have been brought up, or where we live and work, strongly influence our individual and group indentities. But how do we relate to each other within these larger structures? To deal with the larger structures only would miss out the richness and detail of people's lives, how they themselves see society and their own positions within it. Section 5, **Identities and Interaction**, looks at UK society at this level of analysis – people's feelings, their biological and human nature, and the organization of their social interactions. The varied readings include autobiographical accounts by a working-class woman in Yorkshire, a middle-class man from the West Indies, and a young disabled woman, as well as writings by psychologists and other social scientists who adopt various approaches. Some writers, as in Chapter 15, stress the biological basis of human behaviour, returning to one of the concerns of Section 2. This approach, however, is seriously challenged in Chapters 16 and 17, which suggest that people's behaviour is extremely flexible and is heavily dependent on such factors as socio-economic position, personal circumstances and cultural differences. Chapter 18 focuses on therapy for social relationships 'gone wrong' and a particular socio-psychological approach to helping people manage their lives. The readings in this section exemplify some of the variety of methods and types of evidence used in social science.

To complete and round out the picture of UK society, Section 6 – **Localities and Social Change** – looks at internal and international forces which have shaped and reshaped different regions. Understanding the character of particular localities (your own home area for example) involves taking into account the concerns exemplified in all the previous sections, including identities which are specific to the regions. The geographical arrangement of social divisions, economic structures and political institutions affects the way society develops – geographical space is an active ingredient in social processes, not just a backcloth to them. But which space? All social activities occur and have particular locations in space, but the spatial scope and the significance of geographical location varies for different activities. Some operate at a more local level, others are countrywide,

3

continental or even worldwide, and there is a complex and shifting interplay between the different levels. The changing character of regions in Britain is discussed in Chapter 19 in terms of social processes which are simultaneously local and global in nature (returning in more detail to the interaction of internal and external factors which was first raised in Chapter 1).

Different localities – Swindon and Teesside, the subjects of Chapters 20 and 21 – have been affected very differently by the continued growth of multinational corporations, the new prominence of high technology and service industries, and the UK's relative economic decline. While Teesside experienced decline, Swindon had almost the reverse experience of going from slump to boom, but the factors involved and their effects are social, cultural and political as well as economic. In Swindon, for example, older working-class traditions were partly undermined by a new 'enterprise culture' and an influx of higher income people, and this resulted in new political alignments in the area. Teesside also experienced some undermining of traditional cultural patterns but this was due to people having to leave the area in search of work. For the remaining population, the local society and local politics have changed less than in Swindon. The contrasting patterns result from some of the same global trends being played out very differently at a local level. In varying combinations the same or similar patterns have characterized other parts of the UK.

The nature of social science

The second strand of this Reader – the nature of social science – is woven into the depiction of the UK in Part 1, and it is the primary focus of Chapter 22, the essay on traditions of social thought in Part 2. In Part 1 you will see that social science is practised both on a discipline and an interdisciplinary basis. Sections 2 to 6 exemplify some of the concerns of Sociology, Economics, Political Science, Psychology and Geography, respectively. However, the overlaps in the topics also point to the importance of a broad interdisciplinary approach in social science. Most of the really interesting questions about society cannot adequately be answered within the confines of a single discipline. Problems in the real world – such as those associated with food and famine – do not come neatly parcelled in discipline packages. Part 1 also demonstrates that social science operates at different levels of analysis (the levels of the individual, the group or larger social structures, as well as those that vary in geographical and historical scope); and that it is characterized by theoretical disagreements, sometimes within the same fundamental framework (e.g. marxism in the case of Chapter 11 on theories of economic decline). But social science is also characterized by a common body of methods and procedures which to a significant degree are shared by all the disciplines, and by those who adopt different explanatory frameworks. Like other people in society, social scientists may fundamentally disagree about some social issues but, in general, they share common ways of doing research and of constructing and assessing explanations.

They have to be precise about how they define the issues and about the concepts they use to analyse them. They have to test their theories and assumptions against various types of evidence (whether these are official statistics, or the results of a survey as in Chapter 3, or autobiographical accounts as in Chapter 16); and they have to be careful about how they interpret the evidence and about its reliability – all things which other people in society sometimes do not have the time, inclination or training to do.

Modern society needs social science – its specialized knowledge and procedures of analysis, its policy-related research, and its open-ended exploration of social issues. It is both a critical commentary on society and an intellectual activity which helps to mould the ways in which society functions and develops. However it only emerged in its present institutionalized form during the late nineteenth century and, as with understanding UK society, we have to look to the legacies of the past to appreciate its contemporary nature.

The development of industrial capitalism, and the social problems and possibilities it engendered (*see* Chapter 1), called for more detailed and reliable information about society, whether it was to make the economy more efficient, control social conflicts or improve people's living conditions. In the nineteenth century there was a big increase in various types of social research with, for example, a mushrooming of amateur 'statistical societies'. Much of this activity happened outside the universities which continued to be dominated by the study of theology, law, history and the classics. However, towards the end of the nineteenth century, society's need for people trained in social analysis increased, and researchers sought more in-depth knowledge. In consequence, specialization increased and the different disciplines separated from what had previously been the general field of moral and political philosophy. The social science disciplines became institutionalized in university departments and faculties.

The disciplines however continue to be influenced by ideas from moral and political philosophy which pre-date modern social science; and the most influential parts of this legacy are embodied in the four traditions of social thought described in Chapter 22. This essay presents liberalism, marxism, social reformism, and conservatism as 'grand theories' or general conceptions of society. They exist in society independently of social science but social scientists draw on them as explanatory frameworks. The traditions have influenced all the disciplines, though unevenly, and some parts of social science are now more directly affected than others.

These 'grand theories' embody a range of different ideas and assumptions about the way society is structured into groups and classes, about relationships between the economy and the state, and about human nature and the role of individuals. Specific theories and explanations in the various areas discussed in Part 1 have connections with or have been influenced by the 'grand theories'. Chapter 22 has been designed to be read in easy stages: its long second section describes each of the four traditions in turn, and this is followed by shorter sections on their influences on the disciplines, and their manifestations in contemporary society – in political parties and movements, and in popular culture and everyday thinking. For social science, the traditions are thus of interest, in the first place as intellectual systems of thought which shape social science, and secondly as

5

forces on society which social science studies. The existence of different traditions reminds us that there is rarely one uncontested version of 'the truth' where social issues are concerned. It is this above all else which makes social science relevant and interesting. While it cannot escape the fact that there are different conceptions of society and of particular issues, it provides a basis for making informed choices between them.

PART 1

ASPECTS OF THE UNITED KINGDOM IN CONTEXT

SECTION 1

Food for Thought

Introduction

Width of scope and diversity of levels are hallmarks of social science. It ranges from details of personal and family life to social developments at a world level. To understand contemporary society it moves outwards in geographic space and back in historical time, and also down to the details of particular social situations and processes. Some of this scope and diversity is reflected in the three chapters in this introductory section. They provide 'food for thought' about the UK's development, the global causes of 'Third World' famine, and the inequalities of food consumption within British families. Food consumption is something to which we can all relate, and it raises questions regarding the society and world we live in.

Chapter 1 provides a historical perspective on the United Kingdom and its changed international standing. It traces, in broad outline, the internal developments and the growth of empire which suggest why the Industrial Revolution started in Britain and why in a hundred years the UK had become the world's leading political power. It traces subsequent developments and relative international decline, and it suggests how UK society has been shaped by its historical legacy. The text and figures provide background context for material in Sections 2 to 6, and the 'Notes and References' at the end of the chapter fill out some of the detail. The diverse selection of dates in Tables 1.1. and 1.2 provide a broad chronological framework for understanding aspects of the UK's development which you will be studying later.

The other two chapters in this 'Food for Thought' section deal with social and historical factors behind the unequal distribution of food. Although obviously of crucial importance, food has not been chosen as a topic for its own sake however. It has been chosen as a means of examining social processes at different levels, within UK households and at an international level. In Chapter 2 Philip Raikes outlines how the complex intertwining of the history of Africa and Europe, particularly the UK, helps explain contemporary famines in Africa. He identifies two significant historical processes which have had a detrimental effect on Africa's food production – colonialism and the move towards commodity production. He argues that these two processes, in which the UK played a key role, still have a negative effect on the lives of African people today – particularly on the lives of women and children. Their work load, for instance, has increased as commercial deforestation forces them to make longer trips for firewood. Drawing on the work of A.K. Sen, Raikes also argues that there is no simple relation between the severity of a famine and local harvest failures: a variety of factors both historical

9

and contemporary have to be taken into account. Complacent views that famines in Africa are caused simply by local factors or natural disasters and have 'nothing to do with' the UK, are seriously challenged in this piece. We are reminded that food and access to it are intimately tied in with both long- and short-term global processes.

Food consumption within UK households is the subject of Chapter 3. Any idea that food is distributed equally among household members is 'misguided to say the least', according to the authors, Nicola Charles and Marion Kerr. In their study of 200 households, unequal relations of power flowing mainly from gender and age differences seemed crucial in determining the amounts and types of food different household members received. Moreover, and usually related to age and gender differences, the roles that members played outside the home were translated into power within the home. Thus men who were the main breadwinners tended to consume most of the foods ranked by those taking part in the study as 'high status' (e.g. meat such as steak), and they literally got 'the biggest slice of the cake'. Conversely, in unemployed households whatever limited amount of meat was available was shared more equally between different members. Women generally tended to consume less 'high status' foods than men, though more than children who often consumed what was thought of as 'children's food' (e.g. fish fingers). The chapter suggests that roles within the 'public' world of paid work, and important social divisions such as gender and age, deeply affect and impinge upon people's access to food in what we think of as the 'private' world of the home.

James Anderson and Marilyn Ricci

CHAPTER 1

The United Kingdom: Legacies of the Past

James Anderson

Two hundred years ago, in the 1790s, Britain was in the process of becoming the world's first industrialized country. It became, for a time, 'the workshop of the world'. In the 1890s, as the centre of an empire on which 'the sun never set', the United Kingdom was still the world's leading political power. Now, in contrast, it is a middle-ranking European state which in recent years has imported more manufactured goods than it has exported. However, the epoch of empire and industrial revolution has had a lasting influence on the UK. Despite all the subsequent changes, this legacy continues to affect contemporary issues and attitudes.

To appreciate the UK's rich mosaic of different regions, cultures and identities, we need to be aware of the impact of the past on the present. To understand its political or economic problems, we need to understand the interplay between developments at home and changes abroad. It is a complex story of continuity and change, but in this essay we have space for only a 'thumbnail' sketch.[1]* A selection of important dates in British history up to 1900 is given in Table 1.1. overleaf; dates since 1900 are given later in Table 1.2.

Before industrialization

Even before the Industrial Revolution, which started around the 1760s, Britain was already a world power. The kingdom of England had, through diplomacy and military conquest, united the separate kingdoms of Scotland and Ireland, and the principality of Wales, into a unified state ruled from London. Its rule was periodically threatened by rebellions in Ireland and Scotland (e.g. in 1688–89, 1715 and 1745), and it would continue to be contested, especially by Irish nationalists whose first bid for independent statehood occurred in 1798. But by the eighteenth century the UK state was already in place.

The English Revolution of the 1640s and the Glorious Revolution of 1688 had established a constitutional monarchy. This contrasted with the absolutist monarchies based on 'the divine right of kings' which still dominated much of continental Europe. Political power in the UK had been largely transferred to parliament. Until the nineteenth century, however, it was a very limited form

* See Notes at the end of this chapter.

Source: article commissioned for this Reader.

Table 1.1   Selected dates up to 1900

1534	Henry VIII asserts control over the English Church, confiscating much of its lands and properties – the Dissolution of the Monasteries (1536–39).
1536	Wales integrated into Kingdom of England; Welsh-speakers banned from public office.
1542	Henry VIII proclaims himself King of Ireland.
1560	Scottish National Church established (the state church from 1567) – Calvinistic Protestantism led by John Knox.
1588	The Bible translated into Welsh, helping to preserve the Welsh language (particularly with the non-conformist religious revival of the 18th century).
1600	East India Company established.
1603	Union of Scottish and English crowns: James Stuart, King James VI of Scotland, becomes James I of 'Great Britain'. Irish rebellion ends with conquest of Gaelic Ulster.
1607	'The Flight of the (Gaelic) Earls' leads to the Plantation of Ulster with Scottish and English settlers. The founding of Jamestown consolidated the North American English colony of Virginia.
1620	English Puritans – the Pilgrim Fathers sailing in the 'Mayflower' – establish the New England colony of Massachusetts.
1642–8	The English Civil Wars lead to the execution of Charles I (1649), the establishment of a republic in England and Wales (the Commonwealth), and Cromwell's control over Ireland and Scotland by 1651.
1652–4	First Anglo–Dutch War (others in 1665–7 and 1672–4).
1655	Britain captures Jamaica from Spain.
1660	Restoration of the monarchy. Charles II marries Portuguese princess whose dowry includes Bombay (1661).
1667	New Amsterdam acquired from the Dutch and becomes New York.
1688	The Glorious Revolution – Protestant William of Orange replaces Catholic James II, firmly establishing consitutional monarchy with the defeat of James at the Battle of the Boyne (1690).
1690	John Locke publishes his *Treatises on Government*, important in the development of liberalism.
1694	The Bank of England established.
1695	Legal freedom of the press achieved in England.
1707	Union of Scotland and England, with single parliament for Great Britain at Westminster.
1715 & 1745	Jacobite uprisings in Scotland attempt to restore French-allied Stuart dynasty to the British throne.
1756–63	Seven Years' War with France, including victories by Clive in India (1757) and Wolfe in Quebec (1759).
1760	Lloyd's Register of Shipping established – Lloyds had developed as the main centre for maritime trade and insurance from its beginnings in Lloyd's coffee house in the City of London in the late 17th century.
1760–90	Beginning of the Industrial Revolution in Britain, particularly the development of the factory system for cotton spinning around Manchester, the building of a canal network for industrial transport, and the war-related growth of iron industries in areas such as South Wales.
1776	The United States of America declare their independence from Britain. Adam Smith publishes *The Wealth of Nations*, a cornerstone of liberal economics.
1789	The French Revolution begins.
1790	Edmund Burke publishes a criticism, *Reflections on the Revolution in France*,

a key text in conservative thought; Thomas Paine replies with *The Rights of Man*, 1792.

1791	Wolfe Tone and Ulster Presbyterians found The Society of United Irishmen in Belfast, to gain full political independence from Britain. Opposed by the Orange Order (established 1795), they are militarily defeated (1798), despite belated help from revolutionary France which is at war with Britain (from 1793).
1801	Irish parliament abolished and the United Kingdom of Great Britain and Ireland established.
1805	Battle of Trafalgar secures Britain's naval supremacy.
1807	Abolition of the British slave trade.
1815	Battle of Waterloo confirms Britain's dominance among European powers in the 19th century.
1819	The Peterloo Massacre – peaceful Manchester meeting for parliamentary reform dispersed by military means.
1824	Repeal of Combination Acts permits trade unions.
1825	Opening of the Stockton–Darlington railway heralds the age of railway building.
1829	Catholic Emancipation – the removal of voting and public office restrictions on Catholics.
1832	The First Reform Act – extension of voting rights to middle-class males.
1834	The Tolpuddle Martyrs – agrarian trade unionists – deported to Australia.
1837	Victorian era begins (ends 1901).
1838	The Chartists, an early political movement of workers, demand voting rights for all men.
1841	Hong Kong gained from China after the Opium Wars.
1842	The first general strike by workers attempted by the Chartists. In Wales the agrarian Rebecca Riots against 'alien' (English or anglicized) landlords.
1844	Frederick Engels writes *The Condition of the Working Class in England*. The Rochdale Pioneers found the co-operative movement.
1845–7	The Great Famine in Ireland.
1846	Repeal of the Corn Laws – a victory for free trade when import duties on food largely abolished.
1847	The British Museum in London opened.
1848	Revolutionary uprisings in various European countries, including the Young Ireland rebellion against British rule. Karl Marx and Frederick Engels publish *The Communist Manifesto*.
1851	The Great Exhibition of the UK's industrial and commercial supremacy.
1854–6	Crimean War – the UK and France invade Russia.
1857–8	The Indian Mutiny, and the East India Company superceded by direct rule of India by the British Government.
1867	The Second Reform act further extends voting rights, mainly to skilled male workers. Marx publishes the first volume of *Capital*.
1868	The Trades Union Congress established by skilled workers.
1870	The Education Act introduces general elementary education for almost all children (in 1880, school attendance made compulsory for children aged 5 to 10 years).
1871	The first Football Association Cup competition – 15 teams enter.
1873	Lawn Tennis invented.
1875	Legalization of industrial action by trade unions. The UK purchases the Suez Canal.

1877	Queen Victoria assumes the title 'Empress of India'.
1882	The Married Women's Property Act gives them legal right to own separately property of all kinds.
1884	The extension of voting rights to virtually all adult males. At the Congress of Berlin the main European powers divide up large parts of Africa between themselves.
1886	The UK Liberal Government of Gladstone defeated after attempting to grant Home Rule to Ireland. May Day becomes international workers' day after a strike in Chicago for the eight hour working day.
1888	The English Football League established by 12 football clubs. Women workers – the 'Matchgirls' – strike at Bryant and May's factory in east London – leads to:
1889	The London Dock Strike which furthers the unionization of less skilled workers and the politicization of trade unions. The Scottish Labour Party established.
1890	The Housing of the Working Classes Act gives local authorities the power to build council housing if they so wish.
1892	Keir Hardie becomes the first Labour Member of Parliament; elected in east London.
1893	The Independent Labour Party founded in Bradford.
1898	West Ham in east London becomes the first local authority in Britain to be controlled by working-class political parties.
1899–1902	The Boer War – the UK enlarges its territory in South Africa.
1900	The TUC decides to support Labour rather than Liberal candidates for Parliament, effectively establishing the British Labour Party.

of democracy, confined to the landed classes and other substantial property owners who had to be male and members of the established Church.

By the 1760s key parts of the Empire were also in place. The UK had gained supremacy over the Portuguese, Spanish and Dutch states by military and commercial competition. There had been victories over France in India, and in North America. A network of trading companies and institutions had been established and the UK had extensive trading links in the Far East and in Africa. The UK's trade included the infamous traffic in slaves to its sugar-producing islands in the Caribbean and to other parts of the Americas. The USA, with French help, won independence in 1783; but after victory over France at Waterloo in 1815, the UK was established as the dominant European state. During the nineteenth century it further consolidated its Empire in the Far East, Australasia and Africa. (Figure 1.1).

Developments overseas and at home were mutually reinforcing, though various interpretations are offered to explain why Britain was the first country to industrialize.[2] Overseas trade stimulated economic development within the UK – the growth of west coast ports such as Bristol, Liverpool and Glasgow for instance. With the rise of commercial or merchant (mercantile) capitalism in the seventeenth and eighteenth centuries, London (with a then huge population of three-quarters of a million) became the world's major trading and financial centre.

Another pre-industrial source of wealth was the early commercialization of agriculture. The selling off of monastic and church lands, following Henry VIII's

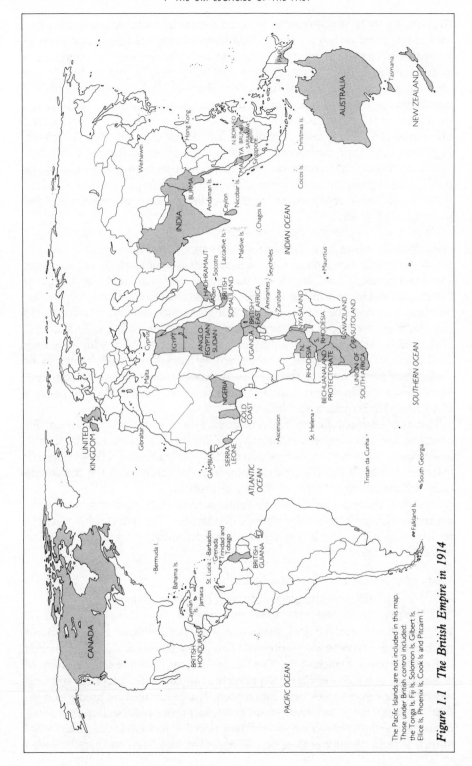

The Pacific Islands are not included in this map. Those under British control included: the Tonga Is, Fiji Is, Solomon Is, Gilbert Is, Ellice Is, Phoenix Is, Cook Is and Pitcairn I.

Figure 1.1 The British Empire in 1914

'Dissolution of the Monasteries' in 1534, meant that land was increasingly bought, sold and worked for profit, rather than simply being held by feudal grant or inheritance. The feudal order of nobles and serfs was replaced by a commercial system of landlords, tenant farmers and labourers, a system which still characterizes extensive areas of Britain's countryside. The commercialization of agriculture meant that large numbers of people had been deprived of land as a direct source of food and livelihood. They were dispossessed by the 'enclosures' of common lands for capitalist farming (the 'clearances' of people from the Scottish Highlands and their replacement by large-scale sheep farms are a dramatic example). For several centuries, self-sufficiency had been giving way to the production of goods for sale as *commodities*, whether by large landowners, tenant farmers, or small independent producers in the case of handicrafts and manufactured goods.

Thus a mid-eighteenth century observer of the UK would have seen a comparatively advanced or 'modern' society by the standards of the time, but it was still largely agrarian and rural. Before 1760 none of England's cities except London had more than 50,000 people (the size of a present day Corby in Northamptonshire or Chester-le-Street, County Durham). Manufacturing was dominated by craftsmen organized in traditional guilds and also by artisans and their families working in their own homes or in small workshops. At least half of all manufactured goods were produced in the rural areas. Political life, excepting the occasional rebellion, was monopolized by landowners and merchants or professional people acting as their agents. In general the members of the different social classes lived in close proximity to one another with well-established patterns of authority, paternalism and deference.

This pre-industrial society has significant echoes in today's UK – in, for example, the constitutional monarchy, the high social status associated with landowning, the separate nations within the UK, the continuing links with former colonies, London's leading position as a financial centre, and the continuing overseas orientation of much of British investment.

However, these pre-industrial continuities have to be balanced against the enormous changes associated with industrialization. The Industrial Revolution transformed UK society in a series of widespread social and political as well as economic changes.

Industrialization and economic changes

Industrialization involved the introduction of the factory system and generalized mechanization of production. It occurred first in textiles, particularly in the cotton industry around Manchester. The 'domestic' or 'putting-out' system of production, in which merchants supplied the raw cotton for people to spin and weave in their own homes, was superceded. It was replaced by production in, first water-powered, and then steam-powered factories.[3] The factory-owning industrialists employed women and children as well as men (and sometimes *instead* of men as their labour was cheaper). Whereas the merchants had simply traded the products of others, the industrialists now directly controlled the actual production process. Work was controlled by the speed of machinery, life by the clock and factory hooter.

The era of *industrial* capitalism had arrived. The small independent producers and those forced off the land by agricultural 'enclosures' and 'clearances' became the employees of industrialists.[4] Production became concentrated in towns and cities, and there was a rapid growth of an urban working class. Manchester's population grew to 80,000 in 1800, 230,000 in 1830 and 400,000 by 1850. In 1830 there were already five provincial cities of over 100,000 people, and the industrial work force of Britain had trebled in size since the 1760s.[5]

From the 1830s mechanization spread to many other industries, especially those producing metal goods. Production became concentrated in larger factories, using coal-fired steam-power and, in the twentieth century, electricity. Transportation too was revolutionized, first by the building of a canal network after 1760, then a railway network after 1820,[6] and in the twentieth century a more sophisticated road network. As new industries developed (and some older ones declined), the 'centre of gravity' and the regional spread of production shifted: textiles and coal up to 1830, then shipbuilding and heavy engineering, were all mainly concentrated near the coalfields of northern England, Scotland and Wales. In the 1930s light engineering and vehicle manufacture became concentrated in the English midlands and south-east. In recent decades, the growth of computer-related technology and financial and other service industries has been mainly centred in London and other parts of the south-east. This growth, together with the decline of older northern industries, resulted in the so-called 'North–South divide' in the 1980s.[7]

Competition for markets, and the need for individual firms to maintain or increase their profits, has stimulated continued technological improvements. This brought enormous increases in the productivity of labour and in society's wealth.[8] Relatively fewer workers are now required in manufacturing industries. Conversely, increasing numbers of white collar workers, many of them women, are employed in the service sector (Figure 1.2). Competition also brought a concentration of ownership as many small firms lost out to larger ones, and today the market in each industry tends to be dominated by a small number of large multinational corporations.[9] They organize production and marketing on a European or worldwide basis, as can be seen in the car industry, or in the different parts of the UK food chain (Figure 1.3).

Social and political changes

Industrialization, and later changes within capitalist production, were associated with equally dramatic social and political transformations both at home and abroad. The geographical distribution of the population, its occupational structure and social composition, all underwent a series of changes. There was a general movement of people from countryside to town and city, and later from city to

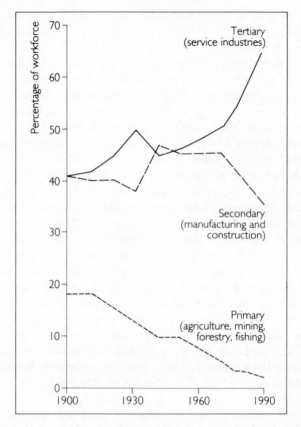

Figure 1.2   Changes in employment sectors: the UK 1900–1990

suburb. Their regional distribution ebbed and flowed as employment in particular industries grew or declined. Agricultural employment dwindled to about 3 per cent of the workforce by the mid-twentieth century; while the artisan class producing consumer items in small workshops almost vanished in the nineteenth century, unable to compete with factory-made goods.

   In the nineteenth century most industrial jobs were occupied by men, as were office jobs which had a higher status than today. In some regions women worked in textile and clothing factories. More generally they worked as domestic servants for the new middle classes which, as owners, managers or investors, had expanded with the factory system. Domestic service remained a major source of female employment until it too dwindled with the labour shortages and changes in social attitudes associated with two world wars. However, by the 1980s women workers comprised nearly half the paid workforce. In a gender-stratified society they are still concentrated disproportionately in lower-paid jobs, particularly in the welfare services and routine office work. But with an ageing population in the UK, women may become an even more important source of paid labour in the 1990s.[10] Work in the home, on the other hand, has changed less since the nineteenth century. Despite modern appliances and more reliance on prepared foods, housework

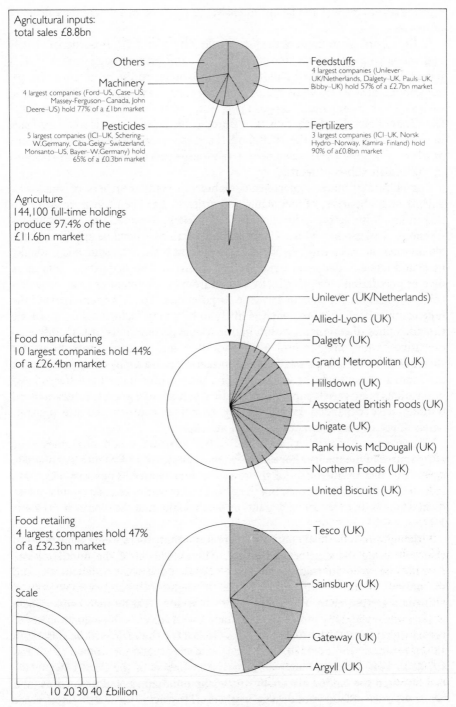

Agricultural inputs:
total sales £8.8bn

Others

Machinery
4 largest companies (Ford–US, Case–US,
Massey-Ferguson–Canada, John
Deere–US) hold 77% of a £1bn market

Pesticides
5 largest companies (ICI–UK, Schering–
W.Germany, Ciba-Geigy–Switzerland,
Monsanto–US, Bayer–W.Germany) hold
65% of a £0.3bn market

Feedstuffs
4 largest companies (Unilever–
UK/Netherlands, Dalgety–UK, Pauls–UK,
Bibby–UK) hold 57% of a £2.7bn market

Fertilizers
3 largest companies (ICI–UK, Norsk
Hydro–Norway, Kamira–Finland) hold
90% of a £0.8bn market

Agriculture
144,100 full-time holdings
produce 97.4% of the
£11.6bn market

Food manufacturing
10 largest companies hold 44%
of a £26.4bn market

Unilever (UK/Netherlands)

Allied-Lyons (UK)

Dalgety (UK)

Grand Metropolitan (UK)

Hillsdown (UK)

Associated British Foods (UK)

Unigate (UK)

Rank Hovis McDougall (UK)

Northern Foods (UK)

United Biscuits (UK)

Food retailing
4 largest companies hold 47%
of a £32.3bn market

Tesco (UK)

Sainsbury (UK)

Gateway (UK)

Argyll (UK)

Scale

10 20 30 40 £billion

Figure 1.3   *The UK food chain, 1987*
Source: Marsden, 1989

remains largely manual and labour-intensive, unpaid and mainly the responsibility of women.

A disproportionate share of the lower-paid jobs – and disproportionate levels of unemployment – are also the experience of immigrant workers from the UK's former Empire and of their children born in Britain. In the nineteenth century the immigrant workers were mainly Irish but they were joined by other groups, such as Jews escaping East European pogroms, and twentieth century immigrants from Italy, Poland and other parts of Europe. With the severe labour shortages in the post-war boom of the 1950s and 1960s there was large-scale recruitment of labour from the overseas colonial territories especially in the Caribbean and in the Indian sub-continent.[11]

The culturally more homogeneous eighteenth century society of landlords, tenants and labourers, of merchants and artisans, has been transformed into a new multi-cultural but still class-divided society. New ethnic and religious divisions – black and white, Christian and Islamic – have been added to the old divisions between English, Welsh, Scottish and Irish, Protestant and Catholic, male and female. The class structure has changed. The majority of this more diverse population now gains its livelihood from employment as blue- or white-collar workers for the state or for large corporations. Today's counterpart of the nineteenth century factory owner is likely to be a paid factory manager. In the extended lines of command within multinational corporations, it is mainly paid executives who now control the workforce and ensure profitability for shareholders. Their high salaries (and in many cases a grant of shares) further differentiate them from the workforce; and the workforce itself is differentiated into various managerial, supervisory, clerical and manual grades. Education and training have expanded greatly in the twentieth century and are a major determinant of employment and social status.

The structures of privilege have altered but inherited wealth continues to be a key source of inequality. For example, extensive areas of Britain's countryside are still owned by members of the aristocracy or gentry. They may also have industrial or financial interests, but the basis of their wealth rests on an inheritance often dating back to feudal land grants or the dissolution of the monasteries (Table 1.1).

Although pre-industrial continuities are important, there were major political changes during the nineteenth century. The expansion of the middle classes ('middle' between the traditional landed classes and artisans or labourers), and the growth of the working-class, broke the eighteenth century monopoly of parliamentary power by Protestant landowners and wealthy merchants. There was a gradual widening of the electoral franchise as reform campaigners achieved voting rights for wealthy male Catholics (1829), for the male middle classes (in 1832), for male workers (1867 and 1884), and eventually for women (1918 and 1929). In 1846 industrial interests achieved the repeal of the Corn Laws which had favoured the landed classes by artificially inflating agricultural prices (and hence the price of food for industrial workers). This victory over state interference in the market firmly established a period of free trade, but the landed gentry and aristocracy retained substantial political power, effectively sharing their parliamentary dominance with the middle class.[12]

The growth of the working class, living separately from the middle and upper classes in large urban concentrations, required new forms of social control. The development of modern industries required a more skilled and stable workforce. These twin requirements gave rise to a series of developments in the second half of the nineteenth century – the establishment of a regular police force, the Education Act of 1870 which brought compulsory primary schooling, the institutionalization of male workers' recreation (e.g. brass bands and football clubs). Much of British working-class culture dates from this period, though in recent decades it has been eroded by the decline of traditional industrial communities and by modern consumerism.

The initiative for nineteenth century developments came in part from the workers themselves.[13] They established their own institutions and to a substantial extent were self-policing. At first trade unions were the preserve of skilled men, but they grew from the 1880s when many of the less skilled workers, male and female, increasingly organized themselves into unions (though membership declined in the inter-war slump and again in the 1980s – Figure 1.4). Initially allied to the Liberal Party, they demanded state welfare provision,

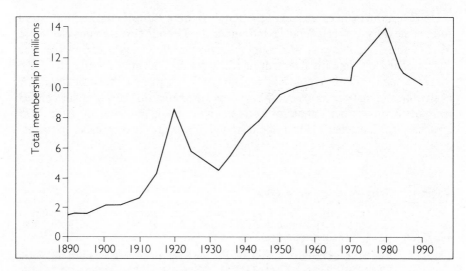

Figure 1.4   Changes in trade union membership: the UK 1890–1990

especially in housing; and in the early 1900s they founded the British Labour Party with the objective of reforming capitalist society by state intervention (though substantial numbers of workers continued to support the Conservative Party – Figure 1.5). State welfare provision was increased from the 1880s to 1914, and in many other ways this was a key period in the formation of modern UK society. Many aspects which are often seen as traditional – the liberal democratic state and political parties, the British public school ethos and the civil service – are to a significant extent inventions of this period.

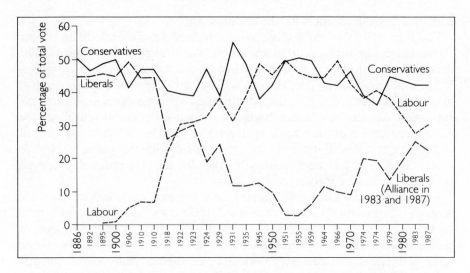

Figure 1.5   Voting support for the three main British political parties – general elections 1886–1987

However, the main extension of the state's welfare, educational and industrial roles came during World War II and under the Labour Government elected in 1945 (Table 1.2). The post-war boom from the late 1940s to the early 1970s was characterized by state involvement or collectivism. The state co-operated with the trade unions and the employers' organizations in managing the mixed economy of private and state enterprises. With some variations this corporatism applied irrespective of whether Labour or Conservatives were in government. After 1979 however, Mrs Thatcher's Government started to reassert the dominance of private enterprise and market forces over state involvement and planning.[14]

Table 1.2   Selected dates since 1900

1900	The setting up of the Labour Representation Committee with TUC support leads to the establishment of the British Labour Party; over 20 MPs by 1906.
1901	Death of Queen Victoria.
1906	The Trades Disputes Act establishes the legal framework for trade unionism up to the 1980s. Suffragettes begin demonstrating for female suffrage – voting rights for women (granted to women over 30 years of age in 1918; equal suffrage for women and men achieved by 1929).
1909	Old age pensions introduced in the UK.
1911	Power of the House of Lords substantially reduced. National Insurance introduced for unemployed or sick workers.
1912	British Government decision to grant Irish demands for Home Rule opposed by the majority of Ulster Protestants, British Conservatives, the House of Lords and sections of the British Army. Constitutional crisis and danger of civil war averted by World War I.
1914–18	World War I.

1915	A rent strike by housing tenants on Clydeside leads to the Government introducing controls on the rents charged by private landlords.
1916	Irish nationalist Easter Rising in Dublin gains widespread sympathy when its leaders are executed.
1917	The Russian Revolution, later followed by invasions by western powers and civil war.
1918	Sinn Fein gains 73 of Ireland's 106 parliamentary seats and sets up an independent parliament in Dublin; war between the IRA and British forces follows.
1920	Government of Ireland Act leads to the partition of Ireland, six counties constituting Northern Ireland with limited powers devolved to a Belfast parliament, and twenty-six counties forming the Irish Free State with its parliament in Dublin. The UK becomes 'The United Kingdom of Great Britain and Northern Ireland'.
1924	Stalin beats Trotsky and others for leadership of the USSR on Lenin's death, creating a personal dictatorship by an extreme centralization of power, forced industrialization from 1928, and having former associates in the Russian leadership murdered. The UK's first Labour Government formed with support from the Liberal Party.
1926	General Strike in Britain.
1931	The British Commonwealth formally established; it includes the Dominions of Canada, Australia and New Zealand, but the colonial status of British territories in Africa, Asia and the Caribbean remains unchanged.
1933	Hitler and the Nazi Party gain control of Germany.
1936	John Maynard Keynes publishes *A General Theory of Employment, Interest and Money* which provides the main theoretical foundation for the 'full employment' policies of post-war UK governments up to the mid-1970s.
1939–45	World War II.
1942	William Beveridge publishes *Social Insurance and Allied Services*, a foundation for the post-war 'welfare state'.
1945	The World Bank and the International Monetary Fund are set up in Washington; the United Nations Organization in New York.
1945–51	The UK has a Labour Government (under Attlee) which establishes the National Health Service, and nationalizes the Bank of England and various industries including coal, steel and railways (1945–47).
1947	India and Pakistan gain their political independence and become members of the British Commonwealth.
1948	The 'Empire Windrush' brings 492 skilled and semi-skilled Jamaican workers to the UK, the first in a UK government scheme to recruit labour in the West Indies, to meet post-war labour shortages.
1949	The western military alliance, NATO, established in Washington.
1950–3	The Korean War. The on-set of the post-war economic boom and steady growth enjoyed by western economies up to the 1970s.
1951–64	Conservative Governments (under Churchill, Eden, Macmillan and Home) in the UK.
1953	The coronation of Elizabeth II.
1955	The USSR forms the military alliance of the Warsaw Pact.
1956	The Suez Crisis – the USA opposes the invasion of Egypt by the UK, France and Israel; Eden resigns as UK Prime Minister and is replaced by Macmillan. Britain's first atomic power station at Calder Hall starts operation. Third-class travel abolished on British railways. Krushchev denounces Stalin. Soviet forces invade Hungary.

1957	The European Economic Community or 'Common Market' is formally established.
	Ghana becomes the first of Britain's colonies in black Africa to gain its independence.
1963	The UK's application to join the European Economic Community is vetoed by France.
	Civil rights 'freedom march' on Washington addressed by Rev. Martin Luther King.
	President Kennedy assassinated in Dallas, Texas.
1964–70	The UK has a Labour Government (under Wilson).
1968	The UK drastically reduces its role as a world military power by withdrawing from military bases east of Suez.
	The 1968 Commonwealth Immigrants Act tightens entry restrictions to the UK for Commonwealth citizens – considered racially biased by the European Commission on Human Rights. Enoch Powell makes his 'rivers of blood' speech and is sacked from the Conservative Shadow Cabinet by Edward Heath. Soviet invasion of Czechoslovakia ends the 'Prague Spring' led by the reforming Alexander Dubchek.
	May uprising by students and workers in Paris and large demonstrations in London against the Vietnam War and British Government support of the USA. Northern Ireland Civil Rights Association established to combat discrimination suffered mainly by Catholics – a well-televised police attack on its peaceful demonstration and on one of its leaders, Gerry Fitt, MP, heralds the 'Troubles' which continue into the 1990s.
1969	The British Army is sent to maintain order in Northern Ireland following attacks on civil rights demonstrations and on Catholic neighbourhoods. The police are reorganized with the disbanding of the part-time 'B Specials', and fairer electoral laws are introduced. The Republican movement and IRA split into the left-inclined 'Officials' and the then more conservatively-minded 'Provisionals'.
	The Open University established (first students admitted 1971).
1970–4	The UK has a Conservative Government (under Heath).
1970	Equal Pay Act – aims to ensure equal pay for women and men doing comparable jobs.
1973	The UK joins the European Economic Community.
1974–9	The UK has Labour Governments (under Wilson and Callaghan).
	The revival of nationalisms within Britain is confirmed by the Scottish National Party getting 30% of the vote in Scotland (from under 2% in 1945; in 1970 Plaid Cymru had got nearly 20% of the Welsh vote, from 1% in 1945).
1974	Northern Ireland's separate parliament is abolished and direct rule imposed from London.
1976	Economic crisis forces the Labour Government to rely on the International Monetary Fund, and effectively to abandon post-war 'full employment' policies and initiate monetarist measures subsequently identified with Mrs Thatcher's Conservative Party.
1979	Mrs Thatcher's Conservatives elected to government and, following the Falklands (or Malvinas) War, again in 1983 and 1987. Departures from the general policies of previous post-war governments include the circumscribing of trade union power by legal constraints, the privatization of state-owned enterprises, and the replacement of local rates by a community charge or poll tax.
1985	Mikhail Gorbachev comes to power in the USSR, initiating internal reform policies – *perestroika* and *glasnost* – and a thawing of the Cold War with the USA and its allies, including the UK.

| 1989 | Pro-democracy demonstrators massacred in Peking. Collapse of USSR-satellite regimes and dictatorships in Eastern Europe, the beginnings of German reunification and the eastward extension of the European Community's influence. Growing tensions within Russia itself and the upsurge of nationalist independence movements in the Baltic and southern republics of the USSR. |
| 1992 | The European single market leading to greater political unity of the European Community. |

International changes

As in the pre-industrial era, the economic, social and political development of the industrialized UK involved the interplay of changes at home and abroad. The internal changes were conditioned by the international rise and decline of the UK and restructuring of the world order. In the 1890s the British Empire, near its zenith, was the largest empire in world history, covering about a fifth of the globe (Figure 1.1). The UK also had a large informal or purely commercial empire.[15] However, from the 1870s the monopoly position enjoyed by British industry in world markets was challenged by growing competition from other industrializing countries such as Germany and the USA. The UK's *relative* share of world industrial production (Figure 1.6) has been in long-term decline ever since.[16]

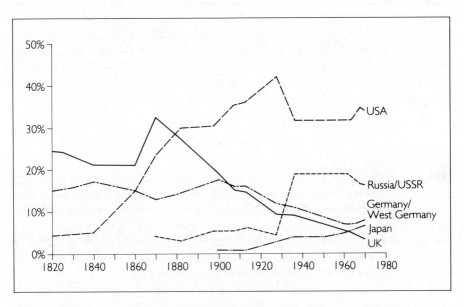

Figure 1.6 Changing shares of world industrial production, 1820–1970
Source: Rostow, 1978

The two world wars brought changes (e.g. the increased employment of women, increased state planning) which helped modernize UK society, but they also undermined its economic strength. After World War II the UK was incapable of sustaining its previous worldwide military and political commitments. Instead, it was obliged to play a supporting role to the USA, which by 1945 was clearly the leading industrial, financial and military power in the world. The nineteenth century Empire was transmuted into a loose confederation of independent states – the Commonwealth. Independence struggles and colonial withdrawals stretched from India and Burma (in 1946), to Malaya and Cyprus (in the 1950s), and on to the Zimbabwe settlement (1980), though British politics was still bedevilled by some of the remnants of an imperial past (e.g. the Falkland Islands and Hong Kong).

For much of the post-war period the UK's international politics were dominated by the problems of readjusting to its reduced international standing – the withdrawal from Empire, the subordinate role as a junior partner of the USA, and being refused entry to the European Economic Community in 1963. As junior partner it played an important part in the Cold War between USA-led market capitalism and Russian-led centrally planned economies. The use of British troops to police various parts of the world fitted in with an imperial past, though some argued that defence spending was now disproportionately high and a drain on the UK economy, an argument bolstered by the better economic performance of Germany and Japan whose defence spending was relatively small by comparison.[17]

The repeated sterling crises, the associated decision to withdraw troops from east of Suez in the 1960s, and the greater prosperity of other European countries in the 1970s and 1980s,[18] all underlined the UK's reduced status and its lack of capacity to reassert an independent world role. In 1973 it joined the European Community without enthusiasm, though that is where its future has increasingly seemed to lie.

The 1990s

How the UK will be affected in the long term by European union, or by the changes in Eastern Europe which started in the 1980s, remains to be seen. The *detente* between East and West, and the decline of US economic strength relative to that of Germany and Japan, have brought significant changes to the post-1945 world order. It has become a more multicentred system in which the USA is but one of a number of important powers. The European Community will be another and the UK's fortunes are now bound up in it.

But will the strong separate identity of British nationalism allow the British to become fully 'European'? Will the legacy of the Empire and early industrialization allow the UK to compete successfully with those who have 'modernized' more effectively? Or will the sheer scale of nineteenth century infrastructure now archaic and outmoded, or the lingering attitudes of superiority which no longer reflect actual political and economic power, prove insurmountable obstacles? Indeed will the UK maintain its present integrity as a 'United Kingdom'? The south of Ireland broke away to form a separate state in 1921; governing Northern Ireland is a major problem for the British state; and there has been a resurgence of nationalism in Scotland and Wales.[19] Will the British identity be reshaped to accommodate these tensions and the greater ethnic and cultural diversity of the UK population, or will the old and new divisions lead to further internal strife?[20]

NOTES

1   A broad sketch of the UK's history and changing world position is adequate for a *general* understanding of how contemporary society was formed. It also provides background to the intellectual history of the *traditions* which is found in Part 2.

We cannot deal here with different interpretations and debates about UK history, but some of them are referred to in subsequent footnotes and later chapters. Further optional readings are suggested for some of the issues.

The footnotes contain additional factual details. They help to substantiate the general story and they introduce some of the issues dealt with later. The notes, and the tables and figures in this chapter, were compiled from a wide variety of sources – books, articles, and official statistics, including the annual HMSO publications *Social Trends*, *Regional Trends* and *Key Data*. These are a useful source of more up-to-date information and are available in public libraries.

2   For example, some explanations focus on Britain's naval power and overseas possessions as providing the necessary wealth and markets (e.g. A. Calder, 1981); others on internal political stability and freedom from absolutist monarchy as facilitating a pioneering economic role (e.g. Barrington Moore, 1967).

3   This social process was accompanied by a series of important technological developments in cotton spinning and weaving from the 1760s. By 1788 there were over 40 water-powered spinning factories in the area around Manchester, and steam-powered weaving was first introduced in 1784.

4   The advent of *industrial* capitalism meant that labour too became a generalized *commodity*. A growing majority of the UK population had nothing to sell in the market-place except their own ability to work for others. They had to exchange their labour for a wage or salary income, rather than being self-employed or self-sufficient.

5   In 1890 Britain was by far the most urbanized part of Europe – 62% of the population lived in cities, compared to only 28% in Germany and 26% in France.

6   In 1750 it took 10 or 12 days to get from London to Edinburgh, in 1850 – 17 hours.

7   By 1985 the South-East of England accounted for over 35% of the UK's total economic output; Scotland accounted for about 9%, Wales for under 5%, Northern Ireland for 2%. Conversely, unemployment rates in Scotland, Wales and northern England were roughly twice as high as in the South-East, in N. Ireland nearly three times as high.

Unemployment in the UK doubled between 1979 and 1982, from 1.3 million people to 2.7 million. Subsequent figures have to be treated with care – between 1982 and 1989 there were over 20 changes to the way unemployment was officially measured. In 1988, 2.4 million, or 8.8% of the UK workforce, were unemployed according to official figures, but using the pre-1982 definition of unemployment the figures were over 3 million or 12% of the workforce.

8   The total output of the UK economy (the Gross National Product) has more than doubled since 1950.

9   In the 1890s the 100 largest manufacturing firms in the UK accounted for less than 15% of total manufacturing output; by the 1990s the 100 largest accounted for over 50% of total output.

10   In 1921, married women made up only 4% of the paid workforce, by 1976 over 25%. In the 1980s there were further increases in female employment, particularly in part-time jobs. In overall terms the UK faces potential labour shortages. The UK's population increased in every decade from the 1790s to the 1970s – from about 17 million in 1790, to over 34 million in 1890, and to over 55 million in the 1970s. But by then growth had become minimal. With falling birth rates the government predicted in 1988 that there would be 23% fewer school-leavers by 1995, and that the proportion of the population which was of pensionable age would rise from 18% in 1988 to 25% by the end of the 1990s. In 1990 there were already about five times more over-65-year-olds than in 1890.

11   In 1971, nearly a third of the UK's immigrant population was born in the Indian sub-continent, the West Indies or Africa; nearly a quarter in the Irish Republic; and another quarter in other parts of Europe. In 1985, the ethnic minority population with Asian and Afro-Caribbean roots was approximately 1.9 million (or 3.4% of the UK population); over 40% of this minority population was then composed of people born in the UK.

Ethnic minorities, particularly their younger members, suffered unemployment rates well above the national average. Department of Employment figures for 1988 showed that in the 16–24 years age group, unemployment was 17% for white youths (twice the national average), but over 30% for Asian and Afro-Caribbean youths.

12   Landed gentry and aristocrats remained the most numerous group in all British Cabinets up to 1906, but there is a debate about the significance of prolonged aristocratic power. Some argue that it prevented the UK from becoming fully 'modernized' and that it accounts for the archaic nature of many of Britain's institutions. Others point to the social mixing of urban merchants and industrialists with the landed classes: many landowners became involved in finance and industry (e.g. they developed coal-mines on their estates); conversely urban wealth bought, or married into, country estates. It is argued that the aristocracy had ceased to be a separate or distinct social force, and that many British institutions which may seem archaic or 'feudal' date only from the formative period between 1880 and World War I. (For an introduction to this debate by marxist historians and others, see C. Barker and D. Nicholls, 1988).

13   There are also debates about the extent to which social developments should be explained in terms of decisions by ruling powers – a history of monarchs, elites and governments (e.g. J.C.D. Clark, 1985); or in terms of 'pressures from below' – a 'people's history' (e.g. E.P. Thompson, 1963). Clark emphasizes the stability and continuity of English society between 1688 and 1832 (see Table 1.1). In contrast, Earle (1989) stresses the rise of the middle class between the 1660s and the 1730s. He shows that London was developing capitalist forms of social organization – in production as well as in trade – long before the Industrial Revolution.

14   As a proportion of the Gross National Product, state expenditure dropped to under 10% in the era of free trade in the nineteenth century. In the twentieth century it climbed to nearly 50% by the 1970s. It remained high in the 1980s despite Government aims and the privatization of nationalized industries. There were significant decreases in some areas (e.g. housing expenditure, overseas aid) but *increases* in other areas (e.g. on social security with the rise in unemployment, and on defence).

15   For example, in 1913 under half of all British overseas investment was in the former Empire, and roughly a quarter was in Latin America.

16   In the 1890s Germany surpassed the UK in steel production, only to be surpassed in turn by the USA a decade later. There is a large amount of literature with debates about the causes of the UK's *relative* economic decline (see Chapter 11; also Coates and Hillard, 1986; and Sked, 1987). P. Kennedy (1988) provides an interesting account of the rise and decline of world powers, particularly the USA.

17   In 1983, 5.6% of the UK's Gross Domestic Product was spent on defence, compared to France 4.2%, West Germany 3.4%, Italy 2.8%, Japan 1%. UK defence spending was increased by 13% between 1981 and 1988. As a proportion of UK investment in research and development, defence accounted for 28% in 1980, compared to 23% in the USA and in France, and only 2% in The Netherlands, Italy and Japan.

18   Taking average European Community living standards as equalling '100', the UK at 104 was slightly above average in 1985, roughly on a par with Italy but significantly below West Germany (116) and France (109). The South-East region, including London, was well above the Community average, but well below the richest regions of Germany, France and several other European Community countries. Most parts of the UK had lower living standards than the poorest region in France. The UK average was overtaken by West Germany's around 1969, and by France's around 1972. Wealth was growing in the UK (see note 8), but not as fast as in other countries. There were big increases in consumer credit – excluding the *largest* item, house mortgages, the *average* debt per household in the UK in 1987 was about £1,000.

19   The nationalists' share of the vote in Scotland rose from 1.3% in 1945 to over 30% in 1974; in Wales from 1.1% in 1945 to over 19% in 1970. In both instances it subsequently declined, but the devolution of rule from London, and – for sizeable minorities – complete political independence, are still very live issues. The long conflict in Northern Ireland has not only caused great suffering there, it has also led to an erosion of civil liberties in Britain and has damaged the UK's reputation abroad.

20   *Suggestions for further reading*: The references cited here provide a starting point if you wish to follow up some issues in more depth. The annually published statistical booklets cited in Note 1 give the latest data on a wide variety of current aspects of UK society. A snapshot of the UK in the recent past is provided by S. Fothergill and J. Vincent's *The State of the Nation: an Atlas of Britain in the Eighties* (Pan Books, 1985).

E.J. Hobsbawm's *Industry and Empire* (Penguin, 1969) gives a stimulating account of Britain's industrial rise and decline, its changing international relationships, and their effects on life in the UK. The development of the world economy and the UK's role in it are described in N. Rowling's *Commodities: How the world was taken to market* (Free Association Books, 1987). *The Making of Britain: Echoes of Greatness* (L. Smith ed., Macmillan, 1988) covers a range of issues including the histories of women, ethnic minorities, the mass media, and working-class political organizations. *Britian in Decline* by A. Gamble (Macmillan, 1985) gives a political interpretation which can be complemented by other accounts such as those in Coates and Hillard (1986) and Sked (1987).

References

Barker, C. and Nicholls, D. (eds) (1988) *The Development of British Capitalist Society, a Marxist Debate*, Northern Marxist Historians Group, Manchester.

Calder, A. (1981) *Revolutionary Empire*, Dutton, New York.

Clark, J.C.D. (1985) *English Society, 1688–1832*, Cambridge University Press, Cambridge.

Coates, D. and Hillard, J. (eds) (1986) *The Economic Decline of Modern Britain: The Debate between Left and Right*, Harvester Press, Brighton.

Earle, P. (1989) *The Making of the English Middle Class: Business, Society and Family Life in London 1660–1730*, Methuen, London.

Fothergill, S. and Vincent, J. (1985) *The State of the Nation: an Atlas of Britain in the Eighties*, Pan Books, London.

Gamble, A. (1985) *Britain in Decline*, Macmillan, London.

Hobsbawm, E.J. (1969) *Industry and Empire*, Penguin, London.

Kennedy, P. (1988) *The Rise and Fall of the Great Powers*, Unwin Hyman, London.

Marsden, T. (1989) 'Exploring the key dynamics of capitalist food systems', Urban Change and Conflict Conference, University of Bristol.

Moore, B. (1967) *Social Origins of Dictatorship and Democracy*, Penguin, London.

Rostow, W.W. (1978) *The World Economy: History and Prospect*, Macmillan, London and Basingstoke.

Rowling, N. (1987) *Commodities: How the world was taken to market*, Free Association Books, London.

Sked, A. (1987) *Britain's Decline: Problems and Perspectives*, Blackwell, Oxford.

Smith, L. (ed.) (1988) *The Making of Britain: Echoes of Greatness* Channel Four/London Weekend Television, Macmillan, London.

Thompson, E.P. (1963) *The Making of the English Working Class*, Penguin, London.

CHAPTER 2

Food Shortages and Famine

Philip Raikes

It is worth considering some of the long-term factors generating hunger and food shortage. This discussion will start with colonialism, not because it is my purpose to attribute all the current ills of Africa to that phenomenon, but because colonialism set in motion a number of highly significant social processes which have certainly altered the nature of societies and thus of food shortage. There can be no doubt that there were famines in Africa before the colonial period, and before the centuries of slave-trading which preceded it. But the nature of both food shortage and the responses to it has changed drastically, and many of the processes initiated then still continue.[. . .]

The colonial incursion itself and the accompanying violence and disruption had disastrous effects on food production and the general quality of life (as did the slave trade before it). In many parts of Africa, this was compounded by the first introduction of rinderpest, a livestock disease which killed up to 90 per cent of all cattle in the worst affected areas. This led to widespread loss of human life and significantly affected the colonization process.[. . .] Wars of colonial conquest and the 'requisitioning' of food led to food shortage, epidemics and significant population decline in East Africa. In most parts of the continent, people lost land, had their crops and villages burned, suffered forced labour and were generally impoverished. Local social and political structures were either smashed or forced into submission.

The following phase, that of the imposition of 'order' and early incorporation into commodity production, had less unambiguously negative effects, but local societies were weakened in a number of ways. Political structures were replaced by, or subordinated to, those of the colonial power and re-oriented towards its aims. Taxes in cash were imposed, having the specific aim of forcing peasants to migrate for labour or produce export crops to pay them. Unlike the previous tributes, they were seldom related to harvest levels, thus weighing more heavily in years of shortage. The capacity to redistribute food in time of need was thus diminished, while the responsibility to do so was transferred to the colonial power. The imposition of administrative boundaries severely limited movement, previously a common response of pastoralists to drought. The latter were further weakened by expropriation of dry season grazing lands for settlers or cultivating

Source: *Modernizing Hunger*, 1988, London, Catholic Institute for International Relations, pp.72–84. (Title of original article: 'Food shortages and famine: how do they occur, where and to whom?')

peasants. In the major settler colonies of eastern and southern Africa, this was accompanied by alienation of huge tracts of the best and most fertile land. The extreme in this sense was South Africa, where whites control 85 per cent of the cultivable land and virtually all the good land, but enormous proportions were also taken in Zimbabwe, Mozambique, Angola, Kenya and other countries.[. . .]

Migrant labour took men away from farming without regard to the effect on production or women's labour burden. Transfer to export crops diverted land and labour from food-crop production. This often affected the quality of the diet more than the quantity. Nutritious but labour-intensive crops (often legumes) were dropped out of cropping patterns. In other cases cereals gave way to cassava, reducing cultivation labour at the expense of lower protein content and more processing work for women.[. . .]

Commoditization of peasant production was one major effect of colonialism, and has accelerated in the period since independence, especially in former settler colonies, where the requirements of settlers for cheap labour acted as a brake on peasant production and accumulation during much of the colonial period. Production of cash crops initiated or hastened the accumulation of land and other resources by rich peasants, businessmen and the politically-favoured. Initial efforts to generate export-crop production through increased labour input were later supplemented by 'modernization', increasing productivity through use of improved seeds, fertilizers, chemicals and machinery, and leading to increased emphasis on the more fertile and better-watered areas.

Alienation of land, accumulation of holdings by commercialized peasants and population increase put enormous pressure on available land with varying effects. In highland and other fertile areas, the effect was enormously increased population density, leading either to fragmentation of holdings or to the emergence of a clear division between the landed and landless. In other cases, pressure stimulated movement into marginal areas, or the previous dry-season grazing reserves of pastoralists, thus further reducing the grazing lands available to the latter. Another response was urbanization.[. . .]

This generated three main social groups of poor and vulnerable people: those whose holdings had declined in size to the point where they could barely (if at all) sustain minimum subsistence (whether directly or through sale of cash crops); those who had been pushed into increasingly marginal areas; and those who had been pushed right off the land into urban poverty. In the first two cases, a common response is (male) migration for labour, whether full- or part-time. Evidently the degree to which these processes operated has varied widely, with the pre-existing availability and quality of land (and level and reliability of rainfall), with the degree of concentration of land and other resources, with the level and impact of investment in both agriculture and industry, and with population growth. But apart from this, there is one large section of society whose diet and general conditions probably suffered more than most.

Women and children

It seems likely that women ate less well than men in most pre-colonial societies in Africa. With few exceptions, these were heavily male-dominated. Male household heads decided (as they still generally do) on the overall disposition of resources, labour and products, and generally to their own advantage. Their ideologies quite specifically assigned an inferior position to women and undervalued their labour. It is true that, in many cases, man and wife or wives operated in different spheres, with women having partially independent control over the production of food for themselves and their children. True also that women were generally those who controlled (and had the skills in) gathering – an important source of food, especially in times of shortage, and still important today. All the same, it seems likely that overall male dominance would have been reflected in better male diets.

Several aspects of colonialism and commodity production have had especially detrimental effects on women, notably through increasing their labour obligations. Labour migrants were mostly male and this left the migrant's farm work for the women remaining behind. Both absence of male labour and increasing shortage of land have led to longer periods of cultivation and shortened (or completely absent) natural fallowing, increasing the burden of weeding, generally an overwhelmingly female activity. Cash-crop production shifted the emphasis of farming towards earning cash, most of which accrued to the male household head. In many cases, this was accompanied by a shift in labour patterns in which the man took care of cash crops (and the income from them), while the woman took on an increasing burden of work producing food for the family. At the same time the shift of land to cash crops left less on which to feed the family. Shifting from production of grains to cassava increases the calorie yield per acre, and lowers the labour requirement for cultivation and for this reason has been a common response to land and the labour shortage where climate allows. But two-thirds to three-quarters of the total labour input consists of processing (crushing, steeping and washing to get rid of the cyanide in the 'bitter' cassava which is most common since wild pigs eat the 'sweet' varieties). This work is done almost entirely by women.[. . .]

In addition to this, household tasks require increasing labour. In many, if not most, parts of tropical Africa, forest and bush cover has been drastically reduced by clearing for cultivation. This means longer trips and more work collecting firewood. Another effect of deforestation is to increase run-off during rainy seasons, acclerating soil erosion and increasing the seasonality of stream-flow, so often implying longer trips to collect water in dry seasons. Where corrugated iron replaces thatch for roofing, insulation deteriorates, requiring more firewood in cold areas (though reducing the labour burden of water collection). Clothes and kitchen implements mean more washing and this means collecting more water, often taking up to several hours per day. Schooling means the loss of child labour and throws the burden on to women.

Most of these factors imply extra work rather than any direct decline in nutrition for women, though reduced land and increased household labour requirements probably reduce food production. But there is clear evidence of a negative impact on child nutrition.[. . .]

There are also plenty of reasons for supposing women to be less well fed than men in general. Men still control the disposition of household resources – the more so, the greater the proportion of cash in total income. Women's rights in land are generally weaker – in some cases almost non-existent. In many parts of the continent, meat is eaten (if at all) largely by men, often as a snack to accompany drinking in bars, a heavily male province. Wheat products like bread and chapatti are especially attractive to single men who lack the skills, facilities and inclination to cook. Within households men tend to eat first and best. Food taboos more commonly limit women's consumption – as, for example, that against pregnant women eating eggs in parts of Tanzania.[. . .]

Whether more women starve than men during famines, I do not know. I suspect that it is not possbile to generalize, since it would depend on the means of survival. One would expect women to have superior skills in gathering and gleaning, in preparing food to avoid waste and in eking out what there is to best effect. There seems to be evidence that women, especially with children, fight harder to survive – perhaps because they have more practice in it from 'everyday life' and because their socialization places more stress on it. Women are possibly less hampered by pride and consciousness of status from seeking means to survive. These factors would seem to offset some part of their general disadvantage. But this is largely speculation. It appears also that famine-relief feeding programmes give preference to women and children, presumably seeing them as more essential to the long-term survival of the society.[. . .]

Immediate factors in the generation of major food shortages

Just as increased food imports do not always imply declining local food production, it is not always the largest harvest shortfalls which generate the greatest food shortages. A topical example of this is the Sudan, which is thought to have had a record harvest in 1985/6. Despite this, emergency assistance was still needed for the huge numbers devastated by the previous year's famine. During this famine, their incomes and livelihoods were largely wiped out, leaving the survivors without means to pay for food, even at lower prices.[. . .]

The concept of 'entitlement to food' was introduced by A.K. Sen in a book about the causation of famine. Sen's major purpose is to show that the standard [FAO] analysis of famine in terms of (national) 'food available decline' (FAD) is not only insufficient but often just plain wrong. This he shows theoretically and by looking at four major famines [the Great Bengal Famine of 1942–4, two Ethiopian Famines of the early 1970s and the Sahelian Famine of 1973].[. . .] He concludes that in only one out of four [the Sahelian Famine] was the aggregate decline in food production sufficient to be considered a major cause of failure. In the other three cases, the decline in national food production was significantly less than in previous or subsequent years in which famines had not occurred.

What did happen in every case was that specific sections of the population had their entitlement to food wiped out, and many starved as a result.[. . .] Three main processes seem to emerge from Sen's survey of these famines:

(i) Workers (urban or rural) suffer from food shortage when the price of food increases in terms of money wages; or the level of money wages (and probability of getting work) falls; or both.

(ii) Peasants face food shortage with harvest failure because this not only wipes out food but their direct entitlement to it as producers. But how serious the food shortage will be is still dependent upon market entitlement. Peasants also produce for sale, so that their access to food will be affected by the production and exchange-value of non-subsistence products.

(iii) Pastoralists and people partially dependent upon livestock, living in low-rainfall areas, are especially vulnerable since the livestock which form their insurance against drought lose their exchange-value against cereals in times of drought.

[. . .] While Sen's analysis is very useful, it is not without its weaknesses. It is strongest where it treats the processes occurring immediately before and during a famine, and weaker on the longer-term factors lying behind it. There is, however, nothing to stop one combining the two.[. . .] To summarize briefly some of the contributions of Sen's entitlement model and some of the conclusions which can be drawn from it:

(i) While there is no doubt that poor harvest and low production are very important factors, they may be restricted to particular areas of a country, yet still have a devastating effect. Moreover there is no simple relation between the extent of harvest failure and the severity of the famine − that depends on a variety of other factors, including the degree of speculation and the government response.

(ii) One thing which emerges clearly is the effectiveness of the private market − in *aggravating* the situation. To some extent it seems that the more integrated the national cereals market, the more effective it is in sucking food from the worst-hit areas and generating price spirals. One of the major contributions of Sen's analysis − and of its application to the details of famines − is to give a picture of the operations of such processes.

(iii) Another clear conclusion is that inappropriate and delayed responses by governments can contribute, and have done so, to the severity and devastation caused by famines.

CHAPTER 3

Gender and Age Differences in Family Food Consumption

Nicola Charles and Marion Kerr

The research and its theoretical context

Anthropologists have long been aware of the social and symbolic importance of food, recognizing that it is an important marker of social relations, and a conveyor of complex messages about social occasions and their participants [. . .] But it is only recently that similar methods of analysis have begun to be applied to advanced capitalist societies [. . .] Such analyses provide evidence that food is a particularly clear indicator of social status and this, together with the increasing evidence of unequal distribution of resources within households [. . .] suggests that the assumption that family food distribution takes place according to egalitarian principles is misguided to say the least.[. . .]

During 1982 and 1983 we interviewed 200 women, all mothers of young children, about their attitudes and practices in relation to food provision and consumption.[. . .]

Analysis of the interview transcripts provided confirmatory evidence of certain aspects of the social relations of food consumption which are widely assumed; for example, it became clear that it is almost always women who carry out the tasks of food purchase and preparation within the family. Our own assumption of this of course provided the rationale for focusing our attention specifically on women's attitudes and experience at the outset. But it may be less well appreciated that connected with these practices are ideologies of food provision and proprieties of consumption which the women also revealed to us in all their complexity yet with surprising unanimity. Thus it became clear that there are cultural expectations about what food is appropriate for men and for children and that in the provision of such foods, women display their ability to be 'good' or 'proper' wives and mothers. Furthermore, it emerged that foods were ranked hierarchically in terms of their social status and that their distribution within the family reflected the relative power and status of family members.[. . .]

The vast majority of our sample families ate three meals a day, one of which was regarded as the main meal. [The] women felt that the provision of a proper

Source: M.J. Brannen & G. Wilson (eds), *Give and Take in Families*, 1987, London, Allen and Unwin, pp. 155–174. (Title of original article: 'Just the way it is: gender and age difference in family food consumption.')

meal was important for men and many men were reported as expecting that this type of meal would be prepared for them. Furthermore, they felt that it was important to ensure that children ate 'properly' through regular consumption of such meals.[. . .]

Women themselves almost always subordinated their own food preferences to those of their partners and children. A great many always bought the food they knew their partners would enjoy for the main meal, while for breakfasts and non-main meals, when men were absent, children's food preferences often held sway. This lack of attention to their own likes and dislikes combined with their intensive involvement in the preparation and serving of meals often led to a situation in which women lacked enjoyment in the food that they cooked, and sometimes even missed out on meals. In general, it was apparent that the women's responsibility for feeding their families did not render their position as purchaser and cook powerful. These observations form an important backcloth to our later discussion of food distribution as they begin to indicate the unequal relations of power and authority within which food consumption takes place.

Food and social status

We now turn to an examination of the social values placed on food by the women. As we might expect, foods of high social status were primarily associated with celebratory eating, but the social status of foods also had a relationship to the 'proper' meal described above. Fresh foods were always valued more highly than convenience foods. Beyond this the food hierarchy apparent in the women's accounts was: [. . .] red meat is the most highly valued food followed by poultry, fish, eggs, cheese, fruit, leaf vegetables, root vegetables and cereals in that order. Thus while eggs, cheese, fruit and cereals might be seen to have considerable nutritional value by many women they did not appear to have the same social value as meat and fish for any but the four vegetarians in our sample. Boiled or roast potatoes and other vegetables were of course essential components to a proper meal, and to substitute chips or baked beans would be to lower the status of the meal, but it was primarily meat which endowed a meal with status. In addition, all the women were highly sensitive to gradations in the status of meat. They voluntarily proposed a hierarchy in which a joint, first and foremost, but also steak, chops and fowl were awarded the highest status. Mince, stewing meat, meat sauces, liver and bacon were regarded as medium status with the lowest status being awarded to sausages, beefburgers and similar meats. The latter category was often not regarded as proper meat and it did not constitute a proper meal.[. . .]

Our brief excursion into the food and drink of everyday meal eating and treats has highlighted the differential status attached to various foods and provides a framework for interpreting the significance of our findings on the distribution of these resources within families. To convey these findings we move away from the qualitative material derived from our discussions with women to a summary of the quantitative evidence from their diary records. At the outset we should point out that these quantitative findings are based on a count of the *incidence* of consumption of specific foods and do not relate to the *amount* of each food consumed at any one time. Despite the fact that this method therefore fails to take into account differences in the size of helpings between family members,[. . .] it nevertheless reveals important patterns of food distribution within families and points to significant status differences between men and women, adults and children.[. . .]

Table 3.1 **Average incidence of consumption of main food items over a two week period (Women's standardized food consumption = 100)**

	Men (N = 151)	Women (N = 157)	Children (N = 289)
High status meat	4.9 (109)	4.5 (100)	3.1 (69)
Medium status meat	9.0 (132)	6.8 (100)	5.3 (78)
Low status meat	6.8 (133)	5.1 (100)	5.2 (102)
Whole fish	1.9 (112)	1.7 (100)	0.9 (53)
Low status fish	1.5 (94)	1.6 (100)	1.7 (106)
Eggs	5.1 (116)	4.4 (100)	3.5 (80)
Cheese	5.8 (104)	5.6 (100)	3.8 (68)
Green leafy vegetables (cooked)	2.8 (97)	2.9 (100)	2.1 (72)
Other vegetables (cooked)	8.2 (104)	7.9 (100)	6.8 (86)
Raw vegetables	5.3 (106)	5.0 (100)	2.3 (46)
Fruit	5.2 (88)	5.9 (100)	7.3 (124)
Potatoes (boiled/roast)	6.6 (103)	6.4 (100)	6.3 (98)
Chips	7.0 (100)	7.0 (100)	4.0 (57)
Bread	21.6 (114)	19.0 (100)	17.4 (92)
Breakfast cereal	5.3 (102)	5.2 (100)	10.4 (200)
Cake	7.3 (109)	6.7 (100)	4.9 (73)
Biscuits	6.4 (80)	8.0 (100)	11.3 (141)
Puddings	7.0 (100)	7.0 (100)	9.3 (133)
Sweets	2.6 (74)	3.5 (100)	8.1 (231)
Crisps	2.4 (133)	1.8 (100)	4.0 (222)
Baked beans, etc.*	2.0 (105)	1.9 (100)	2.9 (153)
Milk	6.3 (105)	6.0 (100)	21.5 (358)
Soft drinks	2.0 (74)	2.7 (100)	22.5 (833)
Tea/coffee	54.3 (94)	58.0 (100)	13.4 (23)
Alcohol	4.4 (163)	2.7 (100)	0.2 (7)

* This category includes tinned spaghetti, tinned ravioli, 'noodle doodles', baked beans, and so on – foods which are frequently given to children at the non-main meal.

From Table 3.1 it is clear that there are strong age and gender differences in the consumption of foods even at this relatively crude level of analysis. While the differences in average incidence of consumption do not always appear to be very large, the proportional differences are more significant taking adult female consumption as a baseline of 100.

We can see that there are some foods predominantly consumed by adults and others which are predominantly consumed by children. On average, adults of both sexes consume high and medium status meat, whole fish, eggs and cheese more frequently than do children. They also tend to consume vegetables more frequently than children and this is particularly noticeable in the case of raw vegetables. Chips are more frequently consumed by adults than children as are tea and coffee, while alcohol consumption is almost totally confined to adults. Interestingly, the only sweet food predominantly consumed by adults is cake. Children on the other hand, are the predominant consumers of biscuits, puddings and sweets. They also consume fruit, breakfast cereal, crisps, low status fish and foods like baked beans more frequently than adults. Soft drink consumption is almost totally confined to children and they drink milk with much greater frequency than do adults.

A variety of explanations may be put forward for such age differences in consumption. Most obviously, some foods are commonly thought of as 'children's food' within contemporary British mainstream culture and are commercially marketed as such. Included within this category are foods such as baked beans, sweets, crisps and soft drinks as well as many breakfast cereals, biscuits and puddings. Children's relatively high consumption of low status meat and fish (the only forms of meat and fish they consume with equivalent or greater frequency than adults) can also be explained in this manner, as included here are such foods as beefburgers, sausages and fish fingers. A further explanation is that women feel that some foods are particularly important for children's health. Milk is perhaps the most obvious example in this category but fruit, too, was commonly cited as being of especial importance for children particularly in view of their frequent dislike of vegetables. This helps to explain children's lower consumption of cooked vegetables, especially the green leafy variety which were particularly disliked by children. Raw (salad) vegetables, on the other hand, were often thought too difficult for young children to manage, while tea and coffee as well as alcohol were often thought to be too strong-tasting and intoxicant for children's consumption. Children were, however, given milky tea and coffee on occasions and also 'tasted' the alcohol that their parents or other adults might be drinking. Usually, though, they drank squash when their mothers drank tea or coffee and a special non-alcoholic drink, such as fizzy grape juice or lemonade, when their parents were drinking alcohol in their presence.[. . .]

The link between the status of foods and the status of those who consume them [is] further illuminated if we consider gender differences in food consumption. Referring again to Table 3.1, we find that those foods which are consumed with greater frequency by men than women include meat, cake and alcohol, while the foods more frequently consumed by women than men include fruit, biscuits and sweets. As we have already indicated, the former foods enjoy a relatively high status within British food culture while the latter foods do not. Again this distribution of food conveys messages about differential status and power within the family. Thus, in families where women and children are financially dependent on the male breadwinner, he is given the best cuts of meat and the largest slice of the cake – literally.[. . .] Many men's consumption of cake was higher than that of their partners and children because it was reserved for them to take to work in their 'pack-up'. And men drank alcohol, usually in the form of beer, more frequently than women. A regular trip to the pub in a good many families was seen as a man's right and just reward for a day at work, while in general men had more opportunity to enjoy a drink than women, as they were relatively free from the demands of childcare.

Women's higher consumption of lower status foods, as well as reflecting their relative lack of status when compared with men in families, is also a product of the fact that most of the women we spoke to were with their children during the daytime. This made it likely that they would share the food their children were eating – be it fruit, sweets or biscuits between meals or a non-main meal of bread and jam or fish fingers. However, women's consumption when their partners were at home was usually more similar to men's. Overall, their food consumption occupies an intermediate position between that of men and children. Their consumption of high status foods was lower than that of men but higher than that of children, while their consumption of low status foods was higher than that of men but lower than that of children.

[. . .] An important exception to this pattern [. . .] is that men's consumption of low status meat was higher than that of women and children. This can be explained by their higher consumption of such items as meat pies which, again, were often included in their 'pack-ups'. They also sometimes ate low status meat as a substantial fourth meal in a day. It was not uncommon, for example, for men to help themselves to a 'snack' of, say, beefburgers and baked beans in the evening. Women and children, on the other hand, hardly ever ate in the evening after the main meal, with the exception of the odd biscuit with a drink.

Thus far it is clear that the distribution of food within our sample families displays a differentiation according to gender and age. Living and working patterns influence food consumption and help to ensure that men eat more and often 'better' than either women or children. Perhaps we should emphasize at this stage that we are not arguing that men's diets are nutritionally superior, or for that matter inferior, to those of women and children. We are not qualified to comment on this. Our point is that, given the social and cultural values that are attached to food and their position within the food hierarchies, the diets of men enjoy a higher social status than those of women and children.

An important question which remains to be answered is whether the age and gender differences in food consumption which typify the sample as a whole apply to all families regardless of their social and economic circumstances. In order to explore this dimension we examine patterns of food distribution within families according to seven occupational groups of the male partners in preference to a social class classification of the household.[. . .] This classification allows us to portray a more refined picture of the occupations themselves – for example, separating professional from managerial workers – and it enables us to differentiate between families where men are employed and where they are unemployed. Secondly, the type of work men undertake, particularly if it is heavy manual labour, is often the rationale used by the women we interviewed for differences in men's and women's food consumption. In fact, very few men in our sample were involved in heavy manual work and usually it was sufficient that men went out of the home to work for women to think they deserved and needed greater quantity and higher status food.

Bearing in mind the point that differential consumption may be a product of poverty and the necessity to limit access to scarce resources, we have found in fact that the inequalities we have described remain a persistent and enduring feature of household food consumption. However, the precise form these take does seem to vary with men's occupations. To explore this in more detail we focus on [meat consumption] which seem[s] to be most sensitive as [a] status indicator and which, according to the women's accounts, [is] most likely to be affected by exigencies of income.[. . .]

Table 3.2   Average incidence of consumption of meat over a two week period within families by men's occupation (average rates of consumption: women's consumption = 100)

	Men (N = 146)	Women (N = 146)	Children (N = 271)
High status meat			
Manual unskilled	4.1 (111)	3.7 (100)	2.7 (73)
Manual skilled	5.4 (108)	5.0 (100)	3.4 (63)
Non-manual	4.6 (102)	4.5 (100)	3.0 (67)
Managerial	4.7 (118)	4.0 (100)	2.5 (63)
Professional	5.0 (104)	4.8 (100)	3.3 (69)
Self-employed	5.7 (116)	4.9 (100)	3.3 (67)
Unemployed	2.2 (100)	2.2 (100)	2.0 (91)
ALL	4.9 (109)	4.5 (100)	3.1 (69)
Medium status meat			
Manual unskilled	11.1 (173)	6.4 (100)	5.6 (88)
Manual skilled	10.1 (131)	7.7 (100)	5.6 (73)
Non-manual	8.5 (128)	6.6 (100)	4.4 (67)
Managerial	8.2 (149)	5.5 (100)	6.1 (111)
Professional	7.4 (109)	6.8 (100)	5.4 (79)
Self-employed	7.5 (123)	6.1 (100)	4.7 (77)
Unemployed	7.2 (100)	6.7 (100)	6.1 (91)
ALL	9.0 (132)	6.8 (100)	5.3 (78)
Low status meat			
Manual unskilled	8.4 (187)	4.5 (100)	4.3 (96)
Manual skilled	7.2 (141)	5.1 (100)	5.8 (114)
Non-manual	8.9 (135)	6.6 (100)	6.8 (103)
Managerial	6.2 (127)	4.9 (100)	4.5 (92)
Professional	5.1 (111)	4.6 (100)	4.6 (100)
Self-employed	5.6 (140)	4.0 (100)	4.4 (110)
Unemployed	6.7 (116)	5.8 (100)	5.2 (90)
ALL	6.8 (133)	5.1 (100)	5.2 (102)

We can see from Table 3.2 that men consume meat most frequently and children least frequently in all these families. However, the quality and quantity of meat consumed varies according to men's occupations. Men in the professions consume meat less frequently than other male workers and it is noticeable that their consumption is closer to that of women. This relatively low meat consumption reflects the fact that we found rather less importance being attached to meat within these families. The women were less inclined to stress the social and nutritional benefits of meat eating and these views would seem to have been shared by their partners.

The highest meat consumption for men and the greatest disparity between men and women is evident within the families of manual unskilled workers, although the meat consumed is not as often of high status as that consumed in other families. But it is in the families of unemployed men that high status meat consumption is lowest. Indeed, consumption of any meat is relatively infrequent for men within this group when compared with their working peers; all these men had previously been engaged in manual work. Furthermore, it is clear that women's and children's meat consumption is closest to that of men in the families of unemployed men. These findings need to be treated with caution for the numbers involved are small. Nevertheless they are interesting because they seem to suggest a different response to the problem of limited resources according to whether or not men are engaged in waged work. We say this because a good many families of manual unskilled workers existed on a low income. Yet it would appear that women in these families limit the meat they give to themselves and their children to ensure that men receive a disproportionate share of what is available. In the families of the unemployed, by contrast, a limited amount of meat seems to be shared more equally.[. . .]

Conclusion

The evidence we have presented here clearly demonstrates that the distribution of food within families is dependent on age and gender throughout the occupational structure. Food is not a resource to which all family members have equal access. On the contrary, [. . .] access is determined by the relative power and status of family members. Thus men consume high status food and drink more frequently than do women and children. Adults of both sexes consume it more frequently than do children. Children, on the other hand, consume low status food more frequently than do adults. These inequalities are more marked in some families than others but they nevertheless appear to typify all families at this life cycle point when most women and children are financially dependent on men. The consumption of food therefore conveys messages about the status of those that consume it and depends upon relations of power between family members, with the most powerful consuming the most and the best. The fact that in most of our families women did the food shopping and cooking does not necessarily lead to their wielding power in their own interests. As providers of food for their families they come to subordinate their own needs and interests to those of their partners and children. Often unwittingly, sometimes reluctantly, women are themselves instrumental in reproducing the social and sexual division of labour so clearly demarcated in the way in which food is distributed within the household.

SECTION 2
The Divisions of Society

Introduction

The word 'society' carries two basic, but opposing, meanings in social science. 'Society' can mean *association* – individuals and groups combining together to reproduce their material and cultural life. This is also how society reproduces itself through space and time. Groups and individuals organize themselves together, forming social relationships, modifying their activities in order to take account of other individuals and groups, towards whom they must orient their actions.

But societies are also fundamentally *divided*. Within any social process, or institution, groups and individuals are divided into different categories – for example, according to the material wealth and goods they have at their disposal, the power they wield, the social status they hold, their gender as men and women or their racial and ethnic background. Groups are positioned differently in society according to which of these categories they belong. The activities in which people engage have different results or outcomes, depending on the ways in which they are grouped. Economic processes, for example, do not have an equal outcome for owners and workers, for men and women, for white and non-white people, or, for that matter, for young and old, or for people who do different kinds of jobs, manual or non-manual, skilled or unskilled.

Social relations in society work as much *through* these divisions as in spite of them. Fundamental inequalities are linked to them. We know no organized society in which some division of material goods, power, status and position does not exist. Taken together, these social divisions provide society with its basic, underlying structure. Social divisions cut through and across the population creating, among the groups which share the same place or position in the social structure, common social experiences, common chances of success and failure in life, and common expectations of what life holds for them.

This section, then, focuses on three fundamental social divisions – those associated with class, gender and race or ethnic origin. Modern societies are divided along many other lines, but these three are pervasive, affecting the lives and life-chances of every individual and group. Hence, we must study social divisions – how they work and what their impact is – if we are to identify the patterns into which social activities and behaviour fall, and explain why those activities function as they do. Social divisions of class, gender and race are the principal ways in which social science data are organized and presented; they are a key component of all social science explanation.

The first of the three readings in this section (Chapter 4) is taken from *The*

43

Black Report, a study of inequalities in health in Britain, and one of the most comprehensive reports of its kind to be produced. Its findings were so controversial and startling that the publication of the Report was delayed by the Government for some months. *The Black Report* (and its follow-up, *The Health Divide*, which was published together with it) demonstrates conclusively that, though the patterns of death and illness have a great deal to do with physical, genetic and biological processes affecting the body, they also clearly reflect the influence of social factors. We cannot explain the causes of ill-health without looking at social factors. We certainly cannot understand how good and ill-health are distributed across the population without understanding the way society is socially divided. However, even if we accept the surprising proposition that illness, and indeed death itself, is – as social scientists say – 'socially constructed' (i.e. people in different classes, gender or racial groups actually die at very different rates), the actual ways in which these social divisions operate in practice are exceedingly complex.

Some of this complexity is brought out in the extract from *The Black Report*. It examines the impact of two ways of looking at social divisions on the distribution of health and illness: that of 'social class' and of what researchers call 'life-style'. 'Class' refers to all those inequalities which arise from the unequal distribution of material wealth, goods and resources and fundamentally arises from (though in most definitions is not restricted to) economic process. 'Life-style' is a broader and looser term, referring to those cultural patterns and ways of life which influence our health.

Much depends, as you can see, on how these difficult concepts are defined. 'Class' and 'life-style' are among the most complex ideas in social science and have been the object of a great deal of theorizing and debate. The extracts spend some time on this question of definition. This is not simply a matter of the need to define clearly the concepts we are using. It also affects how these divisions can be 'operationalized' in research, when we are trying to offer explanations as to why the patterns of distribution are as they appear to be. In a great deal of this kind of social research, the principal measure of social class is occupation; not only because the conditions associated with a person's job can influence his or her health but because a range of other inequalities – income, earnings, living conditions, housing circumstances, education, amounts of leisure time, quality of diet and so on – are indirectly related to occupation. *The Black Report* examines critically this concept of what is called 'occupational class'.

'Class' is essentially about social relations between different groups and principally affects relative standards of living measured in material terms. 'Life-style' often carries more the ring of individual choice about it. We cannot easily choose what class we belong to; but we seem more able to 'choose' our life-styles – whether or not to smoke, or to take exercise, for example, are felt to be more matters of individual will and choice and such decisions can and do have consequences for our health. Chapter 4 examines this rather simplified distinction critically, showing not only how complex the influences of 'class' and 'life-style' are in determining the patterns of health but how intricately they *interact* with each other.

44

The second extract, from John Nicholson's book *Men and Women*, (Chapter 5) explores the social divisions which arise from the sexual differentiation between men and women. This reading starts in more or less the same place as the reading on health inequalities. Like health, sexual differentiation seems to have its roots in physical, genetic and biological 'facts'. And yet, the social distinctions between men and women and the inequalities of wealth, income, social position, status and power which follow from them are *social* and need to be socially understood and explained. They cannot be reduced to or entirely explained with reference to biology.

Social science makes an important distinction between those differences which are due to physical and genetic characteristics and those which can be attributed to social factors, and this distinction is expressed in the difference between the concepts of sex and gender. Men and women do have, broadly, different sex characteristics – though, as the article shows, at the genetic level these distinctions are by no means simple or clear-cut. Very few, if any, of these strictly physiological characteristics are sufficient to explain, either differences in social behaviour or position between men and women, or even the traits and attitudes which we, in our common-sense way, stereotype as typically 'masculine' or 'feminine'.

These stereotypical assumptions about men and women are, nevertheless, exceptionally strong. They seem so obvious and compelling that we are often tempted to trust what we think is the evidence of our eyes, of common sense. Because some physiological differences exist, we extrapolate and project these to explain features of the social relations between men and women which cannot be attributed to them, and whose causes must be sought in the socially-constructed, historically-variable gender divisions of society.

For many decades, 'race' too had its apparently impeccable biological foundations. In the nineteenth century, 'race' came to be understood as, essentially, a genetic phenomenon. Each race was assumed to have clear, distinct biological characteristics. However, in the light of subsequent research, these theories (like those concerning the biological basis of gender) have had to be modified. In any sample, there will be as many common genetic features *across* races as within them. Exclusive boundaries between races are now virtually impossible to draw. The idea of a biologically-guaranteed 'racial purity' does not stand up to scientific inspection.

This discrediting of the biological foundations of 'race' has led to a greater understanding of race (like gender) as a socially constructed category, into which many different things have – quite unscientifically – been collapsed. In actual usage, the term 'race' includes physical characteristics, behavioural characteristics *and* social stereotypes. The scientific explanation of race came to prominence at a specific historical moment, as Miles shows in the third extract (Chapter 6). It functions more as ideology than as a scientific proposition. Thus, its claims to scientific status attempt to establish phenomena which are, in fact, open to challenge and alteration (such as the domination of non-white, non-European peoples by white Europeans) as being part of the laws of Nature, and therefore fixed and unalterable.

Miles treats 'race' not as fact but as a set of representations. It is a way of representing historically-created differences between peoples as if they have some exclusive biological foundation and guarantee. It is also a way of representing non-white or non-European peoples as, inevitably, 'other' – that is, less intelligent, less rational, primitive, more prone to barbarism and violence, and hence necessarily and naturally lower on the evolutionary scale than the white 'races'. It justifies these differences of power and position, as having been created, not by the actions of men and women, but by Nature itself. According to this ideological discourse, in matters of racial inequality as in gender division, 'biology is destiny'.

All three readings, then, undermine the efforts to ground social divisions exclusively in biology. They question the scientific foundations of a purely genetic or 'natural' explanation of social behaviour. They demonstrate the socially-constructed character of the categories and divisions associated with class, gender and race. And they explore some of the complexities of the ways in which these fundamental aspects of social structure function in our societies today.

Stuart Hall

C H A P T E R 4
Inequalities in Health

Sir Douglas Black et al. *and Margaret Whitehead*

4.1 The Black Report

Sir Douglas Black, J.N. Morris, Cyril Smith and Peter Townsend

Concepts of inequality

The distribution of health or ill-health among and between populations has for many years been expressed most forcefully in terms of ideas on 'inequality'. These ideas are not just 'differences'. There may be difference between species, races, the sexes and people of different age, but the focus of interest is not so much natural physiological constitution or process as outcomes which have been socially or economically determined. This may seem to be straightforward, but the lengthy literature, and widespread public interest in the subject of inequality, show that factors which are recognizably or discernibly man-made are not so easy to disentangle from the complex physical and social structure in which man finds himself. Differences between people are accepted all too readily as eternal and unalterable. The institutions of society are very complex and exert their influence indirectly and subtly as well as directly and self-evidently. For some the concept of inequality also carries a moral reinforcement, as a fact which is undesirable or avoidable. For others the moral issue is relatively inconsequential. For them difference in riches or work conditions are an inevitable and hence 'natural' outcome of the history of attempts by man to build society, and they conclude that the scope for modification is small and, besides other matters, of little importance.

Central to the development of work on inequality has been the development of concepts of 'social class': that is *segments of the population sharing broadly similar types and levels of resources, with broadly similar styles of living and* (for some sociologists) *some shared perception of their collective condition.* This too has been controversial and there remains considerable controversy within sociology about the origins and relative importance of class in relation to social inequalities and social change.

Source: *Inequalities in Health*, 1988, Harmondsworth, Penguin, pp. 38–41 and 289–305. This book contains: 'The Black Report' by Sir Douglas Black, Professor J.N. Morris, Dr Cyril Smith and Professor Peter Townsend, edited by Peter Townsend and Nick Davidson; and 'The Health Divide' by Margaret Whitehead.

The problems of choosing indicators of inequality

Traditionally inequalities have been portrayed through a characterization of class obtained by ranking occupations according to their social status or prestige. Of course, a variety of other factors may be said to play a part in determining class: income, wealth, type of housing tenure, education, style of consumption, mode of behaviour, social origins and family and local connections. They are interrelated and none of them should be regarded as sufficient in itself. But historically occupation has been selected as the principal indicator, partly because it has been regarded as more potent than some alternatives, but partly because it was the most convenient for statistical measurement and analysis. Occupation not simply designates type of work but tends also to show broadly how strenuous or unhealthy it is, what are the likely working conditions – for example, whether it is indoors or outdoors and whether there is exposure to noise, dust or vibration – and what amenities and facilities are available, as well as level of remuneration and likely access to various fringe benefits. Pay will also determine family living standards and, while members of a family will not be exposed to some features of the working conditions experienced, there are others which may affect them indirectly, like the risk of intermittent unemployment, or the stress of disablement and of shift work.

Throughout this report we shall employ occupation as a basis of class because of its convenience. In particular we shall use the Registrar General's categories as follows:

I. Professional (for example accountant, doctor, lawyer) (5 per cent)*

II. Intermediate (for example manager, nurse, schoolteacher) (18 per cent)

IIIN. Skilled non-manual (for example clerical worker, secretary, shop assistant) (12 per cent)

IIIM. Skilled manual (for example bus driver, butcher, carpenter, coal face worker) (38 per cent)

IV. Partly skilled (for example agricultural worker, bus conductor, postman) (18 per cent)

V. Unskilled (for example cleaner, dock worker, labourer) (9 per cent)

But in doing this we should also be aware of its limitations. *We believe an effort should be made to make this classification in the rankings of occupations as objective as possible, by taking into account current and lifetime earnings, fringe benefits, security, working conditions and amenities.* Our intention is to shift attention from the more elusive subjective rating of 'prestige' or 'general standing' of occupations that have been traditionally used, to their material or environmental (and more measurable) properties. *Second, it would be desirable for the term 'occupational class' to be used rather than 'social class' when the current occupation of the individual is used as the basis of the classification* (and we shall do this throughout the report when we use this definition of class). *Third, it will become increasingly important*

---

* The percentages are of the total number of economically active and retired males.

to use the married man's occupation in combination with the married woman's occupation in analysing various health conditions and experiences, for example infant and child mortality. *Fourth, the need for a 'social class' measure for analysis of the health of the family unit as a whole or of individual members of the family unit will become increasingly important.* One possibility is using the current occupations of both parents, together with information, where it can be obtained, about the main occupations of the husband's father and the wife's father.

Finally, use of occupation as an indicator of social class has become so widespread in Britain in recent decades that the pre-occupations of some pioneer health. statisticians have been forgotten. Some, however, were particularly concerned to relate health experience to riches or poverty (for example, Stevenson, 1928). Efforts should be made to restore this tradition, and not only because of the difficulties of taking occupation as a reliable indicator of a family's social class. The growth of absolute levels of resources, the spread of employer welfare benefits in kind and of social service benefits, and the increase of owner-occupation among the working classes makes a measure of 'resources' all the more important. The term 'resources' seems to be more appropriate than 'income' because of the present-day impact of wealth and both employer welfare and social service benefits-in-kind upon living standards. Considerable sums are spent each year on official annual surveys – including the Family Expenditure Survey (FES), the General Household Survey (GHS) and the National Food Survey. The FES provides the best measure of income, and although some information is collected about employer welfare and social service benefits it is incomplete and rather rough. Valuable data about the distribution of health are collected in the GHS, and although the information collected about income has, since 1979, been the same as in the FES, it is not supplemented by information on other resources. The development of a more adequate measure will not be easy, and the Royal Commission on the Distribution of Income and Wealth took a very cautious view in some of its reports about the possibilities of linking income and wealth in surveys (see especially Reports Nos. 1, 4 and 5). However, its Seventh Report took a more positive view about the need to develop joint distributions of income and wealth as a priority (p. 160) and about the desirability of sample surveys of personal wealth holdings.

We recommend that in the General Household Survey steps should be taken (not necessarily in every year) to develop a more comprehensive measure of income, or command over resources, through either (a) a means of modifying such a measure with estimates of total wealth or at least some of the most prevalent forms of wealth, such as housing and savings, or (b) the integration of income and wealth, employing a method of, for example, annuitization.[. . .]

4.2 The Health Divide

Margaret Whitehead

Cultural/behavioural and materialist/structuralist explanations

The cultural/behavioural explanation stresses differences in the way individuals in different social groups choose to lead their lives: the behaviour and voluntary life-styles they adopt. In this explanation inequalities in health evolve because lower social groups have adopted more dangerous and health-damaging behaviour than the higher social groups, and may have less interest in protecting their health for the future.

The structuralist/materialist explanation emphasizes the role of the external environment: the *conditions* under which people live and work and the pressures on them to consume unhealthy products. Inequalities in health in this context would come about because lower social groups are exposed to a more unhealthy environment. They do more dangerous work, have poorer housing, and have fewer resources available to secure the necessities for health and to use the available health services. At a more general level, the whole structure of society is implicated.

But several commentators are beginning to question whether the distinction between the two approaches is artificial, as behaviour cannot be separated from its social context (e.g. Blane, 1985). The classic example of childhood accidents has been quoted to illustrate the point. The observation that children from lower social groups have more accidents than children from higher groups may be explained by the behavioural view as due to more reckless, risk-taking behaviour in this group and inadequate care by parents. The materialist view would highlight the unsafe play areas, the lack of fenced-off gardens and the greater difficulty of supervising children's play from high-rise housing. In the latter view, the environment is dictating the behaviour of both mother and child.

The following new evidence supports the behavioural and the structural/materialist explanations but shows that the two are interrelated rather than mutually exclusive.

Evidence on cultural/behavioural differences

Latest evidence confirms previous observations that there are life-style differences between the social classes which are related to health. Cigarette-smoking would be a prominent example.

Smoking habits

Table 4.1 gives the percentages of cigarette-smokers in each social-economic group over the period 1972–84. It is clear that in every year the percentage of smokers increased steadily from the professional group through to the unskilled manual group. For example, in 1984 17 per cent of professional group men and 15 per

50

cent of professional group women were smokers compared with 49 per cent of men in the unskilled manual category and 36 per cent of women in that category.

Table 4.1 Prevalence of cigarette-smoking in Great Britain, 1972–84, by sex and socio-economic group[1] (persons aged 16 and over[2]): percentage smoking cigarettes

	Professional	Employers and managers	Intermediate and junior non-manual	Skilled manual and own account non-professional	Semi-skilled manual and personal service	Unskilled manual	All aged 16 and over
Men							
1972	33	44	45	57	57	64	52
1974	29	46	45	56	56	61	51
1976	25	38	40	51	53	58	46
1978	25	37	38	49	53	60	45
1980	21	35	35	48	49	57	42
1982	20	29	30	42	47	49	38
1984	17	29	30	40	45	49	36
Women							
1972	33	38	38	47	42	42	42
1974	25	38	38	46	43	43	41
1976	28	35	36	42	41	38	38
1978	23	33	33	42	41	41	37
1980	21	33	34	43	39	41	37
1982	21	29	30	39	36	41	33
1984	15	29	28	37	37	36	32

[1] Members of the Armed Forces, persons in inadequately described occupations, and all persons who have never worked have not been shown as separate categories. They are, however, included in the figures for all persons.
[2] Aged 15 and over in 1972.

Source: OPCS (1986d). Crown Copyright.

The table also shows that there has been a decline in the prevalence of smoking in most socio-economic groups, but the decline has been more rapid in some groups than in others. For example, prevalence in women in the manual groups has shown very little reduction over the decade, whereas that in the professional group has shown a pronounced decline.

Smoking habits varied with economic status, too. For example, in 1984 36 per cent of men in work were smokers, compared with 61 per cent of unemployed men. The corresponding figures for women were 34 per cent and 48 per cent. Table 4.2 gives an indication of the regional variations in smoking in 1984 (although the data have not been standardized for age).

Class trends in mortality from lung cancer and coronary heart disease show some similarity to the smoking trends. Thus there is a social class gradient in mortality for both diseases, with lower rates in the professional classes to highest in the unskilled manual class. In addition, mortality over the decade has been declining faster in non-manual groups than in manual groups [. . .] (Marmot and McDowall, 1986).

Mortality from lung cancer and coronary heart disease is higher in the unemployed than in the employed population, and regional variations in mortality from the diseases mirror the smoking variations to a certain extent.

In the case of coronary heart disease, there are further similarities. Before 1950 mortality from the disease in men was marginally higher in classes I and II than in IV and V, but during the 1950s the gradient reversed and mortality became higher in classes IV and V than in I and II (Marmot *et al.*, 1981; Morris, 1979).

Table 4.2   Prevalence of cigarette-smoking in Great Britain, 1984, by region[1] (persons aged 16 and over)

Region	Percentage smoking cigarettes	Base = 100%
England		
North	36	1,020
Yorkshire and Humberside	39	1,662
North-West	35	2,133
East Midlands	31	1,334
West Midlands	33	1,791
East Anglia	24	651
Greater London	37	2,090
South-East	31	3,415
South-West	30	1,383
Wales	37	925
Scotland	39	1,801

[1] It should be noted that the data in this table have not been standardized to take accocunt of differences in age-structure between regions.

Source: OPCS (1986d). Crown Copyright.

Alcohol

Drinking habits also vary between the social groups, but in a much more complex way. Heavy drinking is more common among manual groups than among non-manual groups. For example, 26 per cent of unskilled manual group men were classed as heavy drinkers in 1984, compared with 8 per cent of professional men. At a regional level the highest proportion of heavy drinkers was found in the North (including the North-East) and Wales, and the lowest in East Anglia and the outer South-East of England. However, the pattern varied considerably in relation to other categories of drinker. For example, the unskilled manual group had the highest percentage of abstainers as well as the highest percentage of heavy drinkers. This group also had a lower proportion of 'frequent light drinkers', whereas the professional and managerial groups, both men and women, had the highest proportion of this type of drinker (OPCS, 1986d). Which pattern of drinking would ultimately be more detrimental to the health of each group is debatable. There is some evidence that mortality from chronic liver disease and cirrhosis was lower in class I men and high in class V men in 1979–83, but apart from that the situation is unclear.

Food and nutrition

There are differences between social groups in the quantity and nutritional quality of the food they eat. In this context comparisons are made between income groups. Groups A to D represent households with at least one earner. Group A contains the richest 10 per cent, group D the poorest 10 per cent, and groups B and C are intermediate, each representing 40 per cent of households with one earner. Table 4.3 shows consumption of some of the main food categories by income group in 1976 and 1984. It is interesting to note how the pattern has changed over that period, bearing in mind that recent nutritional advice has stressed the

Table 4.3 Food consumption by income group (Great Britain, 1976 and 1984) (oz./person/week)

Income Group	White bread		Brown bread, incl. wholemeal		Sugar		Total fats		Fruit (fresh)		Vegetables (fresh)		Potatoes	
	1976	1984	1976	1984	1976	1984	1976	1984	1976	1984	1976	1984	1976	1984
A	19.8	12.3	4.1	8	12.3	8	9.8	9.1	22.5	25.3	27.3	30.7	29.8	33.4
B	26.2	18.3	3	6	13.4	9.4	10.5	9.5	18.3	19	24	24.4	35	36.5
C	30.4	23.0	3	5.9	14.5	10.9	11	10.4	15.2	16	24.8	25.5	38.2	42.4
D	29.9	26.0	2.7	5.2	15.7	11.5	11	10	15.2	13	24.9	21.5	42.3	48.3

Source: MAFF (1977, 1986).

need to eat more fibre (for instance in bread, particularly brown and wholemeal), more fresh fruit and vegetables including potatoes, and to cut down on sugar, salt and fat, particularly animal fat. In both years the richest group consumed more brown and wholemeal bread, more fresh fruit and vegetables, and less white bread, potatoes, sugar and fat than the poorest group. By the mid 1980s all income groups had increased their consumption of brown and wholemeal bread and potatoes, and had cut down on sugar. (By 1986 brown and wholemeal bread accounted for 25 per cent of all bread consumed, compared with 10 per cent in 1976.) However, consumption of fresh fruit and vegetables had increased only marginally in groups A, B and C, and in the poorest group had actually declined. There was a small reduction in the consumption of total fats across all income groups, but a substantial change in the *type* of fats consumed. Butter, lard and compound cooking fat consumption declined markedly, and there was a corresponding increase in margarine and 'all other fats' consumption in all income groups (MAFF, 1977, 1986). Thus in terms of the foodstuffs listed the richest income group continues to have a healthier diet than the poorest group. However, there are signs that, within the limits of their income, the poorest group may have responded to nutritional advice to the same extent as other groups, for example in wholemeal bread consumption. How much the poorest group's choice of food is restricted by low income is discussed in greater detail [below].

There is also evidence of higher consumption of sweets by children in lower social groups (Charles and Kerr, 1985).

The links between nutrition and health are many and varied, ranging from effects on growth, to links with specific diseases like coronary heart disease and obesity, to general resistance to infections, and all of these show higher rates in lower social groups.

Exercise in leisure-time

Data on leisure-time activities by socio-economic group were available in the 1973, 1977 and 1983 General Household Surveys. Table 4.4 shows two of the most popular activities: walking and swimming. In both, the professional group had the highest participation rates and the unskilled manual group the lowest. There was an increase in participation from 1977 to 1983 for all groups, but the social gradient remained.

Exercise may be linked to health in several ways, including a possible protective effect against coronary heart disease mortality, which is, of course, class-related (Morris, 1981).

Table 4.4   Exercise in lesiure-time in Great Britain by socio-economic group. Persons aged 16 and over (1977 and 1983): % participating.

Socio-economic group	Walking (over 2 miles)		Indoor swimming	
	1977	1983	1977	1983
Professional	29	30	9	12
Employers and managers	23	24	6	9
Intermediate – non-manual	27	27	7	11
Junior – non-manual	20	22	5	10
Skilled manual	15	16	4	5
Semi-skilled manual	12	15	1	4
Unskilled manual	10	13	2	3

Source: OPCS *General Household Survey* for 1977 and 1983.

Poorer take-up of preventive services by lower social classes has already been noted; it is clearly a possibility that this is due to cultural norms and voluntary behaviour choices rather than to material barriers to take-up, such as limited access.

How much of the differential does life-style explain?

The evidence outlined above suggests that differences in life-style can indeed account for some of the class differential in health, but how much of it do the life-style factors account for? A more systematic investigation of coronary heart disease risk factors was carried out in the Whitehall study (Marmot *et al.*, 1984b). The two major smoking-related diseases, coronary heart disease and lung cancer, were related both to smoking and employment grade. Of the top grade, 29 per cent were smokers, compared with 61 per cent of the lowest grade. However, it was found that even for non-smokers coronary heart disease was strongly associated with grade, with higher rates in lower grades. Table 4.5 shows what happened to the class gradient for coronary heart disease when controlled for age, smoking, systolic blood pressure, plasma cholesterol, height and blood sugar.

The risk associated with employment grade reduced by less than 25 per cent. Likewise, controlling for exercise in leisure-time had little effect on the differential. In addition, steep gradients were found for diseases thought not to be related to smoking.

Table 4.5 Relative risk* of CHD death in ten years controlling for (a) age, and (b) age, smoking, systolic blood pressure, plasma cholesterol concentration, height and blood sugar.

	Administrators	Professional/ executive	Clerical	Other
(a) Controlling for age	1.0	1.6	2.2	2.7
(b) Controlling for other risk factors	1.0	1.5	1.7	2.1

* Calculated by multiple logistic regression.
Source: Marmot et al. (1984b).

In the United States similar results have been found from an important cohort study, the Alameda County Study in California (Berkman and Breslow, 1983; Kaplan, 1985). The study has been assessing levels of health in the sample and trying to determine factors associated with health since 1965. When family income was studied, those with 'inadequate' income had much poorer survival chances over eighteen years of follow-up. For example, compared with the richest group, the poorest group had more than double the risk of death over that period. The study went on to analyse whether harmful behaviour patterns accounted for the increased risk. Even when the data were adjusted to take account of thirteen known risk factors including smoking, drinking, exercise and race, there was still a substantial gradient of risk associated with income. For example, the poorest group still had one and a half times the risk of death as the richest group. They concluded that behaviour patterns were not the major factors related to the increased risk of death, and suggested that factors related to the general living conditions and environment of the poor were more likely to be implicated. This line of enquiry is continuing.

Likewise, in [a] study of unemployed and employed groups [. . .], excess mortality in the unemployed group was still evident when the study controlled for smoking and drinking (Cook et al., 1982).

All these studies suggest that the differences in life-style between social groups account for some, but not all, of the observed health gap. Indeed in some cases most of the difference in health is not explained by these factors.

Several new studies have touched on the cultural aspect of this explanation – the suggestion that beliefs about health and health care may differ among social groups. The 'culture of poverty' idea – that poorer groups have more negative concepts of health and a lack of orientation towards the future which inhibits preventive health action – has been re-examined. For example, Calnan and Johnson (1985) compared the health beliefs of women from social classes I and II with those of social classes IV and V on two issues: concepts of health and perception of vulnerability to disease. Both of these issues are claimed to be related to decisions to take action on health. Findings showed that there was no social class difference in theories about vulnerability, or in concepts of health when defined in relation to personal health. Only when health was defined in the *abstract* were there marked social class differences and this may have been because middle-class women found it easier to express abstract ideas.

Similarly, Blaxter and Paterson (1982), in a study of disadvantaged mothers and daughters in Scotland, found no evidence that would fit a simple 'culture of poverty' model in either generation. Problems in health service use in the younger generation seemed to stem more from a lack of skill in dealing with the system rather than from adverse cultural beliefs. These and other studies (Pill and Stott, 1985a, 1985b) suggest that the importance of the 'culture of poverty' model as an explanation of poor service use and health-damaging behaviour may have been over-estimated in the past, and new appraisals of health behaviour are needed.

Evidence that material factors affect health or health-related behaviour

Several studies published recently have investigated how material and structural factors affect health. Others have looked at how such factors influence behaviour or limit choice about health. The evidence of higher mortality in the unemployed which cannot easily be explained away other than by some direct or indirect effect of unemployment has already been presented. The strong association with aspects of material deprivation and ill-health in small area studies has also been discussed [. . .]. This section therefore concentrates on a number of additional factors, such as housing and income, to add to the evidence.

Housing conditions and health

This subject has been badly neglected until recently and is only beginning to be studied again, mainly in the public sector. Some of the studies look at aspects of poor housing, like damp and mould, in relation to physical health. Others are concerned more with the stress and safety aspects imposed on people by poor design.

A study in Gateshead was carried out in 1983 on eight council housing areas, from the very best to the very worst in the district. Controlling for age, there were marked and consistent differences in self-reported health between individuals from different areas. People from 'bad' housing areas reported poorer health, more long-standing illness, more recent illness and more symptoms of depression than those living in 'good' housing areas. The position was reversed for the over-65s because of a local authority letting policy which gave priority to the less-fit elderly. Nearly a third of households reported defects in houses which they thought affected health, and these came disproportionately from the three 'bad' areas, especially in connection with respiratory conditions. 'Bad' council housing areas did not necessarily conform to the stereotype of non-traditional construction and high-rise flats. Location, poor environment and low quality of construction were the important factors (Keithley *et al.*, 1984).

A further paper by the same team looked in greater detail at respiratory conditions in council house tenants. It was found that smoking, an unhealthy working environment and age were the most important determinants of respiratory problems. When these were held constant, people in areas of 'bad' housing reported more respiratory conditions than those in 'good' housing areas. The problems were associated with flats rather than houses, and with older accommodation (McCarthy *et al.*, 1985).

A large-scale study investigated whether the design of buildings could lead to social malaise among the inhabitants. It covered over 4,000 blocks of flats and 4,000 houses in London, with additional information from around the country and abroad. Fifteen design variables in blocks of flats were identified which affected the behaviour of at least some of the residents, especially children. The degree of social malaise was indicated by the extent of litter, graffiti, vandalism, children taken into care, and urine and faecal pollution. Circumstances worsened with larger buildings and grounds, as the number of interconnecting walkways increased, and also where residents could not see or control the approach to their dwellings. The study concluded that such badly-designed blocks 'made it difficult for normal people to cope', and thus contributed to social malaise (Coleman, 1985).

Also of relevance is the growing problem of infestation of housing estates, with the associated health risks. It has been pointed out that the design of high-rise buildings, with their interconnecting ducts and heating systems, allows rapid spread of vermin over which the individual tenants have very little – if any – control (Young, 1980).

An analysis of 'difficult to let' council housing in Liverpool concluded that the unsatisfactory housing conditions on one estate were contributing to high rates of infectious diseases, respiratory disease and mental illness. One source of infection was traced to unhygienic mobile food vans which residents used because no shops had been provided on the estate. Respiratory illnesses were aggravated by ducted warm-air heating and the practice of drying clothes indoors because of inadequate facilities (Department of the Environment, 1981a). Another study of families living in flats found that serious accidents among children were linked to the design of the building (Department of the Environment, 1981b).

The Housing and Environmental Health Departments of the Wirral, Merseyside, identified serious design and construction faults in their high-density housing. Water penetration, ventilation, heating and insulation problems, inadequate under-floor electric heating, deck access and high child-densities 'combined to produce disaster'. These faults resulted in dangerous and severely limiting conditions for the tenants, including lack of privacy and play facilities, noise, lack of clothes drying facilities, dependence on lifts, inadequate refuse disposal, and the obvious safety aspects of the height of buildings (Darley, 1981).

On the subject of damp, a study in South Wales suggested that respiratory symptoms may be aggravated by damp housing and by open coal fires which were thought to cause some pollution of the air inside the house (Burr *et al.*, 1981). Another found clear effects of damp housing on the health of children in a deprived area of Edinburgh in 1986. In particular, respiratory/bronchial symptoms, headaches and diarrhoea were much more common among children living in damp housing. The effect of damp was independent of the effect of low income or smoking in the household (Hunt *et al.*, 1986). A previous study in Edinburgh in 1984 had also found an association between respiratory problems in children, reported by their parents, and damp or mouldy housing. However, such environmental factors were not linked to GP consultation rates for these illnesses. This highlights the dilemma of which measure of morbidity to use in community studies (Strachan, 1986).

Income

There have been few studies in this country of the direct effect of income on health, partly because of the enormous difficulties encountered and partly because of political sensitivity. To be meaningful, all sources of income would have to be assessed, including the value of fringe benefits, property, etc., and such statistics are not readily available in this country. A preliminary analysis has been carried out on occupational incomes and mortality in twenty-two occupations, comparing 1951 and 1971. Over twenty years those occupations which had increased their income relative to average earnings tended to experience a relative decrease in mortality rates. In occupations where income had gone down relative to the mean, mortality rates tended to go up relative to the mean. The death rates of old people also seemed to vary in a similar way with changes in the real value of state pensions over the years from 1965 to 1982. As Wilkinson notes, this work will have to be repeated and extended before firm conclusions can be drawn (Wilkinson, 1986c).

Another study has looked at the effect of income, but this time on children's height. A study of families in poor areas in London in 1973–6 found that a low amount of money spent on food/person/week in a household was highly correlated with poor growth in children. Among these children protein intake was 92 per cent of the recommended daily intake, iron 80 per cent and vitamin D 40 per cent of that recommended. Of the children in the survey 11 per cent were mildly or moderately malnourished (Nelson and Naismith, 1979).

The *indirect* effect of income on health, for example on choice of diet and eating habits, has been more widely investigated. As outlined [above], people from low-income households tend to eat less fruit, vegetables and high-fibre foods, and more fat and sugar, than people from high-income households.

Studies of why this should be so have found lack of money to be a major factor, restricting food choice as well as limiting the quantity of food consumed. For example, a study of sixty-five families living on supplementary benefit in 1980 found that some parents went without food to provide enough for their children, and lack of money was frequently cited as the reason for lack of fruit and vegetables in the diet (Burghes, 1980). In a study of 1,000 low-income people in the North of England in 1984, approximately a quarter of respondents reported that they did not have a main meal every day. One third of these said this was because of cost. Four out of ten unemployed people went without a main meal because of lack of money (Lang *et al.*, 1984). An in-depth study of 107 women living with pre-school children in Milton Keynes in 1984 found that 51 per cent of single parents and 30 per cent of low-income mothers in two-parent families were cutting down on food consumption for financial reasons. Of low-income women, 67 per cent found it difficult to afford what they considered to be a healthy diet for their children (Graham, 1986).

It is commonly found in such studies that food is treated as a flexible item in the household budget (unlike rent and rates); when money is short, spending on food tends to be cut back. Unfortunately the cheaper foods are often higher in fat and sugar.

A number of 'desk-top calculations' have been carried out to estimate the cost of following advice on a 'healthy diet', to see whether recommendations are realistic for people on low incomes. One, looking at the cost of an 'adequate' diet in pregnancy, concluded that the cost may be beyond the means of families dependent on low wages or benefits. For example, an average couple living on supplementary benefit in 1984 spent 9 per cent to 10 per cent of their income (excluding housing) on one person's food. However, it was estimated an 'adequate' diet for a pregnant woman would have taken up 28 per cent of the couple's income (Durward, 1984). The British Dietetic Association has considered the dietary problems of special groups at risk of malnutrition – children, pregnant women, ethnic minorities, the handicapped and elderly – and concluded that existing benefits for some members of these groups were insufficient for their dietary needs (Haines and de Looy, 1986). One recent study, basing the 'healthy diet' on the advice of the National Advisory Committee on Nutrition Education, calculated that the recommended diet could cost up to 35 per cent more than the typical diet of a low-income family (Cole-Hamilton and Lang, 1986). Some would dispute the figure of 35 per cent and suggest that community studies are now needed to check how valid these calculations are in real-life settings.

In recent years an increasing number of studies have gone out into the community to do just that: to document how people in different circumstances live and how they cope with aspects of health. In the field of family health care, Graham (1984) has collected and reviewed over 250 studies relevant to the question: 'How do parents meet their responsibility to family health?' This provides a valuable insight into the literature. It becomes obvious from such studies that all household resources have the potential to influence health – income, housing, fuel, food and transport. The pattern of spending on these basics varies between rich and poor families. For example, in 1985 poor households spent 56 per cent of income on necessities (food, fuel, housing), whereas rich households spent 36 per cent of their income on these products (Department of Employment, 1986). While 95 per cent of professional households have at least one car available, only 38 per cent of unskilled manual households have one (OPCS, 1986d). It is found that the poorest families may have little choice of fuel, and often have to rely on the most expensive kind (Boardman, 1986). Families who are economizing on fuel risk making their homes cold, damp and prone to condensation. Even within families, there is evidence of resources not being shared out equally. For example, parents may go without food to provide for the children, and the adult breadwinner may be given more food than those who stay at home. If a family has a car it cannot be assumed that women and children have access to it for food shopping and health appointments during the day. Frequently it is found that the male breadwinner in a household has priority over use of the car for work. The issue of transport has been growing in importance as food outlets and medical services become centralized. The time and money spent on travelling becomes a factor to be considered in health service use. One study of pregnant women found that women going to the hospital ante-natal clinic spent twice as long travelling and waiting than mothers going to local GP clinics. They also experienced great problems in travelling with young children (Graham, 1979).

Several studies examine how mothers cope with the stress of caring for the family on a low income, which often involves a juggling act of keeping within a very limited budget while at the same time seeing that the children are well and relatively contented. There is evidence that mothers find a variety of ways of relieving stress in the short term without leaving the child alone. Graham (1984) points out that this often leads to parents going against medical advice. Sweets tend to be used as a quick and easy way of keeping children quiet on shopping trips and on other stressful occasions (Charles and Kerr, 1985), breast-feeding may be abandoned to allow more time for other members of the family (Graham, 1980), and babies' milk may be mixed with cereal to help cope with crying and sleep problems (Graham and McKee, 1980). Cigarette-smoking was used by some mothers as a way of easing tension without leaving the room (Graham, 1976). Another review has also recently highlighted the use of smoking by women to help them survive their stressful workload (Jacobson, 1986).

Graham (1984) points out that such actions, which would be labelled irresponsible by some professionals, may be the only way in which mothers can stay sane and act responsibly towards their family. Poor attendance for preventive health services is also examined in terms of costs and benefits. Graham concludes: 'For poor families in particular a *rational* decision may be one which rejects professional care. The mother may choose instead to invest her limited resources of time, money, and energy in other areas of family health' – in food for the family for example, or in keeping her children warm (Graham, 1984).

These studies on family health, in particular, indicate a complex relationship between individual behaviour and structural and material factors. When researchers start to ask why behaviour differs between classes, it becomes clear that socio-economic circumstances do play an important part. It is far too simple an explanation to put it all down to ignorance or laziness.

Explaining sex differences in health

Parallels can be drawn between the explanations of social class inequalities and those of sex inequalities in health. The artefact, natural selection, behavioural/cultural and materialist/structuralist explanations have all been applied to sex differentials.

For instance, some of the sex differences in morbidity (with high rates for women) have been attributed to artefact, though the exact extent of this is unknown. Morbidity may be under-estimated for men relative to women due to more proxy reporting for men in surveys; or women may have a greater predisposition to report illness. Additionally, women may be more inclined to take care of their health, resulting in increased consultation rates or days of restricted activity for the same amount of illness (Waldron, 1983). All these points need further investigation and, of course, none of them can explain away the sex differential in mortality.

The natural selection or genetic explanation suggests that women's greater longevity and low mortality rate is an intrinsic feature of the human species. This view is supported by the fact that even before birth female foetuses have better survival rates than male foetuses (Hart, 1988). Whatever the merits of the genetic explanation, evidence that the sex differential in mortality is reversed in less developed countries (like Nepal and Bangladesh), and that even the morbidity differential is not a fixed phenomenon in the same country, suggests that the social and cultural environment and health services can play a powerful part in modifying the differential. If that is so, then there should be scope for improvement in health for both sexes.

Very little work has been published on the causes of the sex differential in Britain, though studies in the United States and Europe attempt to answer the question: 'Why do women live longer than men?' Male mortality exceeds female mortality by 100 per cent for seven of the major causes of death in the United States: coronary heart disease, lung cancer, emphysema, motor vehicle and other accidents, cirrhosis of the liver and suicide. These causes account for 75 per cent of the sex differential in mortality in the United States. Reasons for the differential have been analysed at the behavioural/cultural level. It was estimated, for example, that well over half the difference between male and female death rates could be accounted for by differences in behaviour, for example cigarette-smoking, alcohol consumption and occupational hazard. The study concluded that sex differences in behaviour are more important causes of higher male mortality than genetic factors (Waldron, 1976).

A comparison of sex differentials in health and illness in Sweden, Denmark, Finland and Norway found great variation in the morbidity differential. For example, the sex differential in symptoms of anxiety was much smaller in Finland and Sweden than in Denmark and Norway. Type of employment also had an effect on the differential. There was excess female morbidity in agricultural and manual workers. In white-collar groups, students and pensioners, however, men and women had similar standards of health. In some countries, like Finland and Norway, white-collar women were healthier than their male counterparts. Overall, the excess female morbidity rate was mainly due to higher rates for female manual workers and full-time housewives (Haavio-Mannila, 1986). In general it was concluded that in countries where many women work outside the home, rates of illness and hospitalization for women are lower than those for men. In countries, and at certain periods of time in the same country, when women mostly stay at home, women's illness rates are higher than for men (Haavio-Mannila, 1986). In Britain employment outside the home was found to be a benefit to some groups of women and a burden to others, depending on their social circumstances [. . .] (Arber *et al.*, 1985).

Another study in 1985 was interested in the causes of the difference in life expectancy between men and women. The authors argued that if much of the difference between males and females was due to environmental factors, then there may be situations where the difference could be reduced. They hypothesized that kibbutz life might be capable of narrowing the gender gap in life expectancy by providing a closely matched environment for men and women with less difference in gender roles than in other developed countries. Calculating the expected gap in life expectancy from international data, they found that in the kibbutz the observed gap was much smaller – at birth the gap was 4.5 years instead of the expected 7.1 years, and at age fifty the gap was 2.7 years instead of the expected 5.1 years. The gap had been reduced by improvements in male life expectancy rather than by a reduction in female life expectancy (Leviatan and Cohen, 1985).

These recent studies open up intriguing possibilities for improvements in the sex differentials in health, though investigations are only at a preliminary stage. They certainly illustrate the potential importance of social and environmental factors on the health of both men and women.

Conclusions

The four possible explanations of inequalities in health put forward by the Black Working Group have been reviewed in the light of new evidence. From the evidence, the inequalities between social groups are genuine and cannot be explained away as artefact. Further evidence has confirmed the existence of a health selection effect – in particular, showing that serious illness in childhood can cause a fall in occupational class later on. There is also renewed evidence of selection for height at marriage. Estimates suggest that the selection effect is small and does not account for the much larger differentials in health observed.

The weight of evidence continues to point to explanations which suggest that socio-economic circumstances play the major part in subsequent health differences. For example, the evidence that health-damaging behaviour is more common in lower social groups continues to accumulate, especially concerning smoking and diet. But can such life-style factors account for all the observed differential in health between different social groups? The short answer is: no. When studies are able to control for factors like smoking and drinking, a sizeable proportion of the health gap remains and factors related to the general living conditions and environment of the poor are indicated. In this context there is also a growing body of evidence that material and structural factors, such as housing and income, can affect health. Most importantly, several studies have shown how adverse social conditions can limit the choice of life-style and it is this set of studies which illustrates most clearly that behaviour cannot be separated from its social context. Certain living and working conditions appear to impose severe restrictions on an individual's ability to choose a healthy life-style.

The evidence suggests that policies to reduce inequalities which focused entirely on the individual would be misguided. The importance of social and material factors highlighted by the research suggests that broader policies incorporating structural improvements in living and working conditions would be required in addition.

References

References are listed in the order in which they appear in the chapter: Blane, D. (1985) 'An assessment of the Black report's explanations of health inequalities' *Sociology of Health and Illness*, 7; OPCS (1986d) *General Household Survey for 1984*, HMSO; Marmot, M.G. and McDowall, M.E. (1986) 'Mortality decline' *Lancet*, ii; Marmot, M.G. *et al.*(1981) 'Changes in heart and disease mortality' *Health Trends*, 13; Morris, J.N. (1979) 'Social inequalities undiminished' *Lancet*, i; MAFF (1977, 1986) *Household Food Consumption and Expenditure 1976/1984*, HMSO; Charles, N. and Kerr, M. (1985) *Attitudes towards the Feeding and Nutrition of Young Children*, Health Education Council; Morris, J.N. (1981) *Coronary heart disease*, Update 1 Aug.; Marmot, M.G. *et al.* (1984b) 'Inequalities in death' *Lancet*, i; Berkman, L.F. and Breslow, L. (1983) *Health and Ways of Living*, OUP; Kaplan, G.A. (1985) 'Twenty years of health in Alameda County', Society for Prospective Medicine; Cook, D.G. *et al.* (1982) 'Health of unemployed middle-aged men in Britain' *Lancet*, i; Calnan, M. and Johnson, B. (1985) 'Health, health risks and inequalities' *Sociology of Health and Illness*, 7; Blaxter, M. and Paterson, L. (1982) *Mothers and Daughters*, Heinemann; Pill, R. and Stott, N.C. (1985a) 'Choice or chance' *Soc. Sci. Med.*, 20; (1985b) 'Preventive procedures among working class women' *Soc. Sci. Med.*, 21; Keithley, *et al.* (1984) 'Health and housing conditions in public sector housing estates' *Public Health*, 98; McCarthy, P. *et al.* (1985) 'Respiratory conditions' *J. of Epidemiology*, 39; Coleman, A. (1985) *Utopia on Trial*, Hilary Shipman; Young, B. (1980) 'Health and housing' *Roof*, July/Aug.; DoE (1981a) *An Investigation of 'difficult to let' Housing*, HMSO; (1981b) *Families in Flats*, HMSO; Darley, C.D. (1981) 'High density housing' *Royal Society of Health J.*, 101; Burr, M.L. *et al.* (1981) 'Wheezing, dampness and coal fires' *Community Med.*, 3; Papers by Hunt, S.M. *et al.* and Strachan, D.P. at Unhealthy Housing Conference, Warwick University, 1986; Wilkinson, R.G. (1986c) 'Income and mortality' in *Class and Health*, Tavistock; Nelson, M. and Naismith, D. (1979) 'The nutritional status of poor children in London' *J. of Human Nutrition*, 33; Burghes, L. (1979) *Living from Hand to Mouth*, Child Poverty Action Group; Lang, T. *et al.* (1984) *Jam Tomorrow?* Manchester University; Graham, H. (1986) *Caring for the Family*, Health Education Council; Durward L. (1984) *Poverty in Pregnancy*, Maternity Alliance; Haines, F.A. and de Looy, A.E. (1986) *Can I Afford the Diet?* British Dietetic Association; Cole-Hamilton, I. and Lang, T. (1986) *Tightening Belts*, London Food Commission; Graham, H. (1984) *Women, Health and the Family*, Wheatsheaf; DE (1986) *Family Expenditure Survey for 1985*, HMSO; Boardman, B. (1986) paper at Warwick conference op.cit.; Graham, H. (1979) *Problems in Antenatal Care*, University of York; Graham, H. (1980) 'Family influences on eating habits' in *Nutrition and Lifestyles*, Applied Science Publ.; Graham, H. and McKee, L. (1980) *The First Months of Motherhood*, Health Education Council; Graham, H. (1976) 'Smoking in pregnancy' *Soc. Sci. Med.*, 10; Jacobson, B. (1986) *Beating the Ladykillers*, Pluto; Waldron, I. (1983) 'Sex differences in illness incidence' *Soc. Sci. Med.*, 17; Hart, N. (1988) 'Sex differentials in mortality' in *Inequality in Health within Europe*, Gower; Waldron, I. (1976) 'Why do women live longer than men?' *Soc. Sci. Med.*, 10; Haavio-Mannila, E. (1986) 'Inequalities in health and gender' *Soc. Sci. Med.*, 22; Arber, S. *et al.* (1985) 'Paid employment and women's health' *Sociology of Health and Illness*, 7; Leviatan, U. and Cohen, J. (1985) 'Gender differences in life expectancy among Kibbutz members' *Soc. Sci. Med.*, 21.

CHAPTER 5
Men and Women

John Nicholson

Persons do not exist; there are only male persons and female persons.
Thomas Colley, psychologist

For most of us, the single most important influence on what we feel about another person is whether that person happens to be a man or a woman. We have fixed ideas about what men and women are like, and about what constitutes 'typical' masculine and feminine behaviour.

Given the very determined campaign which has been waged against sexism over the last twenty years, you might suppose that sex stereotypes would have gone out of fashion, or at least that people would have become reluctant to admit that they still use them. But research carried out in the early 1970s, when the influence of the Women's Movement was at its height, suggests that this is not so at all. A large sample of Americans of all ages and both sexes were asked to list the characteristics, attributes and types of behaviour in which they thought men and women differed, and their answers leave no doubt that sex stereotypes are still enormously powerful. Three-quarters of the people questioned agreed that men and women differ on more than forty aspects of behaviour, listed in Table 5.1. And both men and women expressed a clear preference for the behaviour they had designated masculine. The investigators were surprised to find that students were just as likely to use sex stereotypes as their elders, and there is no reason to suppose that people's views about typical masculine and feminine behaviour are more firmly entrenched in America than they are elsewhere. Nor is it easy to get people to change their minds – researchers in both Europe and America have found that taking a course on sex differences at university has no effect on a student's sex stereotypes. So it seems that we expect men and women to behave very differently, and that we value masculine behaviour more highly.

We may *think* that men and women behave differently, but do they? And if so, why? The main purpose here is to try to establish which of the popular beliefs set out in Table 5.1 are justified – that is to say, based on real, observable differences between the sexes – and which exist only in our imagination. However, adult behaviour is the product of a lengthy process of development. We must go back to the beginning of the story to have any chance of understanding the nature and the causes of differences between the sexes.

Source: J. Nicholson, *Men and Women: How Different Are They?*, 1984, Oxford University Press. Oxford. Chapter 1.

Table 5.1 Stereotypic traits.

Feminine	Masculine
Masculine pole is more desirable	
Not at all aggressive	Very aggressive
Not at all independent	Very independent
Very emotional	Not at all emotional
Does not hide emotions at all	Almost always hides emotions
Very subjective	Very objective
Very easily influenced	Not at all easily influenced
Very submissive	Very dominant
Dislikes maths and sciences very much	Likes maths and sciences very much
Very excitable in a minor crisis	Not at all excitable in a minor crisis
Very passive	Very active
Not at all competitive	Very competitive
Very illogical	Very logical
Very home oriented	Very worldly
Not at all skilled in business	Very skilled in business
Very sneaky	Very direct
Does not know the way of the world	Knows the way of the world
Feelings easily hurt	Feelings not easily hurt
Not at all adventurous	Very adventurous
Has difficulty making decisions	Can make decisions easily
Cries very easily	Never cries
Almost never acts as a leader	Almost always acts as a leader
Not at all self-confident	Very self-confident
Very uncomfortable about being aggressive	Not at all uncomfortable about being aggressive
Not at all ambitious	Very ambitious
Unable to separate feelings from ideas	Easily able to separate feelings from ideas
Very dependent	Not at all dependent
Very conceited about appearance	Never conceited about appearance
Thinks women are always superior to men	Thinks men are always superior to women
Does not talk freely about sex with men	Talks freely about sex with men
Feminine pole is more desirable	
Doesn't use harsh language at all	Uses very harsh language
Very talkative	Not at all talkative
Very tactful	Very blunt
Very gentle	Very rough
Very aware of feelings of others	Not at all aware of feelings of others
Very religious	Not at all religious
Very interested in own appearance	Not at all interested in own appearance
Very neat in habits	Very sloppy in habits
Very quiet	Very loud
Very strong need for security	Very little need for security
Enjoys art and literature	Does not enjoy art and literature at all
Easily expresses tender feelings	Does not express tender feelings at all easily

Source: Broverman and others, 1972.

Sexual differentiation

In human beings, the female ovum and the male sperm both contain twenty-three chromosomes. These are tiny threadlike bodies which are found in every one of the billions of cells of which we are composed, and they contain the genetic instructions which make a major contribution to the development of every single characteristic of our bodies – from the colour of our eyes to the length of our toes.

If you start with the belief that men and women are very different, you might expect there to be two quite different sets of genetic instructions governing male and female development. There would be a male blueprint which caused the formation of male genitals, large muscles and extensive bodily and facial hair, and a female pattern which would result in the development of the characteristic female shape and appearance. In fact, this is not at all how things are. Both sexes actually receive very similar genetic instructions, not only for characteristics like eye colour and hair texture which do not distinguish between them, but even for the features we use to tell them apart. For example, the shape and size of a woman's breasts are very different from those of a man, but we all have the same raw material to develop breast tissue. What happens is that both sexes receive sets of instructions dealing with breast development, but in only one sex are the instructions acted upon. The same applies for all the other physical characteristics which obviously distinguish men from women: genitals, shape, muscle growth, voice-box development, body hair and so on.

But it is not simply a matter of luck whether a newly created embryo becomes male or female, though chance is of course involved. So far as genetic sex is concerned, an irrevocable decision to develop consistently along either male or female lines is made the moment the sperm and ovum unite, and it is made on the basis of the composition of the twenty-third pair of chromosomes, the sex chromosomes. Every pair of chromosomes is made up of one from each of our parents, and in all but the sex chromosomes the two are roughly the same in size and structure. But the two sex chromosomes can either be similar or very different. When they are similar, this means that the ovum and the sperm have both contributed what is known as an X chromosome (so called not because of its shape – all chromosomes are X-shaped – but because scientists discovered it after the other twenty-two pairs, and named it X for extra), and the resulting embryo is genetically female. One X chromosome comes from the sperm, and one from the ovum. But an ovum can contribute only an X chromosome to the newly formed egg, since the woman from whom the ovum came has no other sex chromosome. A pair of X chromosomes is the hallmark of femaleness, but in a male the sex chromosome pair consists of one X chromosome plus a different, much smaller chromosome called the Y chromosome, which always comes from the sperm. There is a fifty-fifty chance of the sperm contributing a Y chromosome. Whenever this happens, the resulting embryo will have the XY combination on its sex chromosome, and it will be genetically male. This is how sex is determined genetically, and there is an interesting point to note: the sex of a child is determined solely by its father. If he contributes an X chromosome, the child will have two Xs and she will be female; if he contributes a Y, the child will have an X and a Y and he will be male.[. . .]

Although the composition of the sex chromosomes is determined at conception, a month and a half passes before there is any visible sign as to which of the two sets of genetic instructions is going to be followed. Embryos of both sexes contain tissue which will eventually develop into either male gonads (testes) or female gonads (ovaries). They also have a genital tubercle which will become either a penis and scrotum or a clitoris and labia, and two sets of ducts, one of which will turn into whichever internal reproductive structures are appropriate to the sex of the particular embryo. About six weeks after conception, the genetically male embryo will begin to develop testes. In the female embryo, nothing happens for several more weeks, and then the ovaries start to be formed. Once formed, the gonads begin to secrete the sex hormones. In males, these organize the development of the appropriate reproductive structures and later the external genitals. In females, though this is the time when hormones start being produced, they are not responsible in the same way for the development of the genitals.

The dominant sex hormones in males are androgens, the most powerful of which is called testosterone. The major female sex hormones are oestrogen and progesterone. Calling these 'male' and 'female' hormones is actually misleading, because both sexes produce both hormones, and the only difference lies in the balance between them. At birth, for example, boys have a greater concentration of testosterone in their bloodstream than girls do, but there is no consistent difference between the sexes in the level of 'female' hormones, and the two sorts of hormone are very similar chemically.

At every stage in the process of human sexual differentiation, changes in the male direction occur before changes towards femaleness. There is no neuter sex, and nature's plan seems to be that the embryo will become female unless it has a Y chromosome which leads to the formation of testes which produce testosterone. This is not the case with all species. In birds, for example, the basic blueprint is male, and females are the departure from the norm. The old wives' tale about hens turning into cocks is actually entirely plausible, since if a hen's supply of female hormones dries up for any reason, the basic male pattern of development can reassert itself. Returning to humans, [. . .] if the Y chromosome is destroyed the child will be born female with Turner's syndrome. And if for any reason the testes fail to produce testosterone then the result will be a genetically male child with female genitals.

There is only one conclusion to be drawn from this account of the clearly distinct developmental sequences followed by unborn males and females: your sex is decided long before the time when you officially enter the world, and the decision is made and implemented by biological forces. Nor does the influence of biology stop at birth. At birth, the physical differences between boys and girls are actually very small (except of course for their genitals), but shortly before puberty there is a massive increase in sex hormone production which leads to the physical divergence between the sexes. Notice, however, that we have so far established only that there are fundamental biological differences between males and females.

It is quite possible that the only significance of these differences is that they equip men and women for their different reproductive roles. As yet we have no evidence that they cause men and women to behave differently in any other respect.[. . .]

Beware biologists

The interplay of biology and culture, and how far each is responsible for sex differences, will be one of the central themes of this [chapter]. I do not want to play down the importance of biology, tempting though it is to try and counteract the biological determinism of writers such as Desmond Morris and Konrad Lorenz. But before turning to the influence of culture on children's ideas of masculinity and femininity, I would like to point to the folly of two assumptions made by those who detect the influence of biology in everything we do. The first assumption is that the study of animal behaviour can explain human behaviour, and that what goes for rats probably goes for man too. The second is that behaviour which made good sense for Stone Age man is 'natural', and that we abandon or seek to change it at our peril, however different our life-style is from that of our ancestors.

So far as the first assumption is concerned, you need look no further than the sex hormones we have been talking about to see the pitfalls. If a group of rats is castrated, they lose their sex drive. Inject them with sex hormones and they will show normal sexual behaviour. So sex hormones govern sexual behaviour. But do the same thing with a group of monkeys and the results are not nearly so predictable. A group of female talapoin monkeys may be treated in such a way that each has exactly the same level of circulating hormones. But only one of them – the dominant female – will make any attempt to interest a male, and her attentions will be directed exclusively at the dominant male (and his attentions only at her). The explanation of this is that the effect of sex hormones is drastically reduced in species which have any form of social organization. Sex hormones may have an effect on what a monkey is ready to do, but what he or she actually does depends entirely on the situation. Since human social and cultural organization is still more complex, we are unlikely to learn much about human sexuality from experimenting with rats, and it is for this reason that I don't have much to say about their behaviour.

As for attempts to explain behaviour in terms of the pressures which operated on primitive man, it strikes me as ironic that those who are most ready to point to the biological importance of particular customs seem to ignore the fact that evolution has not stopped. The most successful species are those which modify themselves to accommodate changes in the environment – the race is won by the swiftest to adapt. When trying to explain the differences between men and women, some writers make a lot of the fact that a clear delineation of separate tasks and status along sex lines had a number of advantages for primitive hunter-gatherer societies. But external circumstances have changed so dramatically since then that changes in the way we behave may not only be possible, but very likely desirable. Attempts to conserve hunter-gatherer behaviour in modern society – as some biologists recommend – may actually be dangerous.[. . .]

Gender roles and culture

So far we have been talking mainly about sex – maleness or femaleness – which tells us a lot about how men and women come to be different physically. But when we think about what is meant by being a man or a woman, we are usually less interested in biological sex than in gender, the concept which covers masculinity and femininity, so we must now try to establish how a child comes to think of himself or herself as a boy or a girl, and how children develop the idea that it is masculine to behave in one way and feminine to behave in another.

Babies appear to have very little sense of self-awareness, so presumably they start life oblivious of what sex they are. Their parents, however, take a very different view of the matter, and their attitude clearly cannot be disregarded since they are going to play a crucial role in the child's development. We know that parents are concerned about the sex of a child even before it is born.[. . .]

This suggestion was confirmed by the results of a study carried out recently in a London hospital, which showed that first-time mothers who had had a boy baby felt a greater sense of achievement than those who had given birth to a girl.

When it comes to what babies actually do, there is little difference between the sexes. Not all babies behave in exactly the same way; on the contrary, signs of a distinct individual personality can be seen in the way a child behaves from the very beginning. But an infant's sex is not a particularly strong predictor of what sort of behaviour it is likely to show. There is far more variety of behaviour amongst babies of the same sex than there is between a 'typical' boy and a 'typical' girl – an observation which applies to virtually every sex 'difference' between adult men and women.[. . .]

However, the way things are is not always the way people think they are, and there is a great deal of evidence which suggests that most people firmly believe that little girls and little boys are – or ought to be – very different creatures. In the study of first-time mothers referred to earlier, more than half of them said during pregnancy that they believed the behaviour of boy and girl babies was different. After giving birth, thirty-eight per cent said they felt their relationship with the baby was affected by its sex. Nor is it just mothers who think that boy and girl babies are different. You can discover this yourself by carrying out the following simple experiment.

Take a baby out into the street, stop the first twenty people you meet and tell them you are conducting an experiment to find out how people react to babies, and then ask them to hold 'Mark' and tell you what sort of baby they think he is. Repeat the procedure with twenty more people, only this time ask them what they think of 'Mary'. The baby will be the same in both cases (you can add an extra frill to the experiment by covering 'Mark' with a blue blanket and 'Mary' with a pink one), but the responses you get from the two sets of people will be quite different.

Whatever the baby's real sex, 'Mark' will be described as bouncing, cheeky, mischievous and strong, while 'Mary' will be seen as lovely, sweet, gorgeous and cute. Of course these are the reactions of strangers to a baby they are meeting for the first time, so the experiment does not tell us anything about what parents think of their own children. But it has been carried out a number of times, usually with the results I have described. As you might expect, the effect is strongest amongst adults with traditional attitudes, and it depends to some extent on the degree to which 'Mark/Mary's' behaviour conforms to the popular stereotypes of how little boys and girls should behave. But it is a powerful effect which leaves no doubt that such stereotypes exist, and that they influence the way we perceive boy and girl babies.

Does the fact that our spontaneous reactions to baby boys and girls are so different mean that we actually treat them differently? To answer this question, researchers at Sussex University invited thirty-two mothers into their laboratory, invited them to play with a baby they had never seen before, and filmed the results. As in the previous experiment, the same baby was presented to different women as either a girl or a boy, and once again this had a marked effect on how 'he' or 'she' was treated. As you might expect, the women's first choice of toys was governed by what sex they thought the baby was: a toy hammer for the 'boy', for the 'girl' the inevitable doll. But even more striking was the fact that they interpreted exactly the same behaviour by the child in a different way when they thought 'he' was a boy than when they thought 'she' was a girl. When 'he' became restless and started to wriggle, they took this as a sign that he wanted to play and went along with what they took to be his wishes. But when 'she' made the same movements, she was assumed to be upset and in need of soothing.

If this is typical of the way mothers respond to babies, it seems likely that boys and girls, from an early age, will form very different views about their ability to influence other people and to dictate the course of events. We can assume that if boys are allowed to call the tune in this way, they will be encouraged to behave independently and to expect that if they make their wishes known, they will get what they want. But the only lesson girls can learn from their treatment is that they are expected to lie quietly, passively waiting for things to happen before reacting.

Of course, this experiment [. . .] only tells us how mothers react to other people's children. Researchers have found it much more difficult to show that mothers treat their own boy and girl babies differently. This is not because mothers treat all their own children in exactly the same way, but because mothers treat each child according to his or her individual personality, regardless of whether it is a girl or a boy. She may believe in sexual stereotypes, but these seem to be much more influential when she is confronted by an unknown child. However, there *are* differences in the way mothers treat their own boy and girl babies, and one of these ties in with the results of the experiment we have been discussing.

Studies show that mothers spend more time holding and soothing their baby daughters than they do their sons, despite the fact that boys actually cry more and sleep less than their sisters. Both parents make a greater investment in encouraging their daughters to be sociable: they smile and talk to them more.

encouraging them to smile and gurgle back, and they tend to be more verbally affectionate towards girls, using terms like 'honey', 'precious' and 'angel'. With boys, less time is spent on these embryonic conversations and more on stimulating them to be active and outgoing.

Fathers may be particularly important here. There is some evidence that a small child would rather play with its father than with its mother. Part of the explanation for this must be his greater rarity value. But fathers also tend to be more physical and imaginative playmates than mothers, particularly when playing with boys. When children find a task difficult, fathers are more likely to give them practical assistance, while mothers tend just to offer general encouragement. The role of fathers in bringing up children is something researchers are only now beginning to investigate, but it looks as though they are more influenced than their wives by the sex of a child. Fathers touch new-born sons more than daughters, and are especially attentive to first-born boys. Later, it is they rather than their wives who are more concerned that their daughters should be 'feminine' and their sons unmistakably 'masculine', and they have more rigid ideas about the different sorts of games it is appropriate for boys and girls to play.

How do children become aware of their gender and start thinking in terms of masculinity and femininity? [. . .]

The role which television plays in inculcating sexual stereotypes in children is hard to assess. Expert opinion seems to have swung quite sharply away from the once popular view that children are not much affected by what they see on the screen. On the other hand, there do seem to be some grounds for cautious optimism about the willingness of at least some TV directors to present a less biased view of the adult world. For example, [a] survey of American TV commercials carried out at the end of the 1970s found that women were more often shown working in traditionally masculine jobs than in earlier studies. However, men were never shown in traditionally feminine occupations outside the home, and although they were sometimes seen to be cooking and cleaning, this was invariably being done under the supervision of their wife, usually to make a humorous point.

Where children's books are concerned, we might expect the media to exert a more liberal influence. But this does not seem to be the case, at least where the USA is concerned. Researchers who investigated how men and women were depicted in nineteen prize-winning children's books published between 1972 and 1979 detected few signs of the considerable changes which had taken place in sex roles in the real world. Comparing these books with prize-winners from the period 1967–1971, they found that although the ratio of male to female pictures had changed dramatically (from 11:1 to 1.8:1, for human characters), the authors, regardless of their own sex, still seemed to be locked into traditional sex-typing when it came to what the characters actually did. Almost without exception, the female characters were presented as warm, caring and affectionate, but dependent and incidental to the plot. The male characters, on the other hand, were tough, self-sufficient and aggressive, and it was around them that the stories revolved.[. . .]

Since children are surrounded by adults with preconceptions about masculine and feminine behaviour, it is tempting to assume that they first become aware of gender as something adults seem to think is important. But some theorists have suggested that children would take on a gender role without any outside assistance, as an inevitable consequence of the biological differences between the sexes, specifically in their genitals. Psychoanalysts claim that there is a connection between people's genitals and their personality. The fact that the penis is an organ which intrudes into the world is said to lead to men being outgoing, adventurous and aggressive, while the internal reproductive system of a woman is alleged to make her passive, receptive and peaceful. When parents talk to their children about the difference between their genitals, they sometimes give the impression that girls are people who lack penises. According to Freud, this leads to the condition of penis envy, which he claimed is one of the most powerful influences on the developing female personality, and at the root of women's feeling that they are inferior to men. But while it is true that children are keenly interested in their genitals and anxious to understand why there are two different models available, the psychoanalytic explanation of gender roles cannot account for all the facts.

An alternative explanation is that masculinity and femininity develop in the same way as the physical differences between the sexes [. . .] as a result of the action of the sex hormones which circulate in our bodies. The problem with this explanation is that children start responding to gender at a time when the overall production of sex hormones is at a low ebb, and when there is very little difference between the sexes in hormonal activity.

In fact, when children of different ages are asked questions to discover what they think about masculinity and femininity, it transpires that the concept of gender is not something which just becomes clearer and clearer as the child grows up. On the contrary, the willingness of children to accept gender roles seems to wax and wane as their thought processes change, and no single principle – whether of biology or learning – can explain what actually happens. Instead we are confronted with a complicated mixture of biological change, the influence of parents' and teachers' views about boys and girls, and a child's own determination to make sense of the world and of other people's attitudes and behaviour.[. . .]

Conclusion

The question is often asked, is it biology or culture which makes men and women what they are? We have yet to tackle the job of deciding what men and women in fact are, but I hope that my description of how we come to think of ourselves as men and women will have convinced you that the question is based on a false distinction. The process of becoming a man or woman begins at conception and never really stops. We can no more escape from our biology than we can avoid being influenced by the norms of the society into which we are born, though we know that the message carried by a person's genes about his or her sex can sometimes be modified. We also know that the relative weight an individual attaches to the biological or sociological aspects of masculinity and femininity depends on the way [s/he] interprets them, and that this varies predictably, according to what stage of development [s/he] happens to have reached.

Finally, notice that we have not so far come across any evidence which forces us to accept that men and women must *behave* differently because they *are* different biologically.

References

Broverman, I.K., Vogel, S.R., Broverman, D.M., Clarkson, F.E. and Rosenkrantz, P.S. (1972) 'Sex role stereotypes: a current appraisal', *Journal of Social Issues*, **28**, pp. 59–79.

Downs, A.C. (1981) 'Sex role stereotyping on prime-time television', *Journal of Genetic Psychology*, **138**, pp. 253–8.

Hines, M. (1982) 'Prenatal and gonadal hormones and sex differences in human behaviour', *Psychological Bulletin*, **92**, pp. 56–80.

Hwang, C.-P. (1978) 'Mother-infant interaction: effects of sex of infant on feeding behaviour', *Early Human Development*, **2/4**, pp. 341–9.

Kolbe, R. and LaVoie, J. (1981) 'Sex role stereotyping in preschool children's picture books', *Social Psychology Quarterly*, **44**, pp 369–74.

Maccoby, E.E. and Jacklin, C.N. (1975) *The Psychology of Sex Differences*, London, Oxford University Press, chapter 9.

Manstead, A.S.R. and McCullock, C. (1981) 'Sex-role stereotyping in British TV advertisements', *British Journal of Social Psychology*, **20**, pp. 171–80.

Oakley, A. (1980) *Women Confined*, Oxford, Martin Robertson.

Parke, R.D. (1981) *Fathering*, London, Fontana Paperbacks.

Perry, D.G. and Bussey, K. (1979) 'The social learning theory of sex differences: imitation is alive and well', *Journal of Personality and Social Psychology*, **37**, pp. 1699–1712.

Scheibe, C. (1979) 'Sex roles in TV commercials', *Journal of Advertising Research*, **19**, pp. 23–7.

Singleton, C.H. (1978) 'Sex differences', in B.M. Foss (ed.), *Psychology Survey No. 1*, London, George Allen & Unwin.

Smith, C. and Lloyd, B. (1978) 'Maternal behaviour and perceived sex of infant: revisited', *Child Development*, **49**, pp. 1263–5.

Ullian, D.Z. (1976) 'The development of concepts of masculinity and femininity', in B. Lloyd and J. Archer (eds), *Exploring Sex Differences*, London, Academic Press.

CHAPTER 6

Representations of 'Race'

Robert Miles

The idea of 'race' took on a new meaning with the development of science and its application to the natural world and, subsequently and more narrowly, to the social world from the late eighteenth century (Banton, 1987). From this time, 'race' increasingly came to refer to a biological type of human being, and science purported to demonstrate not only the number and characteristics of each 'race', but also a hierarchical relationship between them. Thus it was claimed that all human beings, and therefore every single individual, either belonged to a 'race' or was a product of several 'races', and therefore exhibited the characteristics of that 'race' or those 'races'. Moreover, science purported to demonstrate that the biological characteristics of each 'race' determined a range of psychological and social capacities of each group, by which they could be ranked.

Thus, stated in its most extreme form, 'race' determined economic and cultural characteristics and development (Barzun, 1938; Banton, 1977). This was a discourse of 'race' that may be described as an instance of biological determinism (Gould, 1984; Rose, 1984). Thereby, the Other was represented as a biologically distinct entity, as a 'race' apart, whose capacities and achievements were fixed by natural and unalterable conditions which were common to that collectivity. There is now a considerable literature on the ideological career of the idea of 'race' (Gossett, 1965; Banton, 1977; Stepan, 1982), and here I draw attention only to those aspects relevant to this general survey of representations of the Other and to the subsequent argument.

First, the scientific assertion of the existence of different biologically-constituted 'races' led eventually to a clash with religious epistemology and religious discourse about the nature and development of the world and the human species.[. . .] Biblical interpretation suggested that the human species was a divine creation and that all human beings, past and present, were descended from Adam and Eve, implying some ultimate homogeneity of the human species. One method of resolving this problem without questioning the legitimacy of Biblical explanation was to claim that God had responded to the commission of human sin by damnation, and that the descendants of those damned were marked by distinctive features (such as a black skin). Another, with an equally long pedigree, placed less emphasis on divine intervention, maintaining that environmental factors (such

Source: R. Miles, *Racism*, 1989, Routledge, Chapman & Hall, pp. 32–40. (Title of original chapter: 'Representations of the other'.)

as the influence of the sun) had modified the original and single biological form represented by Adam and Eve, creating a number of different types which had subsequently become permanently established by hereditary means. Using this latter argument, many 'race' scientists of the eighteenth and nineteenth centuries were able to claim that their explanation for 'race' differentiation was consistent with Christian theology.

But in the late eighteenth century, scientific analysis revived an objection which had been articulated in the late sixteenth century in Hakluyt's collection of travel writings (Sanders, 1978). The counter-claim was that the phenotypical features designated as evidence for the existence of 'race' did not change when members of 'races' moved to different geographical locations and were subjected to different environmental conditions. The case of Africans forcibly moved to, and enslaved within, the United States was often cited to support this view, as was the experience of Europeans resident in the tropical colonies. Both instances were interpreted in such a way as to conclude that the environmental factors, including climate, were incapable of altering the physical features of 'race'. The implication was that distinct 'races' of human beings had always existed and that the hierarchy of inferiority and superiority was therefore natural, inevitable and unalterable. This assault on environmentalism led to a more fundamental conflict with Christian theology (Stanton, 1960; Stepan, 1982). The conclusions to which it gave rise were accorded even greater legitimacy as science occupied an increasingly ascendant position over theology. By the middle of the nineteenth century this theory of polygenism was dominant, and many of its key assumptions survived into the post-Darwinian era (Stocking, 1968).

Second, the scientific discourse of 'race' did not replace earlier conceptions of the Other. Ideas of savagery, barbarism, and civilisation both predetermined the space that the idea of 'race' occupied but were then themselves reconsititued by it. Thus, as I have demonstrated elsewhere (Miles, 1982) extant imagery was refracted through the representational prism of 'race', with the result that environmentalism as an explanation for the sense of difference declined in importance. For example, the idea of civilisation emerged in the later part of the eighteenth century. It was a capacity or achievement that was initially considered to be attainable by all human beings, including those thought to be the most savage peoples, given sufficient time and assistance. This implied a plasticity of human characteristics which was challenged in the later nineteenth century by the scientific idea that the human species was divided into permanent and discrete biological groups. As a result, savagery became a fixed condition of the 'Negro' or African 'race', a product of a small brain, and civilisation became an attribute of large-brained 'white' people (Stocking, 1968).

Third, the generation and reproduction of the idea of 'race' was a European and North American phenomenon (Gossett, 1965). Many scientific writers contributed, and they drew upon and criticised each other's work, seeking new methods of measurement and solutions to emergent anomalies. The writings of the British theorists, Lord Kames and Charles White, were critically reviewed in the United States by Samuel Stanhope Smith in a book, *Essay on the Causes of the Variety of Complexion and Figure in the Human Species*, published in 1787

(Fredrickson, 1972). The science of phrenology originated in the work of Franz Joseph Gall and Johan Gaspar Spurzheim in Germany and was developed by George Combe in Scotland (Gossett, 1965). In turn, George Combe was a friend of Samuel George Morton, an American who published *Crania Americana* in 1839 and *Crania Aegyptiaca* in 1844 (Gould, 1984). The cephalic index (a measurement of skulls which involved dividing the length of the skull by the breadth) was invented by Anders Retzius in Sweden (Gossett 1965: 76) and was a stimulus to a significant proportion of the work (much of which was critical) of Paul Broca in Paris (Gould 1984: 98–100).

F. Tiedeman, a German anatomist, measured brains in order to establish differences between 'races', his results stimulating a critical reply from Josiah Clark Nott in the United States (Gossett, 1965). Louis Agassiz was a Swiss naturalist who was influenced by Georges Cuvier (himself a French anatomist) and who migrated to the United States in 1846 where he collaborated with Josiah Nott and George Gliddon (Stanton, 1960). These two had a major impact on 'race' theory with their book *Types of Mankind*, first published in 1854, which appeared in at least nine editions before the end of the century (Gossett, 1965; Banton, 1977). Thus the increasingly international character of the scientific enterprise was demonstrated by, and facilitated the formulation of, the discourse of 'race'. The consequences were that, as a form of human classification, the scientific idea of 'race' had a widespread circulation, and that all its proponents represented various Others (Africans, North American Indians, Indians) as instances of different and inferior 'races'.

Fourth, although the interrelated ideas of biological type and hierarchy remained a constant feature of the discourse of 'race', the forms of classification and the content of attribution and determination changed over time. For most of the late eighteenth and early nineteenth centuries, 'race' classifications were based upon the phenotypical characteristics of skin colour, hair type, and nose shape, but there was an increasing emphasis upon the dimensions of the skull (Benedict, 1983). The latter figured prominently in investigations from the early nineteenth century [. . .], and considerable effort was expended in assessing, for example, cranial capacity, facial angle and cranial index. Indeed, there was much debate about the relative validity of these different measures. The science of 'race' therefore underwent a complex evolution. In part, this complexity was a function of the essential error of the idea. As each attempt at classification broke down under the weight of logical inconsistency and empirical evidence, a new classification was formulated. But it was also a function of increasing sophistication of measurement (Stocking, 1968).

For example, in Germany in the late eighteenth century, Peter Camper claimed to distinguish between 'races' by facial angle, the angle that a line drawn from the chin to the top of the forehead forms with a horizontal line at the base of the chin. He drew the most extreme contrast between 'Greeks' and 'Negroes' (Gossett, 1965). Somewhat different arguments, but leading to the same conclusion, were advanced by phrenology, the science of the mind, the central claim of which was that the brain was divided into a number of sections, each of which was the basis of a different faculty. It was argued that each 'race' was distinguished by a distinct variation in size and interrelation of these different sections, and not by the weight of the brain or capacity of the skull (Stepan, 1982). As Fryer expressed it succinctly, on this basis 'phrenology justified empire-building' (Fryer, 1984).

Samuel Morton measured difference between 'races' by filling skulls with mustard seed or lead shot, from which he derived a measure of cranial capacity. He claimed to demonstrate significant differences in cranial capacity between five different 'races' (Caucasian, Mongolian, Malay, American, and Ethiopian) although in his final conclusions, these 'races' were further subdivided into 'families' (Gould, 1984). Morton's craniometry was a major influence upon Nott and Gliddon (Stanton, 1960; Gould, 1984) who assumed that there was a correlation between increasing cranial capacity and a higher level of innate intelligence. Louis Gratiolet offered evidence that the coronal suture of the skull closes, thereby arresting the growth of the brain, at different times for different 'races'. He concluded that this closure occurred earlier amongst 'Negroes' than amongst 'Whites' (Gossett, 1965; Gould, 1984). The problems are most evident in the increasing complexity of the measurement systems evolved by Paul Broca in his attempt to identify a phenotypical feature that would systematically and consistently demonstrate the existence of a hierarchy of 'races' (Gossett, 1965; Gould, 1984).

Fifth, the scientific notion of 'race' had a universal application. Not only did those who formulated the idea consider themselves to be members of a 'race' but they also identified a hierarchy of 'races' within Europe. Efforts were made in the late nineteenth century, for example, to identify the different 'races' of which the British population was composed, using hair and eye colour and skull measurements (Beddoe, 1885). Concerning Europe as a whole, various classifications were devised, the most common being a distinction between Teutonic (or Nordic), Mediterranean, and Alpine 'races' (Ripley, 1900). In the USA, this classification was combined with an argument that human intelligence was a fixed and hereditary characteristic in order [. . .] to produce a hierarchy of acceptable and unacceptable immigrants (Gould, 1984).

Within Europe, representations of the Other as an inferior 'race' focused, amongst others, on the Irish [. . .] and Jews [. . .]. This was sustained partly by claiming a biological superiority for the Nordic 'race'. In Germany, Günther [. . .] interpreted European history in a book titled *The Racial Elements of European History* (first published in 1927) using the scientific idea of 'race' to refer to human groups with distinct and measurable physical and mental characteristics. He identified the Nordic 'race' as especially creative, with a need for conquest, a special aptitude for military science and a low crime rate, and he feared social decay in Europe as a result of 'the running dry of the blood of the . . . Nordic race' (1970: 198). Portentously, he stated that 'the question put to us is whether we have courage enough to make ready for future generations a world cleansing itself racially and eugenically' (1970: 267). Günther was only one of a large number of German (and other European) scholars (and political activists) who employed the scientific discourse of 'race' to assert simultaneously the superiority of the Nordic 'race' and the inferiority of Jews [. . .].

Sixth, the scientific conception of 'race' has now been shown to be mistaken, although a number of scientists continue to this day to assert the key ideas in various forms.[. . .]

When the human species was located in evolutionary theory in Europe in the latter half of the nineteenth century, the idea of 'race' was retained, the argument being that each 'race' could be ranked on an evolutionary scale. Thus, what came to be known as Social Darwinism [. . .] asserted that there was a struggle for survival amongst the different human 'races', in the course of which those with lesser intelligence or capacity for 'civilisation' would eventually disappear, their elimination being evidence of their natural inability to evolve. Thus, rather than leading to the rejection of the idea of discrete biological 'races', evolutionary theory was developed initially in a way which endorsed this conception, and the classifiers of the human species (notably the physical anthropologists) continued to produce their typologies (Banton, 1977; Stepan, 1982).

A further decisive development was the articulation of the statistical limitations of phenotypical measurement by those who continued to defend the utility of such measurement. The work of Boas in the early twentieth century is particularly important because he also demonstrated the influence of the social environment on physiological features by use of the cephalic index (Boas, 1940). Boas, then, asserted the existence of biological 'races' but rejected the argument that they were fixed, because of evidence that phenotypical features such as head form did respond to environmental influences (Stocking, 1968). He also argued that although the world's population could be divided into a number of 'races' using various phenotypical criteria, each such category contained within it a range of variation that overlapped with the variation of any other category. He said, moreover, 'With regard to many characteristics of this kind, we find that the difference between the averages of different races is insignificant as compared to the range of variability that occurs within each race' (Boas 1940: 42). It follows from this that although it may be the case that two populations can be shown to have a different average height, it does not follow that any two individuals selected from these two populations will demonstrate the same difference. In other words, groups differences do not correspond to individual differences (Stocking, 1968).

The full implications of Darwin's evolutionary theory could only be explored with the emergence of the science of genetics which identified the biological basis of evolutionary processes. Genetics shifted attention partly away from phenotypical differences such as skin colour and analysed biological features which were not evident to the naked eye and which, in a complex interaction with the environment, determined biological changes in the human species. It was generally concluded after the Second World War that the scientific conception of 'race' grounded in the idea of fixed typologies and based upon certain phenotypical features such as skin colour and skull shape does not have any significant scientific meaning or utility. Moreover, it was concluded that there is no causal relationship between physical or genetic characteristics and cultural characteristics. In a phrase, genetics demonstrated that 'race', as defined by scientists from the late eighteenth century, had no scientifically verifiable referent [. . .].

This has not, however, prevented the continuing use of the term in scientific and everyday language. Concerning the scientific community, some physical anthropologists have continued to assert a 'race' classification using phenotypical features in spite of the genetic and other contrary evidence [. . .] and the famous UNESCO statements on the nature of 'race' gave some varying, but heavily qualified, approval to this approach [. . .]. On the other hand, many geneticists have argued that populations can be better distinguished from each other by identifying different frequencies of variable genes, although they acknowledge that the point at which it is decided to distinguish between populations is determined arbitrarily [. . .]. They argue that these populations, distinguished not by phenotypical features but by genetic frequencies, should be labelled 'races'. In the light of these different conceptions, and of the claims by other scientists that the 'race' idea has no scientific value at all, it is difficult to identify any utility in continuing to use the term scientifically (Miles, 1982).

Concerning the latter, in many different contexts, people have continued to identify the Other by reference to phenotypical features (especially skin colour) which therefore serve as indicative of a significant difference. Moreover, they have continued to use the idea of 'race' to label that difference. As a result, certain sorts of social relations are defined as 'race relations', as social relations between people of different 'races'. Indeed, states legislate to regulate 'race relations', with the result that the reality of 'race' is apparently legitimated in law [. . .]. Thus the idea of 'race' has continued to be used in common-sense discourse to identify the Other in many societies, but largely without the sanction of science.

Conclusion

[. . .] First, the process of representing the Other entails a dialectic of representational inclusion and exclusion. By attributing a population with certain characteristics in order to categorise and differentiate it as an Other, those who do so also establish criteria by which they themselves are represented. In the act of defining Africans as 'black' and 'savages', and thereby excluding them from their world, Europeans in the eighteenth and nineteenth centuries were representing themselves as 'white' and 'civilised'. Moreover, by using the discourse of 'race' to exclude and inferiorise, that same discourse, but with inverted meanings, served to include and superiorise: if the population of Africa was represented as a 'race', then the population of Europe is simultaneously represented as a 'race', albeit a supposedly superior one. Hence, the act of representational exclusion is simultaneously an act of inclusion, whether or not Self is explicitly identified in the discourse.

Second, for the European, the Other has not been created exclusively in the colonial context. Representations of the Other have taken as their subject not only the populations of, for example, Africa, the Indian subcontinent, and the Americas but also the populations of different parts of Europe, as well as invasionary and colonising populations, notably from North Africa and the Middle East. Moreover, the Other has been created not only externally to the nation state but also within, most notably in the case of the Jews. Consequently, debate about the nature and origin of representations of the Other cannot be confined to the analysis of European colonialism (although this is not to claim that the colonial experience is of no relevance to understanding the nature and origin of European representations of the Other).

Third, representations of the Other are holistically neither static nor unitary. They have undergone transformation over time, in response to changing circumstances, including the economic and political position of those producing and reproducing the representations. The characteristics attributed to the Other, the evaluation of those characteristics, and the explanations offered for difference, have therefore been altered, although again rarely in a holistic manner. Thus, in the case of the European representation of the African, while skin colour has remained a constant distinguishing feature, representations of savagery and bestiality have been historically variable. Indeed, the evaluative content of European representations has not been consistently negative, and we have seen examples where the qualities identified and attributed have been largely positively evaluated. Moreover, those people who constitute the object of representation, who are created as the Other, also change over time. For example, for a long period of time in European history, the primary Other was found in the Islamic world rather than central and southern Africa.

Hence, when analysing representations of the Other, it is necessary to be alert to the class position of those producing and reproducing them, and to their dynamic and heterogeneous nature, as well as to their more constant features. The analytical implication is that one cannot assume the existence of a simple process of representational reproduction whereby contemporary representations are inherited from the past. Rather, contemporary representations are always the product of historical legacy and active transformation in the light of prevailing circumstances, including the pattern of class relations.

Fourth, for the European, as well as for other populations, somatic features, and particularly skin colour, have been used to represent the Other long before European colonisation. However, exteriorisation by reference to blackness has not consistently correlated with the attribution of additional, negatively evaluated characteristics, and hence the representation of the African within the Greco-Roman world during the third and second centuries BC differs in a number of important respects from that created and reproduced in north west Europe from the seventeenth century. Moreover, representations of the Other have not been based on somatic characteristics alone. Cultural characteristics have also been used, and sometimes to the virtual exclusion of phenotypical features: European representations of the Islamic world extensively utilised images of barbarism and sexuality in the context of a Christian/heathen dichotomy.

Fifth, the development of the discourse of 'race', and its subsequent incorporation into the discourse of science did not entail a complete break with earlier representations of the Other and therefore the creation of completely new means of representational inclusion and exclusion. Within Europe, scientific discourse, and its application to the human species took place in a context of an existing pattern of representation and inferiorisation which it incorporated and theorised by new criteria of secularised validity. Because the emergence of science did not displace these earlier hierarchies of inferiority, including those which used somatic differences to identify the Other, analyses of the representations of the Other which focus exclusively on the career of the discourse of 'race' arbitrarily detach that history from its roots.[. . .]

References

Banton, M. (1977) 'The Concept of Racism' in S. Zubaida (ed.) *Race and Racialism*, London, Tavistock.

Barzun, J. (1938) *Race: A Study in Modern Superstition*, London, Methuen.

Beddoe, J. (1885) *The Races of Britain: a Contribution to the Anthropology of Western Europe*, Bristol, J.W. Arrowsmith.

Benedict, R. (1983) *Race and Racism*, London, Routledge and Kegan Paul.

Boas, F. (1940) *Race, Culture and Language*, New York, Free Press.

Fredrickson, G.M. (1972) *The Black Image in the White Mind: the Debate on Afro-American Character and Destiny, 1817–1914*, New York, Harper and Row.

Fryer, P. (1984) *Staying Power: The History of Black People in Britain*, London, Pluto Press.

Gossett, T.F. (1965) *Race: The History of an Idea in America*, New York, Schocken Books.

Gould, S.J. (1984) *The Mismeasure of Man*, Harmondsworth, Penguin.

Miles, R. (1982) *Racism and Migrant Labour: A Critical Text*, London, Routledge and Kegan Paul.

Ripley, W.Z. (1900) *The Races of Europe: A Sociological Study*, London, Kegan Paul, Trench, Trübner and Co.

Sanders, R. (1978) *Lost Tribes and Promised Lands: The Origins of American Racism*, Boston, Little, Brown and Co.

Stanton, W. (1960) *The Leopard's Spots: Scientific Attitudes Towards Race in America, 1815–59*, Chicago, University of Chicago Press.

Stepan, N. (1982) *The Idea of Race in Science: Great Britain 1800–1960*, London and Basingstoke, Macmillan.

Stocking, G.W. (1968) *Race, Culture and Evolution*, New York, Free Press.

SECTION 3

Work, Markets and the Economy

Introduction

Now we come to focus on the economy. The readings in this section cover a diverse field but each one is engaging with important economic issues of the 1990s. The background for each of these discussions is the changing economic landscape of the 1990s that has evolved out of previous decades, but which is increasingly becoming a shared international landscape uniting many countries. A feature of this landscape that threads its way through all these readings is the renewed questioning of the influences determining the health of the supply side of an economy, both the national economy and the international economy. These are the questions surrounding the growth performance of an economy, the way that its work processes are organized, the most appropriate set of market arrangements for promoting efficiency and consumer choice, and the proper role for governments in providing a framework for efficiency and competition. These questions are now being asked anew in Europe – East and West – and in the Soviet Union.

In the UK this renewed interest in efficiency and productivity is especially acute, both in view of the perceived structural problems of the UK economy, and as part of the continuing assessment of the effectiveness of market-led supply side policies. For a long time, rates of growth in the UK have fallen behind those in many other advanced countries. Decline may have been reversed for short periods, but inevitably the improvements seem to be stopped in their tracks by the recurrent problems of inflation and the balance of payments.

The first reading, *The Future of Work* by Alan Warde, considers whether there has been a major change in the way that production and work are organized. The traditional picture of capitalist production, Warde argues, has been based on large scale factory production with standardized consumer products coming off the assembly line. This is the world associated with Braverman's deskilling hypothesis and Taylorist scientific management. But is all this changing, Warde asks? Some authors have pointed to the new demands for small batch production, rather than mass production, and to the reorganization of factory work on a more autonomous and subcontracted basis. Associated with these new trends, it is argued, is the new technology of micro-electronically controlled multipurpose machines and the ubiquitous microcomputer. This 'post-Fordist' regime, as it is sometimes called, is also connected with the move towards 'deindustrialization', defined here as the declining proportion of jobs in manufacturing industries and the relative, as well as absolute, increase in jobs in the service industries.

On the whole, Warde is sceptical about post-Fordism. Some changes are evident along these lines of flexible specialization, but Warde doubts whether they are empirically well-developed in Britain, although other countries such as Germany and Japan have travelled further along this particular road. Warde is also sceptical on theoretical grounds as he is not sure whether the changes that do exist have an identifiable common cause or whether they are a series of untidy, ad hoc reactions to many different kinds of circumstances. Generalizing across manufacturing and services may also be hazardous given the changing sectoral composition of the enonomy; for example, part time working has been important in many low-paid, low-tech sectors (such as catering) for a long time, and it is hard to see this as a move towards a new high-tech flexibility.

Warde's discussion is one that questions the patterns of future development for the most innovative and high-tech industries; are they going down the mass production assembly line or along a more diversified route that is not clearly mapped as yet? Some of these issues also appear in *Myths and Realities of the European Market* by J.A. Kay in his picture of the likely course of events in Europe after 1992. Kay's article is questioning what he sees as the mainstream view that the completion of the single European market will deliver even more extensive economies of scale for the large Euro-firms producing standardized Euro-goods for the mass Euro-market. Kay argues that the much vaunted economies of scale have already been more or less fully exploited for many industries, although he does note some important exceptions to this, such as telecommunications and power generation.

Kay argues that the European market is not a single market in the economic sense at all, even though it may be turned into one in an administrative and legalistic sense. In an economic sense, Kay argues, the European market is a highly differentiated market displaying all the variety that one would expect given the rich diversity of European cultures and habits. He expects therefore that this diversity will be enhanced in the years after 1992, enabling a greater range of goods to be available to meet the varied demands of the consumer market. The impetus for increased competition that he sees comes not from the merging of national giants into even bigger Euro-firms, but as a springboard for new firms to enter a diversified European market.

What Kay is trying to do here is to work out the implications for European market structure post-1992, from what he knows already about the characteristics of market demand both internationally and on a European basis. He welcomes the opportunities for increased competition in Europe and hopes that these potential benefits won't be whittled away by over-enthusiastic merger policies between national giant corporations. Thus, Kay has a clear idea of the benefits that can accrue to a competitive market in forcing firms to be more efficient and responsive to consumer demand. Time will tell as to what happens in Europe, but the confidence in the competitive market that Kay illustrates and which has inspired much European thinking has also had a tremendous influence in the Soviet Union and Eastern Europe. Mikhail Gorbachev's policy of *perestroika* and *glasnost* has opened up a new wave of thinking about the market in a society which had for many decades been accustomed to thinking of markets as capitalist rather than socialist forms of economic allocation.

This new wave of thinking is evident in the *perestroika* debate in the Soviet Union. The extract *Plan and Market: 'Perestroika' in the USSR* by Abel Aganbegyan, Chief Economic Adviser to Mikhail Gorbachev, represents the view of a supporter and architect of *perestroika* in its first phase in the late 1980s. Here Aganbegyan tries to formulate a new socialist approach to markets, appreciating their efficiency properties but also regulating them as part of the overall socialist plan. Aganbegyan argues that it is wrong to see markets as quintessentially capitalist, as markets and market prices have a positive role to play in the Soviet economy alongside and as part of the socialist plan for the economy. He emphasises that there is no contradiction or tension between the market and the plan, but that both must be seen as necessary elements in a socialist society, together with prices that sometimes include 'social costs'. Thus Aganbegyan, together with Kay, looks to the influence of competitive market pressures in keeping down costs and improving efficiency, but at the same time Aganbegyan is trying to develop a concept of 'socialist markets' that is distinctively different from what he sees as captitalist markets.

The policy of *perestroika* is thus seen as a way of improving the supply of goods in a country where there is substantial excess or 'frustrated' demand. Another way of seeing it is as a way of improving the supply side of the economy and improving the rate of growth. These supply side issues are also addressed in *British Economic Growth over the Long Run* by Nick Crafts; post-war rates of growth are good by historical standards but weak when compared with other advanced countries, and there has been plenty of debate attempting to explain this weakness.

Crafts is sceptical about the value of general theories of growth which attach particular significance to the sectoral composition of output. In particular he argues that there is little empirical evidence to support the view of Bacon and Eltis that growth is improved when the proportion of output in the non-marketed sector falls, nor is there evidence to support the view that growth is improved when a larger proportion of output comes from the manufacturing sector rather than the service sector. Crafts points to the evidence that shows that productivity improved in the 1980s after the substantial fall in output in the early 1980s, and that this improvement was accompanied by a rise in the non-marketed sector (because of the increase in benefit payments during a period of high unemployment) and a relative increase in the service sector.

Much of Crafts' explanation centres on industrial relations problems and the inheritance of craft unions into the post-war period when automation, standardization and large plants became important but whose efficient operation was impeded by inappropriate union and managerial structures. In addition he also emphasizes the significance of inadequate vocational and technical training, and the shortfalls in research and development into new products and processes. These results are summarized in Table 10.2. Crafts also argues that the evidence suggests that Keynesian demand management policies were not of themselves contributory factors in the pattern of low growth during the post-war period.

In surveying the years of the Thatcher governments, Crafts welcomes the changes that have been made on the supply side, particularly in industrial relations, privatization, a more selective industrial support policy, and vocational training, but he doubts whether these policies have been pushed far enough or pursued in the right direction. He suggests that in a number of cases the Conservative governments were more interested in going for political payoffs against the Labour Party than in radically restructuring the economics of the supply side. For example, some privatizations made more sense as a political policy aimed against the Labour Party's traditional commitments, rather than as an attempt to increase competition in the market – which is where economists would see the main benefits. Another example would be the policy of selling off council housing and reducing the number of council houses for rent, as this policy makes little sense from the perspective of promoting labour mobility.

The final reading *Theories of Economic Decline in the UK* by Bernard Stafford summarizes a number of marxist explanations of the relatively poor performance of the UK economy. These explanations all highlight the importance of the structure of class relationships, but within this common framework, Stafford reviews the differences. Eric Hobsbawm had argued that the loss of UK competitiveness after 1860 was the result of the export of British capital into trade and finance overseas rather than building up and modernizing the manufacturing base at home. This has led to a long debate about the relationship between industrial capital and financial capital, and whether the interests of the former have been sacrificed to the latter by the overwhelming power of the City of London in determining the direction of economic policy. As an example consider the use of a high interest rate policy: this, it is argued, favours finance but penalizes manufacturing.

This debate about the role of financial and manufacturing capital is a debate about conflicts between different sections of capital, and whether the historical and institutional inheritance of the UK favours one rather than the other. Other marxist analyses, though, concentrate on conflicts between capital and labour, and this debate is similar to non-marxist accounts such as Crafts' discussion of the role of the trade unions. These analyses argue that it is the strength of labour, not an aggressive financial capital, that weakened domestic capital, and that it was for this reason that capital found it more profitable to go overseas, if indeed it did do so. Stafford's final point is to note that the Hobsbawm thesis and the worker strength thesis are incompatible; both may be wrong, but if one is correct then the other must be false.

In these readings you will find different approaches and emphases in discussing the issue of the longer term trends in UK performance and productivity, and the wider international issue of appropriate market structures for promoting efficient, profitable enterprises that can compete in European and international markets. You will find differences in emphasis and in the range of focus of the readings from the shopfloor to the aggregate economy, and from the Soviet Union to the European market.

Vivienne Brown

CHAPTER 7
The Future of Work

Alan Warde

Capitalist societies are characterized by constant economic innovation, as firms continuously reorganize their operations and reinvest their profits. The penalty for not doing so is to be put out of business by their competitors. As a result, the last 15 years have seen many dramatic changes in UK industry. Jobs have changed as unskilled manual work has declined and professional occupations expanded; unemployment has increased very considerably; women make up a larger proportion of the workforce; the largest corporations have increased the size of their operations, usually on a world-wide scale; new technologies associated with microchips have radically altered production processes and consumer goods.

One particular set of issues has greatly interested sociologists – changes in the social organization of the factory in manufacturing industry and their impact on work, occupations and industrial relations. Sociologists have always been fascinated by the factory. The images that many of us associate with industrial activity is that of disgruntled people working on assembly lines. Huw Beynon's well-known graphic account of *Working for Ford* or Ruth Cavendish's excellent descriptions of assembly line work in the production of automobile components in *Women on the Line* are but two incisive depictions of factory work. The most important modern debate in the sociology of work -- that which followed the publication in 1974 of Harry Braverman's *Labor and Monopoly Capital: the degradation of work in the 20th century* – concerned the question of whether more and more jobs were becoming like assembly line work.

Braverman argued that there was a tendency for jobs to become 'deskilled' as the techniques of Frederick Taylor's scientific management were more widely introduced. 'Taylorism' aimed to regulate work very tightly, redesigning jobs by breaking them down into their smallest component elements and transferring control from worker to management. Perhaps the most thorough implementation of this strategy was in the car factories of Henry Ford, but there were many examples in other manufacturing industries, and in offices too, of Taylorist managerial strategies which produced fragmented, narrow, repetitive, work tasks.

Braverman has been criticized for overestimating the extent to which Taylorist techniques have been adopted, and for failing to appreciate that many newly created jobs required as much or more skill than those disappearing. The emergence of 'flexible production methods' in *manufacturing* industry, much commented upon recently, appears to support the critics.

Source: *Social Studies Review*, Vol. 5, No. 1, September 1989, pp. 11–15.

'Flexibility' in industrial production

A general tendency for increased flexiblity has been identified in four aspects of industrial production: changes in technology, products, jobs and employment contracts.

(1) **Technology** New technologies provide new opportunities for organizing production. Recent technological advances concern computerized control of manufacturing processes: computer aided design and computer aided manufacture (CAD/CAM); the use of robots alongside computer control; and the combination of personal computers and communications networks to make working from home a real possibility for certain workers. In association with social reorganization on the factory floor, these developments permit more efficient small-batch production. On old-fashioned assembly lines it was very difficult to change from one product to another. The machinery was 'dedicated' to producing a very large volume of identical products which could, by virtue of the economies of scale that underlay mass production, be sold fairly cheaply. Micro-electronics allows machine tools to be reprogrammed very quickly in order to shift from making one product to another (see Sayer, 1986).

(2) **Products** It is therefore possible to produce small quantities of much more specialized products, sometimes called 'customized production', for particular market niches, whether these be specialist chemicals or fashionable clothes. The phenomenon of the 'Third Italy' has attracted much attention (see, for example, Scott, 1988). Here there is a growing concentration of small firms in the textile, clothing, pottery and engineering sectors, based on use of the latest technology and craft labour, producing for quickly changing consumer tastes in world markets. The franchised Benetton chain supplies clothing in Britain produced in this flexible way in north-east Italy.

(3) **Jobs** This new organization of production needs more versatile workers. The routinized and fragmented jobs disappear along with the old dedicated assembly lines; fewer workers are employed to carry out more tasks; and the new processes work most efficiently where workers are responsible for programming and maintaining the machines themselves. These developments are referred to as increasing 'functional flexibility', which may mean the removal of demarcation barriers between different crafts and hence the 'multi-skilling' of workers. This is most evident within Japanese industry.

(4) **Contracts** One final way of achieving flexibility is by reducing the number of workers doing nothing at any point in time. 'Functional flexibility' describes the ways in which workers are moved around from job to job within the factory as required. An alternative is what is called 'numerical flexibility'. Here firms employ on a permanent and full-time basis only those workers who can be fully occupied for 40 hours per week. All extra capacity is achieved by one of two means. Either firms employ workers on a temporary, part-time or casual basis, thereby avoiding paying wages for wasted time. Or they sub-contract out certain activities for which there is insufficient demand on a permanent basis. It may

be cheaper and more efficient, for instance, to use external firms of designers or caterers than to employ such people directly. Similarly, specialist parts may be bought in from another firm. Such firms will typically be relatively small, and in some cases large companies set up their own ex-managers in small businesses with guaranteed contracts for a period of time in order to establish networks of sub-contractors.

Post-Fordism

Some authors consider the growth of flexible organization and working practices so significant as to constitute the basis for a major new phase in the development of capitalist societies. Various terms are used to describe the new phase – 'flexible accumulation', 'neo-Fordism' and 'post-Fordism' all imply slightly different scenarios (see Wood, 1989) – but each identifies a transition away from Fordism to a more flexible *system* of production, the ideal-typical characteristics of which are listed in Figure 7.1.

	Fordist	Post-Fordist
1 Technology	• fixed, dedicated machines	• micro-electronically controlled multipurpose machines
	• vertically integrated operation	• sub-contracting
	• mass production	• batch production
2 Products	• for a mass consumer market	• diverse specialized products
	• relatively cheap	• high quality
3 Labour process	• fragmented	
	• few tasks	• many tasks for versatile workers
	• little discretion	• some autonomy
	• hierarchical authority and technical control	• group control
4 Contracts	• collectively negotiated rate for the job	• payment by individual performance
	• relatively secure	• dual market: secure core, highly insecure periphery

Figure 7.1 Ideal types of production system

As can be seen, the characteristics of Fordism are precisely those that Braverman argued were becoming more general in the late twentieth century. Fordist production describes a system of mass production in mechanized workplaces (including offices) where work is routinized and closely supervised and where deskilled workers come to share a common proletarian condition.

Post-Fordism offers a different prospect. If the new scenario is accurately identified, then it certainly sweeps away many of the industrial conditions identified by Braverman. In some cases it entails the return of the craftworker: the pattern of work described in the case of 'the third Italy' is one in which craftworkers use their experience and very advanced technology to work in small quasi-domestic workshops. In all instances, flexible organization and working practices entail the abandonment of the technical control that contributed to the degradation of labour on the dedicated assembly-line. It means the contraction of mass production and, some authors suggest, a significant change in patterns of consumption as new products, designed to suit special tastes or needs, are made available. Also it signifies the end of secure full-time employment for a substantial portion of the labour force.

In many respects, accounts of the new flexible practices are, as was Braverman's, diagnosing *tendencies*. Flexible production describes the leading edge of industrial innovation on a world scale. Scarcely anyone thinks that mass production has yet been superseded; it is, rather, that this is the way things are going. Employment figures show a decline in unskilled manual work and an increase in white-collar occupations. Sub-contracting has increased somewhat (see Imrie, 1986). There has also been a considerable increase in the number of small businesses in Britain. Hakim (1988: pp. 427) records that 'between 1981 and 1987, the number of people in Britain who were self-employed in their main job grew from 2 million to almost 2.8 million, or from 9% to 12% of total employment'. A growing proportion of jobs are part-time and there are more temporary jobs than there used to be. However, there are two kinds of objection that may be raised about this view of the future of industry. First, there is an empirical problem of how many people are being affected by these changes. Second, there is an explanatory problem: do these things have anything in common, are they a unified set of changes with a common cause or is the apparent power of this trend more a function of the sociologists' concepts.

The empirical objection to post-Fordism

The extent to which these tendencies have developed, particularly in Britain, remains doubtful. In Britain there are relatively few firms that have introduced a complete flexible package on the model of the Japanese, for example. Jones (1988), studying the engineering industry, argues:

'that British industry has not yet made a systematic shift to flexible automation. The systems that have been implemented have not yet been accompanied by a corresponding revolution in work roles, or the functional and authority aspects.' (p.453)

This may be an indication of Britain being somewhat backward. Comparative studies show far more examples of integrated flexible production systems in

Germany (Lane, 1988) and of course in Japan. In all countries there can be no doubt that mass production survives in many industries, for instance in food processing. In addition 'the new international division of labour' has seen some of the most routinized of mass production processes developed in factories owned by the western multinational corporations but located in the Third World. For certain labour-intensive firms – for example, electronics assembly and textiles – can take advantage of very low rates of pay for unskilled and semi-skilled labour and weak union organizations. The fragmented jobs identified by Braverman are, so to speak, exported.

The explanatory problem of post-Fordism

It is not entirely clear that these changes are part of a new, coherent or unified system of manufacturing production, still less that they are the harbinger of a new age. In Britain, conditions of employment have altered in the last 10 years, with some functional flexibility and many more insecure jobs. However, these features may have other causes than attempts by firms to move towards flexible accumulation. Part-time work has been increasing since the early 1960s, before flexible production had been thought of, and has more to do with the movement of more low-paid women workers into the labour force. Moreover, most part-time work is not in manufacturing industry, where it has been declining recently, but in the service industries. Agency work, a form of flexible contract, is largely restricted to a couple of occupations – nursing and secretarial work. Temporary contracts are more prevalent in the public sector than in the capitalist sector, contrary to the logic of competitiveness that lies behind flexible accumulation. This suggests that changes in employment conditions may have more to do with state policy than capitalist reorganization. Indeed, it might be proposed that in Britain at least what we have seen in the last 10 years is less a consequence of advanced technology and new products, more a change in the balance of power between employers and unions. Declining membership, the loss of legal immunities, unemployment, and fewer jobs in traditional manufacturing industries with high union density have swung the balance of industrial power significantly in favour of employers.

The service sector and polarization

It is ironic that the growth of less secure forms of employment should be seen as indicative of a *new* employment scenario, for casual and temporary work was very much the norm in Victorian times and probably until the mid-twentieth century. What is more, outside the manufacturing sector there have always been plenty of jobs that are seasonal or temporary – for instance, in the tourist and catering trades. In this context it is equally ironic that so much attention is being paid to changes in manufacturing industry, since it now employs a relatively small proportion of the labour force.

Sociologically speaking, if we want to understand the effects of industrial change on the British population we are unlikely to get a reliable general picture from manufacturing establishments. Today, just over five million people work in manufacturing, less than a quarter of the British workforce (see Figure 7.2). Twenty-five years ago the figure was around eight-and-a-half million. The number of people in service industries has increased by about four million in the same period and now employs about 65 per cent of all workers. Of course, many people in service industries are providing services to manufacturing companies: for example, banking is a service industry, but it clearly performs services essential to effective manufacturing. The same might be said of many others: contract

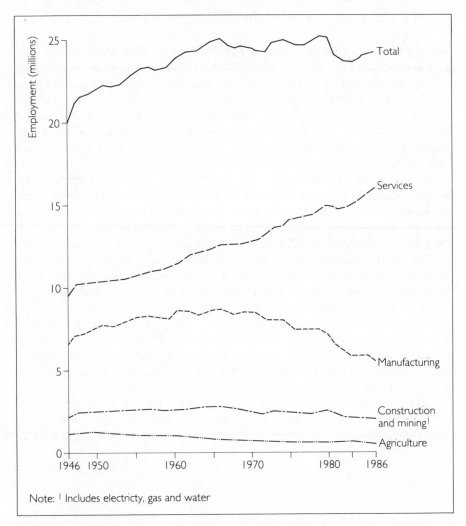

Figure 7.2   Declining levels of employment in manufacturing industry (Britain 1946–86)
Source: Data from Ministry of Labour and Department of Employment. Allen and Massey, 1988, p.52

cleaning, design, legal services, scientific research, etc. are all services that may be sold to a manufacturing firm by outside contractors and they would then appear in the national statistics as services.

Nonetheless, these service industries are the ones that primarily hold the key to future employment opportunities. This is *not* because fewer goods are produced. Deindustrialization does not entail lower output: Britain produces a similar volume of manufactured products in 1989 as it did in 1973 but with only two million fewer workers. But the process of the fragmentation of work described by Braverman has meant the loss of many jobs through mechanization and relocation.

Post-industrial society

There are few sociological studies of work in services. Some good studies have emerged recently, like those of Crompton and Jones (1984) on clerical workers in financial services and Gabriel (1988) on catering, but nothing like the same attention has been paid to services as to manufacturing. Yet it would appear that some of the features attributed to flexibility in manufacturing are more pronounced in service industries. The growth of service industries has sparked off some very optimistic sociological accounts, in, for instance, Daniel Bell's famous 'post-industrial society' thesis.

For Bell, deindustrialization, or more precisely the declining proportion of jobs in manufacturing industries, had major positive consequences. He envisaged work becoming more pleasant, as dirty routine manual graft gave way to more work with people, more professional occupations, etc. But, while it is true that the growth of professional jobs has been a continuing feature of the last 20 years, the number of menial servicing jobs has also grown. Some authors have seen the quest for numerical flexibility in manufacturing leading to increasingly sharp distinctions between a *core* workforce (workers who have skills and experience crucial to their employers and thus improved, secure and well-paid conditions of work) and *peripheral*, or secondary, workers (who make up the numbers when required but are really casuals – insecure, doing unskilled jobs, poorly paid and little valued) (see, for example, Atkinson, 1985). Yet this process seems more prevalent in service industries than in manufacturing. Prominent among industries with low average wages are catering, retail distribution and motor repairs. On the other hand the 'yuppies' of the City of London are extremely highly paid. Such contrasts support one depressing view of contemporary social change which sees social polarization occurring in Britain as inequalities in living standards become ever greater.

Conclusions

Service industries do not guarantee good jobs: they frequently entail sub-contracting and numerical flexibility without any compensating qualities. In general, workers in service industries are less densely unionized, so that even among better placed workers the capacity to sustain the positive conditions supposedly associated with 'core' jobs may be missing. In Britain, at least, the evidence for the arrival of post-Fordism employment practices may primarily indicate the continuing process of deindustrialization. As secure full-time employment for men disappears from older manufacturing industries, like steel and ship-building, the proportion of workers who are women in part-time jobs in service industries inevitably increases.

Industrial conditions *are* changing. Factories are becoming smaller, new products emerging, craft demarcations declining, employment contracts becoming less secure, worker solidarity less prominent. This makes Braverman's projections seem implausible. It need not, however, be convincing evidence of a new era of flexible production (except insofar as it is impossible to imagine a system less flexible than Fordism). The difficulties of adapting flexible production systems to different national industrial cultures (see Turnbull, 1988), the peculiarities of the conditions that have nurtured the foremost examples of flexibility (for example, see Murray, 1987, on the Italian case) and the uncertainty that the evidence reflects a single, unified process (see Legborgne and Lipietz, 1988) leaves considerable room for doubt.

References and further reading

For a detailed survey of the debate about the impact of flexibility see Wood (1989: pp. 1–43). For a broader overview of related economic trends in the UK see Allen and Massey (1988). On the employment effects of deindustrialization, see Abercrombie, Warde *et al.* (1988: pp. 82–90).

Abercrombie, N., Warde, A. *et al* (1988) *Contemporary British Society*, Cambridge, Polity.

Allen, J. and Massey, D. (eds) (1988) *The Economy in Question*, London, Sage.

Atkinson, J. (1985) 'The changing corporation' in Clutterbuck, D. (ed.) *New Patterns of Work*, Aldershot, Gower, 13–34.

Crompton, R. and Jones, G. (1984) *White-Collar proletariat: deskilling and gender in clerical work*, London and Basingstoke, Macmillan.

Gabriel, Y. (1988) *Working Lives in Catering*, London, Routledge.

Hakim, C. (1988) 'Self-employment in Britain: a review of recent trends and current issues', *Work Employment and Society*, 2(4), 421–50.

Imrie, R. (1986) 'Work decentralisation from large to small firms: a preliminary analysis of subcontracting', *Environment and Planning A*, 18, 949–65.

Jones, B. (1988) 'Work and flexible automation in Britain: a review of developments and possibilities', *Work Employment and Society*, 2(4), 451–86.

Lane, C. (1988) 'Industrial change in Europe: the pursuit of flexible specialisation in Britain and West Germany', *Work Employment and Society*, 2(2), 141–68.

Legborgne, D. and Lipietz, A. (1988) 'New technologies, new modes of regulation: some social and spatial implications', *Environment and Planning D: Society and Space*, 6(3), 263–80.

Massey, D. (1988) 'What's happening to UK manufacturing?', in Allen, J. and Massey, D. (eds), *The Economy in Question*, p. 45–90, London, Sage.

Murray, F. (1987) 'Flexible specialisation in the "Third Italy" ', *Capital and Class*, no. 33, 84–96.

Sayer, A. (1986) 'New developments in manufacturing: the just-in-time system', *Capital and Class*, no. 30, 43–72.

Scott, A.J. (1988) *New Industrial Spaces*, London, Pion.

Turnbull, P.J. (1988) 'The limits to "Japanisation" – just-in-time, labour relations and the UK automotive industry', *New Technology, Work and Employment*, 3(1), 7–20.

Wood, S. (ed.) (1989) *The Transformation of Work?: skill, flexibility and the labour process*, London, Unwin Hyman.

CHAPTER 8

Myths and Realities of the European Market

J.A. Kay

Introduction

This report looks beyond the – often absurd – hype which has surrounded the discussion of 1992 in the last year, and assesses the realities of what the programme means for business opportunities and business behaviour. We do so with some qualms.

There is a sense in which the real significance of 1992 lies in the hype, rather than the programme itself. The marketing campaign has enjoyed a success far beyond its promoters' dreams in alerting business to the potential of European markets and the opportunities for European ventures, and in restoring self-confidence in the European ideal. Objective reality may not have changed, but the manner in which it is perceived has:

'Nothing new has happened except that this time these joint projects worked. 1992 has changed things. People have woken up.' (Lord Weinstock, quoted in the *Financial Times*, 30th December 1988).

In this way, the spirit of 1992 may have taken on a significance greater than the detail of the programme. And the spirit is at once wider and narrower than the programme itself. Wider because it is already apparent that opportunities will be seized which were not taken before, not because there were official obstacles to them, but because business horizons were too national in outlook. Narrower, because in specific areas – such as public procurement or financial market liberalization – it is the sincerity with which governments pursue the ideals of 1992 that matters, rather than the content of Commission directives themselves.

But this emphasis on the spirit of 1992 is not in any way a justification of the woolly generalization that surrounds much discussion of the impact of 1992 on both public and business policy. It is important to understand both what the spirit of 1992 does involve and what it does not. While phrases like 'the creation of a single market of 320 million people' are effective ways of firing the public imagination, they are profoundly misleading as a guide to the real significance of economic integration. The cliché is dangerous because it invites business to

Source: E. Davis, *et al.*, *1992: Myths and Realities*, 1989, Centre for Business Strategy Report Series, London Business School, Chapter 1. (Title of original article: 'Myths and Realities'.)

believe that the European market will be more homogeneous after 1992 than it is now, in the same way as the British market is today more homogeneous than the European market (and, indeed, more homogeneous than the market in a large federal state, such as the United States, or the Soviet Union). But there is not, and cannot be, anything in the 1992 programme that will bring about such an outcome. Trade liberalization has its primary effects on supply, not on demand. The reason why demand for many products varies across the European community is mainly because of differences in preferences, habits, language, culture, climate and incomes which will be wholly unaffected by 1992. In this context, economic integration is about the creation of greater product diversity within national markets, not about the elimination of product diversity in international markets.

It follows that the view that the likely consequence of 1992 will be the standardization of European production in a smaller number of plants, offering consumers a reduced choice of products but also the benefit of lower prices from greater scale economies, is in most cases mistaken. It also follows that the idea that an appropriate immediate response to the approach of 1992 is to promote transnational mergers with a view to benefitting from such rationalization is also erroneous. If there were advantages in concentrating production on a small number of varieties of eurobeer, eurocars, eurobiscuits and eurochocolate, there are few obstacles now to such concentration. The reason these developments do not occur is that the variety of consumer tastes – within countries as well as between them – demands a wider range of products. At the same time there are few scale economies that would become available by extending production beyond the levels of output which are already attained in a fragmented Europe. This will be as true after 1992 as before it.

This is not to say that 1992 will have no effects on the structure of markets or production, or that it will not benefit the European economy. The gains derive from the availability of wider product ranges within domestic markets, and this has been the principal consequence of economic integration so far; as a result of the promotion of greater competition through the liberalization of ossified national regulatory structures; and through the breakdown of comfortable domestic cartels. The potentially important effects come, in short, from new market entry, and they come in those industries where entry has in the past been inhibited – by domestic regulation or public procurement policies. It follows that the merger which meets both the business and public policy requirement of 1992 is the merger which provides a springboard for such entry. With a few exceptions, merger between established market leaders in different member states is unlikely to be a sensible business strategy, and where there are business advantages to it, there are public benefits in blocking it.[. . .]

Completing the internal market

The measures which form most of the 1992 programme were first put forward in a Commission White Paper – 'Completing the Internal Market' – in 1985. Some of the proposals aim to reduce obstacles to the rapid and economical distribution of goods within the community. The most dramatic of these is the plan to abolish fiscal frontiers, thus reducing or eliminating border controls on intra-Community movements of goods and people. Many of the provisions are concerned with the elimination of non-tariff barriers to trade – the ways in which differences in national standards and regulations have the intended or inadvertent effect of limiting market access to other community producers. Many of the Commission's proposals are intended to promote the liberalization of public procurement policies – the use of public sector purchasing to promote national champions or to give preferences to local suppliers. The White Paper contains a now famous list of 300 measures designed to promote these several objectives.

The Single European Act, which became effective in 1987, takes these measures further. It requires the Commission to bring forward proposals which would achieve the completion of the internal market by 31st December 1992. Such proposals require the approval of the Council of Ministers and, if adopted, become binding on individual member states. This approval may be given by a qualified majority of the council, except for proposals relating to fiscal policy or the movement of individuals between countries, for which unanimity is required. The Council of Ministers has committed itself to the objective of completing the internal market by 1992, although this does not, of course, require it to approve all or any of the commission's proposals.

There is nothing comprehensive about the Commission's plans. The fact that a practice or a regulation inhibits trade between member states does not necessarily imply that there is any existing or planned proposal to modify it, far less that such a proposal is likely to be adopted. Various examples will be instanced in the course of this chapter. It is, in a way, a measure of the extraordinary political momentum which the 1992 programme has generated that these obvious points come as a surprise to many people. More importantly, 'completion of the internal market' is a description of a legal and administrative process, rather than an economic outcome. It is, nevertheless, by its economic consequences that the programme asks to be judged, and should be judged.

From this perspective, what matters is the scope of the economic market. The relevant economic market is not determined simply by the presence or absence of trade barriers. In this sense there will not be a single European market in 1992, any more than there is a single British market now. For some commodities – such as aircraft – the relevant geographical market is already the world. For other goods and services – such as haircuts or concrete – the market is, and always will be, a local one.

There is a unified European market for some commodities now. There are also many for which it is not. Since the days of Alfred Marshall, economists have measured the extent of market unification by reference to the *law of one price*: in a single economic market, there can only be one price at which any particular commodity is sold. It is apparent that there is no single European market for any of the four commodities illustrated in Table 8.1, even though three of them – cars, domestic appliances, and pharmaceuticals – are subject to extensive and growing international trade. We should not confuse the development of trade with the unification of markets, and the strategies appropriate to a single market

Table 8.1 Prices in European markets (Belgium = 100).

	German cars	Pharma-ceuticals	Life insurance	Domestic appliances
Belgium	100	100	100	100
France	115	78	75	130
West Germany	127	174	59	117
Italy	129	80	102	110
Netherlands	n.a.	164	51	105
UK	142	114	39	93

Source: *European Economy*, March 1988; Nicolaides & Baden Fuller, 1987

are by no means the same as those appropriate to a group of inter-related markets. The issue of whether or not a unified market exists can be resolved only by references to the particular conditions under which particular commodities are sold. The nature of a market is defined by the nature of competition between buyers and sellers, not by governments, commissions, laws or regulations. What governments, commissions, laws and regulations can do – and all they can do – is to influence the nature of that competition.[. . .]

Mergers before, and after, 1992

It may come as a surprise to many people that it has been possible to write at length on the strategic implications of 1992 without so far discussing mergers and corporate restructuring. For many, this is the essence of what 1992 is about.

But it is clearly appropriate to look at the product market first. The implications of 1992 for corporate structure follow directly from its implications for the organization of production. If 1992 leads to increased competition and new entry, then that should be the basis for corporate reorganization. If, on the other hand, the impact of the 1992 programme on the product market is likely to be comparatively small, then mergers in anticipation of changes in the structure of production and distribution are inappropriate.[. . .]

Much discussion of the need for European mergers rests on a belief that economies of scale are pervasive throughout industry, that national markets within Europe are too small to allow these scale economies to be realized, and that major cost savings are to be obtained from the rationalization of European production into a smaller number of plants and companies.[. . .]

There are, indeed, some industries for which this account is true. They are principally industries where fragmentation has been sustained by national purchasing policies. Promotion of national champions in airframe manufacture by the British and French governments failed to produce effective competitors to Boeing, and success in international markets has come only as a result of a European collaborative project. The absurd proliferation of public switching equipment systems in the European telecommunications industry, each designed for the specific requirements of a national post and telecommunications office, has raised costs to European consumers and reduced export markets for all the companies involved.

These industries, however, are very much the exception rather than the rule. Economies of scale are substantial but nonetheless unrealized because governments and their agencies are ready to accept substantial cost penalties in pursuing industrial policy objectives. Private sector customers, in the main, are not. Cars are more typical. This is an industry in which there are substantial economies of scale. As a result, there are indeed cost savings to be derived from the rationalization of production into a smaller number of producers and models.

So why does this not occur? The reason is not the fragmentation of the European market which has been described above. Car sales are effectively segmented into individual national markets, but production is already completely international. There are potential cost savings from rationalization, but it might be observed that precisely analogous 'savings' could be derived from rationalization of the number of producers and models within the unified markets of the United States or Japan. This reduction in the number of models does not occur because the preference of consumers – as revealed in the market place – is for a wider range of products at somewhat higher prices. It is fortunate that this is so, since otherwise European car producers would already have disappeared from the market in the face of lower cost Japanese competition. It is not apparent why the willingness, or otherwise, of consumers to pay more for commodities suited to their particular needs and preferences should be affected in any way by the 1992 programme. Indeed all the evidence we have suggests that the diversity of consumer tastes increases as markets widen and incomes rise.

Thus there are no reasons to anticipate that the completion of the internal market will have the consequence that fewer European car producers will produce larger numbers of cars. If type approval requirements are harmonized, there will be some savings to all producers (including smaller savings to non-Community producers) and some losses to manufacturers (particularly Ford and Rover) if market segmentation is undermined. Otherwise, it is difficult to see major changes in the relative positions of established Community producers. Similar observations can be made in most other markets, and the idea that the 1992 programme is likely to induce substantial structural change in manufactured foodstuffs or alcoholic drinks – where scale economies are exhausted at low levels of production, compared with the demands of 320 million people, and where consumer preferences for product diversity are clearly strong – seems fanciful in the extreme.

There can be no doubt that merger activity within the European Community is set to grow substantially. In just the same way, the internationalizations of the world economy and the prospect of British accession to the Community provoked a wave of domestic mergers which can be seen, in retrospect, to have brought few benefits either to their promoters or to the economy as a whole. 'Buy now while stocks last' is as potent a slogan in the market for corporate control as in any other market, and even the recent disappointments in the City of London do not seem to have diminished its force.

There are very few industries in which mergers between large established producers in different community states are an appropriate response to 1992. It cannot, it seems, be repeated frequently enough that the larger relative size of American and Japanese companies in many sectors, particularly electricals and engineering, is the *result* of their greater success, not the *cause* of it; that such success has almost never been founded on the suppression of competition in their domestic markets; and that the evidence does not exist that there are important unexploited scale economies in many sectors of European industry. There are exceptions to this, and GEC's recently proposed joint ventures in telecommunications and power generation are in sectors which are exceptions – probably, in fact, the only two exceptions of importance. The reason is that these are industries where mistaken nationalism in public purchasing policies has both secured the survival of inefficient producers and fragmented markets in which there are indeed significant scale economies.

There is an obvious implication for European industrial policy. It is that the pursuit at European level of the policy of promoting champions, which has been so remarkably unsuccessful when promoted by national governments, is likely to be just as damaging to the long term health of the European economy as the current nationalism. It is apparent that there are elements in the Commission which would like to develop policies of this kind, and major companies which are positioning themselves to take advantage of the opportunities provided. This is the greatest source of danger that the 1992 programme will prove damaging, rather than beneficial, to the Community. The objective of Community policy should instead be to ensure that the structural changes which would result from a more competitive environment within the community are not frustrated.

The kind of merger which does make sense is that which provides a springboard for new entry, especially into markets where such entry has previously been restricted by domestic regulation, local cartels, or nationalism in procurement policies. It will rarely pay to buy large companies for these purposes, because their prices will reflect the rents which the protection they have received has enabled them to earn. The Spanish joint venture in mortgage lending established by Abbey National [. . .] is an example of what is appropriate in a particular kind of industry and environment.

Another kind of merger which elements of the 1992 programme will facilitate is the growth of a European market in corporate control – the prospect that weakly managed companies, especially in the small European economies, may become vulnerable to hostile take-over from predators anxious to make more effective use of the assets involved. The stalking of Belgium's Société Générale by de Benedetti is the most striking example of what might become a different trend in European mergers. The British experience of the operations of the market for corporate control suggests that this development offers some advantages, but not unmixed or unambiguous ones.

Conclusions

1992 is perhaps the most successful marketing campaign of the decade. It has restored the political momentum of the European Community, and broadened the horizons of many businessmen across the continent. But it should be treated with the intelligent scepticism which should be applied to any marketing campaign. The images and the slogans of the advertisement should not be confused with reality. And nothing in the campaign relieves the purchaser of the obligation to inspect carefully the nature of the product in relation to his particular needs and circumstances. The significance of 1992 is almost entirely to be found in measures which are industry-specific.

CHAPTER 9.

Plan and Market: 'Perestroika' in the USSR

Abel Aganbegyan

In the journal *Novyi Mir* a piece appeared recently from the Soviet economist Popkova entitled 'Whose pies are lighter?' Although confused and seeming like a stream of consciousness the piece defined the nature of socialism as being a centralised society in which the market must not be developed and used to meet people's needs more fully and so end shortages. The market, the author asserted, is a characteristic of capitalism and only under capitalism can shortages be avoided and the market come to be full of goods. The author concludes that there is no third alternative. This primitive view of a socialist economy is fairly widespread in the Soviet Union and more so in the West. In our opinion, this point of view is wrong and contradicts not only theory but practice.

Commodity production and market relations have been characteristic also of socialism. These relations are by no means inherent only in a capitalist economy. Commodity production and market relations have come about over centuries, commencing long before the rise of capitalism in the period of the break-down of early communal systems. In ancient Greece and Rome there were fairly well developed markets, and a money system operated. Market relations were also characteristic of the later feudal societies of the Middle Ages.

Without doubt the full development of market relations occurred under capitalism, when these became universal. In a capitalist society everything is bought and sold, not merely everyday goods, but land, natural resources, whole enterprises and organisations. And in additon to the market for goods there is a stockmarket for capital. Labour also becomes a commodity insofar as there is a fairly free labour market where there is unemployment. Internationalization has strengthened market relations and made them worldwide. In the post-war period the integration of international capital has intensified with the rise of transnational monopolies.[. . .]

Quite a different issue is the new content of these market relations under socialism. The point is that in the exchange of commodities relations are established between people. These can be between private capitalist owners or monopolies and the population, as is characteristic of capitalism, or between socialist enterprises or cooperatives and the population as under socialism. Commodity production, the market and market relations in the socialist conditions

Source: Abel Aganbegyan, *The Challenge: Economics of Perestroika*, Michael Barratt Brown (ed.) Hutchinson Education, 1988, pp. 125–138. (Title of original chapter: 'Plan and market'.)

of the Soviet Union, vary greatly. But in contrast to capitalism commodities and money relations are not universal categories. Land and natural resources cannot be bought and sold. Since there is no unemployment and the economic base of society accords with socialist ownership, there is no labour market. A market for capital is not envisaged as part of *perestroika*. There are no plans for a Soviet stock exchange, shares, bills of exchange or profit from commercial credit.*

A socialist market is a government-regulated market. Through the prescription of set economic proportions, fixed wages and a system of state finance and credit, the monetary income of the population is regulated. On the other hand, prices for most essential products are also to be set by state bodies. Major capital investment and other economic levers and stimuli are in the hands of the state and can be directed at greater or lesser production of certain goods and thus have a major influence on the market.

Up to now the market in the Soviet Union has been both restricted and deformed. Most means of production have been centrally allocated by the state through a material and technical supply system. They are not freely bought and sold. The market is still one in which there are persistent shortages and consumer demand, especially for high quality goods, is not being met. The system of pricing is excessively rigid and centralised, so that prices may not reflect reality because they do not correspond to the costs incurred and efficiency in the production of goods. Since in the past, many types of cooperatives were not permitted to develop and self-employment was not encouraged, representation of commodity producers in the market was incomplete. In such a distorted marketplace the grey economy became widespread with its uncontrolled mechanism for distributing goods and incomes. The so-called black market also grew and speculation became increasingly rife.

During *perestroika* market relations in the USSR will be deepened and broadened. Above all the market is set to more than double in size thanks to the transition from centralized material and technical supply to wholesale trade in means of production, including direct commercial links between enterprises. In this way a well-developed market in the means of production will be created, and the proportion of centrally set prices will be substantially reduced. Centralized pricing will be retained only for the most essential products, to control their rate of growth and to stave off inflation. At the same time the scope of contracted and free prices will grow significantly.[. . .]

The development of cooperatives and of self-employment will supply the socialist market with many goods, and bring the higher flexibility and competitive potency needed to satisfy social needs. The essential attribute of a market is consumer choice. The advantage of a market is lost when monopoly occurs. To give the market its economic effectiveness, competition between producers making similar or the same goods is crucial. Under *perestroika* this question is being given special attention. Monopoly of particular lines of production has to be ended and

[* In *Moving the Mountain* (1989) this argument is revised; it is argued that a Soviet labour market does already exist (although in a different sense from capitalist economies), and that a financial market is likely to emerge as part of *perestroika* (pp. 49–56).]

parallel enterprises or economic organisations created. When designating enterprises as economically effective we now apply the term 'economic emulation', to express the distinctive form of competition between enterprises in Soviet conditions. The growing socialist economy can never become capitalist. Since there is no hired labour, business-owners, exploitation and commodities are not a universal category. There will not be an uncontrolled market. In the light of this the relationship between the plan and market must be examined.

A socialist economy is by its nature planned. Indeed it is based on socialist ownership with state ownership as its main form.* The means of production of society, particularly the land, material wealth and enterprises belong to the whole people, through which their administrative bodies systematically manage them and seek to make good use of them.

Thus the social formation of a planned economy from top to bottom as in Soviet society is overriding and universal. This formation will be conserved even with *perestroika*, but it will take on some new features and, most importantly, new forms to implement the realisation of a planned economy. Planning for the development of the economy will in part be realised through the market. In the market place commodities obtain the social recognition of the consumer – they are bought or rejected. Social valuation is given to the production costs of the goods. Thus the market place acts as a key additional regulator of production within socialist society.

People ask the following question: is the development of a socialist market a step on the road to capitalism? From the above it will be quite evident that the answer to this question is categorically 'no!' We are not developing capitalist production, but a socialist market with a new content and system of operation in a socialist economy. Similarly we are asked: what about 'market socialism', does the ongoing radical reform of management in the USSR equal a step on the road to a 'market economy'? Here the answer depends on what is understood by the terms market economy or market socialism. If by this is understood the universalisation and general spread of the market place, an economic system in which everything is bought and sold, then naturally we are not moving towards such a system and never will since this would not be socialist. In China during their economic reforms the term 'planned commodity economy' is being promoted. My attitude to this term is two-fold, again depending on the meaning ascribed to it. I have tried to describe the place of the market in a socialist economy, its important though limited character. But is this how the market is understood when the whole economy is called a commodity economy? Let us recall what was said earlier, that in the Soviet case a significant number of prices of goods are not determined in the market.

In our radical reform of management the relationship of plan and market is being fundamentally changed. It is changing because the whole centralised system of planning is being looked at differently. It is changing because the market sector is being developed and extended and a new unity and interaction of plan and

[* In *Moving the Mountain* (1989) Aganbegyan emphasizes the importance of a 'pluralist attitude to property' including co-operatives, personal enterprises, and collective leaseholding as well as state enterprises (pp. 168, 170).]

market is beginning. Plans are being implemented by proportional norms and contracts and not by commands.

In the new system of economic management prices become a basic point of reference. Enterprises and associations will evaluate the results of their work through the pricing of their products. The existing system of prices does not give a true valuation because prices do not reflect social cost and the economic efficiency of production. Up to now this common denominator has been lacking in the Soviet Union.

For historical reasons the prices for natural resources and agricultural products have been depressed, since these did not include rents and a realistic valuation of the labour used. Low prices for fuel and raw materials in the past stimulated their wider use in production and assisted their growth. The depressed prices for agricultural products re-allocated resources from agriculture to industry, although subsidised prices guaranteed foodstuffs to the less well-off families. Currently these depressed prices are acting as a brake on development. Low prices for fuel and raw materials led to waste and impeded resource conservation and economies in their use. With prices at these levels, many geological enterprises and even whole extraction branches (like coal mining) are unprofitable and their losses are simply covered by grants from the state. Depressed prices for agricultural products, where their production is relatively costly because of low productivity, have also been covered by state grants. This impairs the stimulating effect of prices on the development of agriculture.

During the *perestroika* this situation must be fundamentally changed. A radical and total reform of price formation is envisaged as well as a revision of all types of prices; wholesale, purchase, retail and supply tariffs, into a unified coordinated system of prices. A substantial increase is intended in the prices of fuel and raw materials, relating them to world levels. At the same time subsidies on the price of goods will be substantially cut. In agriculture prices will be constructed so as to take into account the real cost of fertiliser inputs, of machinery and other equipment, formerly sold to agriculture at depressed prices through state compensation for the actual cost of production of these products.

Prices must be constructed in such a way that improved quality and more efficient production becomes highly profitable. Obsolete products which do not meet contemporary demands of efficiency should become unremunerative and unprofitable for enterprises to produce. [. . .]

At the same time the sphere of contractually set and free prices will rapidly expand, since now enterprises themselves will decide on their own development plans based in turn on agreements with consumers. Thus to a large extent prices will be a matter of agreement. It is possible then that the state will set up a certain method for calculating prices, and the Prices Committee is being invested with the task of assessing the rationale for contractual and free prices. In particular, speculative price increases aimed at excessive profit will not be permitted. Special measures will be taken to combat monopolies. It can be seen that a process of democratising the whole of price formation is underway.[. . .]

If we accept that the most fundamental part of radical reform is the transition from administrative to economic methods of mangement then the basic measures needed still lie ahead of us, namely: the reform of price formation, changes in the finance and credit mechanism, the transition to wholesale trading and to direct links instead of the centralised material and technical supply. One measure without the other will not give the anticipated result and will simply not work.[. . .]

CHAPTER 10

British Economic Growth over the Long Run*

Nick Crafts

Introduction

It is now conventional wisdom that, for some hundred years or so, British growth and especially productivity performance have been deeply disappointing when compared with that of other advanced countries. More contentious, but nevertheless widely held, is the belief that the failures of the post war economy are deeply rooted in the past, presenting successive governments both with an unenviable legacy and a most daunting task in their aspiration to remedy Britain's relative economic decline: thus Eatwell (1982) claims that 'The weakness of the British economy . . . is the cumulative product . . . of the entire history of Britain since the end of the nineteenth century, when it first became evident that Britain was unable, or unwilling, to adapt to a competitive world in which her pre-eminence could no longer be taken for granted'. Certainly complaints about the poor quality of industrial management, trade union obstacles to productivity advance, the inappropriate and inadequate education system in the UK and slowness to develop and apply advanced technology were commonplace at the turn of the century – as they have been in recent decades. Furthermore the twentieth century has seen a constant and often painful need to restructure economic activity in the face of a declining share of world trade and changing comparative advantage, whilst, in terms of Olson's thesis (1982), suffering the sclerotic effect of special interest groups undisrupted by war, foreign occupation or totalitarian government.

There is an understandable but unfortunate tendency among both economists and the general public to look to history for simple answers to what is a complex problem. Thus favourite explanations are put forward for relative economic decline as a result of, say, a history of anti-manufacturing prejudice or amateurish and self-perpetuating management, or an Oxbridge dominated educational system orientated to the academic rather than the technological.[. . .] Such claims are at best in need of severe qualification in the light of the detailed historical record.

*I am most grateful to Christopher Allsopp and Derek Morris for perceptive comments which led to a substantial improvement on an earlier version of this paper. The errors, unfortunately, are mine.

Source: *Oxford Review of Economic Policy*, Vol. 4, No. 1, 1988. (Title of original article: *'The assessment: British economic growth over the long run.'*)

Furthermore, it is extremely important to recognise that, if such factors have been persistent and important, persuasive reasons must also be found for the failure of market forces and/or governments to eliminate them. At the moment this latter task is, to a large extent, still on the research agenda.

Much remains to be done to convince a sceptic that there really are powerful strands of continuity underlying unsatisfactory growth in different periods, or that it really is extremely difficult to escape from the dead hand of the past. Indeed, there may be a danger of a too ready acceptance of caricatures or even myths relating to past economic performance with the result that the lessons of our economic history are misunderstood.[. . .]

The post-1945 economy in historical perspective

The most obvious feature of post-war economic growth is that up to 1973, British performance was very good relative to our own history but very poor compared with other countries. By the early 1970s we lagged a little behind other major European countries in terms of GDP per hour worked and the gap widened further during the 1970s. Rates of multi-factor productivity growth* abroad far exceeded anything Britain, or even the United States, had achieved in earlier eras. The post-war years have seen more rapid technological change than hitherto and, in 1950, a large technological gap between the United States and other advanced economies. A general experience among different countries was that they caught up with the United States to a considerable extent – Britain, however, did so relatively slowly.[. . .]

Levels of government spending as a share of national income can be seen as being 'displaced upwards' during the war and subject to a ratchet effect thereafter (Peacock and Wiseman, 1961). Indeed during the 1960s and early 1970s the public sector expanded further relative to the economy as a whole. This led Bacon and Eltis (1978) to argue that the expansion of the non-marketed sector had 'crowded out' growth, particularly as, combined with militant trade unionism, the funding of public spending had, in effect, severely squeezed profits and hence investment and growth.[. . .] As Table 10.1 shows, however, the general long-run pattern is for the expansion of the non-marketed (public) sector since World War I to have been at the expense of the marketed (private) sector consumption rather than investment.[. . .] In the 1980s profits have recovered, and, arguably, higher unemployment together with faster productivity growth have restrained real wage pressures, although the relative size of the non-marketed sector has continued to expand.[. . .]

Probably the most promising insight of the 'sclerosis' approach is in terms of the economy's heritage in the area of industrial relations, which is to be thought of more in terms of the type of trade unionism than in the level of trade union membership *per se*. In this respect, the legacy inherited by the post-war British

[*Multi-factor productivity is a measure of output per unit of total input, i.e. allowing for capital and land as well as labour.]

Table 10.1 The long-run relationship of the marketed and non-marketed sectors (percentage of marketed output)

	1924	1937	1955	1965	1974	1979	1985
Marketed sector consumption	81.4	76.4	56.7	53.0	51.2	47.0	44.6
Marketed sector investment	6.5	9.4	14.0	17.3	10.0	19.7	17.5
Balance of trade	−3.0	−5.0	−1.8	−0.9	−6.1	0.2	1.2
Government financed consumption	9.3	9.8	20.3	18.8	22.1	21.8	25.3
Government purchases of materials and investment	5.8	9.5	10.7	11.7	13.8	11.3	11.4

Source: based on the identity $Y_m - C_m = I_n + C_n + NX_m + I_m$ where m is marketed and n is non-marketed sector, NX = net exports, I = investment and C = consumption; derived from Bacon and Eltis (1978), Feinstein (1972) and National Accounts Statistics (1986). The rise in Government Financed Consumption since 1979 reflects increased transfer payments to the unemployed in particular and is rather different from, but similar in effect to, the diversion of resources to government expenditure on goods and services which concerned Bacon and Eltis originally.

economy may have been unusually unfortunate. Recent research has stressed the difference between British and American managerial strategies towards trade unions and job control in the early decades of this century, particularly in engineering and related sectors such as motorcars, shipbuilding and iron and steel.[. . .] The impact of highly differentiated markets, legal immunities for unions, fragmented and small-scale employers and strong craft union traditions led British producers to emphasize payment-by-results bargaining, with control over demarcation and intensity of effort shared with workers in a less capital-intensive mode of production. The American strategy involved direct management control over work effort and measured day work under a clearly defined managerial hierarchy designed to exploit large scale plant efficiently. When, after World War II, the advantages of automation and standardization became overwhelming in industries like cars and shipbuilding, the switch to direct management control proved impossible to achieve efficiently, given worker resistance and lack of effective management hierarchies, experience and training. In such circumstances attempts to move to capital-intensive, large plants often proved disastrous and workers' incentives and opportunities to inhibit productivity advance were considerable. Prior to World War II the disadvantages of the British stragegy were considerably less.[. . .]

Reflections of these problems appear in comparative productivity studies done for cross-sections of British industry. Thus the series of reports in the late 1940s and early 1950s of the Anglo-American Council on Productivity, based on visits by British industrialists and trade unionists to the United States, are virtually unanimous in their condemnations of British management practices with regard to work organization, and highly critical in more than half the industries studied of union restrictive practices. The reports were endorsed both by the TUC and management. The econometric work of Davies and Caves (1987) reported in Table 10.2 shows problems of trade unions and related British failures with large plants [which] were especially strike-prone[.] Equally it must be recognized that other factors have contributed to unsatisfactory productivity growth and this is also reflected in Table 10.2. Recent studies have particularly pointed to the poor training and low levels of technical skills of shop floor personnel such as foremen, [and] the continuing failure of educational reforms to make significant improvements to technical training.

Table 10.2 Predicted improvements in relative value added/head from achieving best practice standards throughout British manufacturing in 1967/68 (in percentages)

[. . .]	[. . .]
Eliminating capital shortfall	9.1
Removing substandard educational background of workforce	8.5
No adverse trade union problems	6.7
Correcting plant size	5.5
Making good R & D shortfall	4.7

Source: Davies and Caves (1987, Table 7.4)

With the advantage of hindsight the chief criticisms of government policy should probably be directed at omissions which led to the continuation of these weaknesses on the supply-side of the economy. In particular, early post-war governments were reluctant to intervene to improve productivity advance through trade union reform legislation, perhaps for fear of destroying the 'post-war settlement'. Trade unions entered the post-war economy in a position of unprecedented potential strength with their legal immunities intact, their membership levels high and the labour market at an extremely low level of unemployment. Faced with this situation governments sought cooperative solutions with the TUC to avoid a possible inflationary crisis. Thus, in return for a tacit incomes policy, the Conservatives in the 1950s forswore deflation, labour legislation and explicit incomes policy. For as long as cooperation was pursued as a solution to the changed bargaining power of organized labour there was a major obstacle to attempts at reforming industrial relations in pursuit of a system more conducive to productivity growth [. . .]. In the long term this approach failed as the locus of bargaining switched to the plant level and shop stewards became more important in exploiting the latent wage-bargaining power of workers and perhaps increasing real wage rigidity resulted.[. . .]

At the time, however, more concern was expressed about damage to growth done by destabilizing demand management in the form of 'stop-go' policies. In part, the short-lived National Plan was a policy response to this perception, as by the 1960s government consciously adopted economic growth as an objective. However, not only is it debatable whether demand management in the Keynesian years of the 1950s and 1960s did actually make for greater instability, but in any case detailed study subsequently demonstrated that the UK, in fact, experienced decidedly milder economic fluctuations than the fast-growing economies.[. . .]

Since 1945, of course, the economy has moved much more fully into a corporate stage of capitalism. The share of the top 100 firms in manufacturing output doubled between 1959 and 1970 as, under the auspices of the 1948 Companies Act, restraints on takeover were removed and a major merger movement occurred.[. . .] Particularly in the aftermath of a period of widespread collusion and 'family capitalism', it might have been expected that such developments would be of considerable benefit for productivity; government policy reflected this belief and was distinctly 'pro-merger'. In the event, the evidence seems to suggest both that mergers did not produce productivity gains and that capital markets continued to be permissive of managerial failure to maximize profits, at least through the early 1970s; [. . .] mergers lowered profits and productive efficiency on average in 1954–72.[. . .] At the same time, the educational background of British managers appears to have been inferior to those of other industrial countries.[. . .] Although, on occasion, merger permits the achievement of economies of scale in research (e.g. ICI between the wars), post-war British industry has financed a relatively small amount of research [. . .] and there was a steady decline in patented inventions relative to key rivals; thus in 1958 Britain had 23.4 per cent, Germany 25.6 per cent and Japan 1.9 per cent of all patents granted in the United States, but by 1979 the percentages were 10.1, 23.9 and 27.7 respectively.[. . .]

While in earlier periods Britain showed up as a country with an exceptionally low rate of investment at home, this was less true after 1945, although the share of national income invested at home was some five percentage points lower than the European average. In manufacturing, Britain invested a similar proportion of output to Germany; [during] 1954–72 the difference between Britain and Germany in growth of output per worker was almost entirely due to multi-factor productivity growth. Britain experienced a much lower level of output per unit of capital and thus its investment translated into a lower rate of growth of capital stock and received a lower rate of profit, as Table 10.3 indicates. Indeed the Wilson Committee concluded that this productivity problem was more important as a restraint on investment than were difficulties relating to the supply of funds, notwithstanding the continuing tendency for banks to be less closely involved in financing industrial investment in Britain than in Germany, [. . .] and the substantial and indiscriminate investment subsidies offered by successive governments.

Table 10.3 Investment, profits and capital productivity in British and German manufacturing

(%)	United Kingdom			Germany		
	1964	1973	1979	1964	1973	1979
Investment/output	12.4	11.2	13.2	13.7	11.6	11.2
Profits/output	31.0	26.9	22.4	35.2	31.2	28.8
Output/capital	39.1	34.6	29.0	52.2	52.9	50.0
Profits/capital	12.1	9.3	6.5	18.4	16.5	14.4

Source: derived from Hill (1979) and OECD (1986); note that $P/K = P/Y . Y/K$ where P is profits.

The pre-war pattern of international trade changed radically after 1945, and the British position in the international economy now moved decisively away from that of Victorian times. By the 1960s British exports had become human capital and research intensive, textiles accounted for only 6 per cent of exports [. . .], while the direction of our trade switched towards industrial countries even prior to joining the EC so that in 1971 they received 45 per cent of our manufactured exports [. . .]. Britain's share of world manufactured exports fell from around 25 per cent in 1950 to 7 per cent or so in the early 1980s.[. . .]

The Thatcher government's economic reform in the light of historical experience

It is by now widely perceived that Britain's relative standing in terms of growth of real GDP and productivity has improved considerably since 1979. Table 10.4 provides a brief reminder of this change.[. . .] It is also the case that more sophisticated calculations also show an improvement in productivity trends.[. . .] It is interesting to note that the improved growth performance has not coincided either with a rolling back of the non-marketed sector (see Table 10.1) as Bacon and Eltis suggested, nor with an expanding manufacturing sector.[. . .]

Table 10.4 Growth rates of real output per worker employed (per cent per annum)

	UK	USA	Sweden	France	Germany	Italy	Japan
1964–73	2.6	1.6	2.7	4.6	4.4	5.0	8.4
1973–79	1.2	−0.2	0.5	2.8	2.9	1.8	2.9
1979–86	1.8	0.6	1.3	1.6	1.7	1.2	2.8

Sources: Matthews et al. (1982) and OECD (1986).

In assessing the Thatcher government's achievements in terms of reversing long-term relative decline, both short-run and long-run aspects need to be considered.[. . .]

The effects of exogenous shocks, such as those from oil price rises, can last for a considerable time and in the short to medium term, growth is influenced by the demand effects of government policies and interruptions from problems of external adjustment. Such conclusions complicate comparisons of growth pre- and post-Thatcher [and suggest] that there may be difficulties in sustaining high growth over the next few years [. . .] in the context of the world economic environment.

It is also, of course, debatable whether the [Thatcher] administration's policies have produced a basis for sustained high rates of growth in the long run and the catching up of other previously more successful economies. There has clearly been a substantial shift in supply-side policies with moves towards reform of trade union law, privatization of nationalized industries, the development of a more selective and more innovation-orientated industrial support policy [. . .], and initiatives to strengthen vocational training. Nevertheless it would appear that a number of obstacles arising from our economic history are yet to be overcome.

The Thatcher Government can be seen as having abandoned earlier efforts at cooperative solutions to the control of inflation by means of implicit or explicit incomes policies; thus it has more freedom to manoeuvre in seeking to reform industrial relations in order to give management an opportunity to control restrictive practices, to obtain faster productivity growth and to assert control over the productive process. Signs of improvements along these lines are very clear in recent surveys, although [. . .] about a third of managers are still constrained in their prerogative to organize work.[. . .]

It seems probable that there has been a significant reduction in the overmanning which featured so widely in productivity reports.[. . .] This 'shake-out' has permitted some catching-up of European productivity levels while allowing productivity growth in some sectors to be well above anything sustainable in the steady-state. On the other hand, [. . .] further reform may be necessary to achieve a full resolution of the industrial relations sclerosis to which the 'British strategy' led.[. . .]

To a considerable extent Conservative policies appear to have been motivated by an attempt permanently to dismantle the postwar settlement through seeking to erode Labour's power base by privatization, sales of council houses, reform of the rates, redirection of educational syllabuses etc., taking advantage of the 'window of opportunity' arising from trade union disputes of the late 1970s, fratricidal struggles in the Labour Party and overambitious Argentinian generals. The 1987 election and the reaction to it in the Labour Party suggests that the Conservatives may have been at least partially successful. Though there have certainly been gains from the retreat from the post-war consensus, the accent on defusing the political legacy has caused important opportunities to be missed. Thus, for example, in privatization policy opportunities to promote efficiency through competition have been lost; in the housing market regional mobility has been reduced and skill shortages probably exacerbated; in education, the power struggle seems in danger of jeopardizing the effective provision of the technical and vocational training which [. . .] is of key significance.

More generally, despite clear productivity improvements and substantial gains from the removal of restrictive practices, and despite explicit attention being paid to the obstacles to growth discussed above, there is considerable evidence that the remedies have been inadequate to the scale or persistence of the problems involved, at least so far. Thus it seems unlikely that the skill shortages and vocational training deficiencies highlighted [. . .] as a major reason for the lag of British behind German productivity will be solved in the near future. Certainly the Youth Training Scheme has not proved to be a satisfactory response in terms either of skills acquired or training quality [. . .] and in any event most older workers will continue to work on with no upgrading of their skills. Rather similar comments apply to management skills where Britain remains far behind other countries in training. A recent report concluded that a tenfold increase in management education was required (NEDO, 1987). Moreover, a recent Select Committee report found that defence still dominates the UK's research and development effort, that skilled scientific manpower for other needs is in short supply and that of the five leading industrial nations the UK now devotes the lowest share of GDP to research and development (House of Lords, 1986). The Thatcher Government's policies have, at best, dealt with only some of the supply-side problems which the Conservatives inherited.

References

Bacon, R.W. and W.A. Eltis (1978), *Britain's Economic Problem: Too Few Producers*, 2nd edn., London, Macmillan.

Davies, S.W. and R.E. Caves (1987), *Britain's Productivity Gap*, Cambridge, Cambridge University Press.

Eatwell, J. (1982), *Whatever Happened to Britain?* London, Duckworth.

Feinstein, C.H. (1972), *National Income, Expenditure and Output of the United Kingdom, 1855–1965*, Cambridge, Cambridge University Press.

Hill, T.P. (1979), *Profits and Rates of Return*, Paris, OECD.

House of Lords (1986), *Select Committee on Science and Technology, Report on Civil Research and Development*, vol. 1., London, HMSO.

Matthews, R.C.O., C.H. Feinstein and J. Odling-Smee (1982), *British Economic Growth, 1856–1973*, Stanford, Stanford University Press.

National Economic Development Office (1987), *The Making of Managers*, London.

Olson, M. (1982), *The Rise and Decline of Nations*, New Haven, Yale University Press.

OECD, (1986), *Historical Statistics, 1960–1984*, Paris.

Peacock, A.T. and J. Wiseman (1961), *The Growth of Public Expenditure in the United Kingdom*, Princeton, Princeton University Press.

CHAPTER 11

Theories of Economic Decline in the UK

Bernard Stafford

Marxist analyses are not vulnerable to the charge of inadequacy of scope. None of them may be accurate but each represents an attempt to uncover the underlying political and economic forces which have governed the progress of the UK economy over the post-war period. The most fully developed Marxist explanations rely on a general theory of self-generated decline and crisis which is first applied to the world capitalist economy to account for the rise and fall of the long boom, [. . .] and then extended to incorporate the distinctive features of the UK economy which explain the relative weakness of the long boom and the extra severity of the post-1973 slump[.] Although all Marxist writers attribute the differential performance of the UK economy to differences in the structure of class relationships, there are substantial disagreements about which class relationships have been crucial and about the mechanisms by which class conflict has been transmitted into the observable outcome of slow growth. The major division is between those who put the conflict between capital and labour at the centre of the analysis and those for whom the primary factor is the orientation of powerful sections of the capitalist class and the conflict which this has generated within the capitalist class as a whole.

The argument that the decline of the UK economy is attributable to the orientation of powerful sections of the capitalist class draws much of its inspiration from Hobsbawm's analysis of the decline in the international position of the UK economy after 1860:

> what lay before the eye were the shining pastures of cotton exports to Asia, steam coal exports to the world's ships, Johannesburg gold mines, Argentine tramways and the profits of the City merchant banks . . . what happened therefore, was that Britain exported her immense accumulated historical advantages in the underdeveloped world . . . and had in reserve the exploitation of the 'natural protection' of the home market and if need be 'artificial protection' of political control over a large empire. When faced with a challenge it was easier and cheaper to retreat into an as yet unexploited part of one of these favoured zones rather than to meet competition face to face . . . The

Source: D. Coates and J. Hillard (eds), *The Economic Decline of Modern Britain*, 1986, Brighton, Harvester. (Title of original article: 'Theories of decline'.)

British economy as a whole tended to retreat from industry into trade and finance . . . Britain's annual investments abroad began actually to exceed her net capital formation at home around 1870. What is more, increasingly the two became alternatives . . . The amount of domestic capital formation before 1914, so far from being adequate for the modernization of the British productive apparatus, was not even sufficient to prevent it from running down. Britain we may say, was becoming a parasitic rather than a competitive economy. (Hobsbawm, 1968, p. 161)

Aaronovitch (1981a, 1981b, ch. 2) has applied a much-developed form of this thesis to the post-war UK economy. Detailed comparative material is presented for the UK, West Germany, Italy, France and Japan to demonstrate the cosmopolitan orientation of UK capital which is manifest in three characteristics of the organisation of UK capital: the extent of the overseas operations of UK multinational companies and the City; the historic dislocation between industrial and financial capital in the UK which is institutionalised in the separation of banking and industrial enterprises; and the historic alliance between UK financial capital and the state designed to safeguard the international position of sterling and the City. Aaronovitch acknowledges the relative strength of the UK trade union movement over the post-war period, but judges it to have been of secondary importance – 'this largely defensive posture has certainly interacted with other conditions which have contributed to the relatively low growth rate of the UK but this has been, in our judgment, a secondary rather than a primary factor' (Aaronovitch, 1981a, p. 69). Two mechanisms are identified by which the specified class characteristics have been transmitted into slow growth. The first involves an investment – growth relationship. The claim here is that domestic accumulation and thus growth has been retarded by (a) a shortage of finance arising from the export of capital and the dislocation between industrial and financial capital, and (b) the deflationary and other policies adopted in defence of the overseas interests of UK captial. The second link involves the political and organisational cohesion which capital requires in order to restructure itself and grow. The claim here is that the coordination of UK capital has been seriously weakened by the dislocation between its financial and industrial sections.

Several writers have analysed the post-war decline of the UK economy within the broad framework adopted by Aaronovitch. Jessop (1980) and Longstreth (1979) emphasise the importance of the brake on domestic [investment] which has resulted from the enforcement of policies designed to sustain the political and economic [dominance] of UK financial capital. Jessop also points to the importance of the relative strength of the UK labour movement in retarding industrial reconstruction and in generating the damaging 'stop – go' cycle by its interaction at the political level with the power of financial capital. The London CSE Group (1980) endorses the argument on the structural damage inflicted by the overseas orientation of the City, and also shares Aaronovitch's view on the relative unimportance of the strength of the UK labour movement. Whereas Currie and Smith (1981) see the relative strength of the UK labour movement not as a cause (primary or secondary) but as a result of the decline generated by the promotion of the overseas interests of UK capital – 'the defensive strength and strategy of the British labour movement can then be seen as a result, rather than a cause of this failure of development' (Currie and Smith, 1981, p. 10).

An even more radical interpretation of the significance of the UK labour movement is Rowthorn's claim that the neglect fostered by a strategy of overseas expansion was tolerated by a quiescent labour movement and that a more militant movement could have forced the state to give priority to the restructuring of the domestic economy: 'We reach the paradoxical conclusion . . . that British capitalism declined not because workers were too militant . . . but because they were not militant enough and were willing to foot the bill for a suicidal strategy which put overseas expansion before domestic development' (Rowthorn, 1980, p. 144). Coates (1983) also insists on the importance of the historic relegation of the interests of domestic industrial capital but rejects both the claim that domestic investment has been retarded by capital exports and a shortage of finance and that there exists a systematic causal relationship between the quantum of investment and economic growth. The argument relies instead on a less direct transmission mechanism by which innovation and the productivity of investment has been retarded by the political and managerial weakness of UK industrial capital. Coates also acknowledges the relative strength of the UK labour movement but insists that the 'problem of worker resistance to capitalist restructuring is a secondary and derivative one' (Coates, 1983, section 6). In one way or another each writer in this group traces the post-war decline of the UK economy to the motives, orientation and responses of the dominant section of the capitalist class. Their explanations can thus be seen as expressions of the Hobsbawm thesis.

The fullest statement on the importance of the capital-labour struggle in the post-war decline of the UK economy is that of Kilpatrick and Lawson (1980). Other writers adopting a broadly similar position include Purdy (1976), Glyn and Harrison (1980, ch. 2) and Hodgson (1981, ch. 8). The basic argument starts from the claim that the process of industrialisation in the UK economy relied on pre-industrial craft labour to a much greater extent than elsewhere. The emerging labour movement in the nineteenth century thus became organised on the basis of skill differences rather than industrial categories, and as a result, and in contrast to developments in France, West Germany, Italy and Scandinavia the growth of centralised collective bargaining was inhibited whereas a strong union organisation at plant and company level was encouraged. The strength of European labour movements at the point of production has also been weakened by political and religious divisions in France and Italy, and by state suppression and control in Germany, Italy and France during the war and interwar periods of the twentieth century.

The final claim is that the balance of power in favour of labour in the UK retarded economic growth through its effect on the level and growth rate of industrial productivity—

the UK working class's strong organisation at factory level thwarted many of capital's attempts to increase productivity. New techniques, involving a sharp increase in the technical composition of capital were often effectively vetoed by unions which did not want to lose jobs. Where new technology was installed, its effect on productivity was often reduced because unions insisted on maintaining existing operating levels or line speeds. (Glyn and Harrison, 1980, p.50)

The advocates of this view see the retreat into protected overseas markets as a result of the economic decline of the UK and not a cause of it. The general claim, which appears in one form or another in each of the cited works, is that 'if British capital did turn overseas, this was largely because it was difficult to produce competitively for export from the UK' (ibid., p. 42). The structure of the arguments of these writers suggests that they would not disagree with Kilpatrick and Lawson's specific claim about the relevance to the post-war UK economy of the situation after 1880 in which 'UK exporters found it to their advantage to avoid conflict with workers over an accelerating remoulding of the structure of production, and instead redirected sales to new or protected markets, often with the aid of capital exports' (Kilpatrick and Lawson, 1980, p. 96). This assessment of the relative significance of the strength of the UK labour movement and the overseas orientation of UK capital should be compared to that contained in the arguments of Aaronovitch, Coates, Currie and Smith, the London CSE Group and Rowthorn. The reversal is more or less complete. The factor which is secondary or consequential in these expressions of the Hobsbawm thesis is central to the Kilpatrick-Lawson thesis, and vice versa. [Moreover, the Kilpatrick-Lawson thesis, unlike that of Hobsbawm, is compatible with] the view that the uniquely strong position occupied by the UK labour movement in its struggle with capital has retarded economic growth by setting in train a cumulative process of decline involving slow innovation and productivity growth, a slackening demand for UK products in world markets and a slow rate of accumulation in the domestic manufacturing sector.[. . .]

The comparison presented above makes it quite clear that [. . .] [the Kilpatrick-Lawson] composite thesis is competitive with almost all expressions of the Hobsbawm thesis. It is possible to hold that the decline of the UK economy, the overseas orientation of UK capital and the neglect of the domestic manufacturing sector have been joint products of the relative strength of the UK labour movement, or that capital exports and the overseas orientation of capital have been of fundamental importance with the struggle between capital and labour occupying a secondary or even consequential position. But it is not possible to hold both views at once. In particular it is not possible to subscribe to the view that in a capitalist economy such as the UK, investment is in the long run self-financing and accumulation is the evidence of growth, and also to hold that UK growth has been retarded by low investment induced by the export of capital and a shortage of investment finance. Both claims may be incorrect but if one is correct the other must be false.

References

Aaronovitch, S. (1981a), 'The relative decline of the UK', in Aaronovitch, Smith *et al.*, *The Political Economy of British Capitalism: A Marxist Analysis*, London, McGraw Hill.

Aaronovitch, S. (1981b), *The Road from Thatcherism, the Alternative Economic Strategy*, London, Lawrence and Wishart.

Coates, D. (1983), 'The character and origins of Britain's economic decline' in Coates, D. and Johnston, G. (eds), *Socialist Strategies*, Oxford, Martin Robertson.

Currie, D. and Smith, R.P. (1981), 'Economic Trends and the Crisis in the UK economy' in *Socialist Economic Review 1981*, London, Merlin Press.

Glyn, A. and Harrison, J. (1980), *The British Economic Disaster*, London, Pluto Press.

Hobsbawm, E.J. (1968), *Industry and Empire*, New York, Pantheon Books.

Hodgson, G. (1981), *Labour at the Crossroads*, Oxford, Martin Robertson.

Jessop, R. (1980), 'The transformation of the state in post-war Britain', in Scase, R. (ed), *The State in Western Europe*, London, Croom Helm.

Kilpatrick, A. and Lawson, T. (1980), 'On the nature of industrial decline in the UK', *Cambridge Journal of Economics*, March.

London CSE group (1980), *The Alternative Economic Strategy: a Labour Movement response to the crisis*, London, CSE Books and Labour Co-ordinating Committee.

Longstreth, F. (1979), 'The city, industry and the state', in Crouch, C. (ed.) *State and Economy in Contemporary Capitalism*, London, Croom Helm.

Purdy, D. (1976) 'British capitalism since the war', *Marxism Today*, September and October.

Rowthorn, R.E. (1980), *Capitalism, Conflict and Inflation: Essays in Political Economy*, London, Lawrence and Wishart.

SECTION 4

Politics and Power

Introduction

The politics of the United Kingdom have reflected the striking changes that have occurred at global and national levels over the past fifty years. Perhaps those changes that have taken place globally have been the most dramatic. The British Empire over which the sun never set no longer exists. The UK is no longer a global power. The last few decades have been a period of almost continuous relative decline for the United Kingdom. British politicians have had to deal with the nation's diminished global status, but they have also had to cope with the changes in British society and the economy that have been examined in the previous sections. Some of these changes have been no less dramatic. The use and relative decline of trade union power, the growth of the women's movement and the altered character of British capitalism have all left their mark on the British political process. This section of the book focuses on some of these aspects of British politics.

The three readings in the section examine particular concepts and relationships – power, equality and democracy – that are central to the study of government and politics. The first reading discusses the concept of power; a concept which has exercised political scientists, and indeed other social scientists, for a very considerable time. Who rules? or who governs? are questions that have been frequently asked by political scientists. The answers that have been offered to the questions, unsurprisingly, have been extremely varied and have always aroused controversy and debate. The reading by Steven Lukes is no different. It provides an especially interesting venture into this arena, by offering a strikingly different analysis of this difficult but critically important concept from that suggested by several other political scientists. Indeed, Lukes wrote *Power: A Radical View* in 1974, from which this reading is taken, in response to what he saw as a misunderstanding about the nature of power, that was beginning to dominate the discipline of politics.

In particular Lukes took issue with the work of perhaps the leading American political scientist at the time, Robert Dahl. Dahl had written a book in 1961, which was entitled *Who Governs?* In the book, Dahl attempted to identify the institutions and people who had power and ruled the city of New Haven, Connecticut. He sought to do so by observing the institutions of city government, those actors – local politicians, representatives of interest groups etc. – who were very active in the politics of the city, and those issues that both aroused a great deal of visible conflict within the city and required a decision by the city government. As a result of his observation, Dahl offered a portrait of New Haven that suggested political power was reasonably widely dispersed. In other words,

Dahl's analysis sustained the broadly liberal and pluralist assumptions about power and influence in western democratic societies. However, Lukes contests this conclusion, not by offering us new information about the politics of New Haven, but by arguing that Dahl has misunderstood the concept of power. He suggests that the concept of power is far more complex than Dahl would have us believe. Those political scientists who focus on decision-making and the institutions of government, according to Lukes, can only offer a limited or one-dimensional perspective of power. The limited focus obscures the view of vital and important characteristics that exist within societies. It is a focus that does not permit the observer to note certain more fundamental and structured power relationships. Lukes argues in the section of the chapter, entitled the 'Three-dimensional view', that perhaps the greatest source of power in any society is the capacity of a select few to influence the manner in which others construct and view their world, and this will not emerge from a concentration on political institutions and decision-making.

Lukes's notion of power, of course, emerges out of his own perspectives and beliefs, which are broadly marxist. Those political scientists, to whom Lukes was responding, were of a broadly pluralist persuasion. It is interesting to note that their differing conceptions of power reinforced their very different general assumptions and understandings about the nature of society.

The second reading in this section is written by April Carter. The reading is a passage from her book, *The Politics of Women's Rights*, and deals with the changes and developments that occurred in the political climate between the passage of two important pieces of equal opportunity legislation, the Equal Pay Act of 1970 and the Sex Discrimination Act of 1975. Although in this reading, Carter does examine the decisions made by Parliament, she does not fall into the trap that Lukes was so critical of, by narrowing her focus. She provides an account of the individuals and institutions who were involved in the parliamentary arena, but the thrust of the reading lies in another direction. It suggests the forces that produced the two Acts were very different, because the conditions had altered quite remarkably. The passage of the Equal Pay Act conformed, as it were, to the more traditional and conventional route that has been taken by reform legislation in the UK over the past decades. It was a very long time in coming, it had the support of numerous interest groups, most notably the union movement, and although some of the support was less than enthusiastic, it was endorsed finally by the Labour Party, included in the party's election manifesto in 1964, and finally enacted by a Labour government. Interestingly, the more far reaching and radical Sex Discrimination Act offers a very different account of the British political process. Unlike the Equal Pay Act which had been on the political agenda for thirty-five years prior to its enactment, the Sex Discrimination Act became law extraordinarily quickly. The reason Carter offers for this development is that the political agenda was transformed by the women's movement. Carter suggests it was passed as a consequence of a very sharp change in the climate of opinion in the nation at large; a change that was brought about by the rapid growth of the women's movement and the ideas that were generated by that movement in the years between 1970 and 1975. The political institutions and the mainstream political actors were, to a large extent, swept along by these developments in society. The institutions and the politicians did not control the process but were essentially responding to a dramatic shift in the way in which the issues of equal opportunities and rights were being constructed. The very concept of equality was being altered and extended.

The final reading in this section is by John Dearlove and Peter Saunders which also deals with a similar theme of the relationship between the political process or polity on the one hand and society, and also in this case, the economy. However, in this extract from their book, they reflect on a far wider and more complex relationship, which exists between democracy and capitalism. They trace a relationship that was, at one stage, thought to be inherently antagonistic but which, notably in recent years, has been viewed by those on the New Right in Britain and the United States as uniquely complementary. It is an interesting development which Dearlove and Saunders interrogate, although their own lack of any enthusiasm for market capitalism, which is not disguised, should be kept in mind when reading this extract. Moreover, their book was written before the vogue for markets and liberal democracy swept through Eastern Europe, so it is no longer a phenomenon confined to Western Europe, North America, Australasia and Japan. Nevertheless, Dearlove and Saunders raise a variety of very interesting issues. They raise the problem of defining both capitalism and democracy, which is central when deciding whether a society can be labelled a capitalist democracy. They are particularly good at noting and analysing the tensions between the practices of market capitalism and the values of liberal democracy, and their suggestion that the 'fit' between them is uneasy cannot be readily dismissed. But just in case you believe that their ability to detect this tension is due simply to their dislike of market capitalism, Dearlove and Saunders do indicate that the 'fit' between socialism and democracy is also problematic. The issues and questions they raise over this relationship are both important and provocative.

Richard Maidment

CHAPTER 1 2

Power: A Radical View

Steven Lukes

The one-dimensional view

In his early article, 'The concept of power', Dahl describes his 'intuitive idea of power' as 'something like this: *A* has power over *B* to the extent that he can get *B* to do something that *B* would not otherwise do' (Dahl, 1957, p. 80). A little later in the same article he describes his 'intuitive view of the power relation' slightly differently: it seemed, he writes, 'to involve a successful attempt by *A* to get *a* to do something he would not otherwise do' (p. 82). Note that the first statement refers to *A's* capacity ('. . . to the extent that he can get *B* to do something . . .'), while the second specifies a successful attempt – this, of course being the difference between potential and actual power, between its possession and its exercise. It is the latter – the exercise of power – which is central to this view of power.[. . .] Dahl's central method in *Who Governs?* is to 'determine for each decision which participants had initiated alternatives that were finally adopted, had vetoed alternatives initiated by others, or had proposed alternatives that were turned down. These actions were then tabulated as individual 'successes' or 'defeats'. The participants with the greatest proportion of successes out of the total number of successes, were then considered to be the most influential' (Dahl, 1961, p. 336).[. . .]

The focus on observable behaviour in identifying power involves [. . .] studying *decision-making* as the central task. Thus for Dahl power can be analysed only after 'careful examination of a series of concrete decisions' (Dahl, 1958, p. 466); and Polsby writes:

> one can conceive of 'power' – 'influence' and 'control' are serviceable synonyms – as the capacity of one actor to do something affecting another actor, which changes the probable pattern of specified future events. This can be envisaged most easily in a decision-making situation. (Polsby, 1963, pp. 3–4)

and he argues that identifying 'who prevails in decision-making' seems 'the best way to determine which individuals and groups have 'more' power in social life, because direct conflict between actors presents a situation most closely approximating an experimental test of their capacities to affect outcomes' (p. 4).

Source: S. Lukes, *Power: a Radical View*, 1974, London and Basingstoke, Macmillan, pp. 10–25.

As this last quotation shows, it is assumed that the 'decisions' involve 'direct', i.e. actual and observable, *conflict* [. . .] [Writers in this tradition] see their focus on behaviour in the making of decisions over key or important issues as involving actual, observable conflict. Note that this implication is not required by either Dahl's or Polsby's definition of power, which merely require that A can or does succeed in affecting what B does. And indeed in *Who Governs?* Dahl is quite sensitive to the operation of power or influence in the absence of conflict: indeed he even writes that a 'rough test of a person's overt or covert influence is the frequency with which he successfully initiates an important policy over the opposition of others, or vetoes policies initiated by others, or *initiates a policy where no opposition appears [sic]*' (Dahl, 1961, p. 66). This, however, is just one among a number of examples of how the text of *Who Governs?* is more subtle and profound than the general conceptual and methodological pronouncements of its author and his colleagues; it is in contradiction with their conceptual framework and their methodology. In other words, it represents an insight which this one-dimensional view of power is unable to exploit.[. . .]

The two-dimensional view

In their critique of this view, Bachrach and Baratz argue that it is restrictive and, in virtue of that fact, gives a misleadingly sanguine pluralist picture of American politics. Power, they claim, has two faces. The first face is that already considered, according to which 'power' is totally embodied and fully reflected in 'concrete decisions' or in activity bearing directly upon their making' (Bachrach and Baratz, 1970, p.7). As they write:

> Of course power is exercised when A participates in the making of decisions that affect B. Power is also exercised when A devotes his energies to creating or reinforcing social and political values and institutional practices that limit the scope of the political process to public consideration of only those issues which are comparatively innocuous to A. To the extent that A succeeds in doing this, B is prevented, for all practical purposes, from bringing to the fore any issues that might in their resolution be seriously detrimental to A's set of preferences. (p. 7)

Their 'central point' is this: 'to the extent that a person or group – consciously or unconsciously – creates or reinforces barriers to the public airing of policy conflicts, that person or group has power' (p. 8), and they cite Schattschneider's famous and often-quoted words:

> All forms of political organisation have a bias in favour of the exploitation of some kinds of conflict and the suppression of others, because *organisation is the mobilisation of bias*. Some issues are organised into politics while others are organised out. (Schattschneider, 1960, p. 71)

[. . .] The central thrust of Bachrach and Baratz's critique of the one-dimensional view of power is, up to a point, *anti-behavioural*: that is, they claim that it 'unduly emphasises the importance of initiating, deciding, and vetoing' and, as a result, takes 'no account of the fact that power may be, and often is, exercised by confining the scope of decision-making to relatively "safe" issues' (p. 6). On the other hand, they do insist (at least in their book – in response to critics who maintained that if *B* fails to act because he anticipates *A's* reaction, nothing has occurred and one has a 'non-event', incapable of empirical verification) that their so-called nondecisions which confine the scope of decision-making are themselves (observable) *decisions*. These, however, may not be overt or specific to a given issue or even consciously taken to exclude potential challengers, of whom the status quo defenders may well be unaware. Such unawareness 'does not mean, however, that the dominant group will refrain from making nondecisions that protect or promote their dominance. Simply supporting the established political process tends to have this effect' (p. 50).

A satisfactory analysis, then, of two-dimensional power involves examining both decision-making and nondecision-making. A decision is 'a choice among alternative modes of action' (p. 39); a nondecision is 'a decision that results in suppression or thwarting of a latent or manifest challenge to the values or interests of the decision-maker' (p. 44). Thus, nondecision-making is 'a means by which demands for change in the existing allocation of benefits and privileges in the community can be suffocated before they are even voiced; or kept covert; or killed before they gain access to the relevant decision-making arena; or, failing all these things, maimed or destroyed in the decision-implementing stage of the policy process' (p. 44).

In part, Bachrach and Baratz are, in effect, redefining the boundaries of what is to count as a political issue. For [Dahl and Polsby] those boundaries are set by the political system being observed, or rather by the elites within it: as Dahl writes, 'a political issue can hardly be said to exist unless and until it commands the attention of a significant segment of the political stratum' (Dahl, 1961, p. 92). The observer then picks out certain of these issues as obviously important or 'key' and analyses decision-making with respect to them. For Bachrach and Baratz, by contrast, it is crucially important to identify *potential issues* which nondecision-making prevents from being actual. In their view, therefore, 'important' or 'key' issues may be actual or, most probably, potential – a key issue being 'one that involves a genuine challenge to the resources of power or authority of those who currently dominate the process by which policy outputs in the system are determined', that is, 'a demand for enduring transformation in both the manner in which values are allocated in the policy [. . .] and the value allocation itself (Bachrach and Baratz, 1970, pp. 47–8).

Despite this crucial difference with [Dahl and Polsby], Bachrach and Baratz's analysis has one significant feature in common with theirs: namely, the stress on actual, observable *conflict*, overt or covert.[. . .] The two-dimensional view of power involves a *qualified critique* of the *behavioural focus* of the first view (I say qualified because it is still assumed that nondecision-making is a form of decision-making) and it allows for consideration of the ways in which *decisions* are prevented from being taken on *potential issues* over which there is an observable *conflict* of (subjective) *interests*, seen as embodied in express policy preferences and sub-political grievances.

The three-dimensional view

There is no doubt that the two-dimensional view of power represents a major advance over the one-dimensional view: it incorporates into the analysis of power relations the question of the control over the agenda of politics and of the ways in which potential issues are kept out of the political process. None the less, it is, in my view, inadequate on three counts.

In the first place, its critique of behaviourism is too qualified, or, to put it another way, it is still too committed to behaviourism – that is, to the study of overt, 'actual behaviour', of which 'concrete decisions' in situations of conflict are seen as paradigmatic. In trying to assimilate all cases of exclusion of potential issues from the political agenda to the paradigm of a decision, it gives a misleading picture of the ways in which individuals and, above all, groups and institutions succeed in excluding potential issues from the political process. Decisions are choices consciously and intentionally made by individuals between alternatives, whereas the bias of the system can be mobilised, recreated and reinforced in ways that are neither consciously chosen nor the intended result of particular individuals' choices. As Bachrach and Baratz themselves maintain, the domination of defenders of the status quo may be so secure and pervasive that they are unaware of any potential challengers to their position and thus of any alternatives to the existing political process, whose bias they work to maintain. As 'students of power and its consequences', they write, 'our main concern is not whether the defenders of the status quo use their power consciously, but rather if and how they exercise it and what effects it has on the political process and other actors within the system' (Bachrach and Baratz, 1970, p. 50).

Moreover, the bias of the system is not sustained simply by a series of individually chosen acts, but also, most importantly, by the socially structured and culturally patterned behaviour of groups, and practices of institutions, which may indeed be manifested by individuals' inaction. Bachrach and Baratz follow [Dahl and Polsby] in adopting too methodologically individualist a view of power. In this both parties follow in the steps of Max Weber, for whom power was the probability of *individuals realising their wills* despite the resistance of others, whereas the power to control the agenda of politics and exclude potential issues cannot be adequately analysed unless it is seen as a function of collective forces and social arrangements. There are, in fact, two separable cases here. First, there is the phenomenon of collective action, where the policy or action of a collectivity (whether a group, e.g. a class, or an institution, e.g. a political party or an industrial corporation) is manifest, but not attributable to particular individuals' decisions or behaviour. Second, there is the phenomenon of 'systematic' or organisational effects, where the mobilisation of bias results, as Schattschneider put it, from the form of organisation. Of course, such collectivities and organisations are made up of individuals – but the power they exercise cannot be simply conceptualised in terms of individuals' decisions or behaviour. As Marx succinctly put it, 'Men make their own history but they do not make it just as they please; they do not make it under circumstances chosen by themselves, but

under circumstances directly encountered, given and transmitted from the past'
(Marx and Engels, 1962, p. 247).

The second count on which the two-dimensional view of power is inadequate
is in its association of power with actual, observable conflict. In this respect also
[Bachrach and Baratz] follow their adversaries too closely (and both in turn again
follow Weber, who, as we have seen, stressed the realisation of one's will, *despite
the resistance of others*). This insistence on actual conflict as essential to power
will not do.[. . .] It is highly unsatisfactory to suppose that power is only exercised
in situations of such conflict. To put the matter sharply, A may exercise power
over B by getting him to do what he does not want to do, but he also exercises
power over him by influencing, shaping or determining his very wants. Indeed,
is it not the supreme exercise of power to get another or others to have the desires
you want them to have – that is, to secure their compliance by controlling their
thoughts and desires? One does not have to go to the lengths of talking about
Brave New World, or the world of B.F. Skinner, to see this: thought control takes
many less total and more mundane forms, through the control of information,
through the mass media and through the process of socialisation. Indeed,
ironically, there are some excellent descriptions of this phenomenon in *Who
Governs?* Consider the picture of the rule of the 'patricians' in the early nineteenth
century: 'The elite seems to have possessed that most indispensable of all
characteristics in a dominant group – the sense, shared not only by themselves
but by the populace, that their claim to govern was legitimate' (Dahl, 1961, p.
17). And Dahl also sees this phenomenon at work under modern 'pluralist'
conditions: leaders, he says, 'do not merely *respond* to the preferences of
constituents; leaders also *shape* preferences' (p. 164), and, again, 'almost the entire
adult population has been subjected to *some* degree of indoctrination through the
schools' (p. 317), etc. The trouble seems to be that both Bachrach and Baratz
and [Dahl] suppose that because power, as they conceptualise it, only shows up
in cases of actual conflict, it follows that actual conflict is necessary to power.
But this is to ignore the crucial point that the most effective and insidious use
of power is to prevent such conflict from arising in the first place.

The third count on which the two-dimensional view of power is inadequate
is closely linked to the second: namely, its insistence that nondecision-making
power only exists where there are grievances which are denied entry into the
political process in the form of issues. If the observer can uncover no grievances,
then he must assume there is a 'genuine' consensus on the prevailing allocation
of values. To put this another way, it is here assumed that if men feel no
grievances, then they have no interests that are harmed by the use of power. But
this is also highly unsatisfactory. In the first place, what, in any case, is a grievance
– an articulated demand, based on political knowledge, an undirected complaint
arising out of everyday experience, a vague feeling of unease or sense of
deprivation? Second, and more important, is it not the supreme and most insidious
exercise of power to prevent people, to whatever degree, from having grievances
by shaping their perceptions, cognitions and preferences in such a way that they
accept their role in the existing order of things, either because they can see or
imagine no alternative to it, or because they see it as natural and unchangeable,

or because they value it as divinely ordained and beneficial? To assume that the absence of grievance equals genuine consensus is simply to rule out the possibility of false or manipulated consensus by definitional fiat.

In summary, the three-dimensional view of power involves a *thoroughgoing critique* of the *behavioural focus* of the first two views as too individualistic and allows for consideration of the many ways in which *potential issues* are kept out of politics, whether through the operation of social forces and institutional practices or through individuals' decisions. This, moreover, can occur in the absence of actual, observable conflict, which may have been successfully averted – though there remains here an implicit reference to potential conflict. This potential, however, may never in fact be actualised. What one may have here is a *latent conflict*, which consists in a contradiction between the interests of those exercising power and the *real interests* of those they exlude.[. . .]

References

Bachrach, P. and Baratz, M. (1970) *Power and Poverty: theory and practice*, New York, Oxford University Press.

Dahl, R.A. (1957) 'The concept of power', *Behavioural Science*, vol. 2; reprinted in R. Bell *et al.* (eds) (1969) *Political Power: A Reader in Theory and Research*, London, Collier Macmillan.

Dahl, R.A. (1958) 'A critique of the ruling elite model', *APSR*, pp. 463–9.

Dahl, R.A. (1961) *Who Governs? Democracy and Power in an American City*, London, Yale University Press.

Marx, K. and Engels, F. (1962) 'The Eighteenth Brumaire of Louis Bonaparte', in Marx and Engels *Selected Works*, vol. 1, Moscow, Foreign Languages Publishing House.

Polsby, N.W. (1963) *Community Power and Political Theory*, London, Yale University Press.

Schattschneider, C.F. (1960) *The Semi-Sovereign People: a realist's view of democracy in America*, New York, Holt, Rinehart and Winston.

CHAPTER 13

The Politics of Women's Rights

April Carter

Women's rights achieved widespread publicity in Britain as a result of the writings, demands and demonstrations of a new generation of feminists who came to public attention at the end of the 1960s. Whilst they promoted much greater awareness of discrimination against women, their immediate political effectiveness depended on co-operation with existing campaigners for women's rights and organizations representing women's interests. Individual women MPs had used Private Members' Bills and other parliamentary devices to try to extend women's rights.[. . .] Women's organizations in the Labour Party and trade unions had campaigned consistently on various issues, in particular equal pay, which the Labour Party had been formally committed to introducing since 1964. In addition, bodies dating from the original struggle for women's suffrage, like the Fawcett Society, and organizations representing women's professional interests took the lead in pressing for legislation to end sexual discrimination, though they were joined by new feminist groups in the early 1970s.[. . .] Nevertheless, the Women's Liberation Movement did act as a catalyst to campaign for women's rights, and in addition focused attention on a much wider range of issues affecting women's daily lives.[. . .]

The two most central laws designed to promote women's rights were the Equal Pay Act of 1970 and the Sex Discrimination Act of 1975, and it is the politics of passing these two Acts we compare here.

Although they were only separated by five years, and the Equal Pay Act did not become fully operational until 1975, these two Acts reflected differing pressures for reform and a significant change in the attitudes of political parties to the demand for women's rights. The Equal Pay Act was the culmination of a slow but steady progress towards accepting the formal equality of women at work – equal pay had already been implemented for white-collar workers in public services and in the professions by the early 1960s. The Act reflected international endorsement of the principle of equal pay by the International Labour Organization and the EEC and was a product primarily of long-term pressure within the trade union movement. Demands from women trade-unionists became more vocal in the 1960s when the Labour Government delayed taking action, and the Act followed manifestations of working-class women's militancy in 1968–69; but the Labour Government's decision to legislate in 1969 owed little

Source: A. Carter, *The Politics of Women's Rights*, 1988, Harlow, Longmans, pp. 50–1, 112–124.

to the emerging Women's Liberation Movement. The Sex Discrimination Act by contrast did reflect a greatly heightened public awareness of women's lack of rights, due in part to the new feminism, and was adopted after several years of increasingly active lobbying and attempts by MPs to introduce Private Members' Bills. It was influenced, too, by the precedent of legislation against racial discrimination and by the American approach to enshrining equal rights in law.

The Labour Party had included a promise to introduce equal pay for women in its 1964 Election Manifesto, after the previous Conservative Government had turned down a request from the TUC to legislate on equal pay on the grounds that this was a matter for employers and trade unions to resolve, not for governments. The Labour Party support in principle for legislation reflected an abstract commitment to women's equality, but its failure to introduce an Equal Pay Bill until its last year in office clearly showed that women's rights had a very low priority. Repeated resolutions for equal pay at National Labour Women's conferences did not have any obvious effect.[. . .]

The role of the trade unions in promoting equal pay for women has been ambiguous. When women's entry into traditionally male jobs threatened to undercut men's wage rates, for example during the Second World War, the unions did press for equal pay. The TUC and relevant unions did also back the demand for equal pay in the public service after the war, whilst the TUC raised the basic issue again in the 1960s. But trade unions as a whole did not [. . .] have a good record of backing the interests of their women members – the majority after all had failed to raise equal pay in negotiations with employers. The leadership of the Amalgamated Union of Engineering Workers did commit itself to seek rapid implementation of equal pay in 1964, but most union leaders did not press the issue, and women trade-unionists became increasingly impatient during the 1960s. The Women's Advisory Committee of the TUC drew up the Working Women's Charter in 1963, calling not only for equal pay but equal opportunities for promotion and for training and special provisions for women workers, and the TUC endorsed it at their 1963 conference. Women complained at the 1966 Women's TUC Conference about the lack of urgency shown by the TUC over equal pay, and in 1968 criticism became more vociferous both at the TUC Conference and at a special TUC Conference on Equal Pay.

Two factors are usually cited to explain why the Labour Government did at last introduce an Equal Pay Bill in 1969: the strikes by women workers in 1968 and the appointment of Barbara Castle as Secretary of State for Employment in 1968 to replace Ray Gunter. Both were certainly important.

The Ford women's strike in 1968 hit the newspaper headlines, held up £50 million worth of exports and led to a march on the House of Commons. The strike dramatized an increasing sense of anger and injustice among working women, which in turn influenced trade-unionists.[. . .]

Barbara Castle's personal role was decisive. Several commentators have suggested that the Equal Pay Act would not have been pushed through if there had not been a woman as Secretary of State for Employment, and this is probably true, though Barbara Castle's feminism should not be exaggerated. Her *Diaries* indicate that she did not wish to involve herself closely with women's issues.[. . .] But she did have an interest in women's role at work and in improving the position of working-class women, who would be the most immediate beneficiaries of an Equal Pay Act, and she had joined an equal pay demonstration in the 1950s. Moreover, she had met a deputation from the Ford women during the strike and publicly promised that equal pay would be introduced in November 1968.[. . .] Barbara Castle succeeded because she was an able and energetic minister, keen to make a success of whatever she turned her hand to, and usually good at getting her own way. The Act reflected compromises she accepted under pressure: she was unsuccessful in getting pensions and social security covered, and refused to try to include discrimination in areas like recruitment and training. But passage of the Act did have considerable symbolic importance as well as some practical effects in the mid 1970s, and it paved the way for further legislation on women's rights.

The main obstacle to equal pay during the 1960s was the widespread assumption that women's issues were unimportant, at least in the political arena. Although there was potential ideological opposition on the Right among those who still believed woman's place was in the home, and on the Left from those who saw feminism as a diversion from the central class struggle, within the liberal consensus that embraced the majority of Conservative and Labour party members and supporters the principle of equal pay was unexceptionable.[. . .]

Whereas equal pay had been on the public agenda since 1945, broader measures to ensure equal opportunity had been canvassed by feminists without attracting much attention. When the Equal Pay Act was introduced there was recognition in debates in Parliament that supplementary measures were needed, but a general law against sexual discrimination was a new idea stimulated by the 1960s experiment in legislating against racial discrimination. It was, moreover, inherently more controversial than equal pay, since it raised questions about the desirability of trying to change attitudes through the law, problems about the scope of such a law and difficulties about what women wanted or needed. So it is interesting that the Sex Discrimination Act was passed after only a few years' agitation. One reason must be the spread of feminist ideas and feminist activism between 1969 and 1975, accompanied by a change in attitudes to women's rights by the press, radio and television and among many of the public. There was certainly a marked increase in sympathy and interest among MPs in that period. It could more cynically be argued that the major obstacle to equal pay – fear of increased wage costs – did not apply to the Sex Discrimination Act, since the costs to employers arising from it were less clear cut. But CBI evidence to the House of Lords was markedly unenthusiastic about a Sex Discrimination Act, so there was some employer resistance.

The pattern of the campaign to achieve a Sex Discrimination Act was a series of Private Members' Bills, backed by increasingly well-organized and visible support outside Parliament and cross-bench support inside it. All these Bills eventually failed, but the Conservative Government felt impelled to produce a Green Paper in 1973, even though feminists dismissed it as a token gesture, and the Labour Government got an act passed in 1975.[. . .]

Given the large number of groups involved at various stages in lobbying for equal pay or the Sex Discrimination Bills and in presenting relevant evidence it is impossible here to delineate them in any detail or assess the influence of each group. But it is worth noting the diversity of the organizations involved. There were sectional interest groups representing women at work – professional and business women's associations as well as women in trade unions – and organizations promoting the interests of wives and mothers. In addition to women's bodies there were general professional and trade union organizations that gave particular support to women's rights, for example the NUT. There were in addition numerous promotional or cause groups involved. Some of these were set up specifically to agitate for equal pay or for legislation to end discrimination, for example the Women's Lobby, while there were other feminist groups with rather different aims, for example Women in Media whose primary purpose was to contest stereotypes and sexist bias and demand better jobs for women in the media, who took part in the campaign. Apart from specifically feminist organizations, both old and new, one promotional group which played an important role in campaigning for legislation was the NCCL, which had been persuaded during the 1960s to extend its concern with civil liberties to women's rights by a number of women on its council, and which set up a Women's Rights Unit in the 1970s.

Finally, there was pressure from women within the major parties for equal rights; not only from women MPs with the support of some of their male colleagues, but also from the women's organizations within the parties.[. . .]

CHAPTER 14

Capitalism and Democracy

John Dearlove and Peter Saunders

[M]aking good sense of British politics demands that we 'see' politics, not as a self-contained activity that only occurs in officially designated 'political' organizations and institutions, but in the round and in the larger context of economy and society. Nineteenth-century theorists recognized this; they did not write about politics *or* economics but explored the total political economy and the complex intermeshing of governments and markets, public power and private power. Sides were taken on the appropriate balance between governments and markets. Defenders of free-market capitalism supported a *laissez-faire*, limited state and were anxious as to the implications that might flow from a state based on unfettered mass democracy: would public power eat into private power, and would the voting many use the state to pillage the wealthy few who were dominant in the market? From the other side, those critical of the privilege and power of private property saw, in a popularly controlled public power, the possibility of fundamental change and the emancipation of the masses.

These, then were the questions that were the stuff of theoretical political economy, and they were at the core of politics and political action as well. If you were 'for' the market then you were probably against democracy, and if you were against the market and the power of private interests then you were likely to be optimistic as to what might come from the extension of the franchise to the working class. Simply expressed, prior to the extension of the franchise to the urban working class, theorists explored politics and economics in relation to each other, and most informed commentators saw a polity based on democracy and an economy based on capitalism as in many ways incompatible.

Since those days assessments as to the 'fit' between democracy and capitalism have changed. The extension of the franchise in England did not bring the immediate disasters and transformations that opponents (and even liberals) feared. Indeed, supporters of the free market gradually came to praise liberal democracy as a good in its own right and as posing little challenge to the survival of the economy of capitalism. The point was not lost on Marxists. Marx himself expressed high hopes as to what democracy *could* bring, claiming that universal suffrage was a 'socialistic measure' and its 'inevitable result' would be the 'political supremacy of the working class'. However, he also recognized the limitations

Source: J. Dearlove and P. Saunders, *Introduction to British Politics*, 1988, Cambridge, Polity Press, pp. 436–444.

of *bourgeois* democracy which he believed simply served to incorporate the working class within the prevailing economic order. It was this idea of democracy as a concession that helped to legitimize the system whilst leaving the fundamentals unchallenged which was later to inform Lenin's argument that 'a democratic republic is the best possible political shell for capitalism'.

So, as the practice of liberal, or bourgeois, democratic politics unfolded, reassessments were made as to its implications for the prospects of stability or change on the larger canvas of society. There were intellectual about-turns. The kind of people who once feared democracy learned to love it, whereas critics of capitalism who had once held out high hopes for democracy found them dashed so that the Marxist tradition came to see revolution as the only viable road leading to transformation and socialism. All in all, by the beginning of the twentieth century a new and fudgy consensus had emerged between supporters and critics of both capitalism and democracy. That consensus overturned the view which suggested that democracy and capitalism were in conflict, and held instead that capitalism and democracy were in fact mutually supportive. Defenders of capitalism and democracy argued that they fitted together because freedom, competition, and power dispersal were the essential hallmarks and guarantees of both. Critics of capitalism and democracy argued that they fitted together because a formal democracy of citizens actually served to sustain the economic inequality of the market: workers accepted political rights in return for a general sacrifice of economic ones, and the fairness central to the ideology of liberal democracy legitimized the total system in the eyes of the majority whilst still allowing dominant minority interests sufficient scope to rule from behind the scenes.[. . .]

Now, there is a problem in exploring the relationship between democracy and capitalism in Britain because the terms themselves are contested. Mainstream and liberal opinion is content to see democracy in *procedural* terms – e.g. in the existence of formally free elections and certain civil liberties. Left opinion, by contrast is concerned to define democracy in *substantive* terms – e.g. as involving popular participation in decision-making in both the polity and the economy with that participation inevitably leading to a rough equality of results in terms of the distribution of material benefits. Similarly, apologists for capitalism are concerned to define it in terms of freedoms and opportunities where the bulk of economic activity is organized through private enterprise in a free market, whereas critics of this mode of production (whilst recognizing the importance of private ownership and the market) are concerned to assert the lack of freedom and opportunity which follows from the exploitation and subordination of those who only have their labour power to sell to the owners of capital.

Given the disagreement concerning the definition of capitalism and democracy, it is perhaps not surprising that there are also disputes as to whether Britain is any longer 'really' democratic or 'really' capitalist. Mainstream and liberal opinion would certainly see Britain as democratic – indeed, as too democratic – but tends to see the growth of nationalization and state economic activity as having produced a 'mixed' economy in place of a purely capitalist one. Left opinion, by contrast, generally sees British democracy as partial and crushingly constrained by economic power and the institutions of the secret state, but insists that the economy is still unremittingly tied to capitalist essentials despite the many changes which have occurred since the nineteenth century.

Now, even allowing for the intellectual uncertainty that is part and parcel of these contests and disputes, there is surely something of a paradox in the coexistence of democratic institutions within capitalist societies since the principles of majority rule and political equality (one person one vote) seem inconsistent with the economic reality of minority power and the persistence of marked inequalities with respect to material advantages and benefits that are a feature of all capitalist economies. In our view, it is by no means self-evident that democracy is the 'best possible political shell' for capitalism, nor that capitalism is a necessary condition for the full realization of democracy. Doubts about the supposed 'fit' between the two are reinforced once we realize that capitalism is by no means universally associated with formal political democracy. The burgeoning capitalist economies of Latin America for example, could be cited to support a contrary hypothesis of a 'natural' fit between capitalism and authoritarian and military regimes with limited political freedoms.

Para 8   Nearer to home, it is important to consider the challenging implications of
verbal contemporary New Right thinking on these matters. Here is a body of work vehemently opposed to socialism and centrally concerned to defend capitalism and revive the flagging economies of the West.[. . .] Interest groups and trade unions are accused of contributing to an overload of demands that has made for ungovernability, political parties are criticized as too adversarial, and both these tendencies are said to have made for unstable public policies and to have led to 'too much' state intervention and public spending which has served to provide an unstable base for capitalist development. High taxation has, we are told, crowded out opportunities for economic growth in the private sphere because resources have been pre-empted by the state in order to provide uneconomic social benefits.[. . .]

The fact that it criticizes British democracy and proposes a new constitution of *limited* democracy, and the fact that it justifies these criticisms and proposals in the name of an active and aggressive defence of the virtues of free-market capitalism, surely provides still further grounds for our wondering whether capitalism and democracy have come to the parting of the ways.

What all this suggests is that we should be wary of seeing a tight fit between democracy and capitalism. No absolute and general relation can be constructed between them. It is true that a democracy is a *possible* form of capitalist state, but it is less certain that mass democracy is the *best* or most adequate form of capitalist state (especially when we see it in the context of an increasingly monopolized economy where huge multinational companies need to manage governments in the way in which they manage and manipulate their markets). Democracy, then, is indeterminate in so far as its relationship to capitalism is concerned. Put another way, certain conditions must be satisfied if it is to function in a way that is supportive of continued capitalist development. What are these conditions?

135

1   Harking back to the ideas of Bagehot in 1872 when he was forced to ponder the implications of working-class suffrage, the population as a whole must be 'deferential' and modest in their expectation of politics and of change through politics so that they accept the 'natural' order and inequalities of the market. A deferential politics limits the popular role in the political process at the same time as it limits the claim for rights through the public power of the state.

2   The precise type of democracy should itself be limited to a representative and parliamentary form. If this prevails and secures a legitimacy then the scope for a more participatory democracy involving intra-party democracy and extra-parliamentary action is restricted. Furthermore, pivotal positions within the state system and crucial institutional centres of state power should not be based on the elective principle; should be beyond the effective reach of the elected side of the state; and should enjoy close links to those dominant in the market system of private power.

3   The capitalist economy should be buoyant and subject to steady growth so that there is sufficient 'slack' within the economic system to enable elected politicians to respond to popular pressures for more and better public services and to fund those services through an ability to draw increasing tax revenues from an expanding economy without crowding out opportunities for further growth, and squeezing the economically powerful.

4   Because the danger is ever present that political power will be employed to undermine individual economic freedoms in the market if the 'wrong' people and parties employ the power of the state for the 'wrong' purposes, it is vital that interests sensitive to the need to maintain the essential disciplines of a capitalist economy are politically and ideologically dominant. This occurs if the electorate is firmly attached to political parties that are committed to the rules of parliamentary democracy (with all the limitations this implies) and if the parties are content to develop programmes that are 'realistic' (in that they work within the dominant ideology and accept that certain crucial aspects of economic life lie beyond the bounds of political control).

It should be clear that all these conditions serve to box democracy in to a narrow formalism of particular procedures which fall far short of participatory democracy and which represent a mere shadow of a substantive democracy in which all citizens have relatively equal chances to influence and control the making of decisions that affect them be they in politics or the market. Having said that, it is nevertheless clear that the four conditions relate each to the other and the importance of any one condition for sustaining capitalism varies at particular points in time. For example, if there is substantial slack in the system (condition 3) then there is scope to concede to demands from below. In this state of affairs, deference (condition 1) is less needed to ensure that democratic demands do not press up against the limits of capitalist concession because the limits are themselves expanding. However, if both slack and deference are lacking, then popular politics need to be constrained by a particular kind of public ideology (condition 4), and if that too is a problem, and the limits of the form of democracy are insufficient to restrain people's demands and aspirations, then public power needs to be successfully and legitimately transferred to the secret side of the state (condition 2). Attending to the relationship between democracy and capitalism in contemporary Britain thus involves consideration of the extent to which these four general conditions are satisfied in practice and whether they pull together (or compensate each other) in support of a free economy. What, then, can we say about each condition today?

1 A lot has happened since Bagehot wrote *The English Constitution* over 100 years ago. He feared that the established political parties would bid for the support of the working class, and he feared still more the possibility that the 'lower classes' might combine to form their own political party to advance their own interests ('an evil of the first magnitude that . . . would make them . . . supreme in the country'). He feared, in other words, the breakdown of deference which he saw as the key holding democratic excesses in check. Much has been written about the significance of deference in British politics but there is little doubt that deference is less a force than was once the case [. . .] and popular expectations of the state have risen in the period since Bagehot. Moreover, those who write about adversary politics today are right to remind us that political parties do bid for popular support, and elections have often been auctions of popular policies where the problem of paying for the promises is only faced after the event of victory. In addition, the 'political combination of the lower classes' that Bagehot so feared came into being with the formation of the Labour Party at the beginning of this century. Although the extent to which the party has 'really' transformed Britain when in government is still hotly debated, there is little doubt that elements within the party have always held to an ethic of provision that is challenging of capitalism and market power, and aspects of the welfare state are a concrete embodiment of the ethic of provision according to need rather than according to ability to pay. So, the conditions that Bagehot saw as vital to make democracy compatible with 'property' have largely evaporated.

2 It is true that democracy in Britain is mainly restricted to the representative and parliamentary form but this has not stopped moments of participation which have fallen outside, and challenged, those procedures. Working people, organized in trade unions, have taken action on the streets and in their workplaces. In the period since the 1960s, many people have begun to take local democracy seriously, participating in locally based campaigns of 'community action' in a way that has asserted the legitimacy and credibility of a more participatory democracy, and attempting (as in the Greater London Council and some of the metropolitan counties in the early 1980s) to use local authorities to challenge the power of the centre and to assert an alternative set of values to those of private property and the market system. Again in the 1970s, sections of the Left in British politics were active in an extra-parliamentary politics that often tumbled into anti-parliamentary politics as well. Notwithstanding these challenging developments, however, it continues to be the case that crucial centres of state power are beyond democratic control.[. . .]

3   Democracy is a fragile flower. It is always likely to push up against the confines set by the pattern of social and economic power based on the ownership of property and the control of economic opportunities by privileged groups. The survival of democracy requires tolerance, the inclusion of all classes in the exercise of political power, and a fundamental unity on the part of the people. The problem is that the unity between the classes is contingent on economic success. Harold Laski has not been the only person to wonder 'whether the uneasy marriage between capitalism and democracy is psychologically possible in the period of capitalism's decline' when the 'better classes' no longer feel able to concede. In the twenty years of relative affluence following the Second World War, slow but sustained economic growth provided slack, constraints on public policy-making were comparatively loose, and much could be achieved through parties and pressures and the democratic process. But at times of economic recession, the constraints on popular politics and the democratic process tighten as dominant economic interests look to their profit margins and exert pressures on the state to reduce the cost of the concessions made in the democratic round of politics. At times like this [. . .] capitalism and democracy come into sharp conflict.

However, it is important to remember that recession does not *create* the problem of the fit between capitalism and democracy since it simply serves to *exacerbate* the endemic problem which faces the state in a capitalist economy where democracy entrenches popular expectations and the means to press them that cannot easily be ignored, repressed, or left to be satisfied in the market. In bald outline, the state has to encourage economic growth because if it fails to do so it does not have an expanding base to tax, and tax is the source of its own power. At the same time as the state encourages economic growth through the market it also has to secure social harmony and legitimize its role in the eyes of the larger public whose actions do not directly make for growth. So, the state has to assist in the making of profits and so support the few who can contribute in vital ways to economic growth. But in helping one class at the expense of other classes and in limiting its role in the provision of social benefit, it risks losing its legitimacy as a neutral, fair, and caring agency and so undermines the basis of its loyalty and support. With recession, the Catch 22 problem is heightened as the capitalist economy is unable to deliver the goods as promised and so state efforts at social amelioration become increasingly urgent as popular pressures escalate. However, at the very moment when the state is most pressed to provide social support services it is least able to do so because the surplus is not there and those concerned with the preservation of a lean and fit capitalism see these services as expensive deductions from profits and an obstacle to further growth. Something has to give. Recession seems to highlight many of the problems integral to maintaining a capitalist democracy.

4   So far we have highlighted problems with respect to the fulfilment of the conditions resolving the paradox of the fit between capitalism and democracy. Deference is not what it was; popular politics frequently challenge established democratic procedures; and most profoundly, recession cuts into the slack that gives democracy room to move within the confines of capitalism. This being the case, sustaining the connection between capitalism and democracy at the present

time seems to depend on the fulfilment of the fourth condition – the political and ideological supremacy within democracy of those interests attuned to the need to protect the essentials of the capitalist economy. What, then, can we say about this?

The Conservative Party won the election of 1979 and won again in 1983. The Labour Party was routed in the 1983 election and the Liberal – SDP Alliance secured the support of over a quarter of the voters. Two things are significant about these events. First, the ideological tendency that is supreme within the Conservative Party and that has been endorsed twice at the polls is keenly pro-market and anti-state and so is active in attempting to create the conditions to revive a viable system of capitalism in Britain. Second, the Labour Party is the only mass party committed in principle to an alternative mode of organizing the economy, and yet it failed to secure substantial popular support even in 1983 at a time of mass unemployment when the individualistic philosophy of the market should be vulnerable to challenge. So, the fourth condition *is* roughly fulfilled at the present time, but is this enough to sustain the fit between capitalism and democracy?

Observing contemporary politics rather suggests that rights and freedoms that have been at the core of the democratic tradition are under challenge. The repressive side of the state is being strengthened in support of the free economy while civil liberties are being eroded; trade union powers are being curbed and certain government employees are banned from union membership altogether; popular movements are attacked when they dare to move outside the tight limitations of established procedures and the cost of working within these procedures is itself increased by, for example, raising the candidate's deposit at elections from £150 to £1000; moves to open government are resisted and the powers of the secret state are strengthened and defended; the significance of elected local authorities is being massively eroded and those authorities most vulnerable to control by non- or anti-capitalist interests are being abolished; and those in positions of constitutional authority advocate limiting democracy by law and strengthening the power of the judges.

Writing on the allegedly supportive connection between capitalism and democracy has been causal. What our review suggests is that conditions need to be met if capitalism and democracy are not to come into conflict and those conditions all involve limitations on democracy and limitations on the ends to be pressed on the state by democracy. It is not so much capitalism and democracy that go together but capitalism and *liberal* democracy – the democracy, that is of *limited* participation by a *limited* section of the population which sees the principal role of the state itself as *limited* to the traditional sphere of law and order that does not involve it intervening in the operation of the free market. The trouble is that democracy is not easily contained within the liberal political straitjacket, and it seeks by its own inner impulses to be more and become a social and economic democracy as well. It finds the road barred by the capitalist foundations upon which the political democracy is built and thus inevitably represents a constant threat, now hidden, now manifest, to these very foundations. It is for this reason that we agree with Laski that 'a political democracy which rests upon capitalist foundations has war, open or secret, in its midst'.

One last point needs to be made about all this. To assert, as we have, that capitalism and democracy are locked into a relationship of perpetual tension does not imply that socialism fits democracy any better. With the short and notable exception of Allende's Chile, no country in the world has yet been able to reconcile a socialist system of collective and centralized economic planning with the protection and development of individual civil rights and political freedoms. Socialists themselves tend to argue that, while genuine economic and political democracy is impossible in capitalism, it is possible in socialism since the power of private property has been removed. We doubt this, for it is difficult to see how the detailed planning of a modern complex economy and the power of the planners can be reconciled with an extension of individual liberties and local self-determination.

In pointing to the contradictions between capitalism and democracy, therefore, we should be wary of drawing the all-too-easy conclusion that socialism and democracy go together any better. When we move from the cosy world of studying British politics to the chilly and uncertain world of acting within them, it may well be that, as conservatives or as socialists, we will be called upon to make some very uncomfortable choices between values that we cherish.

SECTION 5

Identities and Interaction

Introduction

A complex society like the UK can be viewed from many perspectives, just as a landscape can be photographed from many different angles. Previous sections of this reader have concentrated on the broad processes and structures which account for the anatomy and distinctive character of the UK. They have emphasized the grand picture and the general scheme, moving from social structures and divisions, to economics, to politics.

It is time we added another dimension to this analysis. This part of the Reader focuses in on the individual women and men who constitute the raw material of a society. Viewed from a distance, often all that is evident are the patterns and shapes formed by collections of people, but what of the particular elements which make up those patterns?

The short readings which follow are all concerned with questions of identity and the development of social relationships, with issues about human nature and the organization of social interaction. There are eight pieces in all, including extracts from the writings of psychologists and other social scientists and autobiographical accounts in which women and men give their own versions of their lives.

Apart from the common emphasis on socio-psychological issues, very little else is shared. The eight selections deliberately present a montage of very different positions on identity and interaction. You will find a biological and materialist view of self-consciousness, for instance, which can be contrasted with readings which stress social position and cultural group as the key to identity and action. Some of the articles argue that identity is determined by factors, such as genes, social roles and institutions, beyond the control of any individual. Other accounts, particularly the autobiographical pieces, give more room to human agency and our capacity to create ourselves and our lives. You won't find that the major debates surrounding identity and human action are resolved here but you will find some indication of the nature of those controversies.

The readings not only differ in their basic assumptions about identity and interaction, they also provide food for thought about method in social science. Procedures which are based on the natural sciences can be contrasted with more interpretative and reflective approaches. The presence of autobiographical accounts also allows some comparison between this mode of knowledge and social science analysis.

The section opens with a reading from an American psychologist, D.J. Levinson, (Chapter 15.1), which indicates the perspective on identity which

141

emerges if we assume human life, from infancy to old age, goes through a number of distinct transitions or developmental stages. Levinson also assumes that the unconscious is an active element in the crises and dramas of identity. His work was clearly influenced by Freud and the psychoanalytic tradition but that influence is tempered by an emphasis on the *psychosocial*. This extract is taken from a book based on detailed interview studies with forty men. In the reading, Levinson discusses confusions in identity experienced by middle-aged men as they move from being young to old. Levinson is fascinated by the inner experience of the individual and with the resolution of tensions caused by biological change and ageing, but he also looks at how the images and opportunities offered by society structure the possibilities for identity and the nature of transitions.

Although this piece is written from a psychosocial perspective, it tends to present a universalistic image of identity. This tendency is characteristic of developmental stage theories. There are few references here to differences and specific social circumstances. It is assumed that all members of a society tend to go through the same type of experiences in the same kind of sequence. For this reason, this approach to identity is often read as individualistic in emphasis. Primacy, ultimately, seems to be given to pyschodynamic processes unfolding within the individual which provide the motor for different experiences of identity.

The second reading in Chapter 15 is by Richard Stevens and discusses the contribution sociobiology can make to understanding identity. Sociobiologists argue that some behaviours shown by animal species can be explained through the action of genes on hormones and motivation systems and, furthermore, that the analysis can be extended to some human actions. The actions of a worker bee collecting honey or a gull feeding its chicks seem far removed from, say, the choice of sexual partners in human societies, or male criminal behaviour, or a helpful response to a stranger, yet socio-biologists suggest that the same biological principles can be used to help to make sense of all these diverse responses.

Sociobiology is controversial because it suggests that social relationships emerge from deep-rooted natural bases and for this reason humans are not as flexible as we thought. It may also seem to justify inequalities between women and men on the basis of biology. For this reason, it is important to be clear and exact about the claims of sociobiology. Stevens not only describes the sociobiological contribution but notes how most sociobiologists place limits on their claims. He also evaluates the usefulness of this approach to the study of identity.

Again, we can see that a relatively universalistic approach is being taken to identity and interaction. The emphasis is on continuities and the persistence of biologically based evolutionary strategies. This is also a more deterministic account. Levinson describes how the middle-aged man can actively and self-consciously construct and rework life transitions whereas the patterns described by sociobiologists suggest the possible pre-determined nature of some identity choices.

The readings in Chapter 16 are very different kinds of accounts. They present autobiographical narratives which give a personal rather than a detached or abstract view of identity. They also take up a theme neglected so far – that people's circumstances and their social positions in the UK vary widely, with decisive effects on sense of self and social relationships. We hear from a working-class woman living in Yorkshire, a middle-class West Indian man who emigrated to Britain as a child, and from a young, disabled woman.

Qualitative material such as interviews or the personal accounts presented in these readings are often used as the starting point for social science theorizing. The readings raise acutely the issue of different types of knowing and the tension in the study of identity between qualitative accounts of particular experiences, which may none the less be representative of a social group, and studies which derive their conclusions from large numbers of individuals, using quantitative measures such as surveys and questionnaires. The choice seems to be between the intensive and the extensive, between richness and generalizability. The debate among social scientists concerns the appropriateness of these different methodological styles in the light of other criteria for conducting a science.

The two readings in Chapter 17 propose a social and cultural analysis of identity. Zimbardo (Chapter 17.2) describes an experiment, another example of quantitative methods, which tries to investigate two possible influences on human action: social factors (the roles people are assigned to play in an institution) and individual differences in personality. Which is more crucial in explaining behaviour – the social situation someone is in or the kind of individual he or she happens to be? Zimbardo concludes that the social situation is primary but obviously Levinson would want to question him further about the role of psychodynamics in the situation he studies. The students in Zimbardo's study are presented with a situation which threatens their image of themselves and psychoanalysts would be interested in how particular individuals might deal with this threat to their identity.

Eisenbruch's article (Chapter 17.1) indicates the contribution culture can make to identity. He presents the case history of a Vietnamese woman now living in the UK diagnosed as suffering from depression. The categories and symptoms of mental illness will obviously be vital to issues of identity and self-perception but Eisenbruch argues that a person's experience of these things is strongly related to the system of reference provided by culture. He contrasts the western psychiatric diagnosis of depression with the diagnosis of 'wind illness' provided by Mrs Xuyen and her family. Headaches, insomnia and incapacitation may be universal but the way they are interpreted and represented, and measures for recovery, are culturally specific.

Chapter 18, the final chapter in this section, turns to questions of the application of socio-psychological research and in particular the kind of therapy clinical psychologists could offer people with disturbed social relationships. This chapter from Judy Gahagan describes one method in detail: social skills training. Social skills therapy assumes that problems in daily life, and problems in getting along with others, may not have deep psychological roots or rather, even if they do, improvement can come about through work on basic interactional techniques. The person can learn a new vocabulary or a new repertoire of behaviour. The key assumptions here are behaviour modification and self-management. Gahagan assumes that what we do, how we behave and how we are perceived by others, are crucial determinants of who we are. If a person, therefore, can be trained to modify their behaviour and thus manage themselves better their identity will change and relationships will change as a consequence. In this sense Gahagan shares the same perspective as Zimbardo and Eisenbruch, and the same emphasis on the social situation and social interaction.

So, there are several competing perspectives in this collection and a very diverse set of topics – sexuality, mid-life crisis, prisons, altruism, mental illness, inadequate social relationships, the experience of racism, redundancy and attitudes to the disabled. I hope you find the mixture stimulating and, in particular, a useful tool for clarifying the different ways some of the most basic building blocks of society – identity and social interaction – have been understood and studied.

Margaret Wetherell

CHAPTER 15

Developmental and Evolutionary Approaches to Identity

Daniel J. Levinson and Richard Stevens

15.1 The mid-life transition*

Daniel J. Levinson

In the Mid-life Transition the Young/Old polarity is experienced with special force. As early adulthood comes to an end, a man is assailed by new fears of the 'loss of youth.' He feels that the Young – variously represented as the child, the adolescent and the youthful adult in himself – is dying. The imagery of old age and death hangs over him like a pall.[. . .]

One important change [. . .] is the decline in bodily and psychological powers. In his late thirties and early forties a man falls well below his earlier peak levels of functioning. He cannot run as fast, lift as much, do with as little sleep as before. His vision and hearing are less acute, he remembers less well and finds it harder to learn masses of specific information. He is more prone to aches and pains and may undergo a serious illness that threatens him with permanent impairment or even death. These changes vary widely in their severity and their effects on a man's life. Reduced strength and agility may be less distressing to an accountant than to a professional athlete (or a fierce competitor at tennis who cannot bear to lose his standing on the local ladder).[. . .]

Reminders of mortality are also given by the more frequent illness, death and loss of others. A man may suffer distressing losses at any age. The meaning they have for him will depend partly on the developmental period he is in at the time. In his late thirties and early forties, the probability of such losses goes up considerably. His parents, now ordinarily in their sixties or seventies, are more likely to die or to be faced with problems of retirement, illness and dependency. A lot more people, it seems, are dying or getting seriously ill. There are more accidents and heart attacks, more divorces, depressions, alcoholism, job failures, troubles with children or parents, suffering of all kinds.

A man's sensitivity to the increase in others' misfortune and suffering is accentuated by his own entry into the Mid-life Transition. He notices these problems more in others, and resonates to them with greater feeling, partly because he is starting to come to terms with his own mortality.

The sense of ageing and mortality is accentuated by the change in generational

---

*Source: D.J. Levinson, *The Seasons of a Man's Life*, 1979, New York, Knopf, pp. 197–8 and pp. 214–18.

status at around 40.[. . .] A man is part of the 'initiation' generation from about 30 to 45. He is establishing his niche in society and pursuing his youthful aspirations. During the Mid-life Transition, from about 40 to 45, he starts taking his place in the 'dominant' generation. By the middle forties, he is clearly in a generation senior to that of the thirties. The question is not whether he will enter a new generation but on what terms – with what degree of satisfaction, respect, competence, status.

Finally, the culmination of the Settling Down enterprise intensifies his sense of mortality. At around 40 a man reaches a turning point. He must now form an enterprise qualitatively different from those of early adulthood. No matter how well or poorly he has done with the ambitions of his thirties, he is likely to experience a letdown in the Mid-life Transition. Even if he has accomplished a great deal and is on the path to greater attainment, his basic orientation toward success and failure normally begins to change. It is no longer crucial to climb another rung on the ladder – to write another book, get another promotion, earn more of the rewards that meant so much in the past.

Giving up the intense concern with success is especially difficult if a man has not attained his earlier goals. He has to deal first with his bitterness toward others, his contempt toward himself, and his illusion that life would now be marvellous if only he had been able to seize the gold ring. A man may be more free to question the real value of success, once he has tasted it. But the man who manages to reach his youthful goals often gets caught up in the excitement of success. He may need a few years to discover how little meaning it has for him.

Every man in the Mid-life Transition starts to see that the hero of the fairy tale does not enter a life of eternal, simple happiness. He sees, indeed, that the hero is a youth who must die or be transformed as early adulthood comes to an end. A man must begin to grieve and accept the symbolic death of the youthful hero within himself. He will gradually discover which of the heroic qualities he can keep, which new qualities he can discover and develop in himself, and how he might be a hero of a different kind in the context of middle adulthood. Humanity has yet little wisdom for constructing the 'portrait of the hero as a middle-aged man.' That archetype is still poorly evolved.

For many reasons, then, at 40 a man knows more deeply than ever before that he is going to die. He feels it in his bones, in his dreams, in the marrow of his being. His death is not simply an abstract, hypothetical event. An unpredictable accident or illness could take his life tomorrow. Even another thirty years does not seem so long: more years now lie behind than ahead.

Why should the recognition of our mortality be so painful? Why can we not come to know it and accept it, once and for all, in childhood or adolescence? Why does it come up in every developmental transition, to be partially resolved and partially denied, only to confront us again in the next?

A primary reason, I believe, is the wish for immortality. This is one of the strongest and least malleable of human motives. It operates with great force during early adulthood as an aspect of the Young archetype. A young man has the desire to live forever, to play a part in some eternal drama, to be assured permanent tenure in heaven or in history. Like other elemental drives, this one is the source of many illusions and self-deceptions. But it is also a fundament for our love of life, our sense of self, our urge to create products of lasting value, our wish to be involved in the world and experience richly what it offers us. It is reflected in the trauma that accompanies every advance toward acknowledging our short-lived existence in this world. We never entirely give it up, though our awareness and understanding of it normally change as we become more individuated adults.

At mid-life, the growing recognition of mortality collides with the powerful wish for immortality and the many illusions that help to maintain it. A man's fear that he is not immortal is expressed in his preoccupation with bodily decline and his fantasies of imminent death. At the most elemental level, he feels that he is fighting for survival. He is terrified at the thought of being dead, of no longer existing as this particular person. In the words of the old song, 'Everybody wants to go to heaven, but nobody wants to die.'

Beyond the concern with personal survival, there is a concern with meaning. It is bad enough to feel that my life will soon be over. It is even worse to feel that my life has not had – and never will have – sufficient value for myself and the world. The wish for immortality plays a powerful part in a man's reappraisal of his life at 40. He often feels that his life until now has been wasted. Even if, in cooler moments, he finds some redeeming qualities, he is still likely to feel that his life has not enough accrued value. He has not fulfilled himself sufficiently and has not contributed enough to the world. What he has been and what he has produced are of little consequence. In the remaining years he wants to do more, to be more, to give his life a meaning that will live after his death.

A man at 40 may have been so beaten down by an oppressive environment, or so consumed in the struggle for survival, that he cannot make the developmental effort to give his life a new meaning. The inner flame is extinguished and no further potential can be brought into being. He exists without hope or sense of value. Such men often die in their forties or fifties. The immediate cause of death may be illness, accident or alcoholism. The basic cause is that neither he nor society can make a space for him to live, and he just withers away. There are too few available resources, external or internal, to sustain his life. Alternatively, he may live a long and trivial existence if he finds a protective environment and accepts a limited life.

A dramatic example of decline in middle adulthood is Howard Hughes. During this era he converted a small fortune into a fantastic empire. At the end, with all his power, he died of starvation, disease and emotional isolation. He could invest his money with great profit, but he could not invest his self in any enterprise or obtain psychic income from it. He finally suffocated within the cocoon he had built around himself.

Mid-life defeat has been portrayed in countless novels and plays. It is a recurrent theme in the work of Chekhov, Ibsen and Strindberg (especially the plays they wrote after age 40). In *The Iceman Cometh*, Eugene O'Neill depicts the small world of Harry Hope's saloon and boardinghouse. Most of its members are middle-aged men who maintain their youthful illusions but have lost all real hope. The central character, Hickey, a salesman of about 40, visits annually to nourish their dreams and to indulge himself in the role of saviour and Santa Claus. At the end, Hickey gives up the illusory rescue of others and acknowledges his own illusions, his struggle with the archetypal figure of Death (symbolized as the Iceman), and his feelings in the aftermath of killing his wife. O'Neill wrote this play in the aftermath of his own debilitating mid-life crisis.

Lillian Hellman's play *The Autumn Garden* deals with similar themes in a more genteel, Southern world. In a later comment on this play, Hellman said: 'I suppose the point I had in mind is this – you come to a place in your life when what you've been is going to form what you will be. If you've wasted what you have in you, it's too late to do much about it. If you've invested yourself in life, you're pretty certain to get a return. If you are inwardly a serious person, in the middle years it will pay off.' During the Mid-life Transition, it is hard to know how much one has wasted oneself or invested in life, and what kind of further return one will have during the middle years. This was clearly a question for Hellman herself when she wrote the play, in her middle forties.

If his development has not already been too impaired, a man in the Mid-life Transition begins to accept his mortality and to give up his most grandiose illusions of immortality. This does not mean, however, that the wish for immortality disappears. On the contrary, with normal development this wish becomes more conscious, more subject to reflective thought, more modest and realistic in its aims. Making an effort to increase the actual value of his life, he strengthens his claim on the immortality for which he still deeply yearns. Whatever his religious views or his secular philosophy of life, he believes that this claim depends largely on his own self-fulfillment and social contribution. He wants to leave a trace, however small, on the course of humankind.

A man in the Mid-life Transition is troubled by his seemingly imminent death. He is beset even more by the anxiety that he will not be able to make his future better than his past. As he seeks to modify and enrich his life, he has self-doubts ranging in intensity from mild pessimism to utter panic: 'Can I make my life more worthwhile in the remaining years? Am I now too old to make a fresh start? Have I become obsolete? What shall I try to do and be for myself, for my loved ones, for my tribe, for humanity?' The worst feeling of all is to contemplate long years of meaningless existence without youthful passions, creative effort or social contribution. The self-doubts are intensified by the Old, which evokes powerful feelings of disintegration, despair and death. It is his voice within that says, 'There is no more time—the end is here.'

During and after the Mid-life Transition a man tries to transform the Young/Old of youth and create a middle-aged self, wiser and more mature than before yet still connected to the youthful sources of energy, imagination and daring. He comes to grasp more clearly the flow of generations and the continuity of the human species. His personal immortality, whatever its form, lies within that larger human continuity. He feels more responsibility for the generations that will follow his own. Acquiring a greater individuality, a firmer sense of who he is and what matters most to him, he also understands more deeply that he is a drop in the vast river of human history. Slowly the omnipotent Young hero recedes, and in his place emerges a middle-aged man with more knowledge of his limitations as well as greater real power and authority.

In a poem written when he was about 50, the American poet Theodore Roethke portrays his experience of mortality. This poem, entitled 'The Dying Man,' is dedicated to Yeats. It reflects Roethke's struggles, in the flower of middle adulthood, to accept the actuality of death while his own vitality and desire for immortality are at their height:

. . . he dares to live
Who stops being a bird, yet beats his wings
Against the immense immeasurable emptiness of things.

Although a major effort toward the recognition of mortality begins in the Mid-life Transition, a more profound spiritual acceptance of it is not likely to occur until late adulthood. Yeats's poem 'Vacillation' published when he was 67, depicts this process. The title suggests that, despite the fierce pride with which Yeats wishes to approach death, his spirit is still clouded with uncertainty.

No longer in Lethean foliage caught
Begin the preparation for your death
And from the fortieth winter by that thought
Test every work of intellect or faith,
And everything that your own hands have wrought,
And call those works extravagance of breath
That are not suited for such men as come
Proud, open-eyed and laughing to the tomb.

It may have taken Yeats some years longer to imagine entering the tomb neither 'open-eyed and laughing' nor in sadness and fear, but with quiet acceptance of the unknowable losses and gains to come.

15.2 Evolutionary origins of identity*

Richard Stevens

Sociobiological theory is radically different from other approaches in social science. It presents a view of social behaviour premised on the idea that it is biologically based and has evolved over time as a result of its value for survival and reproduction. We are all descendants of successful survivors and reproducers, and behaviour as well as physical characteristics, sociobiologists reason, had a lot to do with this success. By studying and speculating about the likely origins of human social behaviour, we can gain insights into the ways in which we behave today.

As the article's evaluation makes clear, there is much to question about both the conclusions which sociobiologists draw and the nature of the reasoning from which these emerge. Nevertheless, the theory is based on logical extrapolation from well-established principles of evolution and merits serious consideration. As is further noted, an approach of this kind can, at most, offer partial understanding, because we also need to take account of other factors which play a major role in human social behaviour, such as the meanings which stem from the cultural contexts in which we live and the enormous influence of learning and socialization.

Bearing in mind these limitations, this brief account of a sociobiological approach to the origins of identity provides a useful and contrasting supplement to other approaches.

A useful principle is that, if you want to understand something, it is worth looking at its origins, its history. One approach to understanding human behaviour is to look at it as a species pattern. Can we gain any insights into identity by considering how human behaviour might have evolved?

The theory which argues that we can is called *sociobiology*. This is an approach concerned with understanding the social behaviour of animals. Humans are regarded as another animal species and as being, like them, the product of evolutionary development. Sociobiologists are interested in understanding why social behaviours evolved in the way that they did – what functions did they serve in ensuring the survival of the species and passing on genes to future generations?

Sociobiology presents a position radically opposed to other approaches in social science in that it regards the social as inherently biological. Although, as we shall see, there is much to question in the ideas it puts forward, it does provide a provocatively different way of looking at human social behaviour. It relates to identity in that it purports, among other claims, to throw light on the nature and origins of consciousness and why we relate to others in the ways that we do.

Principles of evolution

To understand sociobiological theory, you need to grasp the core ideas of the theory of evolution.

*Source: article commissioned for this Reader.

1 *Genetic transmission.* This refers to the fact that physical characteristics, such as eye colour and height for example, can be passed on from one generation to another by means of genes. It also requires the more problematic assumption that predispositions to behave in particular ways may also be inherited in this way.

2 *Diversity.* While genetic transmission provides *continuity* through the generations, *diversity* is introduced in two ways. As each offspring inherits genes from two parents, every conception produces a new and unique mixture. Every person, apart from identical twins, is genetically unique. A more fundamental source of variation (in that it will be passed on to following generations) is a mutation – a spontaneous change which arises by chance in the patterning of the DNA – the chemical basis of the gene.

3 *Natural selection.* Charles Darwin's breakthrough was to realize that some forms of diversity are more adaptive than others. By adaptive is meant that the characteristics and behaviour in question help the animal to survive and to reproduce and therefore pass on genes to offspring. The idea of natural selection refers to the fact that some individuals are more likely to survive than others. Sexual selection refers to the fact that some individuals are more likely than others to mate and have offspring. Those characteristics which facilitate both physical survival and having offspring are going to be selected because they will be passed on more frequently to the next generation.

4 *Time.* We should, perhaps, also include this fourth ingredient. Evolution is a slow process. For substantive changes to occur, a great many generations are required, and human beings are the outcome of an enormously long period of evolutionary development. Imagine that the time elapsing between the beginning of life on this planet and the present time were represented as twenty-four hours. At what time do you think your ancestors, the first humans, would have made their appearance? (Read on for the answer.)

The logic of sociobiology

It is well established that anatomy and physiology (for example, bone structure and sense organs) evolved over time as a result of their usefulness in adapting to different environmental circumstances. We can trace similarities in skeletal structure and many other features from species to species as each evolved through evolutionary time (see Figure 15.1). Such patterns can be traced in the fossil record and by comparing the characteristics of existing species which we know originated at different stages in the past.

Unlike physical characteristics, behaviour leaves behind in the fossil record no direct and few indirect traces, but, clearly, it must also have been an important factor in evolutionary success. There is some reason to think that predispositions for some behaviours at least can, like physical characteristics, be inherited. Certainly this is the case in other species and there is some evidence of a genetic component in some behavioural characteristics such as extraversion and emotionality in humans too (see, for example, Eaves *et al.* 1989). If this is the case, then reasoning about the origins of behaviour in terms of evolutionary principles may yield some useful insights into why we behave and feel as we do.

That, at any rate, is the view of sociobiologists. Most of their attention has been directed at the social behaviour of other species where such assumptions, and tracing the adaptive value of changing behaviours, are less problematic. Some sociobiologists, though, have turned their attention to look at human social behaviour in this way. Wilson (1978), for example, claims, '. . . the biological principles which now appear to be working reasonably well for animals in general can be extended profitably to the social sciences'. Their general approach is to use the principles of evolutionary theory to explain and, in a few cases, predict the social behaviour of our species. They do this partly by comparing human social behaviour with that of other species to see if there are similarities. More importantly, they try to work out why a particular pattern of behaviour might have evolved by considering how it might have been useful in helping members of that species to survive and reproduce.

It is very important to bear in mind in the discussion which follows that we are *not* talking about the adaptation of present-day people, but of what possible factors in our distant past may have favoured some inheritable, behavioural predispositions over others. Bear in mind also that it is *not* implied that people

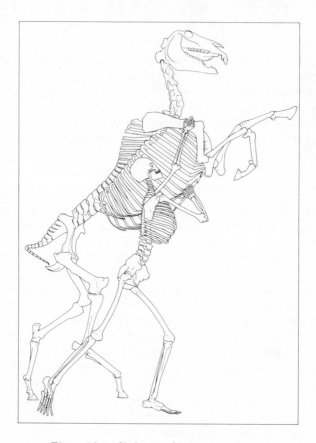

Figure 15.1 Skeletons of horse and human

152

have developed in this way because they realized a particular way of behaving would lead to reproductive success: only that the ones who happened to behave in this way were the ones who passed on more of their genes. For example, a famous study of pepper moths found a much higher density of dark-coloured ones in industrial compared with rural areas. These have survived more effectively because of the greater camouflage their dark colouring has provided against soot-coated trees. The moths did not, of course, purposely change their colouring. Rather, those which happened to be darker were more likely to survive predators and produce offspring until eventually they dominated the population.

Remember also that, in thinking about evolutionary development, enormous periods of time are involved. The answer to the question posed earlier is a few seconds to midnight. The age of the earth has been estimated as around 5,000 million years. The first forms of life probably emerged about 4,000 million years ago. Then, after a *very* slow beginning (shellfish did not evolve until about 600 million years ago), the pace of evolution rapidly accelerated. But not until about three million years ago did the first humans emerge. On the analogy of our twenty-four hour clock, humans make their appearance only a few seconds before midnight! But, bearing in mind that the time of Christ was 2,000 years ago and that no recorded history dates back more than 5,000 years, you can see that even our 'few seconds' – three million years – is a long time.

Finally, it is important to remember that a feature of sexual reproduction is that it produces individual diversity. There is considerable variation among individuals on all the characteristics discussed below.

Consciousness and a sense of self

Personal identity depends on consciousness and self-awareness, together with a sense of agency and continuity. Such characteristics are greatly facilitated by the capacity for language.

Language is a uniquely human capacity. In those cases where our nearest relatives, the chimpanzees, have been taught sign language, their achievement has been rudimentary, and there is no evidence of the spontaneous use of language among apes in the wild. (Dolphins have a complex communication system but whether this has the characteristics of a language has not yet been established.) How language emerged in humans is not known. What is clear is that it depends, not only on learning, but also on particular capacities and characteristics of the brain. You cannot teach language to your cat, however hard you try. There is evidence from the fossil remains of skulls of a rapid increase in brain size preceding the emergence of *Homo sapiens* (see Figure 15.2) which would have been consistent with the accelerated development of a cognitive capacity such as language. It has been hypothesized that language probably evolved because of its value for communication in group hunting.

Humphrey (1986) has put forward the idea that consciousness itself evolved in humans because of its adaptive value. In many social species, like ants or bees for example, specific instinctual patterns control social interactions. The social behaviour of humans is of a different order; much greater flexibility and freedom

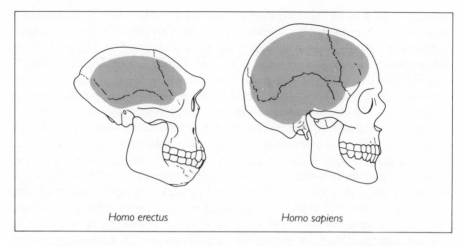

Figure 15.2   Comparative cranial capacity (equivalent to brain size) of early (Homo erectus) and modern (Homo sapiens) humans

from fixed patterns is made possible by language and the far greater capacity for learning and intelligence. Human relationships then become far more varied and unpredictable. In this case, if we assume that, in the distant past of humankind, living in social groups was vital to survival, then any characteristics which enhanced skill in social interaction would have been selected for (i.e. passed on to future generations because they facilitated survival and/or reproduction). Humphrey regards consciousness as a kind of 'inner eye' which gives each of us immediate access to our own mental and emotional states. For such awareness also helps us to infer what other people may be feeling and thinking. Thus, we will be in a better position to predict what they are likely to do.

> In evolutionary terms it must have been a major breakthrough. Imagine the biological benefits to the first of our ancestors that developed the ability to make realistic guesses about the inner life of his rivals: to be able to picture what another was thinking about, and planning to do next, to be able to read the minds of others by reading his own. The way was open to a new deal in human social relationships: sympathy, compassion, trust, treachery and double-crossing – the very things which make us human.

(Humphrey, 1986, p. 76)

It has also been argued (e.g. Crook, 1980) that a sense of identity as well as the capacity for consciousness must also have been of great value in social relationships. It helps us, for example, to distinguish between other people and ourselves and to imagine ourselves in their situations. Because they can influence our awareness of the kind of person we are, other people's opinions can affect our self-esteem and so form a powerful medium of social control.

The origins of a sense of identity have also been linked to altruism – the motivation to help other people. It is not hard to see how a tendency to help those people (such as children, brothers and sisters) who are genetically related to you would have been selected for. Genetic relatives share, in differing degrees, a proportion of our genes. So their survival and reproductive success is a way of passing on at least some of our own genes. As Barash (1979) has expressed it, 'How do I love thee? Let me count thy genes!'.

It is more difficult for sociobiology to explain altruistic behaviour towards people who are not related to each other. Altruism in this case would not confer any evolutionary advantage. Nevertheless, such behaviour is a common feature in human societies. It has been argued (Trivers, 1971) that, even in this case, altruism would have been selected for because, in a relatively stable social group, doing someone a favour may well have predisposed him or her to do a future favour in return. Thus, helping others, in the long run, is likely to facilitate your own reproductive success and hence the prevalence of such a gene will be increased. This is called 'reciprocal altruism'. Such a situation must have depended, however, on a clear sense of identity among the participants so that favours given could be returned in the future to the individual who helped in the first place. The development of identity would thus have been tied in with the evolution of reciprocal altruism.

These arguments are inevitably speculative but they are useful in encouraging us to think about possible reasons for the evolution of consciousness and personal identity.

Gender identity

Looked at from a sociobiological perspective, it may seem self-evident why sexuality is so prevalent in all human societies. Any group or society which failed to reproduce would soon cease to exist. But it is worth noting that sexuality is not the only method of reproduction. This could be achieved, as some species do, by mitosis (dividing into two) or even by cloning (replication of itself by an individual organism). The great advantage of *sexual* reproduction is the diversity in the offspring which results from the mixing of the genes of the two parents. The benefit which such individual diversity confers is the greater adaptability and flexibility it offers to deal with varied and/or changing environmental conditions.

The sociobiological view regards gender identity and behavioural differences between the sexes as originating in the evolutionary development of humankind. From a sociobiological perspective, there is only one fundamental difference between men and women: the number of children a woman can have is limited, say, to twenty; a man, on the other hand, can have as many offspring as he can find fertile partners to inseminate. This, so the argument runs, means that the optimal reproductive strategies (i.e. those behaviours most likely to pass on genes to future generations) would have been different for males and females. This would have had consequences in terms of characteristics, interaction style and which features of the opposite sex each sex is most responsive to.

For a woman, the optimal strategy in terms of passing on genes would have been to try to ensure that the relatively few offspring she had, grew to sexual maturity. The best way of doing this would probably have been through skill in banding together and co-operating with others in the group. As she was investing a great deal in her few offspring, she is likely to have been highly selective in choice of mate, responsive not only to health and strength but also to status and the possession of resources likely to help provide protection for her children.

The optimal strategy for a man (in terms of passing on his genes), on the other hand, may well have been to impregnate as many females as he could. If only a proportion survived to reproductive maturity, the strategy will still be likely to produce more descendants than if he stayed around to bring up a few.

A number of consequences follow from this model. There is an asymmetry between men and women. A woman does not need many sexual partners to produce all the offspring she is capable of. For a man, on the other hand, the more partners he has, the more offspring he is likely to produce. Women would therefore have been a scarce resource for whom men would have been in competition. Because of this, any woman would have had as much chance as any other of producing offspring. For males, however, there is likely to have been much greater variability, a few succeeding in mating with several females and therefore producing many offspring, other males not managing to mate at all and therefore producing none. As it is the bigger, stronger and more aggressive males who are likely to have succeeded in the competition for mates, this would favour the evolution of these characteristics in males (an example of sexual selection). The stronger, bigger males were more likely to mate and so pass on their genes.

Another characteristic which may be differentially selected for in the two sexes is risk-taking. This is a form of behaviour which, while it can produce high rewards, also increases the likelihood of loss, even death. Women would have been essential because nearly all can produce offspring. If females engage in behaviour which increased the probability of their death, the survival of a group could be placed in jeopardy. Men, however, are more redundant in this respect. Only a few males are really needed to produce the maximum number of descendants possible in the group. One might well expect, therefore, that while risk-taking would tend to be selected out (i.e. not passed on) in women, this would not be the case with men. In their case, the benefits for the group of their taking risks would not be outweighed by potential loss of reproductive capacity.

It is very important to bear in mind throughout all this discussion of male – female differences that sociobiologists are *not* talking about all men and all women but about average differences. Because of individual genetic diversity, the distribution of such differences as there may be take the form of two overlapping normal distribution curves (see Figure 15.3). There may be average differences in height (or aggression), for example, but any particular man may be shorter (or less aggressive) than most women.

This, then, is what the model would predict. How consistent is it with what we can observe? Let us consider each prediction.

Men physically more powerful. There are clearly differences in the physical characteristics of the two sexes ('sexual dimorphism'). Men are generally taller and, on average, some 20 to 30 per cent heavier. In sports, male champions outperform women champions in speed and strength (though not in endurance).

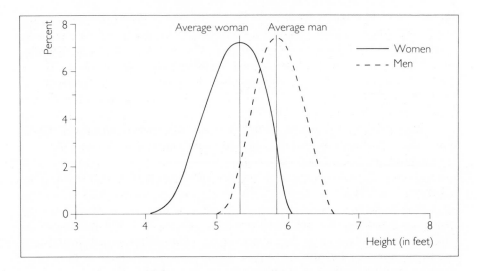

Figure 15.3 Distribution of height differences between men and women showing two overlapping normal distribution curves.

Men more aggressive and risk-taking. In almost all societies, it is men who go to war. Men are much more likely than women to be convicted of criminal offences (and hence presumably to commit crime), particularly crimes of violence. In 1986 in England and Wales, for example, there were more than six men for every woman convicted (and fifteen men for every woman sent to prison) (HMSO, 1988). In the case of violent crime, the difference is even greater; (one estimate is that 93 per cent of all crimes of violence are committed by men). While only some crime involves aggressiveness, all involves taking a risk. Studies of children also indicate that, from an early age, the play of boys is likely to be more aggressive than that of girls (Maccoby and Jacklin, 1974). Clearly many other factors such as socialization and environmental influences play an important role in determining such differences. Sociobiologists are not arguing that genetic predispositions account entirely for the differences observed, but that they play some role.

Asymmetry in sexual style. In all societies (even in those where women have adequate economic resources), where there is prostitution or sex is traded in return for other favours, it is almost always men who are the clients. Where there are male prostitutes, these are usually for the benefit of male homosexuals rather than women. In the UK and other contemporary societies, magazine sales clearly indicated that visual pornography focusing on the physical characteristics of anonymous persons of the opposite sex, is much more the predilection of men. Women, on the other hand, are far more frequently the consumers of Mills and Boon style fiction which portrays an identifiable romantic hero whose attributes are those of mind, status and resource as well as physique. In human societies, sexual relationships come in many forms but, according to Wilson (1978), 75 per cent sanction polygyny (the taking of more than one wife) whereas polyandry (the taking of more than one husband) is found in less than 1 per cent. These are all striking differences. Though particular cultural conventions may, for economic or social reasons, suppress or facilitate them, they are all expressions, sociobiologists will claim, of underlying differences in sexual style.

Women more socially skilled. Studies of child development clearly indicate more rapid development of social skills and responsiveness in girls (Maccoby and Jacklin, 1974). Although the evidence (e.g. Hite, 1989) is more tenuous, many women (over 80 per cent of Hite's admittedly selective sample) appear to perceive their male partners as having difficulty in expressing feelings and in communicating within the relationship.

The aspects of identity for which sociobiologists claim that there are average differences between the sexes, are that men are bigger, stronger and more aggressive, they are inclined to take more risks, they are more inclined to promiscuity and less effective in the subtleties of interpersonal communication. Such differences originate, sociobiologists claim, in the different optimal strategies in the past for men and women to pass on their genes. It should be noted that there are many other aspects of identity for which sociobiologists make no claim for gender differentiation. For most characteristics, the sociobiological model would predict that the variability among men and women would be entirely similar.

Many factors contribute to the complex social behaviours involved in relationships, sex and crime. But there do seem to be some striking differences between the sexes and these would seem to be in line with the sociobiological model. Whether this serves to *explain* them, however, is another matter, and a question we shall consider in the final section.

Summary and evaluation

This article has given a brief account of the kind of arguments which sociobiologists have put forward about the origins of some aspects of identity. Their position is that psychological and behavioural characteristics have been shaped by the process of evolution. Those behaviours which in the past have facilitated survival and reproduction are those which have been selected for. We have looked at:

(a) The way this approach may be applied to thinking about the origins of consciousness and a sense of individual identity. It was argued that these may have developed because of their value in understanding, relating to and co-operating with others.

(b) The proposals by sociobiologists that some differences in identity and behaviour between the sexes may originate in the different reproductive strategies which were optimal for our male and female ancestors.

One of the problems in assessing sociobiology is that often views have been ascribed to it which no serious sociobiologist would support. It has on occasion been used quite invalidly in this way to support positions which seek to justify discriminative practices, for example, and competition as being 'natural'. It is important, therefore, to be very clear about what, in fact, sociobiology does *not* do.

1 Its analysis is not *prescriptive*. It seeks to explain the origins of some social behaviours. In no way does this justify them as being appropriate, desirable or even adaptive today.

2 Sociobiology does not claim that all people (or all men and all women) are the same. In fact, as we have seen, individual genetic diversity is a cardinal principle on which the model is based.

3 Nor does sociobiology claim to explain *all* social behaviours. It makes no statements, for example, about racial differences, for such physical differences as exist in skin colour etc. are superficial and irrelevant to analysis in terms of the behaviours involved in reproductive success. Sociobiologists acknowledge that much, if not most, of our social behaviour requires explanation in sociocultural terms.

In terms of method, sociobiology is quite different from anything encountered elsewhere in both the natural and social sciences. It is based on general principles of evolution which have been well-established by a wealth of evidence. To that extent, we may regard it as scientific. However, it then proceeds to use these principles as the basis for analysing either what the origins of a particular behaviour might have been, or what kinds of behaviour might be expected, given the likely conditions under which humankind must have evolved. Either approach must involve speculation, even if this may be of a reasoned, considered kind. There are several ways in which such approaches are open to question.

The greatest weakness of sociobiology is that, although the model can predict, it is usually used to explain what is already there. You may be forgiven for thinking that, with enough imagination and ingenuity, it is possible to explain *any* social behaviour in this way. Such explanations are rarely open to conclusive test. This problem, however, is in no way confined to sociobiology. It is true of psychoanalysis, for example, and, because it involves understanding complex phenomena, this is also a characteristic of much if not most theorizing in social science. Sociobiology's reasoned speculation *is* grounded, at least, in generally accepted principles of genetics and evolution. Furthermore, the sociobiologist might retort – 'what theory could better explain the often paradoxical and otherwise unexpected patterns of human social behaviour which we have noted above?'

One critical issue in evolutionary sociobiology is whether or not there are inherited predispositions to behave in particular ways. We have little *direct* evidence that genes influence human social behaviour, certainly of the complex kind discussed above. Nevertheless, genes (including those which differentiate the sexes) clearly programme the development and functioning of nervous, sensory and hormonal systems. There is little doubt that these affect what we feel and how we behave. Numerous studies (e.g. Olweus, 1988) have demonstrated that hormones, for example, can influence us in this way. In other species there is unambiguous evidence that genes play a part in determining complex patterns of response and behaviour. Even if we allow for major differences between ourselves and other species, given the continuity of evolution, is it not arrogant, the sociobiologist might argue, to presume that we should be *totally* exempt?

But, of course, humans *are* very different from any other species. What makes them so different is their capacity for language. We exist in a web of meanings created by our culture: beliefs and values which, in a martyr, for example, are sufficiently powerful to contradict even the basic need to live. Language and culture change the whole nature of the evolutionary process. What becomes important are 'memes', as Dawkins (1976) has termed them – the meanings which are transmitted by socializaion and culture from one generation to the next. It has also been argued (Smith, 1983) that, as societies become more complex, so sociobiological analysis becomes increasingly irrelevant. The importance of culturally-based meanings for social life, has led others (e.g. Montague, 1980) to argue that, with respect to human behaviour, the principles of evolution hold no explanatory power whatsoever.

At the most, sociobiology can offer only a *partial* explanation of human social behaviour. The complexities of social and economic life cannot simply be reduced to biological principles; nor would many sociobiologists claim that they could. Sociobiologists see biological process rather as a substratum of a more complex whole – the skeleton of the body social, if you like. To understand how a body works requires knowledge of other processes like circulation, musculature and the nervous system, but the skeleton too is not to be ignored.

This more intermediate position sees human social life as a complex interplay between social process and biological predispositions, each affecting the other in complex interaction. Take weeping – we do not have to learn *how* to cry (Eibl-Eibesfeldt, 1970), and for children in all societies, there are a few situations which spontaneously elicit crying. But we do learn where and when it is appropriate to cry. The meanings attributed to weeping are shaped by social practice and convention rather than by biology. Such interactions are two-way. For example, not only may the male hormone testosterone influence behaviour but behaviour may influence the level of testosterone. It has been found that, if one male monkey is defeated by another, it will show a rapid drop in testosterone level (Rose, 1974). So, not only does testosterone influence aggressiveness, but also whether or not an animal wins influences the hormone. Rather than solely focusing on either cultural process *or* biological process as a basis for behaviour, it may be more productive, as Anastasi (1975) has proposed, to study more closely the interactions between them – no easy task, however!

References

Anastasi, A. (1975) The influence of hereditary factors on behaviour. In H. Brown and R. Stevens, (eds) *Social Behaviour and Experience: Multiple Perspectives*. London, Hodder and Stoughton.

Barash, D. (1979) *Sociobiology: the Whisperings Within*, London, Souvenir Press.

Crook, J.H. (1980) *The Evolution of Human Consciousness*, Oxford, Oxford University Press.

Dawkins, R. (1976) *The Selfish Gene*, Oxford, Oxford University Press.

Eaves, L.J., Eysenck, H.J. and Martin, N.G. (1989) *Genes, Culture and Personality: an Empirical Aproach*, London, Academic Press.

Eibl-Eibesfeldt, (1970) *Ethology: the Biology of Behaviour*, New York, Holt, Rinehart and Winston.

Hite, S. (1989) *Women and Love*, New York, St. Martin's Press.

HMSO (1988) Central Statistical Office: *Social Trends 18*, London, HMSO.

Humphrey, N. (1986) *The Inner Eye*, London, Faber and Faber.

Maccoby, E.E. and Jacklin, C.N. (1974) *The Psychology of Sex Differences*, Stanford, California, Stanford University Press.

Montague, A. (ed.) (1980) *Sociobiology Examined*, Oxford, Oxford University Press.

Olweus, P. (1988) Circulating testosterone levels and aggression in adolescent males: a causal analysis, *Psychosomatic Medicine*, vol. 50, No. 3, pp. 761–72.

Rose, R.M. (1974). Discussed in Archer J. and Lloyd B. 'Sex roles: biological and social interactions', *New Scientist*, 21 November.

Smith, P.K. (1983) 'Human sociobiology'. In J. Nicholson and B. Foss (eds) *Psychology Survey No. 4*, Leicester, British Psychological Society.

Trivers, R.L. (1971) 'The evolution of reciprocal altruism', *Quarterly Review of Biology*, vol. 46, pp. 35–57.

Wilson, E.O. (1978) *On Human Nature*, Cambridge, Massachusetts, Harvard University Press.

CHAPTER 16

Individual Lives: Personal Accounts

A. Coyle, C. Husband and J. Campling

16.1 Phyllis Collins*

I was a machinist at Roger Firth, making up linings. It was part time but it wasn't far off full-time. I used to work from 8.30 to 4.40. I think I used to bring about £35 to £40 home. It worked out to just over £1 an hour. I started there 12 years ago when we moved from Keighley. I didn't know anyone here and I got really depressed. My little lad wasn't more than two. I had worked in Keighley – they used to have an evening shift -- and I thought I'm going to ring this Roger Firth up to see if they've got an evening shift. Anyway I did and they said they were sorry but it took them all their time to fill the machines during the day never mind about an evening shift, but he said if ever I could get through the day to go and see him. Anyway my nerves got worse. I think it was being cooped up and not knowing anybody. I enquired about putting Roger in a nursery and I got him in one that took him at three. So I rang up again and I got the job. I lived on Maple Avenue then. It was walking distance to the bus station on the Leeds Road and I used to pass the nursery on the way, so it was quite handy. He loved it too. I think it did him good because he wasn't any trouble going to school. Then after work I'd just get off the bus, pick him up and walk home. I was there ever since.

We were all upset when it closed, it took a while to sink in. To be quite honest I kept thinking that they'd send for us again. I didn't register as unemployed. I didn't pay the full stamp. It's just something you don't usually do when you're working and you've got kids. They didn't seem to accept it from married women anyway, because you're always on and off when your kiddies are little, there's always something the matter. I wish I'd paid it now, but you don't realise at the time, that little bit coming in would have been better than nothing. I've tried for certain jobs as I've seen them in the paper. I didn't look at first. I thought I'd have a little time at home and my daughter was getting married. I've tried once or twice at the hospital where my friend Mary is working. I've tried for a machinist job although I didn't really want sewing. I've never been in the Job Centre. I suppose I'll have to try in there but my friends go in there and some have got jobs and some haven't. I look through the papers. There are one or two who keep their ears and eyes open for me. If a sewing job came up, I'd take it for the sake of having a job. I'd like to work over at the hospital, though, it's only over at the back of us. Now with bus fares, it's a bit ridiculous going too

*Source: A. Coyle, *Redundant Women*, 1984, London, The Women's Press, pp. 72–7.

far. It was costly enough when I was at Roger Firth. It depends on your wage, if you're not getting a lot it's not worth paying a lot out in bus fares. I'd like a job close to my own home. It's not just the cost. Time adds on to your working hours. If you don't finish work until 4.45 and you've half an hour bus ride, it's going to be six o'clock by the time you get home. I think it gets more desperate to look as time gets on. The first few months were like a holiday. I never thought to look. I think I feel it a bit more because we had a wedding in August and it took the money that we had. I feel now that I need a job more than ever to try and get back on our feet.

It's difficult on one wage, you've just not as much money to go round have you? We never go out. We didn't go out much before. We like country music, both of us and if there were groups on at a club or anything, that's when we went out. We did go out on Saturday to see Andy Williams at Scarborough and that was a real treat because we haven't been out for months. I felt guilty though because I felt we shouldn't be going. I think it's a bit harder living in general but I do miss not being able to afford to go out if you want. I have to make do now a lot more, and probably a lot more as we go on, if things don't get better. It makes you wonder how far it can all go. If it had happened a few years back, it would have been a lot harder, there were four of them to feed then, but now my eldest son lives away, and my two girls are married. I've still got Peter at home. He'd like to have gone in the Navy, but he can't get in so he's going on to further education. It would have been better if he'd got into the Navy. My husband works during the week at the further education college, but on Sundays he has this other job at the hospital. He's a chef, well actually, he's a baker by trade, but he's a chef as well. He gets paid into the bank every month, just over £300 a month and he gets £12 for Sundays. I used to use my wage packet first. I never kept any money for myself, it all went into the house. Now when I was working it was easy, but since I finished work we aren't getting that extra money coming in. Some of my redundancy went on my daughter's wedding, the rest has just gone on living. I used to try and put something away each month out of his wages, but I couldn't.

I'm doing this bit of soldering now. I wouldn't call it work. Last week it brought in about £12 I think. It has all come about by accident. It's my daughter's work actually, she was doing it and not getting it all through. She works full time and she was doing this at home in the evenings. They were waiting for her and she asked me if I wanted some to do. I said yes, I would help. It's nothing guaranteed. They might not want anymore after today. I didn't think it would last as long as this. I thought I would have to get a job after Christmas, but anyway he's kept ringing up. I'm doing plugs right now. Like all homework you have to do about 200 to earn £1.25. I don't do a right lot, because as I say it takes quite a long time to do not many if you know what I mean. The most I ever earn is about £15 a week. It just helps with the weekend groceries. It depends on how many I do, and how many they want. I'd say I do about four hours a day. Sometimes actually, in the evenings, if I'm on my own, I knock up a few for morning. You see when you're working at home you can do that, you can do it when you want. I don't class it as a job actually, not for the bit that I earn, so I just say, I'm just at home, I don't work. Actually I was speaking to my sister-in-law only this weekend, she'd rung up and she said, 'Are you still working?' and I automatically said, 'No'. But I don't tell folk about it, very few, because I don't class it as a job. If I was earning £20 or £30 I would, but some weeks it's only £10.

I wouldn't get a proper job doing this. They're all young girls and they don't pay a right lot. My daughter doesn't like it. It's a case that she sticks it because there is nothing much else to do. It would be no good me trying to get a job down there. I don't enjoy doing it, but to be honest I haven't tried for anything for ages and this [homework] might be one of the reasons. But I keep thinking things will pick up, so I'd wait a bit, which I still think they probably will in time. There seem to be a few more jobs around than there used to be. Sometimes I'll say I'll have to really start looking again. I must seem right lazy, but I've always worked, even when the kiddies were little, so I'm not lazy – I'll say it's my age. Mind you, in the winter, when all the snow comes and the rain, I'd sit and I used to look out and I'd think thank goodness I haven't got to go out. Now even in the summer when it comes right nice, I'm able to go and sit outside.

I've got more time now. I get up and get Roger off to school. He goes for about eight o'clock and then I sit and have my cup of tea and a bit of breakfast. If I do it as I should do, I get this [homework] out of the way early so I can finish after dinner time and then just tidy up. I might watch a film on TV or sit with my knitting. Nearer tea time, I have to start and do the tea. My son comes home at about 4.20 and my husband will be in about six o'clock. Usually I have tea ready for five o'clock and then keep his [husband's] warm until he's home. Otherwise Peter's starving. He's right lanky, like a bean pole and he's always starving. On Wednesday, my husband works late, it's his night for the evening class, so we don't wait for him and me and Roger have our tea early. I used to clean and that when I came in from work and at weekends. My husband used to do a bit but he never bothered really and it doesn't worry him now! I used to do my washing mainly Sunday mornings because he goes to work then. Now I do it all as I come to it. I do it when I'm ready.

Being out of work, I think it gets worse as you go on. I think you lose your confidence. I find that. When I see something in the paper I dread having to go. I'm alright when I get there, but I go through terrible things while I'm going. I really felt sick having to go for that last job, but once I sat down and was talking to him, I was alright. I just think it's confidence and I'm not one for changes anyway. I just like to plod on in my own way. The longer you're out of work the less confidence you've got for going and trying. I think we all need to work. I like to work. I'd prefer to go out to work than be at home, even if it's only part time. I'm not one for stopping at home. I don't like going out socially much, and I won't even go into town unless I'm forced to, but I like to go out to work. I've worked all the time I've been married. I've never been off as long as I've been off this time, even when the kiddies were little. I think what's why I looked forward to being off at first, but it wears off. But to be honest, I think I've stopped looking. It's just gradual, you get out of the habit, you don't bother. My husband used to tease me. He'd say, 'Go on, you don't really want to go back to work.'

We've managed alright. I don't worry about it, but I mean we *just* manage, there's nothing left.

I don't go out a lot. I don't even go out a right lot for shopping actually. Because part of my husband's job is buying in for where he works at college and with us living away from town, he'll say, 'Do you want anything from town?' and he just picks it up. I suppose it doesn't help any. Well you think it's helping, but as time goes on it doesn't really. I think I've really got to push myself and try to do something about it. I see a job in the paper and I think that'd be alright, but I don't do anything about it. Yet I like to go out to work. It's just because I've been here that long my confidence has gone. I've got funny that way. I don't go visiting really, I've no one to visit. My friends have nearly all got jobs, the ones that I bothered with anyway and none of my family are close by, so I can't go and visit my sister. We've no transport now, the car's off the road. I don't really know when I last went out. I think it was around Christmas time. Then again there's not a lot of money to go out spending.

I would like a job. I can feel myself getting into this routine, and I'll have to snap out of it. I know that it's just picking up courage to snap out of it. But you don't just get jobs now, you have to go crawling for them. I hated it at the beginning. I was bored to tears. Every day I used to get fed up, but you get used to that boredom gradually, it's a way of life. I don't know whether I could face a lot of people now. I worried over you coming. I used to feel lonely, but there again I'm used to it. The radio is never off and I talk to my animals. I always have done. I wouldn't say I feel lonely now, six months ago yes, I got that fed up. I don't think about it when I'm on my own but when my husband is in at night, he soon falls asleep if he's sat, and sometimes I say, 'I'm fed up, I'm on my own all day and then you're asleep at night.' When I'm on my own I don't notice it so much I only notice it when someone is there, and I can't talk to them, it's more annoying. It's better to be on your own doing your jobs and letting your mind wander.[. . .]

16.2 A professional black West Indian/British male*

The phone rings. I answer it in my usual confident manner before three European gentlemen are ushered into my office. They are brought in by my secretary. It is very strange that here am I, a black West Indian, speaking about my office and my secretary in this predominantly white society. By all accounts they are all symbols of status and reflect to some degree that I, a black man, have made it in white society. The discussion which followed is centred on a variety of things where, in today's jargon, the black expert is sought to give his advice. Invariably it is the media and they are seeking explanations as to the 'problems' which blacks are 'creating' in this society. The conversation highlights how little white society is aware of the presence of its black members. I remind my visitors that blacks

*Source: C. Husband (ed.), *'Race': Continuity and Change in Britain*, 1982, London, Hutchinson, pp. 180–1.

have been in Britain for almost 400 years and, indeed, in sizeable quantities. A recent booklet suggested to me that in 1774 the black population in London was almost 20,000. Although the numbers of blacks have increased, the attitudes of a predominant white society have not changed since those distant days of slave ships and masters.

By all accounts, my present position would indicate a degree of success in a white man's world. I had the privilege, or more correctly, the right to attend decent schools and colleges and by many whites' standards I must be remarkable in that of the limited blacks at universities, I am currently doing post-graduate work at a second university. The passage between stepping off at Southampton into a grey, dismal-looking English south coast and now sitting in a centrally heated, beautifully furnished, artistically decorated office surrounded by symbols of the black man's world, possibly reflects to many an observer, both black and white – success. The mental torture, the psychic scars are not visible and the sleepless nights and crying days of the white man's pressure seems like a distant dream. The trappings of modern society are only symbols. The torture and pain that white society inflicts upon its black individuals can never be compensated for, in spite of those few black faces one tends to see in so-called positions of authority. White society has little room for black faces and Ellison's *The Invisible Man* and Fanon's *Black Skin, White Mask* epitomizes the frustrations and dilemma of individuals like myself.

Professional blacks are treated as rare specimens by most of their white colleagues. I am no exception. Generally speaking, racist humour is used to make simple conversation and reactions to these generally leaves us, the black individuals, feeling guilty that we have challenged them. It is a continuous process that those blacks like myself, who have moved up (in a manner of speaking) in society, have very often to contend with the labels that not only do we carry 'chips on our shoulders', but we are over-sensitive to racial issues. No one cares if after a hard day's graft the extent of my social pleasures are limited simply because blacks are not allowed; no one cares if I am a professional when I go to the shops and a white employee has no desire to serve me; no one cares if as a black professional, I wish to buy a house in a particular area of the city, when the estate agents would suggest alternatives; and no one cares when as a black professional I question the educational output that is being given to my children and to many of the young people I work with. To white society all that is irrelevant for if I have made it then everyone else can. It confirms their belief that racism is a figment of our imagination and that the benevolence of white society, indeed of British society, is so bountiful that no one should feel they are disadvantaged. To most professional colleagues, the question of colour and discrimination is a theoretical base and is expressed in the fact that society is constructed in a number of classes. It is very difficult for them to imagine that my colour and those of many black, capable individuals, is used as a weapon against us. The fact that we communicate in a common language and that we share loves for the theatre and for other middle-class orientated values, automatically gives them every right to eliminate colour in any discussion. As far as they are concerned all men are equal and so I am continuously reminded that the Bible has said this time and time again.

Today's Britain is a variety of colour and culture. These only reflect customs, rituals and skin colour and there is no resemblance to the harsh treatment that white society metes out to us. As a young boy studying in the West Indies, I recall the words of an English poet whose name escapes me:

Oh England is a pleasant place
For them that is rich and high
But England is a cruel place
For such poor folks as I.

Making it in white Britain is simply a dream for many whites let alone blacks. My colour, my cultural norms and *me* – a person – will always be viewed through white-coloured lenses with all its distortions. To those blacks who would say that they have made it, it must be at a tremendous personal sacrifice and at the end, from my own development, it really is not worth it.

My colleagues leave my office after sipping cups of tea. They are greatly impressed about both my position and knowledge and this is said quite openly. I get a sneaking impression that they are mildly shocked by my performance. This happens almost every day and thus like me, many blacks are contained in a society which sees and hears only what it wants and when it wants. I use the phone to call my secretary and life continues in the same old way.

16.3 Angie*

Angie, who is 21, lived in residential care for fifteen years, but two years ago moved to an adapted flat with her husband. She has cerebral palsy, which means she is unable to walk and gets around in an electric wheelchair. She works as a clerical assistant for the Department of the Environment. She wants to travel to as many places as possible and in a few years would like to have children.

From the age of six years old I attended a residential school for disabled children. The school was very poor on education, so much so that at the age of sixteen I was only at the level of a nine-year-old. I used to go home at weekends and talk to the able-bodied kids about what they were doing at school. I had never even heard of some of the subjects they studied. I felt so ashamed that they knew more than I did and I was a lot older. I decided to ask my teacher why I did not do the same things as my friends did at their school. She told me it was because I was disabled and that there wasn't much point in educating me to 'O' and 'A' level as I would never get a job. I told her I was not prepared to spend my life in a workshop making baskets. I was going to improve my education and get a job in open employment no matter how long it took. Since the age of twelve I had been very bored with school life and started to become rebellious. I felt frustrated and couldn't explain why. Most of the other children were not very

*Source: J. Campling, *Images of Ourselves: Women with Disabilities Talking*, 1981, London, Routledge, pp. 8–12.

intelligent and this made me feel very alone. I could not talk to them as friends. I tried to talk to some of the staff about how I felt, but in their eyes we were all the same whatever disability we had. I was told to go and play and stop bothering them. This was quite common amongst the staff, never explaining what their ideas meant. One idea which most of the staff held was explained to me quite clearly. I was about fourteen years old and had just finished preparing a salad in the cookery class. The teacher came over and said, 'What a good job you have made of that. You would have made someone a good wife.' 'What do you mean, I would have?' I asked. 'Well,' she replied, 'What I meant to say was if you marry a disabled man, you would make him a good wife.' The school had really strange ideas on marriage and the disabled. They believed that if a disabled person got married it should be to another disabled person as it would not be fair on an able-bodied person to burden them with a handicapped partner. Anyway an able-bodied person would not fancy a disabled person. I didn't go along with this idea at all. I knew for a fact that able-bodied boys fancied me. I had proved that when I went home for weekends.

They also seemed to think that disabled people did not have any feelings. Well, that was how it seemed to me. I remember a humiliating experience I had when I was twelve. It was in the physiotherapy room. I was seeing the doctor who came from the local hospital on weekly visits. On this particular day he had brought five male student doctors with him, and I was made to walk naked in front of them and then lie on a mat while in turn they examined my body, opening and closing my legs, poking and prodding here and there and making comments. I was at the age when I was developing from a child into a woman and they made me feel so embarrassed. I used to cry on these visits. Then I started to lose respect for my body but it wasn't so embarrasing for me. There was no one I could talk to mainly because I was too young to understand what was happening. I had learned how to defend myself from an early age. I had to be strong-minded and strong-willed and by the age of fourteen I started to respect my body again. It took a long time and even today I sometimes find it difficult.

I left school when I was sixteen and went to live at a centre for adults. At the centre I tried to improve my education but this was very difficult. The other people at the centre were of normal intelligence and I easily made friends. When I'd been living there for a year I met and fell in love with a member of staff, a care assistant. His name was Tony and he came from my home county. We found we had quite a lot in common and enjoyed each other's company. Before Tony and I got together some of the staff tried to discourage me from going out with him. In the centre, such relationships were frowned upon because most of the staff did not approve of them. However, after a while our relationship developed and each day Tony was doing more things for me. Then he moved into my room and we started living together. This was made easy for us because firstly, as we were living away from home we didn't have any parental pressure and also we did not have the problem of finding somewhere to live. Secondly, the Principal, unlike most of the staff, realised that disabled people had the same feelings as anyone else so he allowed us to be together. Tony had looked after handicapped people for some time so he knew what was involved and anyway we loved each other so we found it easy to adapt.

We lived at the centre for fifteen months and then got married. We lived a further four months there and then we moved to our flat. It is a ground-floor flat which has been adapted to my needs. Tony got a new job and I stayed at home alone. At first I was very lonely as I had never been without people, having always lived in residential establishments. I spent most of my time trying to become more independent and on one occasion I sat on the loo for three hours until Tony came home from work. I just could not get off and I felt so angry with myself but there was nothing I could do. When Tony came home he was worried when I told him how long I had been sitting there. When he realised that I was OK we started to laugh as it was quite funny. At first Tony had wanted to give up his job and stay at home to look after me but he knew it was better for us if he could work and if I could be as independent as possible. Nowadays he doesn't worry because I am really quite independent.

When we had been living in our flat for some weeks, my Mum rang and told me she had met the headmaster of my old school, who had asked about me. She told him that I was now married and living in a flat. He asked what handicap my husband had. When my Mum told him Tony was able-bodied he was quite surprised and didn't know what to say. I have met a number of people who seemed surprised when they find out Tony is not disabled. It is as if they cannot understand how an able-bodied man can marry a disabled girl. One day while Tony was at work the gas man came to read the meter. I showed him where it was and waited in the doorway for him to finish. I always sit with the door open when anyone I don't know comes to the flat, in case they try anything, so I can shout to my neighbour who lives upstairs. As he was leaving the flat he turned and asked if I was married? I told him I was, then a funny look came into his eyes and he asked if I had sex? I was shocked at his question and at first was stuck for words. Then I was angry and said the first thing that came into my head. 'Yes, do you?' He looked embarrassed and hurried away. During the rest of the day I kept thinking what a cheek he had asking me such a question. Since then I have been asked that question several times in different ways, most often by men, and I answer them in the same way. But some people do seem genuinely concerned. For instance, I had some builders in doing some adaptations. One of them was very fatherly and friendly and we had long chats over cups of tea. He was about forty and was married with five children. One day he tried to ask me if I had sex but couldn't find the right words. I knew what he was getting at so I told him not to worry as everything was all right and we were very happy that way. For the rest of the day he never stopped apologising for asking such a personal question. Somehow I did not mind him asking as I felt he was not just curious but anxious about us.

Tony and I are often asked if we are brother and sister. The first time we were asked this was while we were buying some fruit and the shop assistant asked Tony. He replied, 'No, Angie is my wife.' The man seemed really surprised and stared long and hard at me. We left him thinking it over! The next occasion stands out clearly in my mind because of the fuss leading up to it. We were in a restaurant enjoying our meal when we noticed all the waiters watching us. We ignored them hoping they would lose interest but they didn't. Eventually one came over and whispered to Tony, 'Is she your sister?' When Tony said I was his wife, he looked quite incredulous and went off to tell the others. We couldn't help laughing, to think that was why they were standing watching us trying to find the courage to ask us.

Questions like these used to bother us but after a while we learned how to handle them. It would be better though if people would stop and think before they spoke and try and put themselves in our place. How would they feel if someone asked them if they had sex? Or if the person with them is their sister or brother? Why shouldn't disabled and able-bodied people be lovers and marry?[. . .]

CHAPTER 17

Social Contexts and Personal Circumstances

Maurice Eisenbruch and Philip Zimbardo

17.1 'Wind illness' or Somatic Depression? A case study in psychiatric anthropology*

Maurice Eisenbruch

Summary: A 46-year-old mother with a history of chronic headaches and other symptoms and a clinical diagnosis (in western terms) of depression, ascribed her condition to non-observance of Chinese postpartum ritual. The characteristic features of 'wind illness' are described. Western medicine proved useless but acupuncture was beneficial. The case underlines the importance of understanding the patient's own view of his/her illness and its causes in arriving at a correct diagnosis and intervening effectively: this is particularly true when the gap between the doctor's and the patient's cultures is wide.[. . .]

I met Mrs Xuyen, a 46-year-old mother of six, when I called to see her 17-year-old son, who had been reported as suffering from severe depression at school. All available members of the family crowded into the living room – males and females, young and old – and engaged in voluble talk. From time to time, individuals would move about to join groups. At each of my visits, Mrs Xuyen sat huddled in a corner, head averted, her face showing a pained expression. She seemed to have no comprehension of what was going on around her and nobody paid her any attention apart from one niece. This niece, who lived in another household, was always present when I visited: she would sit on the arm of Mrs Xuyen's chair, embracing her and seeming to offer solace, protection and contact.

At first it appeared that Mrs Xuyen's withdrawn behaviour might be acceptable as normal within her own culture, but she remained so persistently unresponsive that I came to believe that she was clinically depressed. This was indirectly confirmed by isolated casual remarks about her made by her children. Reference was made to her bad 'headaches' and numerous other varied bodily pains, to which family members seemed well-accustomed. There was no sense of urgency, or concern that Mrs Xuyen might be ailing, although she had suffered severe headaches for many years. Their onset had coincided with a period of chronic family stress said to be due to the war in North Vietnam: the family had lost

*Source: *British Journal of Psychiatry*, 143, 1983, pp. 323–6.

their house, possessions and livelihood, and had been forced to migrate within Vietnam. A doctor had prescribed tablets, but nobody could recall what they were for. With the trauma of resettlement in England, Mrs Xuyen's headaches became so severe that she was almost incapacitated and her niece visited daily to look after her and care for the family. Mrs Xuyen had no faith in western medicine, and it was only as a result of considerable pressure from the younger members of her family that she finally agreed to see a general practitioner, who diagnosed tension headache and prescribed a course of self-relaxation. Mrs Xuyen emerged from this meeting bewildered and disappointed. Despite the help of an interpreter, she had understood nothing of what had occurred and could see no possible connection between her headache and the prescribed exercise. Nor could she understand why she should now attend the regional hospital to have blood taken from her arm, and for X-rays: in Vietnam, such things happened only in direst illness.

Mrs Xuyen's headaches showed no improvement. They were also associated with insomnia, anorexia, loss of weight, distractibility, inability to concentrate and lack of interest in housework, in her children or in herself, suggesting a diagnosis of depressive illness rather than anxiety or tension headaches.

Because of the cultural gap between Mrs Xuyen and any western observer, it seemed to me to be important to gain information about *her* perception of the nature and origin of her symptoms. She believed, for example, in the power of bad spirits, and it seemed possible that her concepts of health and illness might be based upon notions of humoral imbalance characteristic of Buddhist, Taoist and Confucian cosmologies.

As the weeks passed, Mrs Xuyen made no attempt at the relaxation exercises, but she did make passing reference to 'wind'. Reviewing the history of her headaches, it was learned that their onset dated back sixteen years, far earlier than I had realized. The initial problem was not in fact a headache, but 'something bad'. She explained that after the birth of her third youngest child, she had failed to observe the ritual of 'doing the month'. Consequently, she had become poisoned, and her headaches were a final manifestation of this poisoning. Mrs Xuyen explained that when she was 'dirty' after having delivered the child, she had cleansed herself with a wet towel, and rinsed it out in clean water. Feeling fatigued, she lay down to sleep, placing the moist towel under her head as a pillow. During her sleep, the 'wind' emerged from the towel and entered her head, where it had stayed ever since. It is noteworthy that, of the entire sibship, this child, whom I was first called on to see, is the only one to have developed depressive symptoms and headaches during his childhood. These symptoms have become more pronounced with adolescence. Mrs Xuyen's attitude was fatalistic. She considered that she had already done everything possible to make amends for her carelessness, even trying to right the wrong by more carefully following the ritual of 'doing the month' after the birth of two more children. Herbal remedies had also failed, and she was convinced that there was nothing that she, western practitioners, or anyone else, could do to reverse the situation.

A Vietnamese doctor, well versed in traditional healing, confirmed that headaches caused by 'wind' were notoriously difficult to treat, but Mrs Xuyen willingly commenced a course of acupuncture. After the fourth or fifth treatment, her headaches had diminished and she had become increasingly involved in family life. Her insomnia, however, persisted.

Chinese postpartum rituals

Chinese traditional custom stipulates that a woman should spend a month's convalescence confined to the home after giving birth. During this time she is expected to observe restrictions and proscriptions, referred to as 'doing the month'. Three general principles that emerge from a multitude of details are: anything that might cause disease and specific ailments in the future should be avoided; foetal blood must not be allowed to contaminate others or offend the gods; and hot food (not cold) should be eaten.

These practices are intended to be curative and preventative, but in view of the number of rules and their complexity, it is unlikely that they are always strictly adhered to for the entire month. Failure to 'do the month' correctly leads *ex post facto*, to chronic illness much later in life. Such an affliction may be forestalled by becoming pregnant again to provide the chance to make restitution by 'doing the month' more scrupulously next time.

The cosmological basis to this practice has been the focus of much recent speculation (Gould-Martin, 1978; Pillsbury, 1978; Topley, 1974). Some sources suggest that a poisonous disorder may be caused by contact during the first postpartum month with 'queer' things such as brides, mourners, striking features of the landscapes, demons, and gods, all examples of the Confucian polarisation toward *yin* and *yang*. The catalytic effect of such a meeting of opposites is to produce a powerful 'wind'; a poison is thus generated and a poisonous disorder starts to incubate.

Later, when the disease erupts and declares itself, the sufferer can, it is supposed, contaminate a normally balanced person with her illness. This belief has considerable importance in handling such a condition in a western clinical setting.

Wind illness

'Wind illness' is one of the most common complaints in South-East Asian societies. The term may refer to any combination of organic pathology, psychosomatic disturbance and spirit possessions, disorders of the body, emotions and behaviour all coming under one diagnosis. There are thousands of varieties of wind illness, all treated by the same healers in much the same way.

The relevant cosmology holds that the human body, along with everything else in the universe, is composed of the four basic elements: *earth* (hair, nails and bones, which are hard); *water* (blood and bile, which are cohesive); *fire* (which provides heat and aids digestion); and *wind* (breathing, which causes movement). Imbalance between these elements causes illness.

There are several different points of view of the aetiology of 'wind illness'. Within Buddhist doctrine, the basic cause of all misfortune is bad *karma*, with illness having a fundamental moral significance. In the Confucian perspective, factors leading to humoral imbalance are emphasized: the calendar, the seasons and horoscopes are used by healers. Complementing these formal explanations are the folk beliefs in *spirit possession*. Considerable overlap exists between the presentations of wind illness and spirit possession, making differential diagnosis difficult. This disorder thus provides an example of the way in which explanatory beliefs about a syndrome come together to give not merely a case of multiple aetiology, but one of multiple pathogenesis.

It is possible to distinguish also various aspects of wind illness. First, the *cause* of wind disturbance: hunger, breach of postpartum custom, alcoholism, spirit possession, or drug addiction. Second, the underlying humoral process: wind rises, falls, or gets stuck. Third, the *site* of the congested wind: nerves, chest, brain, eyes. Fourth, the *effects* of the wind disturbance: sharp pain, feelings of faintness, seizures, and episodes of violent or disoriented behaviour.

The category applying to Mrs Xuyen is 'wrong menstrual wind illness' *(lom phit duan)*, caused during the first postpartum month by a maternal breach of postpartum customs; for example, smelling a bad odour, eating the wrong food, or bathing in cold water. 'Manifestations may be acute or chronic, but often they do not occur until . . . ten to thirty years afterwards. Thus (they are) usually diagnosed *ex post facto*, by the women recalling some previous breach of postpartum custom that explains a later occurrence of wind illness.' (Muecke, 1980).

A corollary of the association between parturition and 'wind illness' is that the illness may be transmitted by the breast milk of an afflicted mother. This useful explanation of how some males contract wind illness applies to Mrs Xuyen's son, born at the time she took in the 'wind', and later developing illness in his own right.

According to the indigenous healers, there are four precipitating factors which give rise to 'wind illness', the most dangerous of which is smelling a noxious odour. Poisonous substances enter the body by inhalation, directly with 'wind', and the resultant humoral imbalance produces 'wind illness'. Another cause is eating certain bad foods which, when ingested, affect the abdomen and chest: because wind is situated there, it then rises.

Mrs Xuyen believed herself to have absorbed the wind directly through her scalp by transferring the bad poison directly from her perineum. She had not needed to smell or eat the badness; hers was a far more direct portal of entry to her brain.

The two other precipitating factors are directly connected with the supposed vulnerability of the female sex. The first is their allegedly weaker 'life essence' which makes them less resistant to external stimuli. A specific factor is the impact of menstrual blood flow upon humoral balance: menopausal upsets are attributed to the retention of the element water, leading to disrupted equilibrium of wind. Multigravidae, such as Mrs Xuyen, are considered particularly vulnerable, possibly because of a combination of cumulative blood loss and advancing age. The other factor is a belief that women tend to brood and to have jittery nerves. The most severe forms of 'wind illness' supposedly occur when wind rises to the brain: when a person becomes anxious, depressed, or mad, this is seen as a concentration of disordered wind in the brain, the source of feelings and behaviour. Mrs Xuyen and her family explained not only headaches, but all her symptoms in these terms.

Discussion

Kleinmann (1980) has made a careful distinction between the 'explanatory models' (EMs) held by individual patients, and those held by different practitioners in the separate areas of health care systems. He defines explanatory models as 'notions about an episode of sickness and its treatment that are employed by all those in the helping process.' Explanatory models are different from general beliefs about sickness and health care, which exist outside individual episodes of illness. In the case just described, Mrs Xuyen, the local community, the general practitioner, and I (initially) each held disparate explanatory models for Mrs Xuyen's headache. Understanding Mrs Xuyen's explanatory model, it was possible to harness the available resources more appropriately in offering help.

With the growth of interest in eastern cosmologies, there has been a move toward explaining illness in South-East Asian patients within the framework of Confucian, Taoist or Buddhist philosophy. While I am sympathetic to such attempts at understanding I see two possible flaws in this approach. In the first place, the Vietnamese cannot be taken as a unit culture: they are a pot-pourri of Taoist, Confucism and Buddhist traditions, so that some Vietnamese are more under Chinese influence than others. The second problem is perhaps more challenging: it is to determine in any particular case just what the Vietnamese patient actually says about the aetiology of his/her symptoms. This point is often missed in otherwise illuminating accounts of symptoms which have been found in Vietnamese patients and inserted into a theoretical cosmological matrix for interpretation. Individual patients are usually unaware of the details of their 'great tradition', whereas the well-intentioned western observer, having read the classic texts and surveys of eastern medical philosophy, may superimpose his own construction of eastern beliefs upon his pre-existent western medical viewpoint. This may well distort, rather than clarify, his view of the patient's condition. I would therefore argue strongly for the value of meticulously exploring what the patient thinks to be the explanation of his/her symptoms.[. . .]

Conclusion

All people become sick and require help, sometimes in the physical sense, sometimes emotionally and sometimes both. Every society provides a system of reference to explain the deviations of its members from good health. If the helper does not understand the system used by the patient or client, it becomes very difficult for him to match his intervention with what is sought by the person experiencing the disease. Vietnamese refugees, as a group, employ a broad range of concepts of health and illness: understanding these may increase the efficacy of the health care that we provide for them. The same applies equally to other patients from non-western cultures.[. . .]

References

Gould-Martin, K. (1978) Hot, cold, clean, poison and dirt: Chinese folk medical categories, *Social Science and Medicine*, **12**, pp. 39–46.

Kleinman, A. (1977) Depression, somatizaton and the 'New cross-cultural psychiatry', *Social Science and Medicine*, **11**, pp. 3–10.

Kleinman, A. (1980) *Patients and Healers in the Context of Culture*, Berkeley, University of California Press.

Muecke, M.A. (1980) Wind illness in northern Thailand, *Culture, Medicine and Psychiatry*, **4**, pp. 267–99.

Pillsbury, B.L.K. (1978) 'Doing the month': confinement and convalescence of Chinese women after childbirth, *Social Science and Medicine*, **12**, pp. 11–22.

Topley, M. (1974) Cosmic antagonisms: a mother-child syndrome, in *Religion and Ritual in Chinese Society* (ed. Arthur P. Wolf), Stanford, Stanford University Press.

17.2 Pathology of Imprisonment*

Philip G. Zimbardo

In an attempt to understand just what it means psychologically to be a prisoner or a prison guard, Craig Haney, Curt Banks, Dave Jaffe and I created our own prison [in an experiment conducted at Stanford University]. We carefully screened over 70 volunteers who answered an ad in a Palo Alto city newspaper and ended up with two dozen young men who were selected to be part of this study. They were mature, emotionally stable, normal, intelligent college students from middle-class homes throughout the United States and Canada. They appeared to represent the cream of the crop of this generation. None had any criminal record and all were relatively homogeneous on many dimensions initially.

Half were arbitrarily designated as prisoners by a flip of a coin, the others as guards. These were the roles they were to play in our simulated prison. The guards were made aware of the potential seriousness and danger of the situation and their own vulnerability. They made up their own formal rules for maintaining law, order and respect, and were generally free to improvise new ones during their eight-hour, three-man shifts. The prisoners were unexpectedly picked up at their homes by a city policeman in a squad car, searched, handcuffed, fingerprinted, booked at the Palo Alto station house and taken blindfolded to our jail. There they were stripped, deloused, put into a uniform, given a number and put into a cell with two other prisoners where they expected to live for the next two weeks. The pay was good ($15 a day) and their motivation was to make money.

We observed and recorded on videotape the events that occurred in the prison, and we interviewed and tested the prisoners and guards at various points throughout the study.[. . .]

*Source: D. Krebs (ed.) *Readings in Social Psychology: Contemporary Perspectives*, 2nd edn, 1982, New York, Harper and Rowe, pp. 249–50.

At the end of only six days we had to close down our mock prison because what we saw was frightening. It was no longer apparent to most of the subjects (or to us) where reality ended and their roles began. The majority had indeed become prisoners or guards, no longer able to clearly differentiate between role playing and self. There were dramatic changes in virtually every aspect of their behaviour, thinking and feeling. In less than a week the experience of imprisonment undid (temporarily) a lifetime of learning; human values were suspended, self-concepts were challenged and the ugliest, most base, pathological side of human nature surfaced. We were horrified because we saw some boys (guards) treat others as if they were despicable animals, taking pleasure in cruelty, while other boys (prisoners) became servile, dehumanized robots who thought only of escape, of their own individual survival and of their mounting hatred for the guards.

We had to release three prisoners in the first four days because they had such acute situational traumatic reactions as hysterical crying, confusion in thinking and severe depression. Others begged to be paroled, and all but three were willing to foreit all the money they had earned if they could be paroled. By then (the fifth day) they had been so programmed to think of themselves as prisoners that when their request for parole was denied, they returned docilely to their cells. Now, had they been thinking as college students acting in an oppressive experiment, they would have quit once they no longer wanted the $15 a day we used as our only incentive. However, the reality was not quitting an experiment but "being paroled by the parole board from the Stanford County Jail." By the last days, the earlier solidarity among the prisoners (systematically broken by the guards) dissolved into "each man for himself." Finally, when one of their fellows was put in solitary confinement (a small closet) for refusing to eat, the prisoners were given a choice by one of the guards: give up their blankets and the incorrigible prisoner would be let out, or keep their blankets and he would be kept in all night. They voted to keep their blankets and to abandon their brother.

About a third of the guards became tyrannical in their arbitrary use of power, in enjoying their control over other people. They were corrupted by the power of their roles and became quite inventive in their techniques of breaking the spirit of the prisoners and making them feel they were worthless. Some of the guards merely did their jobs as tough but fair correctional officers, and several were good guards from the prisoners' point of view since they did them small favours and were friendly. However, no good guard ever interfered with a command by any of the bad guards; they never intervened on the side of the prisoners, they never told the others to ease off because it was only an experiment, and they never even came to me as prison superintendent or experimenter in charge to complain. In part, they were good because the others were bad; they needed the others to help establish their own egos in a positive light. In a sense, the good guards perpetuated the prison more than the other guards because their own needs to be liked prevented them from disobeying or violating the implicit guards' code. At the same time, the act of befriending the prisoners created a social reality which made the prisoners less likely to rebel.

By the end of the week the experiment had become a reality, as if it were a Pirandello play directed by Kafka that just keeps going after the audience has left. The consultant for our prison, Carlo Prescott, an ex-convict with 16 years of imprisonment in California's jails, would get so depressed and furious each time he visited our prison, because of its psychological similarity to his experiences, that he would have to leave. A Catholic priest who was a former prison chaplain in Washington, D.C. talked to our prisoners after four days and said they were just like the other first-timers he had seen.

But in the end, I called off the experiment not because of the horror I saw out there in the prison yard, but because of the horror of realizing that *I* could have easily traded places with the most brutal guard or become the weakest prisoner full of hatred at being so powerless that I could not eat, sleep or go to the toilet without permission of the authorities. *I* could have become Calley at My Lai, George Jackson at San Quentin, one of the men at Attica.[. . .]

Individual behaviour is largely under the control of social forces and environmental contingencies rather than personality traits, character, will power or other empirically unvalidated constructs. Thus we create an illusion of freedom by attributing more internal control to ourselves, to the individual, than actually exists. We thus underestimate the power and pervasiveness of situational controls over behaviour because: a) they are often non-obvious and subtle, b) we can often avoid entering situations where we might be so controlled, c) we label as "weak" or "deviant" people in those situations who do behave differently from how we believe we would.

Each of us carries around in our heads a favourable self-image in which we are essentially just, fair, humane and understanding. For example, we could not imagine inflicting pain on others without much provocation or hurting people who had done nothing to us, who in fact were even liked by us. However, there is a growing body of social psychological research which underscores the conclusion derived from this prison study. Many people, perhaps the majority, can be made to do almost anything when put into psychologically compelling situations – regardless of their morals, ethics, values, attitudes, beliefs or personal convictions. My colleague, Stanley Milgram, has shown that more than 60 per cent of the population will deliver what they think is a series of painful electric shocks to another person even after the victim cries for mercy, begs them to stop and then apparently passes out. The subjects complained that they did not want to inflict more pain but blindly obeyed the command of the authority figure (the experimenter) who said that they must go on. In my own research on violence I have seen mild-mannered [female students] repeatedly give shocks (which they thought were causing pain) to another girl, a stranger whom they had rated very favourably, simply by being made to feel anonymous and put in a situation where they were expected to engage in this activity.

Observers of these and similar experimental situations never predict their outcomes and estimate that it is unlikely that they themselves would behave similarly. They can be so confident only when they were outside the situation. However, since the majority of people in these studies do act in non-rational, non-obvious ways, it follows that the majority of observers would also succumb to the social psychological forces in the situation.

With regard to prisons, we can state that the mere act of assigning labels to people and putting them into a situation where those labels acquire validity and meaning is sufficient to elicit pathological behaviour. This pathology is not predictable from any available diagnostic indicators we have in the social sciences, and is extreme enough to modify in very significant ways fundamental attitudes and behaviour. The prison situation, as presently arranged, is guaranteed to generate severe enough pathological reactions in both guards and prisoners as to debase their humanity, lower their feelings of self-worth and make it difficult for them to be part of a society outside of their prison.[. . .]

CHAPTER 18

The Management of Social Relationships

Judy Gahagan

Talk and action are the visible, front-line elements of daily encounters. Behind this front line lie the supply lines of attitudes, values, resources and beliefs, and feelings about ourselves and about others. Helping people to improve their encounters and relationships with others requires attention, both to the front lines but also to the supply lines. Although training programmes for managing social interaction have focused to a large extent on behaviour, we shall also be concerned here with programmes for the analysis and modification of feelings and beliefs. Let us begin by providing some perspective for social-skills training within the broader context of general programmes for personal change.

Two approaches to personal change

Aside from drug and other physical interventions, approaches to personal change are really of two types – action therapies and insight therapies. Insight therapies consist of therapists and clients talking about the client's situations and relationships, both present and past. Present problems are related to each other and to past events, and the therapist interprets the material in terms of certain motivational patterns or themes. The interpretive frameworks vary according to the therapist's orientations; Freud, Jung, Klein, Perls and others have provided theoretical frameworks for understanding the long-term conduct of individuals. Many of these locate the origins of present problems in early childhood, and increasing the awareness of these origins is part of the therapeutic process. In some insight therapies the client's, as opposed to the therapist's, interpretation of underlying themes guides the therapeutic process (as for example in the client-centred therapy of Carl Rogers). The basic assumptions behind insight therapies are as follows: the inadequate or problematic social behaviour is caused by underlying fears and conflicts, that is the manifest symptoms of present problems are caused by latent emotional processes; that changing behaviour will not be

Source: Judy Gahagan, *Social Interaction and Its Management*, 1984, London, Methuen, pp. 140–65. (Title of original chapter: 'The management of social interaction and social relationships'.)

successful without modifying the latent process; that the specialized talk that takes place between clients and therapists and the 'insights' that ensue (and in some cases the emotional processes which take place between the two of them) are both the necessary and sufficient conditions for clients to realize the changes they want in their lives.

One of the main problems with the approaches to personal change through interpretation and insight is that the patterns and themes which the therapist (or for that matter the client) 'sees' may only exist inside their heads (Nisbett and Ross, 1980). [. . .] Much of what we see is determined not so much by what may or may not be there but by our prior *beliefs* about what is there. Thus there is always the possibility that clients emerge with new sets of lenses through which to view their own conduct and circumstances, but with both the latter substantially unchanged. This problem may be partly answered if we find ways to assess and evaluate different approaches, but the technical problems of doing so are very great indeed.

Action therapies on the other hand are aimed at directly changing clients' behaviours, because [. . .] there has been a shift in emphasis towards self-management. One of the reasons for this shift in focus has been the recognition that whatever is learned or changed in a consulting room has to be applied in a variety of situations in the outside world, and from a practical point of view only the clients will encounter and manage those situations. Another reason has been the recognition [. . .] that a sense of control over one's own actions and outcomes is in itself a component of well-being. Self-management techniques are aimed at the client's realization of that control.

Social-skills training is concerned with modifying actual behaviour with others. However, not all action therapies are concerned simply with changing behaviour. They are often aimed also at actually changing what clients are doing, thinking and feeling at the present time. But the problems described are focused on directly as they are presented, rather than interpreted in terms of some other underlying process. Thus clients may be taught techniques for modifying their physiological responses of fear, for example by learning techniques of progressive relaxation to those events which evoke fear. Or they may be taught to monitor particular patterns of thought which accompany depression or anxiety and to modify them, criticize them and substitute other arguments for them.

Who are the clients?

In the past twenty years or so there has been a considerable expansion in the population of people who have voluntarily become involved with techniques for personal change. The most obvious recipients of personal-change therapy programmes are those admitted to psychiatric clinics with severe problems which cripple them both socially and occupationally. In addition to these, however, many become involved for professional reasons because their jobs involve the management of other people – teachers, interviewers for selection and research, psychotherapists themselves, managers, and many others. The distinctions between practitioner and client have in this respect become less sharp. However, it should be remembered that there are people whose social competence is very severely impaired and this is quite apparent simply from observing them in routine situations. Such people can be distinguished easily from the rest of the clinical population with general emotional problems (Trower *et al.*, 1974) in that their social behaviour is lacking in expressiveness and is leaden and unresponsive, and their conversation is sparse and monotonous. Programmes concerned with developing more adequate *behaviour* are particularly relevant to such clients.

Social conduct and values

Except when we are dealing with clients with gross deficits in their social behaviour, and who are extremely isolated on that account, many of the goals of personal change are dependent on particular values being adopted. How we should conduct ourselves with others, the bases of our relationships with others, the relative importance that we attach to our own well-being as opposed to that of others, are questions of value in which professional psychologists have no particular or greater authority than anyone else.

If we look at some of the goals implicit in programmes for increasing social effectiveness we often come across the following: enhancing one's capacity to act autonomously and as individuals rather than collectively (or some would say collusively); asserting oneself rather than being submissive; expressing one's feelings openly instead of hiding them; and so forth. None of these values are written up in the sky to be observed for all time. They are relative to our own culture and moment in history. As psychologists we often imagine that certain patterns of behaviour are synonymous with mental health. We must remember that they are so only to the extent that it is *usually* more adaptive to behave in ways which are generally valued in society than in ways that are not.

Values enter into programmes of change in so far as they are informing clients' behaviours without the latter being quite aware of their doing so. For example some people walk around with hidden agendas in their heads that tell them that they must comply with the wishes of others or that their behaviour ought to be consistent all the time. Failure to recognize such hidden agendas can inhibit people's progress to their other personal goals.[. . .]

Social interaction as a skilled performance

The social-skills model

Reference has been made to social-skills training and the idea of social interaction as a skilled performance. What justification is there for talking about social interaction in this way? We do so because it is possible to consider it as involving many of the components involved in other skills. First there is a hierarchy of sub-skills which with practice become increasingly autonomous and outside the awareness of the actor. In playing tennis, the shifts of weight from one foot to another, the positioning of the feet, the sweep of the arm, the tossing up of the ball and the final strike have to be acquired by the learner, individually and consciously; in the skilled player they become the whole sweep of movement which constitutes the service. Similarly in social interaction the positioning and orientation of the body, the eyebrow movement, the various facial grimaces which signal 'pleasure', 'surprise' and the launching of the first topic seem to the unskilled separate and awkward moves. In the skilled performer, however, they become the smooth sequence of behaviour which is involved in the charming greeting.

Secondly there is the fact that such sequences of action are under the continuous control of feedback. The tennis player adjusts position to adapt to the speed of the ball descending in service and to the position of the other player. If any of these or other variables change, the player will take corrective action, again without awareness. Similarly, if one prepares to greet someone who, before one speaks, yells, 'Hi, I've got to dash for the bus', or returns one's look with an expression of incomprehension, one will, if a skilled actor, short-circuit the prepared greeting without perhaps even being aware of doing so. Seen in this way it is useful to consider social interaction as a form of skill and to design programmes for its development according to the principles found effective in the development of other, non-social skills. These are, in particular, the principles of regular practice, of continual feedback on progress, of isolating the sub-skills and practising them as well as synthesizing them into the larger hierarchies and practising those. This model has provided a basis for programmes for improving social effectiveness, as the following examples will show.

Some skill elements

[. . .] [M]any sequences of interaction are apparently rule-following since they seem so predictable in their formats. Greetings, farewells, the structure of many conversations in terms of adjacent pairs of items, like question-answer, complaint-commiseration, statement-agreement/disagreement. These sequences are below the awareness of most of us because they do not cause us any trouble. Indeed it is necessary to read a book on social psychology in order to become aware of this hidden structure of everyday life. For some, very shy people, however, these elements are no more automated than staying on a bicycle is for a non-cyclist. Failure to perform such lower-order skills clearly impedes the development of higher-order ones like dating and winning arguments or indeed making friends at all. Training in social skills is based, as we said before, on action therapy, that is that clients have to act differently in some way in order for change to occur, and it has to include self-management since ultimately only clients can use their improved skills in the real-life situations where they actually need them.

Professionals may, from their interviews with clients, identify part of the problem as failure to master the basic automatic skills of interaction. Clients then need two things: first an awareness of the common, usually unnoticed sequences of social interaction; and secondly some feedback about where their behaviour omits or distorts such sequences. To meet the first of these needs, clients, like other social scientists, can examine sequences of interaction. These can be recorded on film, described in books like this one, observed *in vivo* at the suggestion of therapists to keep detailed accounts of interaction in natural settings, or simply described and modelled by therapists. Clients will also benefit from observing material which shows these sequences being mismanaged by others. They should by then have caught up with therapists in being able to describe quite accurately these common elements.

Clients also need information about their own typical performances. Like most learning, seeing is a more effective means than hearing about. One of the reasons why we all fail to achieve ideal standards of social performance is that we never have the chance to observe our own behaviour from the perspective of an observer. A crucial element in social-skills training is the provision of that perspective, usually through some kind of hardware like video screening, on a sample of the client's social performance. Preferably this would be obtained unobtrusively, that is without the client's awareness, in order that it be a typical sample. Thus a client might be televised while speaking in a group of other clients or during the initial interview with therapists. Often it is not possible to disguise this kind of observation and one simply hopes that awareness of the recording equipment will diminish after a short while. When clients receive this feedback they need to observe it with the same objectivity and precision as therapists should, that is not in terms of evaluation or criticism, but in terms of what actually happens. Armed with this information, clients may be in a position to formulate their own diagnosis and start to plan a programme for change. Then comes the difficult part. At some point clients have not only to learn but to practise, and to practise until actual conversational sequences are automatic. The difficulty lies in the fact that this kind of exercise can induce exteme self-consciousness in people who are probably most vulnerable to it and least equipped to deal with it. A lot here depends on the qualities of the therapists. Therapists who are themselves unselfconscious about practising social routines and able to show confidence in clients' eventual success will help a lot. Then sheer habituation lessens the effects of self-consciousness, so that routines may have to be practised repeatedly, in the same way as stage actors go through the same sequence many times or the novice learner of a foreign language practises verbal formulae, until they become detached from a sense of self-evaluation (which may well be a critical component for clients anyway).

Here is an example of a greeting routine from the manual for social-skills training developed by Trower *et al.* (1974), in which the therapists and clients role-play a typical greeting sequence, taking it in turns to initiate the sequence:

A [looks, shows recognition, using the 'eybrow flash']
B [greets]Hello, George.
A How are you? [and/or] How's the work going?
B I'm fine, how are you? [or] I'm fine, got a rush job on at the moment, see you.
A I've just been to . . .[or] See you later, cheers.

There are many conversational junctures which can be practised in the same way, with respect both to the verbal elements and the non-verbal elements, like smiling.

Many clients fail with habitual sequences because they are too passive to play the equal role which defines a conversation. For example they may never ask questions, which is a standard practice for maintaining a conversation. One exercise then might be to try out sequences in which they systematically increase the ratio of questions they ask. Similarly, failing to be aware of different types of question, they may not notice questions in which more extended answers would fit and simply reply monosyllabically; and again the conversation falters both for lack of raw material and because the passivity is interrupting some of the normal assumptions underlying conversations. Similar treatment can be accorded to sequences which terminate conversation (see Schegloff and Sacks' work 1973) [. . .] that is clients may have to practise terminating conversation when they want to, with a variety of partners showing a range of difficulties. The components of terminal sequences involve non-verbal elements as well as verbal strategies, and the former too will have to receive specific attention before being put together.

The other normally automated behaviour which a client may have failed to master, and which again shows strong regularity in any given culture, is the non-verbal behaviour involved in meshing skills.[. . .] Normally in conversation the floor passes from one to another via turn-claim signals which involve head nods on the part of the listener and eye signals on the part of the speaker. The topic too passes from one to the other and each has the problem of fading out a topic before introducing a new one. Once again our basic teaching resources are those which make clients aware of the normative nature of many of these devices; of providing them with feedback about their own typical handling of conversations and indentifying where these become unsatisfactory; then practising, either in role play with therapists or through group or dyadic situations with other clients which therapists have set up, the conversational junctures where the talk and topic pass from one to another.

Listening

Communication involves sending signals and receiving them. Social-skills training in these aspects can be considered separately. We all fail at times to listen, for certain common reasons. One frequent reason is that we are actually preoccupied with ourselves or something external to the situation. This often happens even while we continue to give off the automatic signals to the other person that indicate listening. Another reason is that we often believe that we know what the other person is saying anyway, that is we guess what they will say but don't check it out by listening to what they actually do say. Consider the following example:

A Would you mind if I opened the window?
B I'm sorry the air is stale in this room.

B has 'heard' 'This room smells', when A had the heat in mind and asked to open the window. Often we listen only partially because we are concerned only with the evaluation of the message, that is whether we like it or agree with it or not, and not to its specific content. Listening is intrinsically difficult because language [. . .] is based on presuppositions about what others already know and think, and listening reflects these presuppositions just as much as speaking does. A lot of the time we are listening to what we think people mean rather than to what they actually say.

Improving one's capacity to listen involves a number of stages. The first one is that of establishing some estimate of how much we actually do listen, and when we don't what the usual reasons for that failure are. A first step in improving listening is that of making it active by intermittently 'reflecting back' to speakers what we think they said or meant. This process both increases one's attention to the talk and also provides some estimate of the accuracy with which one is hearing other people's messages. Not only that; in 'reflecting back', we can also clarify how the other person feels about the subject they are talking about, for example:

A We have put the house up for sale.
B [who had already heard something of the sort] You have really put it up for sale. Was that a sudden decision?

One exercise one can engage in to counteract presuppositions is to keep a mental note of one's actual or implicit response to remarks and to consider the extent to which they were the only relevant ones possible. Moreover, one can equally heighten one's awareness by carrying out this same activity as one listens to others talking amongst themselves. One ideal milieu for these activities is the encounter or sensitivity-training group, where conversational rules are relaxed so that one can pursue the meanings which people are attaching to one another's talk and the validity of those meanings. Improving listening skills really needs more than a dyadic relationship between client and therapist, even though therapists can point out these common failures of the listening process and the reasons for them and assist in the monitoring process which helps clients to identify their specific failures. Once again it is the small-group context which is particularly helpful.

Sensitivity to non-verbal behaviour

We have described the skill of listening attentively and accurately as if we were simply concerned with the verbal content of the message. But the development of sensitivity to others' messages includes understanding the non-verbal elements [. . .] which communicate information about others' emotional states and attitudes. One of these non-verbal elements is that of voice qualities, another is facial expression and body movement. Again clients need to be introduced to the idea that there are common expressions of the face which can be identified on quite different types of people. The posed photographs and voices which have been used to assess the average experimental subject's accuracy at detecting emotional states, in [. . .] research [. . .] can just as easily be used for training clients in reading and hearing emotional expression. In such training it is particularly important to draw their attention to the components of different facial expressions, for example the role of the mouth, the region around the eyes and eyebrows, and, in the case of voice qualities, to changes in pitch, breathiness, loudness and fading, and so on. In some programmes material can be presented so that only parts of the face are visible. At this stage the clients are simply being given many exemplars of different emotional expressions and analysing their component parts, such as surprised eyes or disgusted mouth. When clients are in groups with others they can also try posing expressions for themselves and allowing others to guess at the expression represented. Then the client can be moved on to actual sequences of expression because, after all, in natural situations people's faces and voices are moving and changing, and change may be the significant point. For example the timing of a smile provides a lot of information about its meaning; a smile which fades soon and rapidly after its appearance seems to hide a less than positive feeling. Some expressions are very fleeting and practice is needed in detecting them. Moreover, sequence is important and clients can interpret such sequences as the smile which has followed the impassive stare as opposed to the smile which has followed a frown; the first usually indicates pleasure or surprise or both, but the latter indicates relief. Then the more advanced skill of detecting hidden feelings can be introduced. The cues to 'leakage' are varied and vary between different people. Close acquaintance with someone enables most of us to learn to spot leakage cues. Nevertheless there are some very common ones. The client can be shown those movements which are customarily less under control because unattended to, like movements of feet and legs, or self-stimulation as in scratching, hair twiddling, hand-to-face movements, avoidance, blinking and of course voice qualities. Film and video material can be used and the client asked to attend specifically to the 'hidden' messages in such leakage cues.

Attitudes about situation, the topic and the other person are also detectable from non-verbal cues. Video-taped sequences in which two people are shown in a variety of relationships can be used for decoding interpersonal attitudes as well as transitory states like agreement, disagreement and approval. These are used initially without the sound so that clients won't be distracted from cues in posture, orientation, proximity, congruency and incongruency of posture and orientation, patterns of gaze, all of which provide so much information about the relationships between people, their relative interest in one another, their status differences, and so on. When the sound is available clients can learn to switch attention from the content of what is being said to the hidden cues described.

Decoding, encoding and balance

What about encoding, that is sending messages? [. . .] All our behaviour is informative in some degree, and the main aim of social-skills training is that of giving clients more control over messages which they may be unintentionally sending or failing to send. There are three stages to the process. First there is the analysis of client's behaviour in interaction. We cannot see our own behaviour and we remain massively unaware a lot of the time of the readings which others make of our behaviour. Feed-back which places clients in the position of observers is crucial. For example, people who avoid eye contact to a chronic degree are often completely unaware of this fact until they actually see it. Then there has to be an acquisition of new elements of communication and these have to be practised and their effects observed. Above all clients have to be endlessly pragmatic and endlessly observant about what effects their signals have, because every encounter is slightly different. There can be no formula of behaviour which will always have the same or the desired effect, for one essential element in managing social interaction is that of flexibility.

Although we consider sending and receiving signals as separate elements in training, at a more advanced level the balance between the two needs attention. Some people upset the conversational seesaw because they never really listen to others and they behave independently of another person's response. Others fail because they contribute neither sufficiently nor sufficiently clearly. Many people who are judged to have poor social skills fall into the latter category. Their behaviour is monotonous and unclear because they just don't behave *enough*. The reason, however, why most clients fall into the passive category is because they are more acutely aware of their deficiencies. People who are over-dominant are less likely to refer themselves for help since they are more of a problem to other people than they are to themselves. Again the critical element in displaying imbalances is real feedback spanning a reasonable period of interaction.

The conversation

We are mostly aware of our talk and its effects. The idea of training people in the art of conversation is hardly new and is an important component of education for upper-class people. Language has the dual function of carrying information about the immediate situation and the relationship between the participants, as well as that of carrying the ideational content. Our capacity to utilize the resources of our own language to narrate, explain, instruct, persuade and generally divert cannot be underestimated, since it probably accounts for more social competence than any other single factor. The skilled talker is a formidable person in any situation. The development of verbal skills is, or should be, a crucial feature of any educational curriculum.[. . .] Two major skills are involved in being effective communicators: one is derived from our understanding of the perspective of others, what they need to know and the effects of our behaviour on them; the other is the capacity to choose words and phrases and to structure our discourse adaptively to the listener and to the situation. What are some common problems that people have with conversations? Typically they find it difficult to keep conversations going, or indeed to start them at all, to maintain the interest of others, to elicit the information they may want from other people, or to provide in adequate form the information that others want from them.

The organization of material for conversation

Clients often complain that on social occasions they can't think of anything to talk about. But often the problem is not one of a deficit of incidents and observation as conversational material; it is more often clients' failure either to remember them or to regard them as relevant for conversational purposes. For clients who complain of this difficulty one step is simply that of keeping a record over a short period of events and observations which they might like to share with others. Then the problem is that of organizing them as conversational material. One of the first objectives here is that of moving from the general to the specific. If we start with general remarks about something we have done, we can then decide to pursue the topic depending on whether the listeners look interested or not, and if they do, orienting them to what is to follow by putting them in the general picture, which we can follow up with more detail. This aspect of conversation training is particularly well-conducted in groups, since it is quite natural to tell people about events even within the context of a training programme. A second task is that of choosing and planning more personally revealing information, like that of opinions and feelings about things as well as other private information about self. Progress in retailing information goes from the general to the particular, and progress in retailing personally relevant material goes from that evoking a slightly emotive response to that evoking a strongly emotive one. That passage in itself is contingent on listeners' responses, both non-verbal and verbal. For example, in our culture it is less risky to make statement 1 than to make statement 2 to someone whom we do not know very well.

1 We arrived back from Edinburgh last night. It's the first time I've been up there, and I found the people different to what I had expected.
2 We arrived back from Edinburgh last night. I must say I really loathe the Scots.

Self-disclosure

Self-disclosure in interaction, perhaps more than anything else, reveals a matching process to which both parties need to be sensitive. We usually move from topics as personal as home life or job to relationships in general, to family and then to sexual relationships and problems (if we get that far, that is). Each party hazards a personal disclosure and one sign of this move being accepted is that the other party makes a disclosure of a similar order of intimacy. The directness and specificity of the formulation is quite important. One way of introducing a personal area is to make a statement about it in general and to see what happens. For example statement 1 as opposed to 2:

1 Christmas is quite a problem for people who are unattached, don't you think?
2 I can hardly face the thought of Christmas on my own again for the third year running.

Choosing conversational style

We should remember that quite a few people fail in their encounters with others because of an overly inhibited, formal and impersonal style. Only clients and therapists together can spot whether this is the case, and they may be aided in their judgements by video material showing people with very contrasting styles in establishing interpersonal relationships. For the person who uniformly keeps everyone at a distance by a frozen style of talk, the following rules have been suggested (Trower *et al.*, 1974):

Use 'I' rather than 'one', 'they' or 'it'.
Try to bring 'I feel . . .' into the conversation more often.
Use more words which refer directly to the emotion, for example: 'I was absolutely furious', as opposed to: 'It was a real shame that . . .'
Use facial expressions to match the feeling being expressed verbally.
Use positive forms rather than negative forms: 'I want to', rather than: 'I wouldn't mind . . .'.

Once again the choice and mastering of particular linguistic styles depends partly on understanding the connotative subtleties of language, [. . .] and is really inseparable from more general linguistic training.

[. . .] We have considered social-skills training in terms of fairly small elements and general processes, relevant to a range of clients, and very much at the level of the average player. We can of course go on to more virtuoso and Olympian tasks like those involved in making amends when one has offended or embarrassed another person; or in resolving very severe conflicts of interest, as is often required between parents and grown-up children; or in holding one's own in conversation with an extremely confident, knowledgeable partner; or in initiating encounters with sexual partners and managing both their acceptances and their rejections; in managing apologies, complaints and arguments with poise. The problems are too diverse and numerous to deal with individually, but there are common elements of training. First, and this is particularly well carried out in groups, there is the listing of critical incidents and situations from real-life experience of clients. Secondly, there is the analysis of actual problems in terms of both parties' perspectives, which often, particularly when focusing on conflict situations, leads on to the strategy of role play, where clients and others not necessarily involved take the parts of the characters involved in the conflict. Thirdly, there is the construction of some actual verbal and behavioural formulae for dealing with the problematic encounters themselves. Fourthly, there is the actual practice either *in vivo*, as a homework assignment, or as a therapeutic exercise. Some excellent and extensive exercises for managing difficult social situations are to be found in *Social Skills and Mental Health* (Trower *et al.*, 1978).

It is at these Olympian heights of social performance that we come to our starting-point – the lay practitioners. We meet them in books, articles and problem-page letters in magazines. These abound with advice and suggestions for handling difficult situations with poise, and indeed charm, and steering relationships into happier fields. It is unlikely that such advice can be easily faulted by any of us. As professionals, however, what we have to offer is precision. We need to be precise about what clients actually do, think and feel. We need to be precise about what they want to change. We need to be precise about whether the changes they do instigate have the desired effects. Above all we want to bring them over to our side and get them to be pragmatic and precise for themselves, effective monitors of and coaches for their *own* social performance. Thus we close on a central theme: [. . .] the close relationship in psychology between scientists and lay persons, and the potential for personal enhancement which can be released when the latter sharpen (with assistance) their own scientific faculties.

References

Nisbett, R. and Ross, L. (1980) *Human Inference: Strategies and Shortcomings*, Englewood Cliffs, N.J., Prentice Hall.

Schegloff, E. and Sacks, H. (1973), 'Opening-up closings', *Semiotica*, **8**, pp. 289–327.

Trower, P., Bryant, B. and Argyle, M. (1974), *Social Skills and Mental Health*, London, Methuen.

SECTION 6

Localities and Social Change

Introduction

In this section of the Reader we take up a further dimension of the making of the modern UK storyline. The nature of that dimension is loosely encapsulated in the market slogan of one of the world's leading finance houses, the Japanese multinational, *Nomura*. The slogan in question is *Local Commitment, Global Capacity*. As a piece of geographical shorthand, its brevity assumes a certain knowledge on our part. It is trying to convey to us that all places are different and yet all can be reached; that there is geographical diversity as well as geographical proximity. What, at first glance, appears to be a set of opposing terms, the local *and* the global, on closer inspection turns out to be aspects of a single interconnected process. The local is part of the global and yet it retains its distinctiveness. Of course, at one level it remains nothing more than a persuasive slogan, a marketing catch-phrase. The company is telling us that it is a global player in the world's financial markets and one that is sensitive to their local features, be it New York, Frankfurt, Milan, London, or even Manchester. As a piece of geographical thinking, however, it represents more than a commercial catch-phrase and is something of a geographical challenge. It challenges us to think through what we mean by such terms as globalism and localism, and encourages us to think of the ways in which the two are interrelated.

The scope of this challenge implies, first, that it is unrealistic to explain what is happening to the UK's cities and regions, without reference to wider, external influences. Chapter 1, on the social forces that have shaped the UK over time, stressed this point. Equally, however, there is the danger of a move too far in the other direction, whereby an attempt is made to explain the UK's uneven and often unequal geography solely in terms of global shifts. Neither framework of geographical inquiry has the analytical power to trace the connections between the global and the local and people's lives.

The three extracts in this section of the Reader don't meet this challenge in full. What they do offer are some of the conceptual tools to trace the social connections that shape the different dynamics of change underway in different localities. All three extracts focus upon an issue that has taxed the geographical imagination for some time -- how to grasp the wider geography of social processes without losing sight of how they work themselves out in particular ways in particular localities. In other words, how we connect the global to the local.

One of the interesting developments within social theory in recent years is the recognition that space makes a difference to the way that society reproduces itself. In part, this theoretical development is itself a reflection of the ways in which global issues increasingly reach into our lives, often in a roundabout manner. Space is no longer regarded as a backdrop against which social change takes place, but rather as an active ingredient of how society changes and reproduces itself. It does matter socially for example that some cities are developing in ways which are quite different from the rest of the country. London is the obvious case, especially the City, with its changing fortunes locked into the global circuits of finance. True, London has always been different in a commercial sense from say, Newcastle, Glasgow or Birmingham, but today that difference is *structured* globally in new ways. In the last century, all of the country's big cities pulled in roughly the same direction, helping to shape a world market in which the UK was dominant. Today, different parts of the country are developing in various directions, some developing around international services and high-technology industries, others around new forms of manufacturing and oil, whilst others attempt to restructure around leisure and selling bits of their past, their industrial heritages. The lines of development reach out to different parts of the global economy. Moreover, what happens economically in one part of the UK may be unrelated to events elsewhere in the country.

These differences matter for the UK as a whole. They matter politically, for instance, and if the economic geography of the UK is shifting, then so too is its political configuration. Whitehall and Westminster are no longer at the political centre of a powerful world empire – on the contrary, the post-1945 period has been one of frantic readjustment as the UK's political leaders have tried to find a new role in a changing world. Since the early 1970s this has involved a reorientation towards a Europe in which the UK is no longer the dominant player.

The differences matter culturally as well, and by this we mean more than the breakdown of long-established community cultures that revolved around particular occupations. Although the fracturing of local cultures is an important dimension of contemporary social change, what is equally important are the new strands of global culture that make up part of today's 'imaginary communities'. Some of these cultural strands reflect patterns of international migration, from the Caribbean, Asia, Africa and also from Eastern Europe. Other cultural shifts are part and parcel of the growth in global cultural products, ranging from fashion and film through to food. What signs and symbols are taken up, however, and by which groups, and in what parts of the country, is a complex geographical issue. Opening up this issue and exploring its different aspects – cultural, political, and economic – is to take up the geographical challenge posed earlier.

In this section of the Reader, we have selected three pieces that engage centrally with the connection between the local and the global. The first article, *Global Local Times* provides an overview of many of the processes and patterns touched upon here. As a piece of geographical thinking, the article attempts to convey the cross-cutting nature of the local–global relationship; that is, it avoids treating the global dimension as something separate and distinct from the local level (which may refer to either a city, a region or a nation) by emphasizing that the global and local are two sides of a *single* process. The other two readings are taken from a book entitled *Localities: The Changing Face of Urban Britain*. The book itself represents an attempt by an interdisciplinary team of researchers in the UK to explore the complexity of social change in a number of different urban locations. What is distinctive about the collection, and indeed why we have chosen to reproduce two of the 'locality' case studies here, is their explicit attempt to move between the different levels of geographical enquiry -- from the local up to the global -- and back. Equally important, for us at least, is the fact that the authors address economic, political and cultural relations in a manner that is sensitive to their separate geographies as well as to the ways in which they interrelate. It is worthwhile here to pick out some of these aspects and in particular, to say a little about how each extract explores the connections between the local and the global.

Global Local Times by Kevin Robins captures in a quite dramatic way the notion that many social processes are simultaneously global and local. This is a rather difficult point to convey, as there is always a tendency to think of global processes as phenomena which operate between countries rather than across them. Robins takes the example of global multinationals to make his point.

Globalization in the economic sphere, he argues, is not a new phenomenon, but rather one that has reached a stage of development in which national boundaries are losing their economic relevance as multinationals compete with one another in a range of differentiated local markets. All of this has been made possible by innovations in information and communications technology. An important aspect of this thesis is that the dimensions of space and time are, as it were, being 'shrunk'. Our relationship to other places, our social conceptions of distance, are in the process of being radically altered, or rather radically shortened. The global is part of the local and vice versa. But, and this is an important qualification, when a Japanese car manufacturer such as *Nissan* sets up production facilities in the north east of England, the local is Europe, not Sunderland. The 'local' here takes its meanings from the geographical markets of the global corporation not the geographical horizons of the factory workforce. If the world's distances are shrinking, they are not contracting at the same speed or to the same extent for all social classes and institutions.

Increasingly, social theorists are recognizing that this way of thinking about economic space also has a political and a cultural counterpart. The European Community, for example, presents us with a different set of questions as to how our lives in different parts of the UK will be organized and shaped politically in the 1990s. Already, there are signs that the nation state is being bypassed by some cities as they deal directly with EC institutions for development funds. But it is in the cultural sphere that some of the strongest claims have been advanced. Here, as Robins argues, the 'stretching' of cultural relations across space has brought together cultural traces and influences from a plurality of cultures. Much of this cultural message comes to us through commodities, media images and various forms of global information, although it is less clear what codes and meanings are attached to these signs by local cultures. American hamburgers and Indian take-aways, Benetton clothing and Laura Ashley wallpapers, 'Dallas' and 'Neighbours', are expressive of a mix of cultures, but in themselves they do not tell us the meanings ascribed to them by, for example, black Muslims in Bradford or middle-class whites living in Hampstead, North London. Nor is it clear what relations of power are inscribed in say, the 'Americanization' of cultural lifestyles and how they are resisted. Local cultures may bear the marks of wider cultural processes, but how they are interpreted and how they are understood is still very much a local issue. Again the local and the global are two sides of a single process. Particular forms of the way local – global relations work can be found in the two case study extracts, *Economic and Social Change in Swindon* and *Coming to Terms with the Future in Teesside*. Comparing the two studies is instructive for a number of reasons. First, the choice of Swindon in the south and Teesside in the north reflect wider changes in the UK economy. As the role of the UK economy in the world economic order has shifted, so too have the fortunes of these regions. In Teesside, the links out from the local economy to the international markets initially to those of the Empire and more recently through the steel and chemical industries to wider export markets, have taken the area through a cycle of growth and decline. In contrast, the local economy of Swindon is on a reverse trajectory, from slump to boom. Much of this success can be traced directly to its new industrial base, that of high-technology and private services, which has integrated the area into a different part of the world economy from that of Teesside. Over time, the global connections of the two local economies have changed and with them their economic prospects.

Culturally the two localities reach out in rather different ways. Swindon is increasingly a cultural mirror of the outer south-east region, with its own working-class traditions and industries giving way to the spread of an 'enterprise culture' across the region. A distinctive middle-class culture is emerging in the south-east region, which possesses all the signs of a class seeking cultural dominance in the country as a whole. The mix of class cultures is still very much in evidence in Swindon, but so too is the direction of change. In Teesside, by way of contrast, the traditions of labourism reflect the old and declining world of industry based on heavy manufacturing. Migration out of the area to seek work down south or abroad has further undermined community and cultural ties. The networks through which people live their lives are now far wider than the locality, but the 'imaginary community' that once was Teesside still gives shape to daily lives.

Politically the two areas have been quite different too. Since the war, Swindon's local politics have been orientated towards growth – to attract jobs and people from outside. Meanwhile, in Teesside, the emphasis has been on defensive alliances between state and local industry to halt decline, although in the context of economic restructuring and a refashioned national politics, the possibility of such alliances has been eroded. Both Swindon and Teesside, it could be argued, are having to adjust to a new politics of growth and decline, reaching out this time to Europe rather than to the UK and its central state.

As was mentioned at the beginning, the three chapters offer various ways in which to think through the relation between the local and global. Each chapter, in related ways, provides an insight into how the geographical imagination works and why today what we know as the global only makes sense in relation to the local. In so doing, as with previous chapters, they provide a further example of *doing* social science.

John Allen

CHAPTER 19

Global Local Times

Kevin Robins

> History emerges on a world level and it therefore produces a space on this
> level: the formation of a world market, an international generalisation of the
> state and its problems, new relations between society and space. World space
> is the field in which our epoch is created.
>
> Henri Lefebvre

Times and geographies are changing. But just how much are they changing? And
what is the process of change all about? One important phenomenon has been
the increasing salience of localities and of localism. Over the past few years a
great deal of attention has been focused on local economies and local economic
development. The various initiatives and strategies undertaken by Labour
controlled authorities (notably in London, Sheffield and the West Midlands)
during the 1980s, are clear examples of this localizing tendency. In their highly
influential book, *The Second Industrial Divide*, economists Michael Piore and
Charles Sabel have gone so far as to argue that the re-emergence of local and
regional economies is actually a defining feature of a whole new historical period.
In their view, the relation between the economy and its territory is changing,
and we are seeing the reconsolidation of the locality or region as an integrated
unit of production. Piore and Sabel point to the growth, throughout the western
world, of new forms of localized production complexes and industrial districts.
Fundamental to the success of local and regional economies, they argue, are
important place-specific resources and endowments: strong local institutions and
infrastructures; relations of trust based on face-to-face contact; a 'productive
community' historically rooted in a particular place; and a strong sense of local
pride and allegiance.

But a resurgent localism is about more than new industrial dynamics and
strategies. It reflects a broader and far more pervasive mood of the times. Thus,
the 'struggle for place' is at the heart of much contemporary concern with urban
regeneration and the culture of cities. Prince Charles' recent crusade on behalf
of community architecture and classical revivalism is the most prominent and
influential example. There is a strong sense that if modernist architecture in the
early twentieth century was associated with universalizing and abstract tendencies,
contemporary architecture and design should draw upon the sense of place and
should be about revalidating and revitalizing the local and the particular. A neo-
Romantic fascination with traditional and vernacular motifs is supposedly about
the re-enchantment of the city. This cultural localism reflects, in turn, deeper

Source: article commissioned for this Reader.

feelings about the inscription of human lives and identities in space and time. There is a growing interest in the embeddedness of life histories within the boundaries of place, and with the continuities of identity and community through local memory and heritage. Witness the enormous popularity of the Catherine Cookson heritage trail in South Tyneside, of 'a whole day of nostalgia' at Beamish in County Durham, or of Wigan Pier's evocation of 'the way we were'.

Localism is scarcely a new phenomenon, of course. There have always been localities. Hence the recognition in the new economic geography that contemporary developments are about the re-emergence, rather than emergence, of local and regional economies. Hence, also, the awareness that new cultural geographies are being shaped around the *re*-valuation of place, the *re*-enchantment of the city, and the *re*-discovery of local traditions and heritage. And yet, for all that, there is something new and original happening. What are significant are the new contexts of locality and localism. If local differentiation once occurred in a national context, it is now being recast in a new continental and international framework. Sub-national localities are giving way to what might be called global localities. The prevailing geographical dynamic in the contemporary period is the logic of globalization. These are global times; times shaped by the increasing globalization of economies and cultures alike. It is the escalating logic of globalization – paradoxically it seems – that is the force behind the resurgence and revaluation of local economic and cultural activity. What seems to be emerging is the centrality of a new global–local nexus.

Historical capitalism has, of course, always strained to become a world system. The perpetual quest to maximize accumulation has always compelled geographical expansion in search of new markets, raw materials, sources of cheap labour, and so on. The histories of trade and migration, of missionary and military conquest, of imperialism and neo-imperialism, mark the various strategies and stages that have, by the late twentieth century, made capitalism a truly global force. If this process has brought about the organization of production and the control of markets on a world scale, it has also, of course, had profound political and cultural consequences. For all that it has projected itself as transhistorical and transnational, as the universalizing force of modernization and modernity, global capitalism in reality has been about westernization – the export of western commodities, values, priorities, ways of life. In a process of unequal cultural encounter, 'foreign' populations have been compelled to be the subjects and subalterns of western empire, while, no less significantly, Europe has come face to face with the 'alien' and 'exotic' culture of its 'Other'. Globalization, as it dissolves the barriers of distance, makes the encounter of colonial centre and colonized periphery immediate and intense.

What is globalization?

In the economic sphere, it is about the organization of production and the exploitation of markets on a world scale. This is, of course, not a new development. Since at least the time of the East India Company, it has been at the heart of entrepreneurial dreams and aspirations. What we are seeing is no more than the greater realization of long historical trends towards the global concentration of industrial and financial capital. Transnational corporations remain the key shapers and shakers of the international economy, and it is the ever more extensive and intensive integration of their activities that is the primary dynamic of the globalization process. It remains the case, more than ever, that 'size is power'. What we are seeing is the continuation of a constant striving to overcome national boundaries, to capture and coordinate critical inputs, and to achieve world-scale advantages.

But if this process is clearly about the consolidation of corporate command and control, it is nonetheless the case that, to this end, we are now seeing significant transformations and innovations in corporate strategy and organization. According to the chairman of General Electric Corporation, 'the challenge is to be able to combine the large corporation's resources and reach with the small company's simplicity and agility'. The limitations of nationally-centred multinationals are now becoming clear, and leading-edge companies like, for example, Procter and Gamble, Hewlett-Packard, Matsushita, NEC or Electrolux are now restructuring themselves as 'flexible transnationals' on the basis of a philosophy and practice of globalization. These companies must now operate and compete in the world arena in terms of quality, efficiency, product variety, and the close understanding of markets. And they must now operate in all markets simultaneously, rather than sequentially. Global corporations are increasingly involved in time-based competition: they must shorten the innovation cycle; cut seconds from process time in the factory; accelerate distribution and consumption times. Global competition pushes towards time-space compression.

Globalization is also about the emergence of the decentred or polycentric corporation. As business consultant Kenichi Ohmae suggests, global operations require a genuine 'equidistance of perspective', treating all strategic markets in the same way, with the same attention, as the home market. He sees Honda, operating in Japan, Europe and North America, as a typical case: 'Its managers do not think or act as if the company were divided between Japanese and overseas operations. Indeed, the very word "overseas" has no place in Honda's vocabulary because the corporation sees itself as equidistant from all its key customers.' This whole process has been associated with a corporate philosophy centred around the 'global product'. A universalizing idea of consumer sovereignty suggests that as people gain access to global information, so they develop global needs and demand global commodities, thereby becoming 'global citizens'. In his book, *The Marketing Imagination*, the pioneer of this approach, Theodore Levitt, forcefully argues that the new reality is all about global markets and world-standard products. This is, of course, no more than a continuation of mass production strategies which always sought economies of scale on the basis of expanding markets. However, whilst the old multinational corporation did this by operating in a number of countries and by adapting its products to national preferences, today's global corporation operates 'as if the entire world (or major regions of it) were a single, largely identical entity; it does and sells the same things in the same single way everywhere'. Transcending vestigial national

198

differences, the global corporation 'strives to treat the world as fewer standardised markets rather than as many customised markets'.

Of course, there is both hype and hyperbole in this. There has been a tendency to overemphasize the standardization of products and the homogenization of tastes. Nonetheless, it would be a mistake to dismiss this globalizing vision as simply another empty fad or fashion of the advertising industry. Levitt's position is, in fact, more complex and nuanced than is generally understood. What he recognizes is that global corporations do, indeed, acknowledge differentiated markets and customize for specific market segments. The point, however, is that this is combined with the search for opportunities to sell to similar segments throughout the globe. These same insights have been taken up in Saatchi and Saatchi's strategies for pan-regional and world marketing. Their well-known maxim that there are more social differences between midtown Manhattan and the Bronx than between Manhattan and the 7th Arrondissement of Paris, suggests the increasing importance of targeting consumers on the basis of demography and habits rather than on the basis of geographical proximity; marketing strategies are 'consumer-driven' instead of 'geography-driven'. What is at the heart of this economic logic of world brands remains the overriding need to achieve economies of scale, or more accurately, to achieve both scale and scope economies – that is, to combine volume and variety production – at the global scale.

Globalization also demands considerable changes in corporate behaviour; the flexible transnational must compete in ways that are significantly different from the older multinational firm. In a world of permanent and continuous innovation, a world in which costs must be recovered over a much larger market base, a world in which global span must be combined with rapid, even instantaneous, response, the global corporation must be lean and resourceful. In order to ensure its competitive position it must ensure a global presence: it must be 'everywhere at once'. This is bringing about significant changes in corporate strategy, with a huge burst of activity centred around mergers, acquisitions, joint ventures, alliances, inter-firm agreements and collaborative activities of various kinds. The objective is to combine mobility and flexibility with the control and integration of activities on a world scale.

Strategic alliances between companies have become an increasingly valued means to achieve this dual objective. Thus, to take the single example of the automobile industry, General Motors has developed an alliance with Toyota; Rover and Honda are jointly involved in design and product development; Nissan and Volkswagen market each other's products; Mazda and Ford have worked out a marketing agreement. In a global environment, few companies have the resources to function across all markets, and it becomes necessary to call upon the expertise of others in the areas of research, design or marketing. In Ohmae's words, 'in a world of imperfect options, alliances are often the fastest, least risky, and most profitable way to go global'. Through this form of agreement the global corporation seeks to position itself within a 'tight-loose' network: tight enough to ensure predictability and stability in dealings with external collaborators; loose enough to ensure manoeuvrability and even reversibility, to permit the redirection of activities and the redrawing of organizational boundaries when that becomes necessary.

The emergence of this global economic field has been associated with the creation of what might be called a new and global 'electronic space' or 'electronic geography'. Global companies need global communications networks. It is on the basis – and only on the basis – of new information and communications technologies that truly global corporate operations have now become viable. Computer-communications systems are fundamental to both the coordination of internal corporate activities and functions, and to the control of external transactions with suppliers, collaborators or customers. Only through the establishment of these information networks, of a new and global communications infrastructure, has it been possible to overcome the time and space barriers to corporate expansion. The global corporation is essentially a 'network corporation'; its coherence and integration are organized around the circulation of information and communication, around what has been called a global 'space of flows'.

These information grids have been described as the new 'electronic highways' of the information society. What must be recognized, however, is that they are being developed by global corporations as private and proprietary systems, available only to a restricted group of end-users. They are private roads, rather than open thoroughfares. Through the new satellite, cable and microwave links, we are seeing the growth of 'customer-specific' and 'dedicated' – that is closed – networks and services. This is the new infrastructure that underpins the globalization process, the infrastructure upon which new corporate monopolies and empires are being built across the world arena.

Cultural globalization

The historical development of capitalist economies has always had profound implications for cultures, identities and ways of life. The globalization of economic activity is now associated with further cultural transformation. We can talk of a process of cultural globalization.

What, then, is the nature of this process? At one level, it is about the manufacture of universal cultural products – a process which has, of course, been developing for a long time. In the new cultural industries, there is a belief – to use Saatchi terminology – in 'world cultural convergence'; a belief in the convergence of lifestyle, culture and behaviour among consumer segments across the world. This faith in the emergence of a 'shared culture' and a common 'world awareness' appears to be vindicated by the success of products like *Dallas* or *Batman* and by attractions like Disneyland. According to the president of the new Euro Disneyland, 'Disney's characters are universal. You try and convince an Italian child', he challenges, 'that Topolino – the Italian name for Mickey Mouse – is American'.

As in the wider economy, global standardization reflects, of course, the drive to achieve ever greater economies of scale. More precisely, it is about achieving both scale and scope economies (volume combined with variety) by targeting the shared habits and tastes of particular market segments at the global level, rather than by marketing, on the basis of geographical proximity, to different national audiences. The global cultural industries are increasingly driven to cover their escalating costs over the maximum market base, over pan-regional and world markets. They are driven by the very same globalizing logic that is reshaping the economy as a whole.

The new merchants of universal culture aspire towards a borderless world. Sky and BSB beam out their products to a world without frontiers; satellite footprints spill over the former integrity of national territories. With the globalization of culture, the link between culture and territory becomes significantly broken. What is being created is a new electronic cultural space, a 'placeless' geography of image and simulation. Cable News Network (CNN) has pioneered global news broadcasting by satellite; its service can now be received throughout the whole world. An axiomatic principle behind the founding of CNN was that the word 'foreign' did not exist. According to spokesperson Paul Amos, 'There has been a cultural and social revolution as a consequence of the globalization of the economy. A blue-collar worker in America is affected just as much as a party boss in Moscow or an executive in Tokyo. This means that what we do for America has validity outside America. Our news is global news.' This new global arena of culture is a world of instantaneous and depthless communication, a world in which space and time horizons have become compressed and collapsed.

The creators of this universal cultural space are the new global cultural corporations. In an environment of enormous opportunities and escalating costs, what is clearer than ever before is the relation between size and power. What we are seeing in the cultural industries is a recognition of the advantages of scale, and in this sphere too, it is giving rise to an explosion of mergers, acquisitions and strategic alliances. The most dynamic actors are rapidly restructuring to ensure strategic control of a range of cultural products across world markets. America's largest broadcasting company, NBC, is now, in the words of its vice-president, keenly 'developing global partnerships' and 'encouraging those companies in Europe and Japan who are interested in working in a partnered or allied way.'

The most prominent example of conglomerate activity is, no doubt, Rupert Murdoch's News Corporation, which has rapidly moved from its base in newspapers into the audiovisual sector. Through the acquisition of Fox Broadcasting, 20th Century Fox and Sky Channel, an (eventually successful) attempt at a joint venture with Disney, and now a renewed interest in the acquisition of MGM/UA, Murdoch is striving to become involved at all levels of the value chain. The most symbolic example of a global media conglomerate, however, is Sony, which is now, according to *Newsweek* magazine, 'buying a part of America's soul'. From its original involvement in consumer electronic hardware, Sony has now diversified into cultural software through the recent acquisitions of CBS and Columbia Pictures. The Sony–Columbia–CBS combination creates a communications giant, a 'total entertainment business', with combined revenues of over $20 billions. The long term strategy is to use this control over both hardware and software industries to dominate markets for the next generation of audiovisual products.

What is prefigurative about both News International and Sony, is not simply their scale and reach, but also their aspiration to be stateless, and 'headless'. These global cultural industries understand the importance of achieving a real equidistance, or equipresence, of perspective in relation to the whole world of their audiences and consumers.

If the origination of world-standardized cultural products is one key strategy, the process of globalization is, in fact, more complex and diverse. In reality, it is not possible to eradicate or transcend difference. Here, too, the principle of equidistance prevails: the resourceful global conglomerate exploits local difference and particularity. Cultural products are assembled from all over the world and turned into commodities for a new 'cosmopolitan' marketplace: world music and tourism; ethnic arts, fashion and cuisine; Third World writing and cinema. The local and 'exotic' are torn out of place and time to be repackaged for the world bazaar. So-called world culture may reflect a new valuation of difference and particularity, but it is also very much about making a profit from it. Theodore Levitt explains this globalization of ethnicity. The global growth of ethnic markets, he suggests, is an example of the global standardization of segments: 'Everywhere there is Chinese food, pitta bread, country and western music, pizza and jazz. The global pervasiveness of ethnic forms represents the cosmopolitanization of speciality. Again, globalization does not mean the end of segments. It means, instead, their expansion to worldwide proportions'. Now it is the turn of African music, Thai cuisine, aboriginal painting, and so on, to be absorbed into the world market and to become cosmopolitan specialities.

Jean-Hubert Martin's important and influential exhibition at the Pompidou Centre, *Magiciens de la Terre* (1989), is an interesting and significant monument, in the world of high art, of this new climate of cultural globalization. In this exhibition, Martin assembles original works by one hundred artists from all over the world: from the major artistic centres of Europe and America, but also from the 'margins' of Haiti, Nepal, Zaire and Madagascar. Here the discourse of high art converges with that of ethnography, the work of the Euro-American avant-garde is contiguous with that of Third World 'primitives'. Martin's aim in developing 'the truly international exhibition of worldwide contemporary art' was to question the 'false distinction' between Western cultures and other cultures, to 'show the real difference and the specificity of the different cultures', and to 'create a dialogue' between Western and other cultures. *Magiciens de la Terre* brings 'world art' into being. Artistic texts and artifacts are pulled out of their original contexts and then reinserted and reinterpreted in a new global context. Martin cultivates an 'equidistance of perspective' in which each exhibit, in equal dialogue with all the rest, is valued for its difference and specificity.

What is the significance and achievement of *Magiciens de la Terre*? Is there something more to it than simply absorbing new products into the international art market? Why does it resonate so much with the times? Well, at one level, the project is genuinely exciting and challenging. This kind of cosmopolitanism is to be preferred to parochialism and insularity, and there is indeed an immediate pleasure and exhilaration in seeing such a juxtaposition of diverse and vibrant cultures. But the exhibition touches deeper and darker chords. In its preoccupation with 'magic' and the 'spirituality' of Third World art, *Magiciens de la Terre* seeks to expose a certain emptiness, a spiritual vacuum, in Western culture. There is, of course, something very suspect and problematical about this Western idealization of 'primitiveness' and 'purity', this romance of 'other' cultures. The exhibition in no way confronts or handles this inadequacy, but nonetheless, even if there is no resolution, it does pose important questions about the nature of cultural identity. How do we now define ourselves as Western? And how does this Western identity relate to 'other', non-Western, identities in the world?

If the global collection and circulation of artistic products has been responsible for new kinds of encounter and collision between cultures, there have also been more direct and immediate exchanges and confrontations. The long history of colonialism and imperialism has brought large populations of migrants and refugees from the Third to the First World. Whereas Europe once addressed African and Asian cultures across vast distances, now they have installed themselves within the very heart of the Western metropolis. Through a kind of reverse invasion, the periphery has infiltrated the colonial core. The protective filters of time and space have disappeared, and the encounter with the 'alien' and 'exotic' is now instantaneous and immediate. The Western city has become a crucible in which world cultures are brought into direct contact. Through this implosion of empire, the certain and centred perspective of the old colonial order is confounded and confused.

As cultures have come to interact with each other, older certainties and hierarchies of identity have consequently been called into question. Of course, they do not disappear. Cultural nationalism and patriotism are always poised to reassert themselves in a storm of jingoism and xenophobia. Little Englandism has become a force to be reckoned with. Nonetheless, in a country that is now a container of African and Asian cultures, the sense of what it is to be English can never again have the old confidence and surety. Other sources of identity are no less fragile. What does it mean to be European in a continent coloured not only by the cultures of its former colonies, but also by American and now Japanese cultures? Is not the very category of identity itself problematical? Is it at all possible, in global times, to regain a coherent and integral sense of identity? Continuity and historicity of identity are challenged by the immediacy and intensity of global cultural confrontations. In these global times, we must confront, more than ever, the responsibilities of dialogue. This is true for all cultures and identities.

Time and distance no longer mediate the encounter with 'other' cultures. This drama of globalization is symbolized perfectly in the collision between Western 'liberalism' and Islamic 'fundamentalism'. How do we cope with the shock of confrontation? What does the responsibility of dialogue entail? These are perhaps the key political questions in this era of space/time compression. One danger is that we retreat into fortress identities. Another is that, in the anxious search for secure and stable identities, we politicize those activities – religion, literature, philosophy – that should not be directly political. The responsibility of dialogue means learning to listen to 'others' and learning to speak to, rather than for or about, 'other' cultures. That is easily said, of course, but not so easy to accomplish. Hierarchical orders of identity will not quickly disappear. Indeed, the very celebration and recognition of 'difference' and 'otherness' may itself conceal more subtle and insidious relations of power. When Martin turns world art into a spectacle in *Magiciens de la Terre*, might this not simply represent a new and enhanced form of Western colonial appropriation and assimilation?

Conclusion

Globalization is the awesome force shaping our times. These global times are about the compression of time and space horizons and the creation of a world of instantaneity and image. Global space is a space of flows, an electronic space, a space in which frontiers and boundaries have become permeable. Within this global arena, economics and cultures are thrown into intense and immediate contact with each other – with each 'Other' (an 'Other' that is no longer simply 'out there', but also within).

If it is globalization that defines these times, then what is the relevance or significance of the localizing forces I referred to at the start of this discussion? It is necessary now to return to our starting point and to reconsider the significance of the local. If it has been necessary to emphasize processes of de-localization, associated especially with the development of new information and communications networks, this should not be seen as an absolute tendency. The particularity of place and territory can never be done away with, can never be absolutely transcended. Globalization is, in fact, also associated with new dynamics of *re*-localization. It is about the achievement of a new global-local nexus, about new and intricate relations between global space and local space. In the words of the president of Nomura Securities of Japan, 'globalization is like putting together a jigsaw puzzle': it is a matter of inserting a multiplicity of localities into the overall picture of a new global system.

We should not invest our hopes for the future in the redemptive qualities of local economies, local cultures, local identities. The local is significant in the context of the emerging new global-local nexus, and we might perhaps describe the present period more appropriately as 'global-local times'. We should not idealize the local. It is important to see it as a relational, and relative, concept, and, if once it was significant in relation to the national sphere, now its meaning is being recast in the context of globalization. For the global corporation, the global-local nexus is of key and strategic importance. According to Olivetti's Carlo de Benedetti, in the face of ever higher development costs, '*globalization* is the only possible answer'. 'Marketers', he continues, 'must sell the latest product everywhere at once – and that means producing *locally*.' Similarly, the mighty Sony describes its operational strategy as 'global localization'. NBC's vice-president, J B Holston III, is also resolutely 'for localism', and recognizes that globalization is 'not just about putting factories into countries, it's being part of that culture too'. The electrical engineering company Asea Brown Boveri (ABB) claims to have mastered 'the art of being local worldwide': 'we are known for being truly multidomestic.'

What is being acknowledged is that globalization entails a presence in, and understanding of, the 'local' arena as a fully-fledged insider. But the 'local' in this sense does not correspond to any specific territorial configuration. The global-local nexus is about the relation between globalizing and particularizing dynamics in the strategy of the global corporation, and the 'local' should be seen as a fluid and relational space, constituted only in and through its relation to the global. For the global corporation, the local might, in fact, correspond to a regional, national or even pan-regional sphere of activity.

This is to say that the 'local' should not be mistaken for the 'locality'. It is to emphasize that the global-local nexus does not create a privileged new role for the locality in the world economic arena. Of course local economies continue to matter, but that is not the issue. The question of their power to act in the new global arenas is another matter. If it is, indeed, the case that localities do now increasingly bypass the national state to deal directly with global corporations, world bodies or foreign governments, they do not do so on equal terms. Whether it is to attract a new car factory or the Olympic Games, they go as supplicants. And, even as supplicants, they go in competition with each other: cities and localities are now fiercely struggling against each other to attract footloose and predatory investors to their particular patch. Of course, some localities are able successfully to connect themselves into the global networks, but others will remain outside. And, in a world characterized by the increasing mobility of capital and the rapid uses of space, even those that manage to become connected into the global system are always vulnerable to the abrupt withdrawal of investment and to disconnection from the global system.

The global-local nexus is also not straightforwardly about a renaissance of local cultures. There are those who argue that the old and rigid hegemony of national cultures is now being eroded from below by burgeoning local and regional cultures. Modern times are characterized, it is suggested, by a process of cultural decentralization and by the sudden resurgence of place-bound traditions, languages and ways of life. It is important not to devalue the perceived and felt vitality of local cultures and identities. But again, their significance can only be understood in the context of a broader and encompassing process. In the cultural sphere, too, these are global times; local cultures are overshadowed by an emerging 'world culture' (and still, of course, by rearguard national and nationalist cultures).

It may well be that, in some cases, the new global context is recreating the sense of place and sense of community in very positive ways, giving rise to an energetic cosmopolitanism in certain localities. In others, however, local fragmentation – remember the Saatchi point about the relationship between populations in midtown Manhattan and the Bronx -- may inspire a nostalgic, introverted and parochial sense of local attachment and identity. If globalization recontextualizes and reinterprets cultural localism, it does so in ways that are equivocal and ambiguous.

CHAPTER 20

Economic and Social Change in Swindon

Keith Bassett, Martin Boddy, Michael Harloe and John Lovering

Introduction

In 1841, with a population of only 2500, Swindon was selected by the Great Western Railway as the site for the rail engineering works which dominated the town up to the last war. Wartime industrial relocation and the postwar boom in consumer goods industries, electrical engineering and the car industry then brought a wave of new employers and a major influx of population. Collapse of manufacturing employment in the 1970s was more than offset by rapid expansion of financial and business services, distribution and new manufacturing sectors including plastics, electronics and pharmaceuticals. The town's workforce has virtually doubled since the early 1950s and its population expanded from 91,000 in 1951 to 151,000 by 1981. Until the last war it had all the characteristics of a northern industrial town, but one in the middle of rural Wiltshire. By the late 1980s it was a key growth centre in the booming M4 corridor.

This account looks first at successive phases of expansion which have reworked the town's economic and employment structure. It identifies the key role of new employers in job growth, the increased 'internationalization' of the 'local' economy, the changing gender composition of the workforce, and shifts in terms of corporate strategy and forms of work. It evaluates the processes underlying these changes, focusing in particular on the role of the local authority and the capacity for local 'pro-activity'. Finally, it looks at the complex interrelationship between economic restructuring and changes in class structure, politics and culture.

Economic change

Swindon's selection as the site for the rail engineering works reflected its strategic location on the GWR network – a junction of two lines where the gradient required a change of locomotives and canals supplied both coal and water (Peck,

Source: P. Cooke (ed.), *Localities: The Changing Face of Urban Britain*, 1989, London, Unwin Hyman, Chapter 2. (Title of original article: 'Living in the fast lane: economic and social change in Swindon'.)

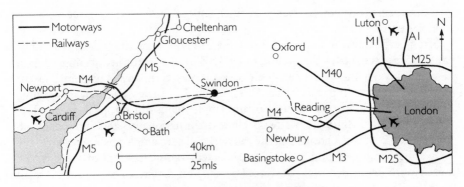

Figure 20.1   The Swindon locality

1983, pp. 8–10). Within a few years, a major, integrated industrial complex had been created. The Works expanded dramatically, producing locomotives, rolling stock and other railway equipment. By 1892 over 10,000 men were employed on one of the largest industrial sites in Europe and the town's population grew from around 7000 in 1861 to 51,000 by 1911, sharply differentiated from the surrounding area in economic, social and cultural terms.[. . .]

Between the wars expansion of road transport, and the collapse of the Welsh coal trade which had been a major source of traffic, brought an end to the era of guaranteed prosperity for the GWR, the railworks and the town. Employment fell from a peak of around 15,000 in the mid-1920s. Decline was, however, more gradual than in other localities dependent on heavy industry, the GWR benefiting from the growth of holiday traffic to the south-west and commuting into London. Apart from the railworks however, there were few significant employers before the Second War – a number of clothing companies, Wills cigarettes, and the Garrard record player company which had moved out from London.

The postwar boom

[. . .] From the mid-1950s [. . .] new employers contributed increasingly to employment growth. The Pressed Steel car body plant was particularly significant. This was established in 1955 after the government denied the company permission to increase capacity at Cowley. Enthusiastically supported by the borough council, the new plant was a major factor allowing the town to capture London's overspill and establish its credibility as a growth point. By 1961 the company employed over 4000, including around 1000 ex-Londoners and 600 skilled men from the railworks.

British Railway's 'modernization plan' largely staved off decline in rail engineering employment, leaving the number of jobs at around 10,000 in the early sixties – only 2000 down on 1950. Overall, therefore, the 1950s was a period of particularly rapid expansion. The town's population increased by around 3000 per year throughout the decade and employment increased by nearly 50 per cent in the ten years from 1952 to 1961. This reflected, above all, the boom in manufacturing, but employment remained concentrated in the engineering and vehicles sectors.

Strong growth was maintained throughout the 1960s, with employment up by 9000 (15 per cent) over the decade to 1971. Within a continued in-migration of new employers, the American high tech plastics company Raychem and the pharmaceutical company Roussel represented a new wave of expanding manufacturing industry. Manufacturing employment did not peak in absolute terms until 1970, four years after decline set in nationally, and significant job loss in the 1960s was confined to the railworks. There employment was virtually halved between 1965 and 1967. This reflected 'rationalization' of the national rail network under Beeching, decreased demand for maintenance and replacement with modern locomotives and stock.

The 1970s

The 1970s saw a fundamental shift in the town's economic and employment base. Heavy manufacturing job loss coincided with in-migration of new companies and marked growth of service employment. Unemployment climbed rapidly, as elsewhere, and heavy manufacturing job loss temporarily pushed the rate above national levels in 1974.[. . .] But, at a time when many local economies faltered and went into decline, Swindon successfully diversified away from manufacturing.[1] With the onset of recession nationally, growth was slower than in the 1960s, but total employment still expanded by 10 per cent over the decade compared with a 2 per cent drop nationally. There were, however, far-reaching economic and social implications. A third of the town's manufacturing employment was lost over the decade to 1981, service employment more than doubled, and there was a major increase in female employment (see below).

Major job losses were concentrated in electrical engineering, vehicles, metal and other engineering [. . .]. Rail engineering employment was relatively stable after major losses over the previous decade. Plessey, among the town's largest employers, disposed of all but one of its Swindon companies, including Garrard: a heavy loss of jobs. Garrard itself, employing 4000 in 1973, was hit hard by Japanese competition and finally closed in 1979. The domestic car industry ran into increasing difficulties in both export and domestic markets. Employment at the Swindon plant fell from around 5000 in 1979 to 3400 by 1981. New technology and major productivity gains also contributed to job loss although the plant, by now part of the Rover Group, remained a major local employer with 1986 employment of around 3000.

Major job gains through the 1970s were concentrated in financial services, distribution, professional and scientific services including education and medicine, and a range of other services. Modest net gains in some manufacturing sectors up to 1978 turned to losses virtually across the board thereafter. In-migration of new employers accelerated through the 1970s, with the emphasis shifting towards office-based employment and distribution. The Post Office established a national supplies centre, W. H. Smith set up a warehouse and distribution facility for its national retail chain, Burmah Oil established a purpose-built administrative headquarters, and Allied Dunbar set up its first Swindon office.[. . .]

The 1980s

Nationally, there was a sharp downturn in the economy in the early 1980s with heavy loss of manufacturing employment. This resulted in rising unemployment locally. Swindon, however, survived relatively well in terms of the national picture [. . .]. Employment grew by seven per cent in the three years 1981–84, compared with a one per cent drop nationally. There was strong growth in service employment – up by nearly nine per cent – and manufacturing employment actually expanded by three per cent, compared with an eleven per cent drop nationally [. . .].

Local job loss was again concentrated in the longer established engineering and metal goods sectors, including rail engineering [. . .]. But there was significant growth (over 2000 jobs) in chemical and non-metal products, and in electrical and electronic engineering: all these sectors recorded strong growth locally, compared with static or declining employment nationally. Service employment growth was concentrated in retailing, up by twenty-one per cent compared with static employment nationally, and in insurance, finance and business services, up by twenty-nine per cent, compared with seventeen per cent nationally. Together they added around 2800 jobs.

After 1984, unemployment remained significantly below national levels. Growth continued in financial services: Allied Dunbar, for example, expanded employment by nearly 500 between 1984 and 1988. Honda set up a UK pre-sales service centre on the old Vickers airport and was also establishing a fully automated engine plant on the site. These decisions were probably influenced by its joint production deal with Austin Rover and [. . .] have raised speculation that car assembly might follow.[2]

In 1984 major redundancies were announced at the railworks followed by closure in March 1986 and the loss of the remaining 2400 jobs. British Rail once again blamed the switch of freight to the roads, and decreased demand for maintenance and replacement. However, rationalization was influenced by the government's requirement that rolling stock be procured wherever possible by competitive tendering, and the unions argued that the main rationale was to make room for the private sector and prepare rail engineering itself for privatization. The flow of new establishments continued but these were primarily smaller companies rather than major relocations – W. H. Smith's retail head office employing around 150 was among the more significant moves.[. . .]

Internationalization

Increased competition in overseas markets, import penetration and inward investment have had marked and varied impacts in different localities. In Swindon's case collapse of export markets, removal of tariff barriers and increased penetration of UK markets, together with lack of investment, led to major rationalization and manufacturing job loss from the early 1970s, in firms like Plessey, Garrard and Austin Rover. Plessey refocused its activities on semi-conductor design and manufacture, employing around 750 locally in 1987, and operating successfully in a highly competitive international market. The Austin Rover plant expanded production for Saab, Volvo and Honda in order to decrease dependence on its parent company.

Inward investment by foreign-owned, particularly US companies (mainly in electronics, plastics and pharmaceuticals), first evident in the 1960s, has been increasingly significant. US multinationals increased their share of manufacturing employment in the town from 15 per cent in 1979 to around 27 per cent by 1985 (firms employing over 100) and total employment in US-owned companies was around 6500. Swindon was thus a major beneficiary of the increasing internationalization of the UK economy, attracting primarily US investment. Other major employers in recent rounds of investment, such as Allied Dunbar or W. H. Smith, are oriented primarily to UK national markets. A smaller number of companies, such as Raychem and the US-owned semi-conductor company Intel, have a more European orientation.

The changing gender division of labour

Increased female participation in paid employment, particularly part-time, has been a marked feature of labour force recomposition nationally. The scale and nature of gender recomposition has varied, however, across different localities. Swindon was until recently characterized by particularly low rates of female participation – 25 per cent locally in 1931 compared with 34 per cent nationally.[3] This reflected the dominance of male employment in rail engineering, which significant employers of women like Wills, Garrards, Plessey and the clothing companies did little to offset. Female employment in manufacturing expanded in the postwar boom, but growth in Pressed Steel and other companies largely maintained the dominance of male manufacturing employment. It was not until the 1960s that female participation rapidly caught up with and overtook national levels.[. . .]

Over the 1970s there was [. . .] a major shift in the overall balance of the workforce towards female employment, reflecting in particular growth in female part-time employment. In the early 1980s, however, male employment grew faster than female employment [. . .] and, in marked contrast to the 1970s, part-time female employment actually fell – by seven per cent compared with continued though modest growth nationally. This reflects a trend common to several of the more prosperous, M4 corridor localities. This loss of part-time female employment was concentrated in public administration, defence and medical services, around 2000 down between 1981 and 1984, only partially offset by an increase in part-time employment in retailing. Full-time female employment, on the other hand, grew strongly.

Changing industrial structure, particularly the switch from manufacturing to services, has been the major factor in gender recomposition in the longer term. Employment has grown in sectors characterized by a relatively high proportion of female employment. This includes sectors in which a significant proportion of employment is in jobs defined as 'women's work'.[. . .] Employment has also expanded in activities such as financial services in which there is significant female employment but where it is concentrated disproportionately in lower grades.[. . .] Examples of 'feminization', in the sense of female inroads into formerly male occupational preserves, are rare. Despite the dynamism of the local economy and rapid employment growth in some sectors, there is little evidence, therefore, that gender divisions at work have been significantly eroded.

Corporate strategies and new forms of work

Economic expansion and diversification have been reflected in major changes in work culture, organization and control. Postwar growth of engineering imported traditional 'Fordist' work practices based on firm hierarchical control, the skilled manual proletariat and large-scale flow-line production processes. These are still reflected in some sections of manufacturing. With continued in-migration, however, and fewer long-established employers than in many localities, forms of work and management-labour relations owe less to earlier rounds of investment and represent a cross-section of more contemporary patterns of corporate strategy and work structure. Incoming employers have imported a variety of pre-existing management practices and work cultures. Relocation and expansion also, however, afford opportunities for social and technical innovation, including the introduction of new technology and work practices.

Rapid decline in manufacturing from the late 1960s hit male, hierarchically structured and heavily unionized employment. Subsequent expansion has greatly increased the number and diversity of employers, forms of work and work culture. Firstly, office-based clerical labour has become increasingly important. Hierarchically structured, this is typically characterized by consensual management styles and an absence of unions. It includes 'career' grades characterized by clear promotional paths, professional identification and a high degree of vertical segregation along gender lines. There has also, however, been a major expansion of routinized clerical employment, primarily female, such that sections at least of some of the larger office-based employers are effectively information processing 'clerical factories' but without the traditions of shopfloor organization. Work pressures can be keen: 'you have to live and die for work, you have to do overtime and to be there when they want you ' (a), and 'although the money's good, they expect you to work like slaves . . . they push you to the limit, it's work, work, work' (b).[4]

Secondly, there has been a major growth of relatively low-paid employment in retailing, cleaning, catering and other services. Much of this is female employment and much of it is part-time. In the private sector, it is predominantly not unionized and offers little job security: 'there's no security, there is no such thing. It doesn't matter how loyal you are to your company now . . . you are just one of a number. If we want you this week, we'll have you. If we don't want you next week, we'll get rid of you' (c). The public sector, on the other hand, is characterized by greater job security and union recognition.[. . .]

Employment growth has also been accompanied by qualitative change in the way in which labour is used. In some cases, use of part-time labour has been increased to achieve flexibility, particularly in the volume of labour inputs.[5] As elsewhere, this is common in contract cleaning and much of retailing, for example. It is also used, however, in order processing activities like the book clubs, and one major employer has adopted an explicit strategy of job splitting for a significant proportion of its lower grade clerical labour. A number of newer employers make significant use of temporary labour to meet seasonal and other peaks in demand. Labour is called in as needed from a pool of temporary workers maintained on company books, and permanent employees are generally recruited from these 'temps' as needed. Other companies have developed quite complex shift systems designed in part to meet company needs in terms of labour inputs and to tap into specific sections of the labour market – women working part-time, for example. Again, this includes employers across a range of different sectors such as electronics, retailing and mail order.[. . .]

Economic expansion of the role of local policy

Local policy, committed to growth and physical expansion since 1945, has played a key role in Swindon's economic and social transformation. It was, however, the town's location within the changing urban and regional system of the UK, and in particular its location relative to the south-east economic heartland, which enabled it to sustain its trajectory of growth and diversification through a number of distinct phases which built on and reworked what had gone before.

Town expansion, 1945–64

There was concern locally, even before the war, over declining rail employment. Wartime expansion and relocation, however, radically altered the policy context and provided an initial basis for town expansion and diversification. Council policy immediately after the war favoured retention of wartime industry, provision of new trading estates, central area redevelopment, new neighbourhood areas and satellite villages – precisely the pattern of development realized over the next thirty years. National policy was not initially favourable. The wartime Barlow and Abercrombie Reports set the context for decentralization of industry and population to new growth centres. Regional policy, however, sought to direct industry to designated development areas, restricting development elsewhere by the use of Industrial Development Certificates, and Swindon was considered too large and too far from London to form the nucleus of a New Town under the 1946 Act.

Election of the 1951 Conservative government, however, and concern over the slow pace of decentralization to new towns, brought a change in the national policy context. The 1952 Town Development Act provided for 'overspill' agreements between designated 'expanded towns' and local authorities in the conurbations. Swindon's designation under the Act, with ministerial approval for expansion by around 23,000 to 92,000, was rapidly accomplished, and agreements were secured with Tottenham and with the London County Council (Harloe, 1975).

Board of Trade approval for Pressed Steel in 1955, for which the local council fought hard, and subsequent relaxation of IDC controls, marked the start of new industrial growth. Policy change was reinforced by its coincidence with the boom in UK manufacturing industry. Initially, relocation of manufacturing firms, particularly from London, was an important component. Decentralization was notably encouraged by the shortage and escalating cost of labour and premises in the capital, compared with Swindon. Engineering skills were readily available, together with an expanding supply of semi-skilled and unskilled labour, facilitated by the provision of local authority housing. Proximity to London was also a factor, many firms seeking to minimize the distance moved. Swindon was particularly successful in its use of the 1952 Act. Initial expansion was rapid, with population overspill from London, around 20,000 on some estimates, an important factor. The pace of growth slackened in the mid-1960s, reflecting tighter IDC controls, slower economic growth and competition from other New Towns closer to London. New employers had been attracted in, but contrary to the council's postwar hopes, only limited diversification away from engineering and vehicles had been achieved.

A strategic place in the south-east, 1964–73

Rapid population growth in the south-east, and pressure for development beyond the London green belt, prompted a series of strategic planning studies, the 1964 South-east Study in particular. In 1965 consultants identified the Newbury-Hungerford area to the east as a possible new city location but this was later rejected in favour of Swindon. Swindon's enthusiastic response to strategic growth proposals, plus its track record of successful expansion, were key factors. This contrasted with opposition from residents and local authorities closer to London. The report proposed Swindon's expansion into a new city with a population of 250,000 by 1981 and 400,000 by 2001.[. . .]

Decisions at national level on infrastructure development consolidated Swindon's position within the western growth corridor. The choice of Heathrow as Britain's international airport in 1941 was a formative early decision. The routing of the M4 motorway, opened in 1971, past the southern edge of town was crucial, and emerged from protracted negotiations in which Swindon's status as an expanding town was a factor (Hall et al., 1987, p. 165). The M4 gave access to Heathrow and London and tied Swindon in to the expanding national motorway net. This emphasized its growth potential in terms of regional and national distribution and services, realized through the 1970s with the arrival of employers like Anchor Butter, Post Office Supplies and W. H. Smith with national distribution networks. Early introduction of the High Speed Train on the Swindon line was important both for business travel back to London and for commuting, whether to Swindon or, increasingly, from Swindon to central Berkshire and London. As Hall et al. (1987) conclude, the M4 corridor and Swindon as a key node within it, 'grew as a result of heavy, if uncoordinated public investment – by a process of disjointed incrementalism, without conscious understanding of its possible consequences'.[. . .]

M4 corridor magnet

With falling birth rates and slower economic growth nationally, the more grandiose 'new city' plans of the 1960s were not fully realized, but there was, nevertheless, major growth in population and employment. The collapse in manufacturing employment and the sharp rise in unemployment in the early 1970s, however, led to policy reassessment locally. In 1977 the council launched a new industrial promotion strategy and set up Swindon Enterprise as a semiautonomous marketing agency headed by a former commercial director from Plessey. His image of Swindon was a town 'fifty minutes by high speed train from London, one hour from Heathrow, next to the M4 in the golden corridor but cheaper than rival towns, surrounded by stunning countryside with lots of old rectories for executives to live in'.[6] The emphasis was on attracting high technology companies and office headquarters, profitable concerns which did not need development area subsidies to survive. Campus-style business park development was explicitly encouraged through the planning process.

By the 1980s, Swindon occupied a particular position within the south-east labour market based on the juxtaposition of an expanding concentration of basic white-collar, clerical and manufacturing employment, with rural Wiltshire and towns (Marlborough, Bath, Bristol) attractive to technical, professional and managerial groups.[. . .]

Housing and lifestyle factors are particularly important for such workers. The consequence is that employers located in Swindon can in turn recruit and retain types of key staff who favour a general M4 corridor location.

Expansion from the late 1960s had been rooted in the strategic planning framework for the south-east. By the late 1970s, however, any form of strategic planning at national government level had disappeared. Continued expansion reflected more generalized pressure for growth in the M4 corridor. Recession deepened after 1979. The south-east, however, consolidated its economic dominance within the UK economy, reflected in the growing 'north-south divide'. Expansion of financial and business services reflected London's role in the international economy and there was a growing concentration of newer manufacturing activity and high technology in the region. Partial recovery in the mid-1980s only served to re-emphasize regional imbalance, again working to Swindon's advantage.

New directions?

By the mid-1980s, however, a combination of factors led to major policy reappraisal. This was summarized in the 1984 consultative document, New Vision for Thamesdown (Thamesdown Borough Council, 1984b). The council's long-held claim that continued expansion, new housing and jobs benefited existing residents, rather than simply fostering in-migration, was increasingly questioned within the ruling Labour group and there were some signs of hostility to continued expansion among existing residents. According to the consultation document, the clear vision which had sustained the strategy of town expansion in the post war years had become increasingly blurred.

In particular, it was felt that the council had lost much of the control and influence which it had previously exercised over the pace and form of town expansion. Central government attempts to control local authority expenditure placed severe financial constraints on the council, and from 1985/86 the council was 'ratecapped' along with overtly left-wing London boroughs and authorities like Liverpool. In Swindon's case, this reflected debt charges resulting from high levels of capital expenditure on town expansion in the past which, ironically, had been explicitly encouraged by central government.

On top of this, the council's landholdings were nearing exhaustion with little prospect of significant acquisitions given not only the new financial constraints but also rising land values which priced it out of the market. The council could no longer, therefore, exercise the degree of control over the development process which it had in the past as a major landowner. Public expenditure constraints posed further problems in terms of infrastructure and service provision. Future development was now therefore largely reliant on the private sector.[. . .]

Pressures for housing development in the south-east were intense in the late 1980s, reflecting the region's economic buoyancy. Opposition to further residential land release from established residents had intensified, however, both in Wiltshire and adjoining western corridor counties and in the region as a whole. There was increasing concern over escalating house prices in the south-east and evidence of labour and skill shortage as a result. Given the regional context there was growing evidence that Swindon was becoming in effect a safety valve for the south-east, taking development pressure off other localities. The motor for growth in the late 1980s was thus increasingly residential development as well as economic expansion per se. Swindon was increasingly seen as a lower-priced dormitory area, particularly for Berkshire and London, indicated by the sharp increase in rail commuting.

Development at Swindon was likely to be politically acceptable to a government keen to demonstrate its faith in comprehensive planning and development led by the private sector. It was, however, caught between pressure from the development industry for land release and vociferous local resistance to further development from predominantly Conservative areas. The problem for the local authorities was one of fulfilling a regional function, but with very limited local resources and powers. Pressure on the Secretary of State to back the development was however strong and approval was granted in 1988. As with earlier phases of development – postwar town expansion and the 'new city' period – the possibilities for Swindon's continued growth again reflected the broader regional context. The nature of these pressures, in particular demands for residential development, and the capacity of the local council to control and influence the pattern of development, were, however, very different by the late 1980s.

Class, politics and cultural change

Economic growth and diversification, and the major influx of population and new employers, have had profound implications for class and social structure, politics and everyday life in Swindon. Social and political change has in turn shaped these processes of economic change.[. . .]

Class and social structure

Up to the 1950s, Swindon's social structure, institutions and community life reflected the dominance of male manufacturing employment, in particular skilled engineering employment in the railworks. Rapid employment growth in the 1950s further emphasized this bias towards skilled and semi-skilled engineering, which left foremen and skilled workers significantly over-represented compared with the national picture, and employers, managers and professional workers under-represented. Between 1961 and 1981 however, employers, managers and professionals increased their share of total employment locally from 9 per cent to 17 per cent while the share of foremen and skilled workers fell from 43 per cent to 31 per cent.[7] This brought the town's occupational structure much closer to the national picture. There was thus a marked decline in traditionally dominant strata of male manual workers. But while skilled manual groups, the 'working class aristocracy', declined, semi-skilled and unskilled manual workers maintained their share of the workforce, as a consequence of a 'deskilling' of the overall manual workforce.

Under-representation of employers, managers and professional groups had largely disappeared by the 1980s. The 'new service class'[8] expanded with the growth of higher-level administrative and financial functions, new manufacturing and high technology industry. Indicative of the increasing importance of white collar employment more generally, intermediate non-manual occupations increased their share of the workforce from 13 per cent to 18 per cent in the decade to 1981.[9] The number of people with degrees or higher professional qualifications doubled.[10]

Growth of routinized, non-manual labour, much of it in the service sector, has greatly expanded the 'white collar proletariat'.[11] In a sense, Swindon is still a working class town. The nature of that working class has been transformed, however. This is reinforced by the fact that many managers and professionals working in Swindon live in the surrounding rural villages – small towns like Marlborough or Cirencester and further afield, for example in Bath, Bristol or Oxford.[. . .]

Local politics

Up to the Second World War, formal electoral politics locally were heavily dominated by the pervasive influence of the GWR. Sir Daniel Gooch, GWR's first locomotive supervisor at the works and later chairman of the company, was the town's MP from 1865 to 1885. Swindon's first mayor was locomotive superintendent at the works and by the early 1920s up to nineteen of the thirty-six local councillors worked for the GWR, including manual and clerical workers and management. The town's petty bourgeoisie – the small traders, professionals and shopkeepers – represented on the council were in any case largely dependent on the fortunes of the town's dominant employer.

Between the wars 'Citizens' League' members and, later, 'Independents' held the majority on the council. Though politically conservative, they were not affiliated to the Conservative Party, did not meet as a formal group, and tended to be strongly 'localist' in outlook. The Labour Party had four seats by 1920 and made significant gains between the wars. It was not until 1945, however, that it won control of the council, major gains reflecting the strength of the unions and labour movement locally – and, indeed, in much of the country at this time. Independents regained power from 1949 to 1951 and remained the major opposition group right through to 1968.

After the war, the locally oriented Independents contributed to strong non-partisan support on the council for town expansion. The policy itself was developed and implemented by a relatively small group of Labour members and key officers, in particular the town clerk, David Murray John. They were, however, able to sustain wide support both within the council and from a broader range of interests locally, including the unions and rail works management. This pro-growth coalition represented a form of territorial alliance with some similarities to the spatial coalition on Teesside in the 1960s committed to 'modernization' [. . .] and support for economic development policies in Lancaster [. . .]. The coalition reflected political patterns established during GWR dominance and the continuing railway presence on the council. With the threat of declining employment in the railworks, the unions argued strongly for the retention of wartime industry and diversification of the town's industrial base, while management saw that expansion would facilitate anticipated cuts in the workforce. Expanding companies, in particular Vickers and Plessey, experiencing labour shortages, were keen to see the town's workforce expand, and urged the provision of local authority housing, though they did not favour increased competition from new employers.

Later years saw local politics increasingly organized and fought on national party lines. The Independents were rapidly eclipsed by the Conservatives in 1968, [and] Conservatives gained control of the Council from 1968 to 1970. Labour, however, regained control in 1971 and have retained it since then, except for a brief period when they lost overall control.[. . .]

The Conservatives did, however, win the Swindon parliamentary seat in 1979 – a surprise result in a long-held Labour constituency. The Conservatives retained it in 1983, and again in 1987 with an increased majority, suggesting a more basic shift in the constituency's political base. The contrast with Labour strength at district council level partly reflects different boundaries. The Alliance gained three seats on the district council in 1987, two from Labour, though whether this is indicative of any longer-term trend is not yet clear. The view is commonly expressed locally that social change must eventually tell against Labour: 'I think they've made a rod for their own backs' (d) and:

'Labour are in grave danger of doing themselves out . . . the prices these houses are going for . . . you're getting commuters to London and they ain't going to vote Labour. One of these days they'll get ousted. As it expands it will become a Conservative town.' (f)

Similar views have however been expressed throughout the postwar period without being realized.

By the mid-1980s a shift was evident within the Labour Group, with the election of younger, more ideologically motivated councillors. The old 'municipal entrepreneurialism' which had carried Labour councils through the 1960s and 1970s began to be questioned by those with perspective closer to the 'new urban left'. The divisions were however, much less sharply drawn than in many Labour councils which shifted to the left in the 1970s. There were signs of change in the Conservative Party as well, with a more Thatcherite outlook increasingly evident.

Thus there was some sharpening of the party political divide in the 1980s, although ambiguities remained. Conservative councillors and the MP Simon Coombs gave at least token support to the campaign against the closure of the rail works, though Labour and the unions made the running on this. In 1985–86 local Conservatives called on Labour to sell land and freeze recruitment to avoid ratecapping, and investigated the possibility of a deal with the minister in return for sale of council assets, a move angrily condemned by Labour. Even so, Conservative views were not clear-cut.[. . .]

Culture and locality

Life in Swindon up to the last war revolved around the railworks: 'just everybody used to work in the railway. GWR was Swindon and that was it' (k). The heavily structured work culture and the rhythms of activity in the works permeated the community to which it gave birth (Williams, 1915; Peck, 1983). Both daily life and major social occasions centred on the works. The annual children's fete, which continued up to the last war, was attended by 34,000 in 1904. In 1905, the annual holiday week, 'the trip', saw 24,500 people, almost half the population, leave the town on 22 special trains. This dominance declined only slowly in postwar years and the feelings of older residents over the final closure of the works in 1986 reflected the loss of something much more than simply jobs:

> 'From a personal point of view, I think we've lost our heritage, because I was born when Swindon *was* railway and I believe that that was real, and I think the high tech is plastic. I think it's made possibly a generation of 50-year-olds feel a bit useless really . . . they were skilled workers . . . very skilled . . . I think the suit and briefcase lady is coming to be. . . . We've lost our culture, the railway culture was a way of life.' (f)

Popular identification of the town with rail engineering remained strong even in the 1980s. Right through from the nineteenth century to the 1980s, if you worked in the railworks you were 'inside'. Over half the respondents to the 1986 survey still associated Swindon closely with railways and rail engineering. The dominant feelings, however, were regret and nostalgia – 'it's sad because we're talking about tradition, heritage' (i) – commonly coupled with more hard-nosed realism: 'Everyone says it's a shame about the railway, and it is. But at the end of the day it's something that had to happen. If it's not making money, it had to go'. (j)

Postwar expansion greatly increased the number and diversity of employers. There was much less overlap between people's work and non-work lives, and the growing population had much less in common in terms of work experiences. With massive in-migration from London and elsewhere, much of the town was marked by the newness of the population and the lack, initially at least, of extended social networks.[. . .]

In terms of urban fabric, there are references back, reconstructions and pastiche: the renovated railway village cottages, the railway museum and the 'Brunel' shopping centre.[. . .] The Western Expansion and planned northern sector development have self-consciously adopted an 'urban village' format. And the planned Tarmac development on the railworks site incorporates high density, disorganized 'village type' housing developments along with 'museumification' of retained buildings.

This postmodernist emphasis on heritage and reconstruction is overshadowed, thus far, by late modernist high tech, the main contender for the dominant image of the locality. Over three-quarters of respondents to the 1986 survey agreed that the town is closely associated with high technology and computers, despite the small percentage of employment actually in high technology defined on the basis of official statistics. The high tech, M4 corridor image has been consciously cultivated by council policy and, importantly, by the private property sector seeking to sell new developments. The council has used the pressure for development and relocation to secure high design standards for both residential and commercial development. Archetypal 'high tech' architecture strongly projects this image of modernity. It includes specific buildings such as the silver and glass Murray John Tower dominating the town centre and symbolically named after the former town clerk, the nationally famous Foster-designed Renault building, futuristic campus-style developments, and the town centre office cluster, a 'mini-Manhattan', dominated by Allied Dunbar.

Things can look very different, however, from the perspective of the seven thousand unemployed, a group which fits uneasily with the images of expansion and modernity. As one unemployed 23-year-old saw it:

'it sounds pretty daft, but in Swindon at the moment, they seem to be recruiting a lot of people from outside, especially with skills, and bringing them all in, and unemployed who actually have lived here virtually all their lives, they are finding it difficult to get work because it's all specialized industry' (h).

Over 75 per cent of people interviewed in the 1986 survey thought that it was no different being unemployed in Swindon than elsewhere. Of those who thought it was different, the majority suggested it was easier to find work, and the feeling that people can find work if they really look for it seems to be stronger in Swindon than in many places. Attitudes to unemployment seem different compared with areas more accustomed to high levels of unemployment: 'there are so many unemployed up at home, in Sunderland, that it is almost the norm, it's accepted, that, and I think that in Swindon, it's an unusual thing not to be working'. (g) [. . .]

Conclusion

Swindon's economic and social transformation demonstrates the central importance of the relationship between change at locality level and the restructuring of the broader urban and regional system, itself inextricably bound up with the shifting nexus of forces at national and international levels. Through successive stages of development, the location of the town, particularly in relation to the south-east region, has been crucial. The nature of this relationship changed, however, through successive periods of economic and social development: the town's strategic location on the GWR network, its location beyond supposed bombing range in the Second World War, postwar town expansion based on overspill from inner London, the 'new city era' linked to broader regional growth pressures and strategic planning policy and, most recently, pressures for economic and social development which reflect the town's nodal position as a key growth centre within the M4 corridor and its integration into the increasingly dispersed urban and regional system of the south-east heartland.

Successive waves of development built on and reworked what had gone before. Wartime relocation of manufacturing and the postwar boom in engineering built on the tradition of skilled engineering. Later service growth drew on the availability of female labour. The different stages of growth and development were, however, to some extent independent in origin and overlaid one on the other. It is more than a truism that, but for its location, Swindon might be little different now from the northern industrial towns which it resembled up to 1945, but which were hit by the collapse of traditional manufacturing sectors. It is the succession of rail engineering, wartime industrial production, postwar engineering boom, growth of services and distribution, and, lastly, M4 corridor growth that is distinctive to Swindon.

At one level, then, the locality is increasingly integrated into the regional and indeed national and international economy and labour market. Internally, however, the picture at locality level is one of increasing fragmentation and complexity, with new employers, new forms of economic activity and new forms of work.[. . .]

Local policy and the particular configuration of local interests in Swindon were necessary factors determining the pace and form of town development. Local policy sharply differentiated the locality from neighbouring areas and indeed much of the outer south-east region. Pro-active capacity should not, however, be thought of as some form of independent ability of local policy or interests to achieve their goals. It reflects, rather, a specific combination of local factors and wider context. The 'pro-active capacity' of the local authority can only be understood in terms of Swindon's place in relation to the south-east regional economy. It lay in the council's commitment and ability to capitalize on the town's growth potential, afforded by its position within the changing urban and regional system of the UK and the consolidation, within this, of the south-east region as the country's economic heartland. Policy at the level of the nation state has also played a key role at different points in time, including planned wartime relocation of industry, reconstruction, protectionism and its demise, as well as specific regional policy and strategic planning. Essentially uncoordinated policy decisions on infrastructure have nevertheless combined to consolidate growth within the western corridor and Swindon's place within this. One can also point to the role of government in supporting and facilitating London's role as a key international financial centre as contributing to continued growth pressure within the south-east. With increased integration into the south-east economy and increasingly centralized government control, the role specifically of local policy, and the scope for local pro-activity, has, however, been undermined.[. . .]

As at the economic level, in social and cultural terms the town has become increasingly fragmented and complex. Working class solidarity, collectivism and community ties have given way to home-centred individualism and social fragmentation. In a sense this reflects the growing homogeneity of local and regional culture and ways of life. The locality has become more like other growth centres in the outer south-east. But this internal fragmentation is all the more marked because of the contrast with patterns of life associated in the past with rail engineering, the scale of expansion and in-migration and the pace of economic transformation. Once everybody, it seemed, was 'inside'. Economic and social change, however, has turned the town inside out.

Notes

1 Overall and sectoral employment figures are from the Department of Employment, Annual Census of Employment. Figures and information relating to individual companies derive from detailed case studies of a panel of local employers carried out in 1986 and 1987. All statistical information relates to the Swindon travel-to-work area, unless otherwise noted. The TTWA extends beyond the area of Thamesdown Borough Council, although the latter includes the major employment centre. The local authority boundary was extended in 1984 to include the Western Expansion and the name changed from Swindon to Thamesdown.

2 The outcome and possible implications of the British Aerospace bid for the Rover Group in March 1988 were unclear at the time of writing.

3 Figures refer to Swindon Borough.

4 Quotes here and following are from semi-structured interviews carried out with a panel of households in Swindon TTWA in 1987. The panel was grouped into five categories: professional and managerial workers, female clerical workers, women working part-time, male workers in traditional manufacturing, and unemployed. The selection frame for this panel was the SCEL survey. Letters in brackets refer to the appendix which gives brief details of respondents quoted.

5 The 1986 SCEL Employer Survey indicated that 23 per cent of employers had increased their use of part-time employment over the previous five years and 10 per cent had replaced full-time with part-time employment. Increased flexibility in terms of labour inputs was the main motive.

6 Quoted in the *Financial Times*, 30 June 1986.

7 Population Census, Swindon Borough, economically active males by grouped socio-economic group.

8 'Those occupations, often characterised by a high level of material reward and considerable autonomy within the work itself, that direct, administer and control . . .

the major institutions of advanced capitalist society, both public and private'. (Crompton and Jones, 1984, p. 4.) See also Abercrombie and Urry (1983).

9 Population Census, Swindon TTWA, male and female, social class.

10 Population Census, Swindon TTWA.

11 See the extended analysis of Crompton and Jones (1984) which emphasizes the fragmentation of the 'office proletariat' by age and qualification but in, particular, gender.

References

Abercrombie, N. and Urry, J. (1983) *Capital, Labour and the Middle Classes*, London, Allen and Unwin.

Atkinson, J. (1984) 'Manpower strategies for flexible organisations', *Personnel Management*, August.

Crompton, R. and Jones, G. (1984) *White Collar Proletariat: Deskilling, and Gender in Clerical Work*, London, Macmillan.

Hall, P., Breheny, M., McQuaid, R. and Hart, D. (1987) *Western Sunrise: the Genesis and Growth of Britain's Major High Tech Corridor*, Hemel Hempstead, Allen and Unwin.

Harloe, M. (1975) *Swindon: A Town in Transition*, London, Heinemann.

Hudson, K. (1967) *An Awkward Size for a Town: A Study of Swindon at the 100,000 Mark*, London, David and Charles.

Peck, A. S. (1983) *The Great Western at Swindon Works*, Poole, Oxford Publishing Company.

Thamesdown Borough Council (1984a) *Employment Information Report*, Corporate Planning Unit.

Thamesdown Borough Council (1984b) *A New Vision for Thamesdown*, Consultation Document.

Williams, A. (1915), *Life in a Railway Factory*, Gloucester, Alan Sutton.

Appendix: Key to interviews

(a) Twenty-eight-year-old female clerical worker.

(b) Twenty-one-year-old female clerical worker, in financial services.

(c) Fifty-eight-year-old female clerical worker, recently made redundant in retail sector following computerization.

(d) Thirty-four-year-old woman, who moved to Swindon from London with parents and lived in Swindon most of her life.

(e) Thirty-two-year-old civil engineer living since 1983 in Purton, a village just west of Swindon.

(f) Forty-four-year-old nurse, working part-time, who has lived in Swindon all her life. Her husband works for British Rail as a train driver.

(g) Thirty-four-year-old-unemployed man living in Western Expansion whose wife works full-time, and who has a history of paid community work. Originally from Sunderland, he moved to Swindon in 1985.

(h) Male in early twenties, came to college in Swindon from North Wales and has been looking for work since finishing his course.

(i) Male field services manager who moved to Shrivenham, outside Swindon about nine years ago.
(j) Twenty-seven-year-old part-time shop-worker who had lived in Swindon for twenty-one years.
(k) Fifty-two-year-old female working part-time as a cleaner in a private nursing home, who had lived all her life in Swindon.

CHAPTER 21

Coming to Terms with the Future in Teesside

Huw Beynon, Ray Hudson, Jim Lewis, David Sadler and Alan Townsend

[. . .] Is 'the game up' for Teesside today? And what do the 'rules' of this 'game' mean for the ways in which people can and do live their lives? Such questions inform this chapter. It explores how international currents of production and trade (not just in shipbuilding, but in other industries like coal, steel, and chemicals, and more recently even in some service activities) have flowed into and out of Teesside. These processes have both shaped and been shaped by the changing social, economic and political character of a changing locality.[. . .]

International and national currents of change and the Teesside economy

'The trouble with most local histories of Middlesbrough,' commented one young supervisor of a Community Programme project dealing with just such a project, 'is that they all seem to ignore the outside world.' Understandable though this is, it is indeed unfortunate, especially given the strong historical ties between Teesside's two dominant manufacturing industries and the national and international markets.

As the iron and steel industry grew and evolved through a process of centralization, the major company to emerge was Dorman Long.[. . .] By 1929 it employed 29,000 men and had the capacity to make 1.5 million tonnes of steel annually. It had diversified into engineering and represented an archetypal example of the 'coal combines' which consolidated their control over a variety of branches of production in the north-east during the interwar period. By 1939 it owned eight collieries in County Durham, employing 9000 men to produce 4 million tonnes of coal annually.[. . .] After 1945 these colliery interests were divested to the National Coal Board and the steel business was affected by the short-lived nationalization of 1951.

As part of the British Steel Corporation (a second, more durable exercise in nationalization) from 1967 [. . .] [to 1989], the future of steel production in

Source: P. Cooke (ed.), *Localities: The Changing Face of Urban Britain*, 1989, London, Unwin Hyman, Chapter 8. (Title of original article: ' "It's all falling apart here": coming to terms with the future in Teesside.')

Teesside seemed secure, especially with the announcement of BSC's Ten Year Development Strategy in 1973 (HMSO, 1973). With world steel demand forecast to grow at 4–5 per cent annually up to 1980, this proposed massive investment in a new steel complex at Teesside with an ultimate annual capacity of 12 million tonnes. Forecast growth in steel demand failed to materialize, though, and world steel output actually fell for the first time since 1945. A halt was called to the 1973 expansion programme, effectively from 1976, formally announced in 1978 (HMSO, 1978). Instead of expansion, employment in steel production on Teesside [was] slashed from 29,000 in 1971 to just 7000 [in 1988]. The truncated development of the BSC South Teesside works has left it in a unique position, the only major steel complex using the basic oxygen route dependent solely upon one blast furnace. A second, projected blast furnace lies rusting in an adjacent field, never constructed. The single blast furnace now used predominantly imported coking coal, with one colliery after another closing on the south-east Durham coalfield in consequence.[. . .] Dependence upon one blast furnace, subject to periodic interruptions of production to replace the refractory brick lining, leaves the works vulnerable to continued plans to cut capacity at BSC. In 1982 and 1983 real fears of complete closure were expressed locally (see for example Cleveland County Council, 1983; Hudson and Sadler, 1984), only (temporarily?) quelled by an elaborate plan to cope with the relining of the Redcar blast furnace during 1986. Additionally, BSC cut back rolling mill capacity, leaving the works deficient in profitable, finished product activities. Its main strength is in semi-finished steel products, open to cost-effective competition from Third World steel industries. BSC also divested itself of the construction and fabrication activities acquired via Dorman Long's earlier diversification, including the sale of offshore construction interests to the Trafalgar House group [. . .]. Since 1981 BSC has been subcontracting out parts of its operations, as it has at the rest of the 'big five' coastal complexes.[. . .]

Similar processes can be observed in Teesside's second major manufacturing employer, the chemicals giant ICI.[. . .] The very name – Imperial Chemical Industries – conjures up images of an industry developing from the outset to serve an international market. As the protected outlets of the old Empire disappeared in the postwar period, the company expanded instead into other international markets. The interwar growth of a major inorganic chemicals complex at Billingham, and postwar development of the organic complex at Wilton, played important roles in this global strategy [. . .]. ICI has invested heavily in the most up-to-date technologies to meet an overall growth in demand for chemicals and to protect its position against competition. From 1962 onwards, for example, major replacement investment took place in ammonia production at Billingham, replacing coal and coke as a basic feedstock first with naphtha, then later with natural gas. Larger production units and cheaper feedstock dramatically reduced costs; in addition, labour requirements were slashed and several thousand jobs were shed. Continuing employment growth in new plant across the river at Wilton, though, meant that in this period most of the job losses could be accommodated through transfers.

In the 1970s, as demand for bulk chemicals slumped, ICI found itself facing a new, intensified set of international competitive pressures. Overcapacity in ethylene production, the basic building block of most plastics such as those produced at the Wilton site, was increasingly in evidence throughout Europe, the USA and Japan. In response ICI initiated a series of plant closures at Wilton, especially after 1980 when the company recorded its first-ever net loss. In a letter to all MPs in 1982, the company even threatened to close the entire Wilton site, claiming it was suffering unfairly from the tax concessions granted to its UK competitors over their supplies of ethane, in contrast to the tax arrangements for its naphtha-based plant at Wilton. Four years later ICI won a prolonged court battle over this issue and, with crude oil prices tumbling, petrochemical profits increased again. Nonetheless, intensive competitive pressures remain from companies and countries with access to still cheaper feedstocks, most especially in the Middle East. Billingham's main product, agricultural fertilizers, is also a market area under great strain in the UK, with demand falling and a strong competitor emerging since 1982 in the Norwegian conglomerate Norsk Hydro.

In response to such pressures in the UK market, ICI has increasingly located production overseas. The Wilton works, for example, now has a parallel production facility at Wilhelmshaven in West Germany. ICI employment in the UK has fallen from three quarters of global company employment at the start of the 1970s to less than a half. On Teesside this has meant a reduction from 31,500 jobs at ICI in 1965 to 14,500 by 1985. In addition, priority has shifted away from the so-called 'bulk' or commodity chemicals of plastics, petrochemicals and fibres, and into speciality chemicals where the emphasis is on high value-added, low-volume production. Employment in the manufacture of these new chemicals is relatively low and it is a high-risk business. The most significant such investment on Teesside, the 'Pruteen' plant, was opened in 1980 but has only operated intermittently – and when it does, it employs a handful of people to produce just 150 tonnes of artificial protein daily.[. . .]

The use of contractors' labour has escalated significantly, especially for maintenance. In 1984 ICI proposed that process workers should do some maintenance work. Whilst this met with strong union opposition, a more portentous move was announced in 1986 and implemented over the heads of trade unions the following year – the hiving off from ICI of the commodity chemicals side to a new subsidiary company, ICI Chemicals and Polymers, in which redundancy and demarcation agreements are completely open to renegotiation. The future prospects for ICI employment on Teesside are grim. Large-scale, continuing job losses [. . .] [in the 1990s] have already been publicly forecast by senior ICI management.

ICI brings a high level of political awareness to this process of managing decline in the UK. 'Resettlement' schemes were established at Wilton from 1981 to encourage workers to find alternative employment or (mostly) retire. The promotional agency Saatchi and Saatchi has been appointed with a £10 million budget to highlight ICI's strengths. In 1987 a science park was established alongside ICI Billingham, with the intention of attracting alternative jobs into small factory units (and deflecting criticism of the company's labour shedding). Throughout its history, and especially recently, ICI has shown itself keenly aware of the need for large employers to maintain a political presence both locally and nationally.

Like ICI, other sectors of the Teesside economy display both continuity and change in decline. Not all sectors of employment in the area are in such drastic decline, of course. *Teessplan* was strident in its insistence that there was a need to diversify the employment structure through expansion as a sub-regional service centre (HMSO, 1969). To some extent this happened, though on nothing like the scale necessary to mop up job losses elsewhere in the local economy. Many of the spaces reserved for office development now stand as vast 'temporary' car parks on the fringes of Middlesbrough town centre, a silent testimony to unfulfilled expectations. A net decline of 20,000 manufacturing jobs in the period 1971–1981 far exceeded a net gain of 4000 service jobs – with most of this latter increase as female part-time employment. Full-time service sector employment actually fell. By 1981 chemicals and steel still accounted for 60 per cent of all manufacturing jobs but over a half of Teesside's jobs were in the service sector. The rise of the service sector, if sometimes exaggerated and somewhat more complex than it is often presented, is nevertheless significant, especially in bringing large numbers of (married) women back into the labour market or into employment for the first time.

Much of this service sector growth was in financial services such as banking and insurance, which increased employment by 80 per cent between 1971 and 1981 [. . .]. This has been vulnerable to technological changes, particularly the increased use of networked computers. Many insurance and finance companies have recently reorganized their operations within the north-east, typically concentrating on Newcastle and closing offices in Middlesbrough. As credit boomed via plastic money, a significant component of financial services employment in Teesside has arisen in Barclaycard, which opened offices at Middlesbrough and Stockton in 1973 and 1974 respectively. In 1985 these employed 700 people, 85 per cent of them women. The main tasks are processing of remittances and sales vouchers – entailing the continuous use of a VDU – and handling customer enquiries.

Service employment in the public sector is typified by the National Health Service. Here too the workforce is predominantly female, but the private sector has not dominated development as it has in financial services. There are no private hospitals in the area and there is a strong commitment to the public provision of health care through the NHS. The industrial and urban legacy of the area is apparent in its relatively large numbers of hospitals and hospital beds, with a standardized mortality rate 22 per cent above the national average.[. . .] In certain areas close to the river, mortality rates are even higher, one impact of long-term environmental pollution. The main planning issue for the South Tees Health Authority concerns the fragmentation among a large number of aging hospitals. Recent years have seen centralization of investment on the new South Cleveland hospital in Middlesbrough and a continuing tension over patient access to facilities in east Cleveland. Centralization in south Cleveland has not been opposed by the trade unions but they have been strong opponents of a more recent development, the planned contracting out, via privatization, of tasks such as catering, cleaning and domestic work.

These changes in steel and chemical production, and in financial and health service provision, represent a series of portraits of the dominant characteristics of change in the economic structure of Teesside. The two major manufacturing industries have acted in a changing and increasingly competitive national and international environment to attempt to secure continuing production, with a considerable degree of state support in the form of investment subsidies and, in the case of steel, nationalization. Regional Development Grant payments and the debt financing of BSC served to underpin investment in new technologies but did not, indeed could not, generate employment gains as in the initial period of absolute expansion of production. Both steel and chemicals industries currently rest on a precarious toehold in Teesside, subject to overseas competition in export markets and import penetration of the UK market. While service sector activities have become, almost by default, of greater significance than manufacturing in terms of the number of jobs, these are often of a qualitatively different character. Service sector growth has been dominated by unskilled and poorly paid part-time female employment, vulnerable to renewed technological change in the case of financial services, and to government-imposed financing limits in the case of the health service.

Such developments in these four different industries mesh together in the character of the Teesside labour market. The dominant feature of this is the shortage of jobs. [At the start of the 1990s] Cleveland County [had] the highest rate of unemployment in Britain. In such a climate, changes in labour practices including the use of subcontractors or the spread of 'flexibility', both in and out of work and within work, are more easily imposed. Pressures in this direction, as we have seen, are evident in both manufacturing and service sectors, and indeed are increasingly apparent nationally [. . .]. On Teesside there is a further emergent trend, one rooted in the earlier prevalence of skilled yet temporary employment in building the new chemicals and steel plants – that of migration of skilled construction workers overseas on lucrative, short-term contract work, to areas such as the Middle East. The irony could not be sharper. As Teesside's industries stagnate or die, Teesside's workers – at least those with the necessary skills acquired in an earlier era – are forced to find employment in precisely those countries where competing industries are emerging. Britain's role within an evolving international division of labour could not be clearer.

Politics and labour in Teesside

Within Teesside these labour market changes, both historic and recent, have recognizable implications. They illustrate how national plans and priorities have varying and sometimes unintended consequences in different localities as state intervention is unable to abolish the contradictions of capitalist production. At different periods, different processes have characterized the development of Teesside as a locality. These have been given order through political apparatuses. Teesside represents perhaps the clearest illustration in the UK of the linkages between capital and labour exemplified by ICI's paternalism, and solidified as a political practice by Labourism. This is most apparent in the provision of housing.

First seemingly endless growth, then more recently economic stagnation, depended upon the construction and reproduction of a series of physical and social relationships between industry and the built environment of roads, housing, schools, shops and other means of subsistence. Much of the early expansion of steel and chemicals production depended upon the construction of successive company towns, first in the early Ironmasters district of nineteenth century development in the heart of Middlesbrough, then later at Billingham and in new estates for steel workers such as Dormanstown. Much of this growth was fuelled by substantial inward migration from other parts of the north-east, or even further afield. At times of labour shortage, such as immediately after 1945, the state also became heavily and visibly implicated in accommodating the labour force required by the expansion of manufacturing industry through the provision of council housing.

Such concerns intertwined with the plans of local authorities to clear a vast amount of run-down housing in this early postwar period. Middlesbrough County Borough Council commissioned a detailed survey partly to cover this task [. . .]. It reported that 'on strictly utilitarian grounds' the old Ironmasters district, the St Hilda's ward, should be cleared completely of its stock of slums (owned principally by a dozen private property trusts and agents). It also recommended that if the town grew strongly through immigration it might consider establishing a satellite community. Both were long-term projects – St Hilda's now has a new stock of partnership trust housing built jointly by Middlesbrough Borough Council and Yuill's, a firm of private builders, whilst substantial growth is currently taking place in the Coulby Newham estate south of the main built-up area. The role of the state in mediating labour and housing markets is clearly apparent in the new conditions under which such policies evolved after 1945.

There is a historical consensus within the area that the way forward is via compromise between capital and labour. This is largely grounded in an argument that what is good for Teesside is good for both employer and employed. In a sense, there exists a Teesside-based coalition of interests, although this is being placed under increasing strain by both the evidence of past failures and the increasing external control of the 'local economy'. Much of this, to be sure, is rooted in the early paternalism of the steel and chemicals employers; but whereas from other similar industries such as coal mining there grew a relatively strong, independent trade union organization, the same cannot be said for Teesside.

From 1945 onwards the Teesside Industrial Development Board (TIDB) was an important cross-party vehicle, incorporating representatives of most local authorities, the local chambers of trade and commerce and trade union organizations such as the Iron and Steel Trades Confederation, the Electrical Trades Union, the Amalgamated Engineering Union and the Confederation of Shipbuilding and Engineering Unions. A revealing insight into its character (and that of the area) was presented when the need for a reorganization of the North-east Industrial and Development Association (NEIDA) was agreed in 1960, after the failure of the region to 'win' any of the 1950s round of new car plant ventures.

The TIDB was concerned to secure three organizations – centred on the Tyne, Wear and Tees – in a federal structure, leaving the Tees considerable autonomy, most especially to cooperate with local industrialists. Such a proposal was not popular with NEIDA, which adopted a new constitution in 1961, forming the North-east Development Council (NEDC). The TIDB reluctantly affiliated to NEDC but some Teesside-based local authorities, including Middlesbrough, did not.

In this period the coalition of interests typified by the TIDB could be held together around a consensus on the need for and possibility of growth through modernization of the sub-regional economy. The economic downturn of 1962 [. . .] represented only a slight hiccup, and if anything the proposed solution served further to coalesce interests and secure agreement. TIDB president, Mr Robson, assured the Board's Annual General Meeting in 1965 that there was 'concrete evidence of great progress on Teesside'. The following year Dorman Long contacted the Ford Motor Company indicating the suitability of the Ironmasters district for a projected new car factory. Teesside was viewed, at least locally, as a prospective candidate for any potential investment project.

With the collapse of such growth policies in the 1970s and their failure to secure *either* employment stability *or* a sound industrial structure, their fragile logic was increasingly apparent and the coalition built around them has come under considerable strain. This was epitomized by James Tinn, Labour MP for Redcar, speaking in 1979:

> I remind the House that in the last decade no less than 10,000 jobs (in steel) were lost on Teesside. In only one closure was there a massive and well-organised protest, and that was not in my constituency but across the river. The Teesside workers recognised that modernisation was inevitable and that a price had to be paid for it. They paid the price before they got the new works. (*Hansard*, vol. 973, 7 November 1979, col. 490).

His concern was with the possibility of further works closures, arguing that this would be unfair on a workforce which had directly cooperated with a decimation of the steel industry for the promised 'new works'. That this was already at risk from competition even as it was being built had been quietly pushed into the background.[. . .]

Whilst some objectives of the strategy in terms of new infrastructural provision, and the restructuring of major capitals engaged in steel and chemicals production, might have been successfully achieved, the employment aims clearly were not. And herein lies the greatest challenge for both industrial policy and Labourism in regions such as the north-east.[. . .]

A coherent local economy in this part of the north-east region has been placed under increasing strain by international processes of change, mediated by national and local policies and politics. In different parts of Teesside, changes in labour and housing markets have historically come together to produce varied conditions of economic and social life. Underlying this variation has been a Teesside-based consensus on the need for growth through modernization, held together only so long as that growth could be maintained, and linked to the adjacent coalfield through a series of transitory transfers of labour and commodities. Today these ties are seemingly broken and the consensus is being torn apart. In the process what are raised are some fundamental political questions to do with the role of state policies, the purpose of production and the conditions of everyday life. These changes are being experienced and expressed by people on Teesside.

Experiences of life in Teesside

[. . .] High unemployment does not directly affect all households to the same degree or in the same way, but the depressed labour market does increasingly have a general effect on those in work or seeking work. One household affected in this way is that of the Cowdreys, a couple in their thirties who live in Acklam with their two young sons. Martin held a variety of jobs, later joining British Steel. In 1982 his part of the works went out to private contractors and he was laid off. It took him two years to find another job. 'I thought I'd probably get another job straight away, but it wasn't to be.' Now he works as a driver on the buses. After two years back at work, he was still struggling to pay off the bills, even though he had invested his redundancy payment wisely. His wife's earnings helped as well, but without the redundancy money "there's no way we could have stayed here with the mortgage – we'd have had to think about moving into the town'. He was relatively lucky – he'd just heard from one of the men laid off from British Steel at the same time, who still hadn't found a job. Carol worked in a number of office jobs, most recently at Barclaycard. She regularly works overtime at weekends, to earn a bit extra for the holidays. She can't see their sons getting a job locally.

'A few years ago you could pick and choose your own jobs, but if you've got a job now you're better off sticking with it. My first job I left because I didn't like the bloke I worked with, but now I wouldn't do that.'

In many ways the Morecambes are a similar household. Richard and Lucy have been buying their council house at Coulby Newham for several years. Richard works shifts at ICI so that they have to negotiate over who has the car because the estate is quite a way out of town. Richard started his early working life in the steelworks before moving around the industrial plant in the area. 'It's a funny thing, that, I always stayed in one job for about two years,' he remarked. In the early 1970s they thought about moving away, but then he got a job with ICI. Some weeks before we first met he was told that his part of the works was soon to be closed, and he was in the process of evaluating his options once he was laid off. He's convinced the chemicals industry is dying on Teesside. 'When I first went to Wilton it took you half an hour to get into the site because of all the cars queuing to get in. Now you drive from one end to the other in a matter of minutes.' At night, the evidence of decline is even more apparent. 'There's plant that should have lights on, and there's nothing. They've closed down – vast open spaces in the middle of the works.' If Lucy didn't work, Richard would work overtime. As it is they've got by, although they're obviously concerned for the future. Lucy said she'll encourage their two young daughters to travel and see the world – 'because I don't think there's going to be anything for them here'.

Even at service sector employers like Barclaycard, the pressures in work are increasing. Irene and Tom Oldham live in Acklam with their two daughters. Irene wants to work and almost always has. 'I have to work, it would drive me mad not to work, just being a housewife. I want something that I can do, a bit of independence. But we were all a lot happier three or four years ago when there was no pressure on.' She recognizes something else: that at Barclaycard, 'few women have husbands who are unemployed. It seems people who work in places like that don't come across unemployment so much. There's different sets of people. Tom has always maintained that if he lost his job he'd find another one.' This he has done successfully on numerous occasions in the past, and both their daughters now also have office jobs.

In their various ways, these households are illustrative of a range of people in Teesside who have evolved ways of coping with the exigencies of its changing labour market. What they indicate too is a growing polarization of society within Teesside between those who are given, or take, the opportunity to adjust to a lifetime of insecure, shifting or intensified employment, and those who do not even get that chance.[. . .] Paula, an unemployed factory worker, expressed her frustration at this growing divide within the area:

'People you meet on the street say "aren't you working yet?" but they don't understand what it's like being unemployed. I think to myself, they read the papers, they see the news, but they don't really know what's going on.'

In a work-oriented society, unemployment frequently brings domestic tensions. One fifteen-year-old recalled how his father was out of work for more than a year.

'He got very depressed; he took up golf, but couldn't stick it. He just started getting depressed and niggly. You couldn't blame him really. You could understand. He was used not so much to a lot of excitement, but pressure. I think my parents nearly split up at that time.'

Becoming unemployed has been an everyday experience for some time now in Teesside. It is an area which has experienced the effects of recession before, in the 1920s and 1930s.[. . .] One man laid off from the engineeering industry put this process into words. He described it as 'just a small item on page seven – you know, the industrial news – and you're out of a job'. Finding another one, or a first one, is not so easy. In the Middlesbrough Job Centre a twenty-three year old butcher, unemployed for two years, commented:

'I've lost count how many jobs I've applied for. I'd say about fifty. Now I've got to force myself to go and look at the cards on the board. A lot of people have given up – just sit at home saying there's no jobs so there's no point looking.'

One reason for giving up lies in a perception of what employers are looking for. Mary, an unemployed catering worker, described one job she had applied for:

232

'At 53 I was too old. The woman behind me in the queue was too young at 20! If you want a job these days you have to be between 25 and 35. If you're old you've no choice. But there doesn't seem to be any jobs for younger ones either.'

Increasingly, finding a job is as much about who you know as what you know. There is widespread, tacit acknowledgement of the significance of informal networks in finding work. 'Through a friend of a friend' is frequently heard in this context. Sometimes these connections extend into the greyer areas of the labour market, although there is more than a suspicion that the extent of the so-called 'black economy' is overstated and the benefits to potential (often waged) consumers under-emphasized, as living 'on the fiddle' is fraught with dangers. One unemployed man put it this way:

'There's a lot of people on the fiddle – but then again a lot are jealous of the money they earn. There's a lot of anonymous phone calls to the DHSS. I wouldn't tell on anybody myself, but I wouldn't take part either for fear of being caught.'

Moving away in search of work is one escape sometimes seen as an inevitable process. A local businessman, for example, felt that 'nobody goes from the South to the North, it's against the natural routes'. Not that there is anything necessarily 'natural' about a journey in the other direction. It has its complications, and can be very traumatic. A school-leaver explained how his father worked in the Middle East on contract work.

'A year ago he came back from Oman. It's expensive to take the rest of the family over there so he has to go out for three months at a time and when he comes back, he's only back for a week and a half or something, so you don't see much of him. You get used to it – he's always away. Now, he's not away, he's working in Watford, down south. He works weekdays and he's back at the weekend.'

As in many parts of Britain, party politics plays little formal role in everyday life, for the waged and the unemployed alike. Part of the reason for this lies in a cynicism, a disbelief in the power, or even intention, of politicians to deliver. This was neatly expressed in the following unprompted dialogue between Tom and Albert, two council workers on the verge of retirement.

Albert: The only way is to get rid of Mrs Thatcher.
Tom: But look what happened when Labour was in – everything was on strike and got paid off after six or eight weeks. At least she's said no, you can go on strike but we're not paying you.
Albert: But at least the money she's spent on strikes would have been better paying people to work.
Tom: It's gone down from one government to another. This one's no better than the last, it's all the same.
Albert: You look back though, history shows the Conservatives can run the country better with more people unemployed.

Tom:　Yes, it's the policy of this government, now, there's no doubt about that.

Albert:　But if Labour got into power tomorrow, they couldn't do a great deal about it.

Tom:　Yes, no doubt.

Given this acute perception of the limits to what government policies can in practice deliver, it seems to make increasing sense for households and individuals to adopt their own (in the final analysis, competitive) strategies of 'getting by'. Yet ultimately, of course, the diverse problems of the area have structural roots.

One reaction to Teesside's new situation is to seek to extend the old; to argue that because the area is experiencing today conditions which the rest of the UK will ultimately have to experience, Teesside should be a testing ground for policies to cope with problems of long-term mass unemployment. One senior local government officer with Cleveland County Council, Reg Fox, put it like this:

'The problem we've got is that we've been the forerunner of changes in manufacturing, and I don't think society generally and the national political scene has caught up with the fact that this is going to be happening in the rest of manufacturing, and until the country comes to terms with that, we'll not have the resources to tackle our problems.'

To which another, John Gillis, responded:

'The sad thing is, for at least the last ten years we've been telling people this. We must cope with these people who are unemployed. What are we going to do with them?'[. . .]

This expression of despair partly masks an unspoken recognition that Teesside as a place both exemplifies national patterns of change and is increasingly marginal to the main currents of the world economy. There is nothing new about Teesside's susceptibility to international change.[. . .] There are limits to what a capitalist nation can and will do in an international competitive economy. One way of coping with this is seen as a reversion to the local: to devise, develop and implement political strategies at a local level knowing they are constrained both in terms of resources and the agenda which they address.

There is a deepening recognition within the area that local economic development initiatives, heavily constrained as they are by a hostile central government policy, are of limited effectiveness. Cleveland County Council's leader Bryan Hanson weighs the balance in this way: 'One year's activity by the county council in the job creation field can be wiped out by one plant closure.' The expansion of make-work schemes by central government, through the Manpower Services Commission, exemplifies national policy towards the unemployed in places like Teesside. [. . .] Whilst it is a significant transfer of financial resources in aggregate (though not to each recipient), the area lacks power to control this expenditure. Yet the unemployed remain a significant, if changing population in Teesside, and the county council has therefore formulated its own unemployment strategy [. . .]. It is based on the premise that 'policies should not be devised *for* or *at* the unemployed, but *with* the unemployed' (Cleveland

County Council, 1987, p. 2). The evolution of this initiative was described by Councillor David Walsh as part of a growing recognition that 'we can no longer rely on government intervention, that with a government which felt the region had played out its historic role, we have to take things into our own hands'. Yet, without adequate finance, it is also clearly accepted that the proposals will not solve the problem of unemployment, or relieve the misery it causes (Cleveland County Council, 1987, p. 3).

In this sense, then, the area is undergoing a potentially dramatic political transition. David Walsh perceives:

'a huge generation gap in the Council Chambers, between people in their twenties, many unemployed, and those in their sixties, who grew up in a different era. People who are in their forties now grew up in a different period again, and didn't get involved politically.'

[. . .] Out with the old guard, in with the new; but what they make of the area is a matter for the future. The outstanding challenge is to inform the (admittedly hard) choices which need to be made if people in places such as Teesside are to avoid hopeless future material deprivation and grim despair.

Some concluding comments

The main features of Teesside's recent economic history are clear and easily understood – a transition from boom town to slump city; an area now of high unemployment where capital intensive investment created few new jobs, where service sector growth was unable to compensate for manufacturing decline, leaving migration in search of work the only realistic option for a substantial minority. Yet the story is also a complex and intricate one, because its plot was written by so many different and competing interests. Diversity in decline is a marked characteristic of Teesside, and other areas of the north, today. In this tension lies a source of polarization and fragmentation.

The evolution of Teesside has been a social process, entailing political decisions. Its current situation poses acute questions, also of a political nature, which are significant both nationally and locally. Different phases of Teesside's development have coincided with different dominant conceptions of the appropriate relationship between national and local government. In the boom years of the 1960s and early 1970s, the area was a highly attractive location for some forms of capital investment in manufacturing. Local authorities in that era were engaged not so much in planning for growth, as responding to growth. Planning was orchestrated nationally whilst, as Cleveland County Council's leader, Bryan Hanson, recalls, local authorities 'were moving like hell to keep up with everything'. He reflects today that 'the amazing thing is that the boom was for such a short period'. The question now is whether such conditions will recur, or whether alternative futures might emerge in and from an area which has seen enough of the social and environmental costs of industrial growth and decline.

References

Cleveland County Council (1983) *The Economic and Social Significance of the British Steel Corporation to Cleveland*, Middlesbrough.

Cleveland County Council, (1987) *Unemployment Strategy*, Middlesbrough.

HMSO (1969) *Teesside Survey and Plan*, London, HMSO.

HMSO (1973) *British Steel Corporation: Ten Year Development Strategy*, London, HMSO, Cmnd. 5236.

HMSO (1978) *British Steel Corporation: The Road to Viability*, London, HMSO, Cmnd. 7149.

Hudson, R. and Sadler, D. (1984) *British Steel Builds the New Teesside? The Implication of BSC Policy for Cleveland*, Middlesbrough, Cleveland County Council.

PART 2
TRADITIONS OF SOCIAL THOUGHT

CHAPTER 22

Traditions of Thought and the Rise of Social Science in the United Kingdom

David Coates

Contents

Source: article commissioned for this Reader.

1 Introduction

Studying the social sciences provides an opportunity to do at least two things. It provides a space within which to reflect upon the nature of the social circles within which we move and with which we are already familiar. It also offers us an opportunity to move beyond the familiar, to explore and come to understand social processes of which we have no direct experience but which nonetheless often impinge upon us in complex ways. If done well, a course in social science can both widen and deepen our social knowledge. It can help us to know more, and so widen our range of information; and it can take us towards a clearer understanding of the origin and character of the information we now know. In other words, it can provide us with a clearer sense of both *how* and *why* the contemporary world is organized as it is.

The widening of our knowledge often comes about in the first instance simply through reading, and reflecting upon, bodies of information that have already been put together by other social scientists. We can learn a lot simply by looking at *social statistics* (on things like unemployment), by reading detailed *histories* (of world trade, or post-war international relations), by absorbing brief *descriptions* of how particular institutions work or key events happened, and by examining *summaries* of important bodies of social research. When we do all that, we can rapidly increase the amount of information we have at our disposal about the character and origins of the contemporary world.

But if this widening of our stock of knowledge is one benefit that can flow from the study of the social sciences, it is not the only one. There is also the matter of deepening our understanding of why social life is organized the way it is, and of how and why it is changing. The determinants of social life, and the patterns of change within it, cannot be fully grasped simply by gathering descriptive material of various kinds. If we want to know what is going on in the social world around us, and why, we have to put some order on that material, pattern it in various ways, and explore the social forces that are giving it shape. We have actively to process what information we have, by approaching it through carefully defined categories of analysis and by relating it to more general bodies of social theory.

So social science involves not simply the gathering of information, the analysis of institutions and the undertaking of social research. It also involves the development and application of social theory. Indeed, the exploration of conceptual distinctions and the discovery of theoretical systems are among the most rewarding and exciting aspects of the study of social science, as I hope you will discover. And I hope you will come to see too the intimate connection between the 'empirical' and the 'theoretical' faces of social science. For even the most apparently straightforward piece of empirical social research is heavily impregnated with assumptions and distinctions that are rooted in particular social theories, and theoretical development in the social sciences is heavily dependent on the gathering and sifting of research findings. In the study of the social you cannot get the 'facts' first and add the 'theory' later. It doesn't work that way. You cannot 'do' social science without using some social theory: and because that is so, there is no way in which we can properly introduce you to social science without introducing you at the same time to at least some of its dominant theoretical systems.

The term 'theory' is often a daunting one – easier to use than to define. It can refer to such a lot of things. When we use it here we normally have in mind *explanatory material* of various kinds. Some of that material will be very broad in scope – whole sets of arguments about the workings of the entire social system. Other theoretical material will be narrower in focus – explaining how a particular part of society or a particular institution operates: how the economy works, or the state functions. Other theoretical material will be more modest still – offering possible explanations of a particular social phenomenon, say unemployment or racial tensions; and some theoretical material will simply take the form of suggested definitions of terms. It will say to you 'why not understand the term social class to mean X or Y, and go off and gather some data using that definition'. In other words, theoretical material in the social sciences comes in different sizes. It comes as grand theory. It comes as specific theories. It comes as particular hypotheses. It comes as different conceptual schemas. But in all its forms it is an essential ingredient of any social analysis; and for that reason anyone coming new to social science would do well to read a general introduction to its overall character and content.

That is what this essay is about. It is a survey of some of the most important examples of what was just termed 'grand theory'. It is a survey organized around three important assumptions of its own. The *first* is that there is an intimate relationship between the levels of theory just described (between grand theory, specific theories, hypotheses and conceptual schemas). Because grand theory informs and shapes the rest we need to provide you with a preliminary specification of the most influential of those grand theories. The *second* assumption at play in this essay is that social science is characterized by disputes at every level of theory. You face different definitions of class, different theories of social division, different explanations of why individuals conform, and so on. Because this is so, any preliminary specification of the theoretical material informing contemporary social science has to cover a range of theories, not just one. And *thirdly*, the essay is designed on the recognition that these disputes are long-established ones. Contemporary theory within social science represents the sifted legacy of more than two centuries of debate in western intellectual circles on the character of modern society. Indeed many of the themes of that debate (on the nature of society in general, and on human potentiality within it) stretch back in western culture further still – to Greece, Rome and Judaea. And because this

241

is so, the broad theoretical positions described here are best understood as *traditions of thought*, each with their own history and internal pattern of development. What you face in this essay is a description of broad packages of theoretical material, each different from the other, and each with its own development over time.

Summary

1   Social science can provide a clearer sense of how and why society is organized as it is.

2   Social theory is an integral part of any social analysis. Theory comes in various forms: grand theory, specific theories, particular hypotheses and conceptual schemas.

3   Social theory in all its forms has a long history characterized by recognizable and persistent controversies.

2 The specification of the traditions

The governing questions in any introductory survey of this kind are 'where to begin' and 'what to include'. These questions could be answered in a number of ways. We could go back – and in a full survey perhaps ought to go back – at least as far as Greece and Rome, to demonstrate the origins of much modern social thought in the debates of Antiquity. We certainly ought to look too – if a full survey was our aim – at the rich reservoir of Christian social thought generated over 2000 years: thought which still informs much modern social theory and practice. And it would certainly be possible – if less valuable – to catalogue the theoretical formulations of a vast range of now long-forgotten nineteenth and early twentieth century social thinkers, whose unopened volumes occupy the basements of many a university library. But time and space permits none of that. All that we can do here is to establish a sense of the broad trends in scholarship produced in response to the emergence of modern society, and to establish a familiarity with the work of key figures within those trends, figures whose formulations continue to have a direct influence on the way contemporary social science is practised.

As we begin, it is as well to be clear about some of the limitations associated with such an approach. The broad trends in scholarship which this essay will explore are retrospective constructions. They are just one way of placing some order on the vast array of theoretical material that has come down to us. They achieve that order at the cost of simplifying (and thereby inevitably distorting to a degree) the intellectual history that they tell. So they must be understood as first approximations, as a preliminary sketch of certain tendencies in western thought in the last three centuries, a sketch that you may well want to refine and amend in important ways as you go on to later courses in the social sciences and the arts.

However, though they are a first approximation they do capture central features of the intellectual universe from which the social sciences emerged. The distinctions that we will draw were recognized, and indeed used, by many of the theorists we will cite, to characterize elements of their own position in the debates in which they were engaged. Those debates were invariably more wide-ranging and more complex than we can do justice to here, and the positions of individual thinkers were more complicated and nuanced than we can capture in a preliminary sketch of this kind. But it will be enough for our purposes to locate some of the core issues in dispute, and to trace some of the major lines of cleavage, in the analysis of modern society in which all these thinkers were engaged. We will locate those core issues and lines of cleavage by distinguishing four traditions of thought, which we will refer to as *liberalism, marxism, social reformism,* and *conservatism*. We will use those four labels to identify broad intellectual positions – positions which are important here because of the influence they have had on the development of twentieth century social science. So the four labels are ours, imposed for our purposes to put order on a story of intellectual development that could be told in other ways; but they are labels which we have chosen to use in part precisely because they were used in the past – and are still used – by many theorists to describe their own intellectual positions.

There is another sense as well in which the selection of these four traditions of thought captures an important feature of the intellectual history of the social sciences. As you will see as you read on, there is an underlying unity to each of the four traditions with which we will deal, a unity which helps to distinguish each from the other. Each tradition is built around the acceptance (by theorists operating within it) of a distinctive set of underlying assumptions about the nature of the human condition and of the knowledge of that condition which it is possible for us to have. These underlying assumptions give to each tradition a characteristic and distinctive set of concerns to be analysed, concepts with which to analyse them, and explanations with which to complete their analysis. As we will see, there is a characteristically liberal way of analysing society, a characteristically marxist one, and so on: and what gives each its characteristic and distinctive approach is this anchorage in a particular set of assumptions, concepts and concerns.

In fact these four traditions can usefully be thought of as 'searchlights' beaming down on to the 'stage' of social life, each originating from a distinct and single source, each fanning out to illuminate some or all of the 'stage' below. They are different beams of light, each coming from different starting points, each using different terms and modes of explanation. But they are all addressed to the same stage. They are all asking the same questions. What is the character of modern society? How do we explain the workings of the major institutions within it? What are the forces of continuity and change at work in the contemporary world? How are we to understand, and even to change, the main social divisions within which we all live? What is the character of the human condition, and the nature of the knowledge it is possible for us to have about that condition? Does that human condition permit the possibility of a better social order emerging in the years to come?

In suggesting to you that broad traditions of thought have shaped the character of contemporary social science, we are encouraging you to think of ideas as relating to each other in distinct 'packages'. We are also suggesting that it makes sense to trace the development of these packages over time, to seek their origins in the writings of particular intellectuals, and to trace the use (and refinement) of their original formulations by later scholars confronted by new and unforeseen circumstances. We are confident that if you do that you will equip yourself with a clearer picture of some of the important continuities in modern western social thought, and acquire a distinct sense of the main frameworks of thought available for social analysis. We are also confident that this will enable you to recognize many of the important building blocks of contemporary social thought, and enable you to establish a firmer critical stance on much contemporary debate.

These are considerable gains, but we must not forget that any schematic presentation of the kind on offer here has real costs as well. Three costs in particular spring to mind. One is the danger of conflating intellectual positions and political movements. All four of the packages of ideas to be discussed here have inspired particular sets of political parties. Each of the four traditions that we will examine as *analyses* of modern society also have a presence within those societies as political *ideologies*. We will look at their role as ideologies in the last section of this essay. Until then we will treat them as they initially were intended to be treated. We will approach them simply as bodies of ideas which are open for our use as social analysts, and pay no heed to the ways in which others have used them as inspirations for political action.

Then there is the danger of 'over packaging'. We will need to remember that not all ideas tie up into these neat packages, and that indeed some of the most intriguing theories often stand outside, and in some tension, to mainstream thought. Moreover, these four traditions, though so influential in areas of social science, are only a part of the wealth of ideas on which social scientists can and do draw. The four we use here are, for example, all predominantly secular in character, and exist alongside traditions of religious thought that will not be discussed in this chapter. The four too have their own agenda of concerns and concepts, and though they differ from each other in many ways, they also share common silences. One of their biggest silences, as we will see, has been on questions of gender – a silence which has then made its own contribution to the reproduction of male dominance. In consequence there is also a two hundred-year-long tradition of feminist thought which lies outside, and in some tension to, the four broad packages to which we will soon turn. In fact the four positions we will establish here also reappear *inside* contemporary religious debate, and *inside* feminist discussion, but with a different inflection that derives from the distinctly religious/feminist sets of concerns and concepts evident there. We lack the time and space to follow those inflections in this essay but once more you may want to pursue them later in your studies.

There is one other question-mark to keep with us as we look at these four traditions; and that is to contemplate the possibility of their contemporary disintegration. The four traditions of thought to which we now turn are currently under review, in the sense that many contemporary social scientists draw on parts of each in quite an eclectic manner, generating new syntheses of thought that do not map directly back on to any one of the original four. You may or may not want to be equally eclectic when you review the value of these four broad positions, but before the old can be synthesized into the new, it must first be grasped in its original form. Twentieth century social science emerged into an intellectual universe shaped in large measure by the development, in the three centuries that had gone before, of four broad bodies of social thought. It is to these four (to liberalism, marxism, social reformism and conservatism) therefore that we need now to turn.

245

Summary

1 We are concerned here with four traditions of thought, each of which is built around a particular set of assumptions, concerns and categories, and each of which addresses a series of important social questions.

2 The traditions chosen tap real divisions between social scientists both now and in the past. They constitute an important set of alternative frameworks with which to make sense of the contemporary world.

3 They are not the only packages of ideas available to us. Much creative thought goes on outside the traditions as specified here, and the dividing lines between them are now under review. Traditions of thought need to be distinguished from the political ideologies that share their names.

2.1 Liberalism

As a fully-fledged way of reading the nature of contemporary society, liberalism emerged out of the vast changes that occurred in Western Europe and North America in the three centuries before 1800. In the sphere of *economic* life, the rise of commerce and the spread of wage labour in the leading economies of Western Europe slowly replaced feudalism with first mercantile and agrarian, and later industrial capitalism. In the sphere of *politics*, the three centuries saw the consolidation of the European system of nation-states, with their recurrent internal battles between absolutist and representative systems of government. *Culturally*, the three centuries witnessed the erosion of the Catholic domination of late medieval Europe by intellectual forces released by the twin initiatives of *Renaissance* and *Reformation*. Liberalism indeed turned out to be among the most potent of those cultural challenges, fuelled as it was by its relevance to the political battles against absolutism and to the economic transformations associated with the rise of capitalism.

The individual in liberal thought

Liberalism, like all the traditions of thought being surveyed here, was and is a working out of very basic assumptions about the nature of the human condition and about the necessary starting point of social analysis. These organizing assumptions were very different from those evident in the dominant belief systems of classical Greece and late medieval Christianity with which liberalism eventually broke. To the vast majority of thinkers whose writings have come down to us from the late medieval period, the individual could only properly be understood as part of a larger social whole. For them, society came first, the individual second. Individuals were seen as part of wider social orders – social orders which were either naturally (in the case of **Aristotle**[1]) or divinely (in the religious case) structured and specified. Liberal thought, as it emerged in the seventeenth century, shattered the stability of the medieval world-view, by placing at the core of its understanding a quite revolutionary emphasis on the importance of the *individual*. Liberal thought did not start its social analysis with God. It did not start with a specification of some natural social order. Instead liberalism's starting point was and is the *individual* – an individual who is driven to act socially by the presence of innate desires/sentiments, and who is able to do so effectively because of the possession of the ability to reason.

Since liberal thought put such weight on the nature of the individual, liberal thinkers were inexorably drawn to explore how individuals learnt about the world in which they acted, and to reflect upon the kinds of motivations and intellectual capacities with which individuals were equipped. Not surprisingly, their answers to such fundamental questions varied somewhat. Early liberal philosophers disagreed about how individuals acquired knowledge of the world around them, or came by the moral codes that guided their action within it. Some saw the human mind as empty and blank until filled with information gleaned from the senses, so finding the origins of knowledge and morality in *experience*. Others insisted that individuals approached their world with minds already equipped with innate intuitions and instincts, and attached greater weight to *common sense* as a source of knowledge and morality than to *reason* as such. There was disagreement too on the nature of the goals to which that knowledge was applied. **Thomas Hobbes**[2], whose writings are often cited as an important influence on the emergence of liberal thought, had individuals driven by totally selfish and self-regarding motives; and was led by the logic of his argument to advocate a most illiberal all-powerful State ('The Leviathan') to keep such selfish impulses in check. Later liberals, including **John Locke**[3], **David Hume**[4] and **Adam Smith**[5], all softened their sense of the anti-social nature of individual desires, so that by Hume's time altruism figured in much liberal thought as a basic individual characteristic.

---

[1]**Aristotle**: 384–322BC. Born in Macedonia, studied in Athens under Plato. Tutor to Alexander the Great. His lectures (on a vast range of subjects from logic and ethics to rhetoric and poetics) re-entered the curriculum of Western European universities from the thirteenth century, and were a dominant presence in university learning for 500 years.

[2]**Thomas Hobbes**: 1588–1679. Philosopher, tutor to the Cavendish family, and in 1647 to the future Charles II. His publications included *Elements of Law* (1650), *De Cive* (1651), and the *Leviathan* (1651).

[3]**John Locke**: 1632–1704. Philosopher, tutor to the family of the first Earl of Shaftesbury, indirectly involved in the resistance to James II, and briefly exiled in Holland in 1683. His highly influential *Essay Concerning Human Understanding* was published in 1690, as were his *Treatises on Government*.

[4]**David Hume**; 1711–1776. Scottish philosopher and historian. Author of, among other books, *Treatise on Human Nature* (1739), *Enquiry concerning Human Understanding* (1748) and *Enquiry concerning the Principles of Morals* (1751).

[5]**Adam Smith**: 1723–1790. Professor of Logic and Moral Philosophy at Glasgow University. Friend of Hume. Author of *The Theory of Moral Sentiments* (1759) and *An Inquiry into the Nature and Causes of the Wealth of Nations* (1776).

However, these internal liberal debates, though important, were essentially ones of detail. What is more significant for us than the answers given is the acceptance by all these theorists of a common approach. For all the participants in the debate were prepared to take 'the individual' as one of their key units of analysis, and to accord that individual certain rights and freedoms. Such a focus on the importance of the individual did not mean that liberal theorists normally based their arguments upon 'the existence of isolated or self-contained individuals, instead of starting from [people] whose whole nature and character is determined by their existence in society'. On the contrary, liberalism's individualistic approach to social analysis was and still is – as one of its most committed contemporary adherents, **F.A. Hayek**[6], insists – 'primarily a theory of society, an attempt to understand the forces which determine the social life of man' (Hayek, 1949, p.6). What unites liberalism as a tradition of thought is the willingness of its participants to build their analysis upon a particular understanding of society and its constituent forces. Liberal thought understands society as an entity composed of *self-interested individuals*. It is with the character and the enhancement of their goals, capacities and action that liberal analysis is primarily concerned.

Summary

1 All traditions of thought are workings out of basic assumptions about human nature and human knowledge.

2 Liberal thinkers made a sharp break with previous modes of thought by taking as their starting point the existence of self-interested individuals.

3 Early liberal thinkers disagreed about the degree of human sociability, and about the role of intuition and reason in the formation of individual action: but they shared a common view of society as composed of individuals in the pursuit of their own ends.

Power and the state

The firm conviction of liberal theorists that individuals know their own self-interest best, infused a consistent liberal opposition to the claims of any other institution (be it Church or State) to know individual interests better. To the liberal mind, individuals had the right to be *free* from the control of kings and priests. Moreover, since those individuals were seen as being alike – in possessing their own private desires, sentiments and rationality – then it became hard to deny in principle their basic *equality*. Not surprisingly therefore, seventeenth and eighteenth century liberalism was a powerfully radical creed, upholding the values of reason and tolerance, the importance of individual freedoms, and the necessity of designing state structures to protect individual rights. Late seventeenth century liberal thought, in the hands of a philosopher like John Locke, characterized those

[6]**F.A. Hayek**: b.1899. Economist, winner of the Nobel prize for economics in 1974, and author of, among other works, *The Road to Serfdom* (1944), *Individualism and Economic Order* (1949), *The Constitution of Liberty* (1960) and *Law, Legislation and Liberty* (3 volumes, 1973).

rights as 'life, liberty and estate' (broadly meaning property), and presented them as 'natural and inalienable' to individuals. People were not 'given' rights by benign political agencies. Rather they 'had' rights because they were human individuals. By arguing in this way, liberal political thinkers were able to assert that these were rights which people possessed *before* entering the jurisdiction of any state, rights which in some sense they sought to protect by making a *contract* with the state.

Seventeenth century liberal political tracts often described the formation of states as *an act of contract* between a group of free individuals and a political authority; and so introduced into western political culture the notion that states had the right to expect obedience from their subjects only for so long as the contract was maintained. The very idea of 'making a contract' carried with it the notion that the contract could be 'unmade'; and liberal thinkers in the seventeenth century – from Hobbes to Locke – disputed only the conditions under which such contracts could in fact be revoked. In the pursuit of that dispute, seventeenth and eighteenth century liberals turned their attention to the question of what kind of state was likely to keep any bargain that was struck; and they began to advocate *representative* forms of government as a solution to their particular formulation of the age-old problem of political obedience and legitimacy. States would keep their side of the contract, protect basic rights of individuals, only if they faced individuals who enjoyed certain vital political and civil freedoms: of thought and expression, of association and participation, and of safety from arbitrary arrest. And states would keep their side of the bargain the better if those citizens were able to place some of their number in charge of the state, as representatives answerable to the people.

By the second half of the eighteenth century liberal thinkers were using the language of 'natural rights' to justify their opposition to government without representation. What, after all, are the opening lines of the American Declaration of Independence, issued in 1776, but a clear liberal call for rebellion against a government to whose policies the colonists had not consented and in whose councils they were not represented.

When in the course of human events it becomes necessary for one people to dissolve the political bonds which have connected them with another, and to assume among the powers of the earth, the separate and equal station to which the Laws of Nature and of Nature's God entitle them, a decent respect to the opinions of mankind requires that they should declare the causes which impel them to the separation . . . We hold these truths to be self-evident, that all men are created equal, that they are endowed by their Creator with certain unalienable rights, that among these are Life, Liberty and the pursuit of Happiness – That to secure these rights, Governments are instituted among Men, deriving their just powers from the consent of the governed – That whenever any form of Government becomes destructive of these ends, it is the right of the People to alter or to abolish it, and to institute new Government, laying its foundation on such principles and organizing its powers in such form, as to them shall seem most likely to effect their Safety and Happiness.

249

Representation and democracy must not however be confused here. Seventeenth century liberals were not democrats in a modern sense. Voting in these representative forms of government was to be restricted to *men*, and then only to *men with property* – to those 'with a permanent fixed interest in the Kingdom', as one of Oliver Cromwell's generals put it in 1647. Such men were apprehensive about the further extension of the franchise, and their 'fear of the "Mob", of the propertyless', was shared by many later liberal thinkers. Before 1789, the fear was one of 'popular discontent, surfacing in occasional disruptions of anger and desperation', (Arblaster, 1984, p.264). After 1789, it took the form of a fear that 'the people', if enfranchised, would use the state to erode minority rights (particularly the rights of those who owned property) and undermine the dominance of middle-class culture and values. Nineteenth century liberals like **Alexis de Toqueville**[7] saw in the emerging democracy of the United States a potential *tyranny of the majority* that would have to be checked if liberty was to be preserved; and in expressing that fear, de Toqueville spoke for an entire generation of early- and mid-Victorian liberal thinkers, politicians and supporters, who favoured representative political institutions but insisted upon a limitation of the franchise to men of property.

In the last century-and-a-half the precise reasons for this liberal unease with democracy have changed, but the apprehension has not gone away. It is still there in the writings of at least some contemporary liberal thinkers (people like Hayek and **Milton Friedman**[8]) who remain troubled by what they see as 'the economic consequences of democracy'. What disturbs them is the propensity of democratically elected governments to indulge in what – to liberal eyes – are unwarranted levels of public spending and economic management. According to many modern liberal thinkers, democracy has its defects as well as its virtues. Politicians find it easy to win votes by spending taxpayers' money, and taxpayers find it easier to see the immediate benefits of government spending than to spot the long-term damage caused by heavy taxation and a large public sector. Friedman put what he called democracy's 'fundamental defect' in this way: that it is a system

> of highly weighted voting under which the special interests have great incentive to promote their own interests at the expense of the general public. The benefits are concentrated; the costs are diffused; and you have therefore a bias . . . which leads to ever greater expansion in the scope of government and ultimately to control over the individual. (Friedman, 1976, p.13)

The normal liberal solution to such democratic tendencies to over-govern is to seal off certain areas of social and economic life from government interference,

---

[7]**Alexis de Toqueville**: 1805–1859. Widely-read nineteenth century liberal thinker: author of *Democracy in America* (1835) and *L'Ancien Régime et la Révolution* (1856).

[8]**Milton Friedman**: b.1912. Emeritus Professor of Economics at the University of Chicago, and author of, among other works, *Essays in Positive Economics* (1953), *A Monetary History of the United States* (1963), *Dollars and Deficits* (1968), *The Optimum Quantity of Money: and other essays* (1969) and, with Rose Friedman, *Free to Choose* (1980).

by 'identifying individual rights which are presumed so fundamental that no government can infringe them and still be called free' (Gamble, 1979, p.8). The precise rights to be so defended vary between theorists, but tend these days to focus on rights of choice in education, welfare, and the bequeathing of property. These liberals are not anti-democratic. They simply point to what they see as dangers endemic to democratic politics, seek constitutional constraints on the freedom of action of elected governments, and keep alive a traditional liberal antipathy to state activity in general.

As we have just seen, when Cromwell's generals defended restrictions on the franchise in the 1640s they restricted voting to those with property; and they restricted voting to men. Women were not to vote, whether they had property or not. The place of women in early liberal thought is a particularly intriguing one. The logic of liberalism's underlying premises – of the freedom and equality of all individuals – is clear enough: that if everyone is equal, then there can be no justification for the subordination of women to men. But few seventeenth century liberal thinkers were prepared to go that far. Instead, residues of earlier ways of thinking were retained, ways that saw women as somehow 'naturally' inferior to men. There was thus an unresolved tension in much early liberal thought between its egalitarian premises and its patriarchal outcome. Hobbes, for example, got round the knotty problem of women's rights by discussing family power relationships almost exclusively in terms of fathers and sons. Mothers 'disappeared' from much of his discussion, and he was largely silent on the status of wives within families. He was honest enough to concede that the terms of the marriage contract favoured men because men had power in the state; and that they had that – he claimed – because they (not women) had made the original contract creating the state. Locke, a generation later, had women consenting to their subordination to their husbands through their voluntary acceptance of the marriage contract. He treated them as 'the weaker sex', whose subordination to men had some 'Foundation in Nature', and whose acceptance of an unequal marriage contract was a rational response to their natural 'disabilities'. Locke's social 'contract', was underpinned by a sexual contract – and if the first guaranteed the liberty of men from state tyranny, the second locked women into a private subordination to their husbands.

This tension in early liberal thought between the equalities of the social contract and the inequalities of the sexual one did not go unchallenged (and later we will look at one of those challengers, when we examine Mary Wollstonecraft's *A Vindication of the Rights of Woman*). But what we need to recognize now is the persistence of this tension in much later liberal writing, in spite of the challenges to it. It remains the case, as Teresa Brennan and Carole Pateman have observed, that '*logically* there is no good reason why a liberal theorist should exclude females . . . [but] *in practice*, for three centuries the "free and equal individual" has been a male' (Brennan and Pateman, 1979, p.184). Liberal thought has consistently asserted the freedom and equality of all individuals, but invariably by that it has meant only the freedom and equality of men. That is why many feminist writers have been prepared to argue that liberalism as a tradition of thought has not been merely sex-blind. Its central category (the individual) has actually been gendered (treated implicity as *male*); and because it has, as liberal thought has asserted the freedom and equality of individuals, that very assertion has itself helped to obscure the extent to which, for women, freedom and equality have yet to be won.

In the three centuries since Hobbes and Locke, few liberal thinkers raised any sustained challenge to the rights of men to exercise power over women. Instead, liberal thought concentrated its energies on the reversal of earlier dominant conceptions of the relationship of the male individual to the state. By positing a world made up of free individuals in existence *before* the arrival of the state, liberalism characterized individual freedom as 'freedom from restraint', as existing where the state was silent, and as guaranteed only by the existence of laws that restrained states and individuals alike. The job of the state was to provide the law within which men could be free: free from violence and anarchy from each other, and free from the capriciousness of arbitrary government. In this way liberal thought divided the world into *private* and *public* spheres, and prioritized the first over the second. It insisted that the public domain restrict its activity to protecting and enhancing the pursuit of individual self-interest in private, or civil, society. Liberal thinkers, that is, offered a conceptual universe divided into private and public spheres, and locked together in popular consciousness the notion that freedom and privacy are indistinguishable.

This sense of the primacy of 'civil society' made politics highly problematic for liberals. If freedom and privacy go together, why have a state at all? Early liberal answers to that question reflected a bleak interpretation of human nature. For Hobbes, since people were naturally egotistical and self-seeking, life without a state would be 'solitary, poore, nasty, brutish and short'. Later liberals, as we observed, disagreed with him by having a more optimistic view of human sociability, and thus a more benign sense of the character of civil society without a state. John Locke argued that people consented to the jurisdiction of the state only to avoid what he termed the 'minor inconveniences' of life without politics. For by then, as thereafter, liberal thinkers were highly suspicious of too much state power. Far from seeing the active state as a precondition of greater individual liberty, they saw political action as inherently dangerous for liberty. This is evident in the characteristic nineteenth century English liberal predilection for a 'night-watchman state', one pursuing *laissez-faire* policies, and acting only as umpire and adjudicator to a world in which individuals were left free to act without direct political supervision. It is evident still in the plea of a contemporary liberal thinker like Robert Nozick for the establishment of what he calls 'a minimal state' – one that 'treats us as inviolable individuals, who may not be used in certain ways by others as means or tools or instruments or resources . . . [one that] treats us as persons having individual rights with the dignity this constitutes' (Nozick, 1974, p.334).

Liberalism has always felt more comfortable with the private than with the public, and has always seen in private action and private institutions a superior capacity to co-ordinate the affairs of self-interested individuals in a mutually beneficial way. States are necessary for law and order, but really they are very dangerous, and become more so the more they do. Private institutions, free of detailed state intervention, are in general, according to liberals, the best guarantee of individual liberty and generalized prosperity: and none more so than the private institution of the *market*.

Summary

1 Liberal thought specified individuals as free and equal, and judged the acceptability of political systems by the degree to which states respected and enhanced individual liberty. Liberal thought divided the world into private and public spheres, and privileged the private, linking its understanding of freedom to that of privacy.

2 Liberal commitments to representative government did not make early liberal thinkers democrats; and even today, some liberal thinkers are uneasy about the tendency of democratic government to 'over-govern'.

3 Early liberal thought equated 'the individual' with 'the male', and either denied, ignored or played-down the rights and freedoms of women.

Economy and society

By the end of the eighteenth century, liberal thinkers were beginning to forge a powerful theory of economic behaviour which enabled them to explain and defend the developments of first mercantile and agrarian, and later industrial capitalism. Again the tight logic of liberal thought was well in evidence, as now economic life, rather than politics, was subjected to an analysis based on the premise of rational individuals in the pursuit of their self-interest. If all that we can know is ourselves as individuals, then what we have as individuals gathers particular significance. The amount of our property becomes a basic measure of how well we as individuals are achieving our individual goals. According to this view, mechanisms which facilitate the growth of our property become vital tools for the enhancement of liberty as a whole. By the time Adam Smith was formulating his arguments in *The Wealth of Nations*, liberal thinkers were confident that the *market* was such a mechanism: that the producing and selling of commodities through individual enterprise would enrich the society in total. Smith himself had an ambiguous attitude to the new society he saw emerging around him, being personally unenthusiastic about the manufacturing and merchant classes who would soon adopt a bowdlerized version of his theory as their own. Yet none the less it was his view that when, in a market economy, an individual seeks

his own advantage . . . and not that of the society . . . he is, in this as in many other cases, led by an invisible hand to promote an end which was no part of his intention. Nor is it always the worse for the society that it was not part of it. By pursuing his own interest he frequently promotes that of the society more effectively than when he really intends to promote it.

(Smith, 1776, Book 4, Chapter 2)

Adam Smith was an early figure in liberal political economy. When he was writing in the 1770s, industrial development had hardly begun, the bulk of the population still worked in agriculture, and it was trade, rather than industry, that attracted much capitalist enterprise. But in the decades after 1780, as an industrial capitalist economy emerged, a whole body of what became known as political economy was developed to explain its inner workings. The economic world described by these nineteenth century economists was quintessentially liberal. It was made up of individuals acting rationally in the pursuit of their self-interest. It was a world of people making and selling things, and of people driven to do so only through their own ambition for personal success. It was a world whose perpetual motion required no central direction, since its dynamism derived from 'the spontaneity of the independent mind and the power of the liberated will' (Manning, 1976, p.16). To the liberal mind, the overriding strength and moral appeal of the emerging capitalist economy lay in just this spontaneity. Its market order was what a much more recent liberal (F.A. Hayek) was to call a *catallaxy* – 'a network of many economies, firms, households etc. . . . not a deliberately made organization but . . . a product of spontaneous growth' which 'because it has no common purpose of its own, enables a great variety of individual purposes to be fulfilled' (Barry, 1979, p.45).

For liberal thought, the self-interest of these individual purposes was all to the good. It was to be encouraged. The only question was how all those personal ambitions were to be co-ordinated: and, more to the point, how were they to be co-ordinated in a way which would bring the maximum benefit to all. Pre-liberal thought might have given that task to the Church or the State. But for liberals neither was necessary for this purpose, and indeed each would only make matters worse. For they believed that the free and undisturbed play of market forces could normally act as *the invisible hand*, efficiently and effectively co-ordinating the activities of free individuals in ways which advanced the interests of all. The interplay of supply and demand, the uninterrupted movement of prices and goods, would – in this view – enhance the wealth of nations and underpin the freedom of the producing and consuming individuals of this new world of trade and industry. All that was left for the state to do was to hold the ring: provide external defence and internal order, and supplement private endeavours with certain public institutions that private profit alone could not sustain (the main example of this, for Adam Smith, was publicly-funded education). To do more would be to *interfere* (and indeed this notion of state 'interference' shows how strongly liberal thought was prepared to privilege the individual and the private over the collective and the public). A 'free market' and a 'strong but restrained state' became liberalism's vision of an ideal economic and political world.

This view of market forces also gave liberal political economists a way of explaining world trade. According to **David Ricardo**[9], economies specialize under the logic of market competition in that for which they are best equipped

---

[9]**David Ricardo**: 1772–1823. Economist, and successful stockbroker. Friend of James Mill (see note 18 below). Member of Parliament 1819. Author of *The Principles of Political Economy and Taxation* (1817).

– in the production of those commodities for which they have a comparative advantage. By specializing in this way, they both enhance the productivity of their own economy and further the growth of wealth in the world economy as a whole. Individual economies, like individuals within economies, best guarantee the interests of everyone by simply looking after themselves. On a liberal view of the world, *competition* between nations, just like competition between individuals, is the key to prosperity for everyone.

Smith and Ricardo were highly representative figures of an entire school of liberal political economy which came to public prominence in the United Kingdom in the decades after 1800. Nineteenth century liberal economists saw a new world of trade and industry emerging, and were conscious of its immense potentiality. Their view of this world had a powerful optimism written into it: optimism about the rationality of individuals and their basic ability to get on with their own lives in ways which benefited everyone; optimism that history was the story of wealth creation and cultural progress if people were free to run their own lives; and optimism that markets were the great clearers and co-ordinators of economic life. By 1820 at the latest their moral vision of an ideal liberal universe was in place. In an ideal liberal world, individuals would be free – free from political constraint, free from monopolies, free to act alone, to produce independently and to trade without barriers, and free to enhance the common good by the unbridled pursuit of their own self-interest. By 1820 the notion of individual freedom and capitalist enterprise were fused in a liberal vision that reinforced the confidence of a rising industrial and commercial class. It was a vision, moreover, which rose to public prominence as that class rose to political power. As Keynes said, 'Ricardo's doctrine conquered England as completely as the Holy Inquisition conquered Spain' (Keynes, 1936, p.32); so that by the third quarter of the nineteenth century the tradition we have just examined was to all intents and purposes the 'conventional wisdom' of an entire society.

For this reason, even when challenged later, this tradition left behind powerful residues of its early dominance. Even today major intellectuals – of whom Hayek is one of the better known – continue to argue for the supremacy of markets as economic allocators and for the freedom of individuals to act in their own self-interest without state intervention. Indeed Hayek was instrumental in creating in 1948 the Mont Pélérin Society, certain of whose members – most notably Milton Friedman and Hayek himself – had a considerable influence on the economic and social policies of a number of leading western governments in the 1970s and 1980s. 'A strong attachment to liberalism unites the members of the Mont Pélérin Society', an attachment to 'the classical brand of liberalism . . . that wants the individual to be free from coercive interferences, especially from interventions by the state' (Machlup, 1977, p.xiv). This is just one indication of what is undoubtedly more generally the case: that the 'classical brand of liberalism' which we have described here needs to be understood not simply as one of the earliest coherent responses to the arrival of modern industrial society. It has also to be understood as one of the most pervasive, influential and tenacious.

Summary

1 Liberal thought came to see 'the market' as an effective and impartial allocator of economic resources and an invaluable arbiter of conflicting interests.

2 The overriding appeal of markets is that they work without human direction, as an 'invisible hand' enabling a multiplicity of purposes to be reconciled and attained.

3 This defence of markets can be applied to international trade as well as to domestic economic activity; and continues to be a major theme in contemporary thinking on state and economy.

2.2 Marxism

This is an appropriate moment in which to pause in our exposition of liberalism since we are beginning to touch on questions of its political impact to which we will return in more detail in Section 4. Our concerns in this section of the essay are with the *history* of ideas rather than with their *influence*; and we will return to our history of liberal thought when we discuss 'social reformism'. But before we do that – before we look at liberalism in its more troubled phase – we need to see the way in which liberalism, even at its moment of highest optimism in the years to 1870, was called into question as an interpretation of modern social life. For however much liberal political economists might assert the superiority and desirability of markets as economic allocators, not everyone was as contemptuous as they were of earlier ways of organizing economic life, nor as enthusiastic about the rise of industrialization. Instead, conservatives of many kinds, as we will see later, tried to stem the emerging social order and turn it back; and many kinds of socialists tried to circumvent the new capitalism – going beyond it, or outside it, to create equally new, but this time non-competitive and egalitarian, forms of social organization. From the explosion of socialist thought and experimentation which the arrival of industrial capitalism precipitated in the first half of the nineteenth century, marxism emerged as the most coherent and comprehensive critique of capitalism as a social system and of the liberalism that would justify it.

The 'real premises' of marxist thought

Karl Marx's[10] own analysis of capitalism began from a quite different point than that commonly adopted by liberal thinkers. Marx rejected as an 'insipid illusion' their belief that social analysis should begin with the examination of the isolated individual. He argued that individuals did not exist in that isolated form.

---

[10]**Karl Marx**: 1818–1883. German philosopher and political economist. Spent the last 35 years of his life in London, and is buried in Highgate Cemetery. His writings include *The German Ideology* (1845–6), *The Communist Manifesto* (with Engels, 1848), *The Eighteenth Brumaire of Louis Bonaparte* (1852), The *Grundrisse* (1857–8) and *Das Kapital* (3 volumes, 1867, 1885 and 1894).

Individuals existed only in relationships with each other – in *social* relationships – relationships which (as he put it) were 'indispensable and independent of their will' (1859). For Marx it was the social relationships into which people were inserted, and not the individuals abstracted from them, that held the key to the character of modern society. Individuals as such did not figure centrally in his work. He did not spend time, as liberal thinkers did, trying to determine their internal psychologies. He was aware of the biological dimension to human behaviour, that 'the first premise of all human history is, of course, the existence of *living* human beings' (1846). But for Marx, individuals were overridingly social beings, and it was their social being that determined their consciousness. He believed that to abstract the individual from that social context, as liberal thought did, was to obscure the way in which individuals and circumstances continually interact to shape each other. It was to miss the way in which people, in order to survive at all, are obliged to act on the natural world, and in the process to change that world and to change themselves within it.

So there is no sense of a constant human nature in Marx. There is, rather, a sense that human beings have a potentiality for fully-altruistic relationships that cannot be completely realized while they remain divided by private property. In liberal thought, property-owning individuals were left free to create their own world by their own actions. Marx too recognized the role of human agency, but was more conscious than liberalism of the constraints operating upon it. As he put it, 'men make their own history, but they do not make it just as they please; they do not make it under circumstances chosen by themselves, but under circumstances directly encountered, given and transmitted from the past. The tradition of all the dead generations weighs like a nightmare on the brain of the living' (1852). For Marx, the realistic options experienced by individual social actors varied between generations, and became wide only as (and to the degree that) the productive forces within society grew over time. Individuals could not be abstracted out of society and out of time, and given constant universal characteristics, as liberal thought suggested. Instead, individuals had to be situated in the definite social relations and in the definite periods of time in which they lived.

Liberal thought had found its starting point in a vision of human beings in competition with one another, and had quickly come to characterize modern society as one in which people traded competitively in commodities. Marx found his starting point – his 'real premises' as he called them – elsewhere: not in competition but in co-operation, not in trade but in human labour itself. Trade may be a feature of only certain sorts of society; but in every sort of society men and women, in order to survive, have had to produce the means of their own subsistence. Marx argued that this need to labour is basic to the human condition, that men and women 'begin to distinguish themselves from animals as soon as they begin to *produce* their means of subsistence' (*The German Ideology*, 1845–6, p.42) – when they begin to work on the natural environment, remoulding it into artifacts (clothing, housing and so on) vital to the continuance of life. Marx argued too that if we look back over time, we see that people's capacity to do this has grown. In other words, the tools and knowledge available to people as they work on their natural environment (what Marx called the *means of production*) have developed over time; and they have done so because of social pressures generated by the other feature of production which Marx also took as basic to the human condition – namely its social character.

He argued that in all human societies, men and women have normally found it advantageous to work *together* on the natural world, and to do so in regular and repeated ways. In other words, people do not simply labour by using the means of production at their disposal. They also enter into social relationships with each other in order to *produce* the things they need to survive – they enter distinct 'social relationships of production'. According to Marx, the form that these relationships take shapes the totality of the society built upon them. The social relationships of production are the defining feature of the *economic base* of society, to which law, politics, religion and culture are best seen as a complex *superstructure*.

Summary

1 Marx rejected liberalism's starting point of 'the individual', insisting instead on the primacy of social relationships.

2 For Marx, individual action was socially conditioned and socially constrained. 'Men make their own history, but not just as they please . . .'

3 Since for Marx human labour is what distinguishes humans from animals, it is the social relationships which surround production which then shape society as a whole. Societies, that is, have an economic base and a social, political and cultural superstructure.

Economy and society

For Marx, epochs of human history were distinguishable one from the other by the way production was organized in each. Each epoch (and he tended to talk, for Europe, of the epochs of *Antiquity, Feudalism* and *Capitalism*) was defined by the way production was organized within it: on the basis of *slavery* in the ancient world, on *serfdom* in feudalism, and on *wage labour* under capitalism. Each mode of production, that is, differed from the one before it; and the key difference lay in the way that those who did the labouring, who actually produced the goods and services, related to those who did not produce at all.

According to Marx, in each epoch to date, production has been organized in a socially divisive way. In each epoch production has been controlled by a tiny class of non-producers (slave owners, feudal lords and now capitalists) who, because they were effectively able to lay claim to the ownership and control of the means of production, could then live off the goods and services provided by and extracted from the vast majority of producers (the slaves, the serfs and the wage labourers) who were denied that ownership. Every mode of production, that is, has been dominated by a class division, by a separation into two main classes, those who own and control the means of production and those who do not. It was Marx's belief that capitalism would be the last mode of production to be divided in this way: that a socialist society would be free of this class division, because it would be free of the private ownership of the means of production which had hitherto set the class of producers and the class of non-producers into struggle against each other.

The existence of the private ownership of the means of production in all complex societies to date did a number of things to those societies, according to Marx. It gave individuals interests in common with others in a similar position in the property system. It turned liberalism's isolated individuals into members of whole social classes, whose individualism was drowned in a shared set of experiences and interests. And it set class against class – with the interests of the owners of property locked into mutual incompatibility with the interests of those denied property. Slave clashed with slave-owner, serf with feudal lord, worker with capitalist in class divisions so basic as to dominate all other forms of social division, self-definition and group struggle. Indeed it was because Marx argued for the centrality of this battle around production that he and **Engels**[11] were prepared to assert in *The Communist Manifesto* that 'the history of all hitherto existing society is the history of class struggles'.

So where liberal thought encouraged us to emphasize the market-based nature of contemporary social life, Marx emphasized instead the capitalist framework of property relationships within which markets were obliged to operate. For Marx, capitalism had two main differentiating features from its feudal predecessor. The first was that in capitalism productive activity was overwhelmingly geared to the sale of what was produced, rather than to the making of things to be directly consumed by the immediate producers. Under capitalism, what were produced were *commodities* – things to be bought and sold. So where Adam Smith emphasizied the novelty and importance of the market as a mechanism of exchange, Marx emphasized instead the novelty of sending everything to market. Capitalism's first distinguishing feature, for Marx, was the generalized commodity production going on within it.

Its second feature for Marx, and the source both of its dynamism and of its ultimate instability as a way of organizing economic life, was its reliance on *wage labour*. The producing classes were no longer tied to the land in various forms of serfdom. Instead they had been separated from any ownership of (or rights to) the land – had been dispossessed – and were now available as 'free wage labour'. That is, they were free to sell their labour power where they could – so they were free, untied labour – but equally they were obliged to do so, having no other means of subsistence – free to move between capitalists if they could, but never free of the need to find some capitalist to employ them. Indeed, Marx's central criticism of liberal political economy turned on this point, their misreading of the 'freedom' of the individual. Liberals focus on markets – and the market-place for commodities is a sphere of individual freedom under capitalism. People buy and sell as they choose, in what Marx characterized as the 'noisy sphere of

[11]**Frederick Engels**: 1820–1895. Marx's colleague for over 40 years. His writings include *The Condition of the Working Class in England* (1844), and *The Origin of the Family, Private Property and the State* (1884).

exchange . . . a paradise of the rights of man. Here liberty, equality, [and] property are supreme' (*Das Kapital*, Volume 1, p.167). But the commodities themselves emerge from a sphere of *production* in which people do not enjoy an equivalent equality: because there what one person is obliged to sell (his/her labour), another is free to buy. Beneath the individual freedom of the consumer lie the class inequalities of the social relations of production.

We should note that major classes, in Marx's way of thinking, normally come in twos. There were slave-owners and slaves in antiquity; there were lords and serfs in feudal Europe; and now, under capitalism, there are capitalists and workers (or bourgeoisies and proletarians -- Marx used both sets of terms). Marx argued that as the European peasantry and independent artisans were proletarianized (were obliged to sell their labour power for money wages in order to survive) the ruling classes of pre-capitalist Europe had to come to terms with a new social force – a class of merchants, industrialists and financiers – who survived only by turning money into more money by the organization of the production and exchange of commodities. Capitalism, that is, brought into existence – according to Marx – a class with the accumulated wealth to organize production: by buying raw materials and machinery (means of production) and by purchasing and utilizing the labour power of the proletariat. Within this class, individuals then prospered only by successfully competing with other capitalists, each attempting to realize his/her profits by the successful sale in Adam Smith's market-place of the commodities produced by the labour power of those they employed.

Marx's attitude to this new system of production was, of course, quite different from Adam Smith's. But it was not entirely negative. Marx realized that the emergence of a class of capitalists competing with each other had developed the productive forces of the society as a whole in ways which the social relationships of production under feudalism had no potential to do. Competition was the great locomotive of economic growth under capitalism, as Smith had recognized. This is Marx, writing in *The Communist Manifesto*:

The bourgeoisie cannot exist without constantly revolutionizing the instruments of production, and thereby the relations of production, and with them the whole relations of society. Conservation of the old modes of production in unaltered form was, on the contrary, the first condition of existence for all earlier industrial classes. Constant revolutionizing of production, uninterrupted disturbance of all social conditions, everlasting uncertainty and agitation distinguished the bourgeois epoch from all earlier ones. . . . The bourgeoisie, during its rule of scarce one hundred years, has created more massive and more colossal productive forces than have all the preceding generations together. Subjection of Nature's forces to man, machinery, application of chemistry to industry and agriculture, steam-navigation, railways, electric telegraphs, clearing of whole continents for cultivation, canalization of rivers, whole populations conjured out of the ground – what earlier century had even a presentiment that such productive forces slumbered in the lap of social labour.

To this degree at least, Marx was at one with the optimism of the early liberal thinkers. For him, as for them, history was the story of progress. It was just that for Marx the route to progress was far stormier and more contradictory than liberalism allowed. Capitalism's historic role, for Marx, was to create the material conditions for a society of abundance. Once this had been created, in the hothouse of capitalist inequalities, more egalitarian and less exploitative sets of social relationships (to wit, socialism) became possible for the first time. It was Marx's view that capitalism would progressively outlive its usefulness and, like all modes of production before it, give way to another in what he termed 'an epoch of social revolution'.

It was Marx's view that such an epoch of social revolution now loomed, put there by the contradictions of the capitalist mode of production itself, by the fact that capitalism had now done its job and needed to go. Indeed, the sharpest point of contrast between liberal and marxist readings of the new market-based industrial economies lay here – in their attitudes to its stability. Liberal thought emphasized the market's capacity to harmonize interests for the benefit of all. Marx emphasized instead the anarchy and crisis-ridden nature of market forces in an economy in capitalist hands. It was his view that economic crises were endemic to capitalism, and that they would intensify over time. They were endemic because capitalism would always be unable to pay its workers enough to buy all the goods that it produced. They were endemic because anarchic competition between capitalists inevitably put first one sector of production, and then another sector, out of proportion with the rest. And they would get worse because capitalist production relied on the generation of profits from the labour of the proletariat, and that rate of profit would fall as machinery replaced human labour in the productive systems of ever larger capitalist units.

A second generation of marxists then began to argue that international activity by capitalist concerns was temporarily alleviating this tendency to crisis, so moving the final resolution of capitalism's contradiction up on to the international stage. If cheap raw materials could be found abroad to lower production costs in capitalism's core areas, then the squeeze on profits could be thereby delayed. If new markets could be found for capitalist goods, then deficiencies in consumption could be held in check; and if new sources of investment could be located in areas of the world not yet totally under the sway of capitalist relations of production, then imbalances between sectors of the capitalist core economy could be assuaged. In other words, marxists in the 1890–1914 period were able to look at the intensification of international economic competition, the scramble for colonies, and the growing military tension between capitalist powers, and argue that this outburst of *imperialism* was a direct response to economic contradictions in core capitalist economies. Instead of foreign trade being to the advantage of all its participants, as Ricardo had argued, many marxists insisted that trade was increasingly structured by the profit requirements of large capitalist concerns, acting in concert with their own state machines to capture markets, outlets for capital, and sources of raw materials, from the capitalist concerns and state machines of other national bourgeoisies. By 1914, marxism offered students of international relations categories of 'inter-imperialist rivalry' and 'capitalist crisis' to explain the drift to war, and to reinforce their own argument that capitalism and world peace were no longer compatible.

Marxists were not arguing here that capitalism would inevitably be replaced by socialism as profits fell and war came: only that capitalism, in its crises, would create the social force which in the end would sweep it away. Its replacement was to be achieved, in Marx's view, by a proletariat radicalized by all this inequality, instability and crisis. In the broadest sense, Marx anticipated that capitalism would simplify and polarize class relationships, and because of its instabilities would not manage ultimately to legitmate itself in the eyes of its proletarian majority. Instead, over time, the size of the capitalist class would diminish (as big capitalists swallowed small ones), so pushing the whole system towards monopoly (what Marx termed the centralization and concentration of capital). In the process, the size of the proletariat would grow (as small capitalists and independent artisans were forced down into its ranks); and its levels of subsistence would fall relatively, if not absolutely, in comparison to the immense wealth of the monopolistic few. This would then radicalize more and more of them over time, and open them to the appeal of revolutionary socialist ideas. Their capacity to implement those ideas would grow as workers were concentrated into larger and larger factories, and as the overwhelming impact of capitalism on daily life drowned out any non-proletarian divisions between workers. On a bad day, Marx was prepared to concede that the radicalization of workers would still be a problematic process, requiring astute political leadership. But on good days, his confidence in the fall of capitalism was quite overwhelming – and to later socialists, highly infectious. As he put it in *The Communist Manifesto*, 'what the bourgeoisie thereby produces, above all, is its own gravediggers. Its fall and the victory of the proletariat are equally inevitable'.

Summary

1 Historically, societies have been divided between producers and non-producers – divided that is, into antagonistic social classes. Different social classes have developed and dominated in different periods. In capitalism the key social classes are the bourgeoisie and the proletariat.

2 The contemporary economy is organized on capitalist lines. Capitalism, for Marx, is a system of generalized commodity production based on free wage labour.

3 Capitalism is more dynamic than earlier ways of organizing economic life, but it is also crisis-ridden. The ultimate source of its instability is the proletariat it creates, which comes to have an interest in its replacement and the capacity to replace it.

Power and the state

Liberal and marxist conceptions of economy and society were, and remain, poles apart. To a liberal vision of a social order composed of free individuals maximizing

262

their personal goals to the benefit of all through market exchange, marxists offered an alternative picture of a society of social classes locked into antagonistic relationships within a crisis-ridden economy. Not surprisingly therefore, liberal and marxist treatments of power and the state were equally divergent.

Let us examine first the power exercised by men over women. As we saw earlier, the conviction of seventeenth century liberal theorists that they faced a world made up of rational, self-regarding individuals provided them with no consistent way of explaining the power that men exercised over women. We saw that they got round this problem either by ignoring it altogether or by retreating to earlier forms of explanation – ones that accepted power inequalities within the family unit, and the family unit itself, as in some way 'natural' in origin. Marxist categories of analysis began, and in large measure remain, equally sex-blind. Marx and Engels were overwhelmingly concerned with the social origins and consequences of tensions between classes rather than between sexes, and in their early writings took gender divisions and the family unit as largely natural in origin. Those early writings – the writings of the 1840s – tended to discuss the character and quality of relationships between the sexes only as an index of human progress. There are many paragraphs there in which Marx takes the treatment of women by men as an indicator of historical development: but in so doing he treats women as nothing more than passive symbols of changes in male society, with their position referred to but in no way explained.

It was left to Engels in 1884 to write the first major marxist account of gender divisions, in a pamphlet significantly titled *The Origins of the Family, Private Property and the State*. The title is significant because it reflects Engels' attempt to explain gender divisions and class divisions as related parts of one single historical process. Drawing heavily on now discredited Victorian social anthropology, Engels wrote of a time in the past, before the arrival of private property, in which sexual relationships were promiscuous and women socially dominant. But as societies generated wealth, he argued, and as that wealth came to be held in the form of private property, it became essential for men to know their heirs, and so vital that they controlled the sexual activity of the women who bore them. Engels did not explain why the women let the men get away with this – what he termed the 'world historical defeat of the female sex' – he seemed to treat that defeat as somehow 'natural'! But he did at least seek to explain the subordination of women to men as a social process, one deriving from the emergence of private property, and by implication one that would not survive the abolition of private property in the communist society to come.

It was the wives of the property-owning class under capitalism, bourgeois wives, who for Engels were the most subordinate, because they were totally trapped inside the family unit, excluded from the public world of paid work, and obliged to trade sexual favours and domestic servitude for a share in the return on capital. Proletarian wives, in Engels' view, were paradoxically in a better position in relation to their husbands. The poverty of the men who would control them was such that women had to engage in paid labour. They had a public existence as well as a private subordination. Engels saw in this proletarianization of women (their entry into waged work) the crucial change that would erode the family as an institution and give women (and their menfolk) a joint interest in the overthrow of capitalism. If early liberal thinkers evaded the 'woman question', Engels reduced it to the character of economic relationships, and so wrote of it as something that would not survive the capitalism with which liberal thinkers were so enamoured.

Liberalism and marxism also demonstrated a quite different attitude to the state. Both shared a sense of the relationship of the state to private property. For liberalism that relationship, as we saw, was essential. Liberal theorists looked to the state to defend the rights of property, and saw in that defence a guarantee of individual freedom. But they were also apprehensive about the power of the state, and conscious that such power could be used against property if the state fell under the control of the propertyless majority. Marx saw that possibility, and welcomed it.

Though he did not develop a fully-rounded theory of the state – to set against those of Locke and Hobbes – Marx wrote enough to indicate his central belief that the state in a capitalist society, no matter what it claimed, always ultimately acted in the interests of the property-owning ruling class. That certainly is the view of the state's role asserted by Marx and Engels in *The Communist Manifesto*, when they wrote that 'the executive of the modern state is but a committee for managing the common affairs of the whole bourgeoisie'. There were occasions on which Marx and Engels were prepared to concede that the state could enjoy a degree of autonomy from the capitalist class: 'that by way of exception . . . periods occur in which the warring classes balance each other so nearly that state power, as ostensible mediator, acquires for the moment a certain degree of independence of both' (Engels, *Origins of the Family, Private Property and the State*). But for them such moments were exceptional, and ultimately transitory, at best only a brief respite from the state's more normal intimate relationship with the personnel and interests of the class who owned the means of production.

The central assertion of the whole marxist tradition has been that state power and class power go together, that 'political power, properly so called, is merely the organized power of one class for oppressing another' (*The Communist Manifesto*). For Marx this was true even of the democratic state in a capitalist society; and he called for the replacement of representative democratic political institutions by the dictatorship of the proletariat. Marx looked to the proletariat to 'make itself the ruling class' and to replace capitalism by socialism. He also anticipated that in what he saw as the 'higher' stage of society that would then ensue – namely communism – all state forms (including the dictatorship of the proletariat) would inevitably wither away.

From Marx's own fragmented observations on the role of the modern state in a capitalist society it is clear that he saw its main job as one of preserving the privileges of the ruling class. The state's ultimate weapon here was force: and many later marxists have been content to think of the state, as Lenin[12] did, as

---

[12]**V.I. Lenin**: 1870–1924. Russian marxist, founder of the Bolshevik Party, and its leader in 1917. Author of many works, including *What is to be done* (1902), *Imperialism* (1916), and *State and Revolution* (1917).

best understood as 'a body of armed men'. But Marx (and indeed Lenin too) was also aware of the role that ideas, rather than force, play in the stabilization of capitalism. He wrote in the 1840s that 'the ideas of the ruling class are in each epoch the ruling ideas, i.e. the class which is the ruling *material* force of society, is at the same time its ruling intellectual force'. He was fairly sure in the 1840s that the bourgeoisie's attempt to sell liberalism to the emerging proletariat as just such a set of dominant ideas would fail, that the horrors of life in capitalism would prevent the mass of workers from accepting a liberal reading of their world. But in the 1920s this idea of the dominance of a particular set of ideas, as a key element in explaining the longevity of capitalism, was picked up again and integrated into a new marxist theory of the state, by the Italian communist **Antonio Gramsci**[13].

By then Marx's optimism about the inevitability of proletarian revolution had been put to a stern test in the revolutionary upheavals that swept central Europe after 1918. It had looked for a moment as though Marx's vision of proletarian power was at hand, but then the wave of working-class and peasant revolutions that had swept Bolshevism to power in Russia unexpectedly petered out in Western Europe. Fascism, not socialism, rose out of the ashes of war and capitalist crisis – first in Italy in the 1920s, then with even more terrible consequences in Germany in the 1930s. Struggling to grasp why all this should be so, Gramsci produced a set of notes on state and ideology which continue to be an important point of reference for contemporary debates among marxists.

Gramsci explained the success of the Bolsheviks in Russia, and the failure of communism in Western Europe, by using a military image from World War I. He argued that unlike Western Europe, pre-revolutionary Russia lacked layers of middle class social and cultural power in a developed 'civil society' behind the Russian State, lacked private 'trenches' of class power to block the socialist advance. Only the Russian Orthodox church existed as a defensive support to Tsarist power prior to 1917: and the church and state fell together in a socialist revolution that each was by then too weak to block. In Western Europe however, with its more developed capitalist economies and its more extensive bourgeois civil societies, socialists faced stalemated trench warfare of the Flanders variety. Here the capitalist state was a more substantial barrier to socialist advance because of its integral relationship to the complex capitalist society behind it. In the West, if the state was the first 'trench' that socialists had to conquer, many other 'trenches' of private capitalist power remained behind it, and they had to be conquered too. For socialists in the West faced more than state power. They faced in addition the entrenched private world of pro-capitalist institutions – not just a world of churches, but also one of education systems, the media, even right-wing trade unionism. It was this world that gave capitalism its stability: by its unity against socialism, by its acceptance and articulation of a dominant set of pro-capitalist ideas.

---

[13]**Antonio Gramsci**: 1891–1937. Italian marxist, founder and briefly leader of the Italian Communist Party, imprisoned by Mussolini. His writings in captivity were later published as *The Prison Notebooks*.

On this view, capitalism was safe from socialist revolution because, and to the degree that, a particular set of ideas ran through all aspects of society, and dominated ways of thinking. Liberal ideas in the mid-nineteenth century had played that role in the United Kingdom, and continued in large part to do so; and the ideas of national glory and imperial expansion were, in the 1920s, attempting to do the same. In each case the state had a crucial role to play in generating such an all pervasive 'national project', and (through its policies) in uniting a bloc of classes behind these particular ideas. Capitalism was stable, according to Gramsci, because and to the degree that the capitalist state managed to integrate significant sections of the working class (and peasantry in the Italian case) into a political coalition united behind a non-revolutionary national project.

Therefore, to overturn capitalism, it was no longer just enough to seize state power. Revolutionary socialists had to build a counter-culture of their own: create their own socialist ideology, wean workers away from anti-socialist ways of thinking, and fuse a bloc of classes behind their revolutionary ideology in the struggle for state power. By the 1920s, that is, marxism had had to realize the important role of *political* and *ideological* forces in stabilizing capitalism, and to recognize that the *economic* contradictions of capitalism would not easily open the road to socialism as earlier marxists had so optimistically thought. They had come to recognize that the contradiction of interests between social classes which capitalism generated in its economic *base* could be ameliorated by political and ideological initiatives in its *superstructure*. They had come to see that capitalism would remain stable until socialist parties managed to dislodge from popular culture pro-capitalist ideas and sentiments.

Summary

1 Marxist sensitivity to questions of power relations between men and women has not been great. However, Engels did attempt to explain gender divisions as products of the emergence of private property, and as such, unlikely to survive the demise of private property in socialism.

2 Marx saw the state as the agent of the dominant class, with at most a limited degree of autonomy from control by the owners of the means of production. He expected the proletariat to establish its own dictatorship in socialism, and for all forms of the state to wither away in communism.

3 Later marxists – particularly Gramsci – emphasized the important role played by the state in orchestrating ideologies to legitimate capitalism and alliances of classes to sustain it.

2.3 Social reformism

Liberal and marxist bodies of thought quickly became, and have remained, important points of reference in the persistent debate about the character of modern society. But as presented here – one unashamedly enthusiastic about capitalism, the other totally opposed to its continuation – it is hardly surprising that they did not exhaust the range of interpretations available to twentieth century social science. It would appear that for many social thinkers what liberalism and marxism gained in the tight internal coherence of their analyses they lost either in comprehensiveness or in subtlety. They shut out the argument of the 'middle ground' that capitalism was a society in need of (and open to) extensive *reform*.

Of all the traditions of thought surveyed here, social reformism is the most 'artificial', in the sense of being a construct that we are imposing on a wide and in many ways disparate range of scholarship. The label 'social reformism' is not an entirely satisfactory one, because it gives priority to a political programme (of reform) rather than to the organizing axes of thought from which the commitment to that programme derived. But we will use it, in the absence of anything better, precisely because the intellectual positions gathered here are more in agreement on their conclusions about reform than they are on the routes by which they arrive at that agreement. Common points of reference do exist to hold these positions together as a tradition, as we will see, including: a generalized commitment to progress, a faith in the capacity of human beings to 'improve', an egalitarian impulse predisposing them to democracy, a faith in the role of the state as an instrument of social reform, a belief in the possibility and desirability of incremental social change and an antipathy to revolutionary movements and revolutionary change. But these underlying predispositions will not bind social reformism into as coherent and internally logical a package of ideas as we found in liberalism and marxism: and this should not surprise us. For the theorists gathered here as social reformists will often want to emphasize the gain to scholarship that comes from a certain untidiness of thought, from the existence of loose ends, and from an openness to a wide range of ideas and influences. Their thought, that is, will invariably be characterized by what **John Stuart Mill**[14] proudly called 'practical eclecticism' and 'a catholic spirit in philosophy'.

Social reformism as portrayed here is *very* much closer as an intellectual tradition to liberalism than to marxism. (Indeed, many of the nineteenth century thinkers cited here as social reformers are often treated as major figures in mainstream liberalism – so close is the connection between liberal and social reformist bodies of thought.) Many of the late Victorian advocates of social reform shared classical liberal assumptions about the importance of the individual, about the growth of markets and about the relationship between freedom and the rule of law. But what many of our social reformists increasingly lacked as time went on, was the confidence displayed by early liberals in the potential of untramelled market forces and unbridled self-interest to generate a stable and just social order. In this centre ground we will find a growing awareness that markets do work well as allocators of economic resources, but also a sense that they do not work perfectly, and that if uncontrolled are likely to generate undesirable social consequences. By the end of the nineteenth century, when a discernible social reformist current became

---

[14]**John Stuart Mill**: 1806–1873. Son of James Mill, economist and philosopher, active political reformer and Member of Parliament. His writings include *System of Logic* (1848), *Principles of Political Economy* (1849), *On Liberty* (1859), *Representative Government* (1861), *Utilitarianism* (1863) and *The Subjection of Women* (1869).

evident in contemporary debate on social issues, the intellectuals within that current would often call themselves liberals – but this time *new liberals*, precisely to differentiate themselves from the unreconstructed advocates of *laissez-faire* with whom they were in such sharp political disagreement. These 'new liberals' looked to the *state*, as earlier liberals had not, to extend the franchise, to implement programmes of social reform, and even (in some cases) to intervene in the running of a market economy.

In this centre ground too we will find a growing sense, shared with marxism, that in a capitalist society the owners of the means of production enjoy a power over the state out of proportion to their numbers in the population, even if that state has a wide franchise. But that recognition, which in marxism sustained a rejection of 'bourgeois democracy' and a preference for a new proletarian state, was combined here with an equally powerful sense that the modern bureaucratic state is itself a potential source of awesome tyranny. So some of the theorists of the centre ground called themselves socialists, but they insisted that they were democratic socialists, not marxists, and were as hostile to the monopoly of power by the communist party in the Soviet Union as they were to the excessive political power of private capital in the West. Our centre ground, that is, is neither liberal nor marxist as we have described those traditions of thought. Its anchorage, if it has a common one, is somewhere between them in a position sufficiently united and different to warrant its own label of 'social reformism'.

The basic premises of social reformism

If there is a common starting point for this third tradition of thought, it lies in some generalized belief in progress – in some sense, as John Stuart Mill put it, 'that the general tendency is, and will continue to be, saving temporary and occasional exceptions, one of improvement; a tendency towards a better and happier state'. There is a general recognition too, among theorists grouped here as social reformists, that 'circumstances maketh the man', that people are good or bad as circumstances allow, that people can be educated to be better, and that circumstances can be reformed. Individual theorists within the tradition arrived at that view from different starting points. For some – the influential English democratic socialist **R.H. Tawney**[15] was one – the belief in the impact of environment on character derived from a serious religious commitment. For others, often referred to as utopian socialists[16] to distinguish them from the marxist variety, the belief stemmed from a condemnation of competition and a preference for small co-operative communities. And for still others, John Stuart Mill again is perhaps the prime example, the source of this belief was the *utilitarian*

[15]**R.H. Tawney**: 1880–1962. Economic historian and Labour Party intellectual, heavily involved in the Workers Educational Association, whose political writings include *The Acquisitive Society* (1921), *Equality* (1931), *The Attack and Other Essay* (1953), and *The Radical Tradition* (1964).

[16]**Robert Owen**: 1771–1858. The best known of the British utopian socialists, he developed his cotton mills at New Lanark in Scotland in line with his commitment to education, improved social conditions and mutual co-operation. He published *A New View of Society* in 1813.

philosophy of his father's circle (that is, of **Jeremy Bentham**[17] and of **James Mill**[18]). Since the younger Mill was such an influence on later social reformists, it is worth closing in on his reasoning in more detail.

In liberal thought as we have presented it, it is individuals who create social institutions and effect social change. In marxism the relationship is much the other way round. Individuals are so shaped by the social relationships in which they find themselves that social analysis rarely needs to go down to the individual level. The marxist story of social change is told at the level of social classes, not at the level of the individuals who constitute those classes in any one generation. There is some kind of continuum of explanation here, from the individual to the social: and though liberal and marxist thinkers often come off their starting point to explore the role of structures or individuals in social causation, their whole mode of thought pulls them away from any systematic exploration of the interplay of individuals and social structures. Yet that *interplay* is at the heart of the social reformist position, and certainly was a central preoccupation of John Stuart Mill. He knew how circumstances mould people, but he was equally convinced that people could rise above circumstance, particularly if educated to do so.

The malleability of human nature was central to Mill's faith in social progress. For him, human nature was not a constant thing. It was something made by circumstances. Mill shared Bentham's enthusiasm for what was known as *associationist* psychology. In that psychology, 'the mind is conceived, as it was by Locke, as a dark room, the senses being the windows which alone provide its knowledge of the external world' (Thomas, 1985, p.24). What we are, what we know, what we value, all that is put together inside our mind (by certain principles of association) from the data flowing into it from outside, via our senses. But of course this doctrine 'of the formation of character by circumstances, as James Mill called it, cuts two ways.' (ibid, p.25) It makes *education* vital, since if the educator can get in first, before the mind is formed, moral development is certain. But it also makes *reform* essential, because the mind also gathers knowledge of the world around it, a world which if unreformed must impair the quality of the morality it generates. Indeed the older Mill applied just this psychology to the education of his son, with the effect both of creating a child prodigy – educated far beyond his years – and of inducing a nervous breakdown in the young John Stuart Mill.

The excesses of the position, when applied in this way, need not however detract from its general importance as an alternative to both liberalism and marxism. To liberal theorists unenthusiastic about state action, social reformists pressed the case for the improvement of 'circumstances'. To marxism convinced that such new circumstances could only be achieved by class-based revolution, social

[17]**Jeremy Bentham**: 1748–1832. Leading philosopher, writer and political reformer. Co-founder, with James Mill, of the influential *Westminster Review*. His writings include *Fragments on Government* (1776), and *Introduction to Principles of Morals and Legislation* (1780).

[18]**James Mill**: 1773–1836. Journalist, employee of the East India company, friend of Bentham and co-founder of the *Westminister Review*. His writings include *Elements of Political Economy* (1821), *Phenomena of the Human Mind* (1829), and *Fragment on Mackintosh* (1835).

reformists argued the case for education, general moral improvement, and incremental change through the building of consensus. There is a strong strand of belief, within intellectuals grouped here as social reformist, that most social problems have a solution, one moreover that can be realized by what J.S. Mill called 'piecemeal engineering'. There is a belief too that most people are sufficiently open to rational argument to be able to see that solution, and sufficiently socially-minded to be willing to compromise their own immediate interests in order to achieve it. So for that reason, the focus of effort should not be on the blanket defence of markets or the generalized advocacy of revolution. Effort should be directed instead to the identification of solutions to discrete social problems and to the creation of the institutions and the public morality through which those solutions can be realized.

Summary

1 Social reformism is a more diverse tradition than liberalism or marxism. It stands closer to liberalism than to marxism. It differs from liberalism in its sense of the inadequacy of unregulated markets and in its associated willingness to advocate state action to enhance individual liberty.

2 Social reformism is united around a belief in the malleability of human nature, in the capacity of circumstances to shape character, and in the role of the state as a reformer of circumstances.

3 Social reformism is united by its recognition of the importance for social life of the interplay of individual action and social structure.

Power and the state

As we saw above, early liberal thought sought to justify its case for representative government by appeals to universalistic principles – to the 'natural rights' enjoyed by all 'men'. But that same liberalism had been reluctant to carry the egalitarianism of those principles to its logical conclusion, had baulked at the advocacy of a state representative of *all* men, let alone one representative of *women* as well. The movement from the 'old' liberalism to the 'new' involved initially a transcendence of just this limitation.

The underlying democratic logic of a system of political representation based on universal rights had not been lost on radical thinkers even in the seventeenth century. When, at the height of the English civil war, Oliver Cromwell had debated restrictions to the franchise with delegates from his soldiers (in what are now known as the Putney debates), Colonel Rainsborough had stood before him to argue the democratic case. In one of the earliest recorded claims for democratic reform in English political history, he said:

> For really I think that the poorest he that is in England hath a life to live as the greatest he . . . and therefore truly, Sir, I think it clear that every man that is to live under a government ought first by his own consent to put himself under that government, and I do think that the poorest man in England is not

at all bound in a strict sense to that government that he hath not had a voice to put himself under.

That same logic would surface, in a different form, more than a century later in the political radicalism of the English utilitarians. Bentham began from pristine liberal premises, of society understood as composed of self-interested individuals, in this case organizing their social life around what Bentham took to be Nature's basic forces: pain and pleasure. The tight logic of Bentham's thought would not allow any possibility that one person's pleasure should have greater value than another's (for Bentham, James Mill reported, 'pushpin is as good as poetry'); and the egalitarianism implicit in this led him to urge the reform of a whole series of institutions in which social privilege still prevailed. In company with contemporary liberal orthodoxy, Bentham believed that every person was the best judge of his/her own best interest, and accordingly best placed to judge who should rule over them. In his later years, Bentham campaigned vigorously against a limited franchise precisely because it necessarily guaranteed that the state would be ruled in the interests of the few. Legislators being as self-interested – in Bentham's eyes – as everyone else, only by making it in their self-interest to rule for the benefit of all could a state hope to escape a decline into government by 'sinister interests'. Bentham argued that it was 'only through equality of power (approached in universal suffrage) [that it was] possible to gain security from arbitrary and tyrannical rule' (Rosen, 1983, p.218). Create a situation in which all individuals vote, vote often and vote secretly, and you would create a state whose representative relationship with the entire electorate would meet the utilitarian test – of generating by its actions 'the greatest happiness of the greatest number'.

So Bentham used standard liberal arguments about individuals and their interests to justify extensions of the franchise: though it should be said that in the hands of his chief ally, James Mill, that extension still stopped short of women and the working class. But in the hands of John Stuart Mill, a generation later, those exclusions were whittled away. Like his father, the younger Mill argued that popular participation in representative government was vital to keep the state under control, and to guarantee individual liberties of conscience, taste and association. This was the standard 'protective case' for democracy: but for the younger Mill there was a 'participatory case' to be made for democracy as well. Democratic participation was also essential to permit the full development of individual potentiality. Participation in political life (including voting, involvement in local administration, and the performance of jury service) was seen by Mill as 'vital to create a direct interest in government, and consequently a basis for an involved, informed and developed citizenry. Mill conceived of democratic politics as a prime mechanism of moral self-development' (Held, 1983, p.17); and opposed barriers to that moral self-development created by the unreformed inequalities of an unregulated market order.

We must remember that behind the early liberal reluctance to carry to their logical conclusion the universalistic principles which they used to justify the rights of property, was a fear of *class*. Early liberals were afraid that a mass electorate would threaten property, by putting government under the control of the 'rude masses', so replacing the tyranny of an aristocratic minority hostile to commercial property by the even more awesome tyranny of a dispossessed majority hostile to property as such. The younger Mill saw that danger and shared that fear: that democracy would produce 'a legislature reflecting exclusively the opinions and preferences of the most ignorant class' (cited in Duncan, 1973, p.228). But Mill was less worried than earlier liberals because he had what would become a typically 'social reformist' view of class. For him, incompatible class interests (between Marx's bourgeoisie and proletariat) were not a permanent feature of life under capitalism. 'Even when he viewed the impact of class as deep and discouraging, he continued to insist that men could be liberated from class by reason, by perceiving the world correctly, and he felt that the tendency for this to happen was increasing with the progress of civilization, which meant [for him] largely the diffusion of intelligence' (Duncan, 1973, p.230). Mill was confident that industrial and social improvements would in the end alter the shape of the class structure, replacing the polarities of rich and poor with a more generally middle-class society. Like many of the intellectuals grouped here as socialist reformist, he felt that class divisions and class tensions would ease over time, that class differences could be reconciled, that the centrality of class to people's sense of the world would diminish as prosperity spread, and that education and rational argument – not class conflict – held the key to social progress.

So for Mill, the 'threat' that democracy posed to property was a manageable one, a threat that could be negated by widespread popular education, and by constitutional innovations within the institutions of the democratic state. He favoured the retention of a Second Chamber, to block the excesses of the popularly-elected Lower House. He favoured extra votes for those with education. He favoured proportional representation, because he thought it likely to generate a higher quality of representative. He even opposed secret ballots, preferring people to have to defend in public their use of the vote. But with these caveats, he was prepared to support a universal franchise, because of his belief that participation in the democratic process would educate the citizenry into a less self-seeking, class-based and avaricious mode of thought. And he was prepared to advocate democratization too because he thought it was 'both inevitable and right that the majority . . . should be the dominant power in a democracy' (Thompson, 1976, p.78).

Nowhere is this sense of the twin imperatives of inevitability and justice more evident in John Stuart Mill's work than in his writings on the position of women. We noted earlier **Mary Wollstonecraft's**[19] *A Vindication of the Rights of Woman*, in which liberal arguments on natural rights, and utilitarian claims on the social benefits of sexual equality, had been combined to discredit arguments about the 'naturalness' of women's subordination to men. As she put it:

If the abstract rights of man will bear discussion and explanation, those of woman, by a parity of reasoning, will not shrink from the same test . . . Who

[19]**Mary Wollstonecraft**: 1759–1797. Educationalist and writer, member of a group of Radicals that included William Godwin, Tom Paine and Joseph Priestley.

made man the exclusive judge, if woman partake with him of the gift of reason
. . . But if women are to be excluded, without having a voice, from a
participation of the natural rights of mankind, prove first, to ward off a charge
of injustice and inconsistency, that they want reason, else the flaw . . . ever
show that man must, in some shape, act as a tyrant [in denying women] civil
and political rights . . . Reason . . . loudly demands JUSTICE for one half
of the human race.

(Wollstonecraft, 1792, pp.87, 89.)

In arguing in this way, Mary Wollstonecraft deployed propositions about natural
rights to insist that 'the female half of the species should be treated first as human
rather than as sexed beings' (Coole, 1988, p.122). She sustained her position by
utilitarian arguments as well, insisting that if women were to be good companions
to men, and capable of rearing the next generation of competent citizens, then
they too would need to be educated. This argument on the education of women
found its way directly into the later writings of John Stuart Mill, particularly
those influenced by his wife, Harriet Taylor. So too did the Wollstonecraft agenda
for women's emancipation: education, civil rights, access to jobs and full political
citizenship. Since Mill believed that participation in public life was vital to the
moral development of those who participated, he was keen to extend that process
of moral development throughout society. He saw that the family had a key role
to play in inculcating such moral values, and that the family could not perform
that function adequately if the women within it languished in a captive privacy,
trapped in ignorance. As Diana Coole observed, for Mill: 'so long as the family
[was] organized along hierarchical lines . . . children [would] be schooled in
tyranny, and public virtue [would] be undermined by the self-love encouraged
in men and the narrow-mindedness enforced in women' (1988, p.142).

For Wollstonecraft and for Mill, sexual equality meant that women should have
the right to participate in public life as well as to work in the private domain.
Neither of them questioned the division of society into those two spheres, nor
challenged the degree to which women were (as they still are) obliged to carry
the burden of domestic responsibilites. But at least after they had made their
arguments, it was no longer so easy for liberal theorists to exclude unchallenged
half the population from the rights they claimed for all.

Summary

1 Social reformism carried the egalitarian logic of liberalism to its logical
   conclusion: arguing for a democratic franchise and equal rights for women.
2 John Stuart Mill recognized the positive impact on human capacities of
   participation in political life, and discounted earlier liberal fears of democracy
   as 'mob rule'.

Economy and society

The writings of John Stuart Mill opened the door through which the 'new
liberalism' emerged. If moral self-development was vital to individual liberty,

then it was *illiberal* to leave unreformed the social institutions and practices which blocked the moral self-development of the poor and disadvantaged. No longer could the definition of individual freedom be restricted to a *negative* one – as the freedom from state-levied restraints on the individual ability to act. Freedom now had to become a *positive* right, the actual ability to do things, with the freedom to participate and develop fully as an individual guaranteed by state action against private barriers to equality. So the state gathered a new role: 'to create those conditions in which self-fulfilment of individuals could occur' (Held, 1983, p.64); and in this way the 'new liberalism' embraced social reform, and reduced earlier liberal dependence on competition as the driving force of human progress.

It is this pursuit of social reform as the prerequisite for the full realization of individual potentiality that has inspired the British non-marxist Left in the twentieth century. Its first political flowering came in the reforming Liberal Government of 1906; and when the Liberal Party disintegrated after 1916, many of the new liberals found their way into senior positions in the British Labour Party. Indeed, social reform inspired by this revitalized liberal philosophy was thereafter largely the preserve of Labour. The Attlee Government's creation of the welfare state – on lines designed by leading New Liberals such as Beveridge[20] and Keynes[21] – is a living testimony to the impact of this way of thinking on twentieth century political and social life in the United Kingdom. It has been an impact which has emphasized the role of the state far more than early liberal thought allowed; and it is an impact which has challenged marxist assertions on the impossibility of capitalist reform.

A fuller discussion of the impact of these traditions of thought on contemporary political life must, however, await the final section of this chapter. What we need to extract now is the contribution of 'new liberal' thinking to the stock of concepts and theories on which we might want to draw in making our own analyses of contemporary life. And here, as in our consideration of earlier traditions of thought, we will need to be selective. We have space to look in detail only at the revision of liberal attitudes to the market that is evident in the thinking of the most influential of all the theorists here labelled social reformist, John Maynard Keynes.

The early liberal faith in the ability of markets to generate prosperity and social stability remained influential throughout the nineteenth century; and indeed (as we have already seen) remains so to this day. Certainly John Stuart Mill retained that optimism throughout his life. But in the United Kingdom in the years after his death (in 1873) early liberal optimism about the inevitability of progress through *laissez-faire* policies began to diminish, as the intensification of international competition from the now rapidly-industrializing German and

---

[20]**William Beveridge**: 1879–1963. Major influence on the development of social policy in Britain, author of the Report on *Social Insurance and Allied Services* (1942) which had a formative effect on the design of the post-war welfare state.

[21]**John Maynard Keynes**: 1883–1946. Economist, member of the Bloomsbury group, his writings include *The Economic Consequences of the Peace* (1919) and *A General Theory of Employment, Interest and Money* (1936).

American economies ended the monopoly of industrial production enjoyed by British manufacturers in mid-century. Later nineteenth century English liberal thinkers became increasingly aware too of the social cost of *laissez-faire* policies to the vast reservoirs of the Victorian poor, locked as they were in the most appalling conditions of industrial and social degradation. Many liberals came to see (and to fear) in that degradation the dangers of radicalization for which marxists were calling; and this same fear of a socialist proletariat stimulated equivalent responses in liberals elsewhere in Europe. Those fears were still very much in evidence in the years after World War I, years scarred by mass unemployment, the rise of fascism and the spread of support for the Soviet Union. By then, the 'middle ground' badly needed an economic theory that could chart its way between the defenders of an unregulated market order and the revolutionary socialist claim that there was no hope of generalized prosperity while private property remained. That is why Keynes is such an important figure in the history of social reformism. For by 1936, when he produced his *General Theory of Employment, Interest and Money*, the 'middle way' had at last found the economic analysis it so desperately required.

Keynes was by then a critic of what he termed 'unregulated capitalism'. In direct opposition to inter-war economic orthodoxy, he argued that the unemployment of the 1930s could not be solved by cutting government spending and money wages, as the Treasury at the time appeared to think. Of course he was aware that cutting wages would enable employers to lower their prices, as his critics emphasized. But he realized that cutting wages had two effects, not one. It enabled employers to reduce their prices, retain more of their income as profits, and hopefully sell more of their now cheaper goods. But at the same time it reduced the purchasing power of the workers whose wages were cut, and left business confidence low, with employers able to sell less. In fact Keynes was not convinced that cutting money wages would actually reduce the real purchasing power of workers, since prices would also fall, to leave the situation unaltered, and the real value of company debts and taxation much increased. It was better, in his view, to tackle the Depression by expanding the economy, and allowing prices to rise; since this too would not only reduce real wages (so long as money wages remained unaltered) but would also ease the burden of corporate debt, so boosting business confidence and investment levels. Against the argument of generalized wage cutting, Keynes insisted that if full employment was to be achieved, it would come only as a consequence of firms somehow being able to produce and sell goods again in large quantities and so employ more people. The question was, how was that volume of output to be generated?

In the conditions of the 1930s, Keynes argued, what the system required was more demand and more spending, not less demand and more saving; and that could best be generated, he thought, both by redistributing income from the high savers (the rich) to the low savers (the poor), and by the government spending more money itself, generating a multiplier effect through the whole economy by an expansion of its own labour force, by its own investment-spending and by its purchasing of the products of the private sector. The Keynesian specification for the role of the state that emerged in the 1930s was one which required the government to manage levels of demand in the economy as a whole (by its instructions to banks, and by its own spending), to keep demand at that level which could generate high levels of employment. It was a specification that gave social reformers for an entire generation after 1945 an answer both to liberal criticisms of state action and to marxist criticisms of capitalism.

We should remember too that, as it did so, it reinforced a characteristic social reformist view that both liberalism and marxism systematically underestimated the complexity of the social structure created by industrialism. Society was not reducible to a billard table on which rational isolated individuals bounced off one another in egotistical competition. Nor was it – to change the metaphor – a battlefield of polarized classes. There were class divisions, of course, and the reality of working-class life, at least in the *early* stages of capitalist development, was as oppressive as Marx had said. But in line with the thinking of John Stuart Mill, social reformists tended to see the *abatement* of class tension over time, to anticipate that class divisions would lose their ferocity and centrality as prosperity grew, and as the democratic process generated universal rights of *citizenship* (to vote, to unionize, to enjoy access to education, health care, pensions and so on) that cut across the experience of class-based inequalities of income and power.

Though John Stuart Mill was one source for such social reformist thinking on social divisions, by far the most important challenge to marxist views on social class came from the German 'new liberal' sociologist **Max Weber**[22]. Politically, Max Weber was heavily involved in German liberal politics, advocating the democratization of the German state and its active involvement in economic and social reform. Intellectually, he saw his own work as in part 'rounding out' marxism by supplementing its explanatory variables. Weber recognized the importance of class divisions in modern society, and the existence of the proletariat and the bourgeoisie. He was prepared to identify the origins of class division in the way the economy was organized, but he resisted Marx's attempts to tie class to property ownership. For Weber, class divisions reflected the relative strength of groups in the market, and was best captured by variations of income, not ownership. Such variations in their turn generated a hierarchy of classes, relating to each other in more complex ways than the simple polarity of incompatible interests emphasized by marxism. And class was not, for Weber, the only form or cause of social divisions. Divisions of *status* and divisions of *power* also set groups apart, and into hierarchical relationships the one with the other; and stratification by status and power was not reducible, as marxism would argue, even in the last instance to questions of property ownership.

Weber was able to argue this because of his sense – shared by others within this broad tradition of thought – of the multiplicity of causal forces at work in society at large. But he was also able to argue it because of his sense, more particular to himself, of capitalism as being merely one, admittedly vital, manifestation of a much broader process at work in modern western society. This

---

[22]**Max Weber**: 1864–1920. German sociologist. His writings available in English include *The Protestant Ethic and the Spirit of Capitalism* (1904–5), *The Methodology of the Social Sciences* (1903–17) and *Economy and Society*.

was a process he referred to as *rationalization*. From his liberal roots, Weber took as central the notion of 'reason', and defined what he termed 'instrumental rationality' as the ability to achieve specified goals by technically efficient means. In his view (and here he stood full-square with both liberalism and marxism) the rationality of western culture in this sense had grown significantly of late, as science had replaced religion as the dominant mode of understanding the natural world, and as the means of production available to successive generations had grown with rapid strides under the force of capitalist competition. Indeed, as we saw, liberal optimism in the future, and marxist certainty on the possibilities of a society of abundance, rested precisely on this view of the desirability of science and industry as 'rational'.

Weber was less sanguine about the potentialities of modern society than Smith and Marx. There was a streak of pessimism in the Weber soul, a sense of trouble that they both lacked. He sensed that western societies were not just more rational in their cultures. They were also more rational in their modes of organization. History was less to be characterized by the struggle between classes than by the growing *bureaucratization* of all forms of social life. The emergence of the modern bureaucracy, according to Weber, gave to contemporary societies the capacity to achieve social ends of unprecedented complexity. They could now run standardized health systems, mass armies, international economies, and so on. But as this technical capacity had grown, as scientific knowledge had developed, the moral certainties of earlier belief systems had slipped away; and life had become so complex as to be literally beyond the capacity of isolated individuals to grasp. Here for Weber was the modern paradox eating away at the optimism of early liberalism and at the certainties of marxism: that modern men and women possessed an enhanced technical capacity to achieve ends that were no longer clear to them, that they were armed with a knowledge-based culture in a world that was now too complex to know. The capitalist oppression of the working class would not forge in the collective mind of the proletariat a vision of an emancipated utopia. It would simply throw up another bureaucracy — that of the revolutionary socialist party — which, if successful, would rule in the proletariat's name. As Weber put it, with the rise of socialism, 'it is the dictatorship of the official, not that of the worker, which, for the present at any rate, is on the advance' (*Essay on Socialism*, 1918).

Summary

1 Social reformers, as new liberals, saw liberty as having both a negative and a positive face; and accepted the need for social reform if people were actually to realize the formal rights accorded to them by earlier liberal thought.

2 Keynes provided social reformism with its economic analysis, rejecting earlier claims that markets guarantee full employment, and advocating state action to stimulate adequate levels of consumer demand.

3 Social reformism emphasizes the complexity of social structure. Max Weber is the key figure here, arguing for a multiplicity of sources of social division, and warning of the danger of the bureaucratization of modern social life.

2.4 Conservatism

There is a fourth reaction to the arrival of industrial society which we need to observe, because it too released into academic scholarship a particular set of concerns and ways of analysing them. That is conservatism. We have held it back to the end not because it is unimportant, but because conservative thought has never generated the scale and detail of social analysis characteristic of the other three traditions, and because its central assertions have in modern times largely been formulated in response to the others – and particularly in reaction to liberalism. So the other traditions of thought need to be in place first if the full significance of the conservative reaction to them is to be grasped.

We should not be surprised by, or see weakness in, the under-developed nature of conservative thought. It is only those who would change the world who feel the need to analyse it in detail; and those who would proselytize who first need an argument. 'Conservatism becomes conscious only when forced to be so' (Scruton, 1980, p.20). Conservatives have come to feel the need for an extended analysis only to counter the proselytization of others; reacting in our period initially to the strident optimism of eighteenth and nineteenth century liberalism. **Edmund Burke**[23] is a key figure here, in English conservatism at least. Indeed it is not too much to argue that the 'philosophical substance of modern conservatism was brought into being in 1790 by Edmund Burke . . .[and that] to a remarkable degree, the central themes of conservative thought over the last two centuries are but widenings of themes enunciated by Burke with specific reference to revolutionary France' (Nisbet, 1986, p.1).

Burke condemned the revolutionaries in France for their excessive arrogance in breaking so ruthlessly with the institutions and practices of the past in their attempt to create a new revolutionary society. History was not to be broken with so decisively; for society had to be understood as a 'partnership not only between those who are living, but between those who are living, those who are dead and those who are to be born' (Burke, 1790). History in all its complexity is there to be learnt from. Customs should be valued as the consolidated wisdom of previous ages. The power of reason and intellect found in just one generation is not enough to justify sweeping away the dominant institutional legacies of the past. Intellectuals, particularly revolutionary ones, would therefore do well to recognize their own limitations, lest their drastic attempts at social engineering degenerate into a tyranny of the 'enlightened' over the rest. According to Burke, societies and their liberties cannot be built just upon a specification of human 'rights'. Such societies also require strong institutions to keep human passions under check; and if these are weakened, the society will inevitably drift towards new strong institutions of a military kind. Believing this, Burke had no time for political systems or social orders consciously based on some metaphysical principle such as 'the Rights of Man'. Such societies, by weakening traditional sources

---

[23]**Edmund Burke**: 1729–1797. Lawyer, politician, supporter of the American War of Independence, but not of the French Revolution. Author of many books and pamphlets, including *Reflections on the Revolution in France* (1790) and *An Appeal from the New to the Old Whigs* (1791).

of private liberty (in the family, the church and the local community) could only pave the way for a new form of tyranny. 'Those who attempt to level, never equalize', Burke wrote, because they fail to grasp the importance of social differentiation and hierarchy as guarantors of both freedom and order.

The bases of conservative thought

Burke's writings on the French Revolution demonstrate clear and characteristic attitudes to human nature and social change. Conservatism has always been a 'philosophy of imperfection', emphasizing the limited capacities of human reason, and counselling caution against the excessive rationalism of reformers and revolutionaries – arguing against what Roger Scruton has called 'the principal enemy of conservatism, the philosophy of liberalism, with all its attendant trappings of individual autonomy and the "natural" rights of man' (Scruton, 1980, p.16). Burke spoke for many conservative thinkers when he wrote that 'we are afraid to put men to live and trade each upon his own private stock of reason – because we suspect that the stock in each man is small, and that the individuals would do better to avail themselves to the general bank and capital of nations and of ages'.

In reaction to the belief in progress and the faith in reason evident in much liberal thought, conservatives have always been keen to emphasize both 'that the world was by no means as intelligible as [people] had come to assume' and 'that pain, evil and suffering were not just purely temporary elements in the human condition, originating in an unjust organization of society' (O'Sullivan, 1976, p.11). In conservative thought, there is always a limit to the capacity of individuals to reshape social life: either because that social life has a higher, more divine, architect, or because contemporary conditions are too complex a product of the past to be easily analysed and amended. The religious basis of human frailty is an important theme for many conservative thinkers: that, as Disraeli put it, 'the most powerful principle which governs man is the religious principle – Man was made to adore and to obey' (cited in Leigh, 1979, p.133). So too is the sense of the individual as occupying a brief moment in time, charged with responsibilities to the past as well as to the present, and under some generalized obligation to justify any alteration to the status quo. 'A Conservative', Pickthorn told us, is a person 'who believes that in politics the onus of proof is on the proposer of change' (ibid, p.20).

So when **Michael Oakeshott**[24] came to define conservatism, he defined it not as a creed, or a doctrine, but as a *disposition*, a propensity 'to enjoy what is available rather than to wish for or to look for something else; to delight in what is present rather than what was or what may be' (1962, p.168).

To be conservative, then, is to prefer the familiar to the unknown, to prefer the tried to the untried, fact to mystery, the actual to the possible, the limited

[24]**Michael Oakeshott**: b.1901. Formerly Professor of Politics at the University of London. His recent publications include *Rationalism in Politics: and Other Essays* (1962), *On Human Conduct* (1975) and *On History and Other Essays* (1983).

to the unbounded, the near to the distant, the sufficient to the superabundant, the convenient to the perfect, present laughter to utopian bliss. Familiar relationships and loyalties will be preferred to the allure of more profitable attachments; to acquire and to enlarge will be less important than to keep, to cultivate and to enjoy; the grief of loss will be more acute than the excitement of novelty or promise. It is to be equal to one's own fortune, to live at the level of one's own means, to be content with the want of greater perfection which belongs alike to oneself and one's circumstance.

(Oakeshott, 1962, p.169)

This is not to say that conservative thought is opposed to change and innovation. On the contrary, such a desire 'to conserve is compatible with all manner of change, provided only that change is also continuity' (Scruton, 1980, p.22). It is simply that for the conservative 'change is something that has to be suffered' and innovation something to be approached with caution. For even 'when an innovation commends itself as a convincing improvement' the conservative 'will look twice at its claims before accepting them . . . Because every improvement involves change, the disruption entailed has always to be set against the benefit anticipated' (Oakeshott, 1962, p.171). That is why conservatives characteristically prefer 'small and limited innovation to large and indefinite' ones, and favour 'a slow rather than a rapid pace' of change (ibid, p.172).

There is also a powerful sense, in conservative thought, of the *differences* between individuals: not just differences of rank, but underlying, innate and irremovable variations in ability and aptitude. Conservative thought is invariably elitist in character, emphasizing the importance of leadership and hierarchy, and dismissive of claims that social inequality can ever fully be removed. This sense of the differences in human beings has led conservative thinkers to resist egalitarianism. As Kirk put it, 'ultimate equality in the judgement of God, and equality before the courts of law, are recognized by conservatives; but equality of condition, they think, means equality in servitude and boredom' (Kirk, 1978, p.8).

Summary

1   Conservatives tend to be reluctant to theorize, reacting instead to the proselytizing of others. Conservatives are wary of excessive rationalism, and conscious of the dangers of radical social engineering.

2   Conservatism is a philosophy of imperfection. It rejects liberal optimism in progress and human reason, emphasizing instead the limits on human capacities, the importance of the past, and the risks involved in rapid social change.

Economy and society

The attitude of conservative thinkers to economic life under capitalism has shown a characteristic development over time. Early conservative thought, in the hands of people like **Coleridge**[25], **Carlyle**[26], and **Southey**[27] was as hostile to industrialization as it was to revolutionary politics; so the emerging capitalist industrial order faced – in its early years – a challenge of a conservative as well as of a socialist kind.

Indeed much of the support for early factory legislation came from conservative circles horrified at the inhuman working conditions created by the new employing class, and disturbed by what they saw as factory work's adverse effects on family life and individual morality. 'Commerce', as Southey said after his visit to Birmingham 'sends in no returns of its killed and wounded'. Its 'watch chains, necklaces and bracelets, buttons, buckles and snuff boxes, are dearly purchased at the expense of health and morality' (Southey, 1807, p.196). But as industrialization became established, conservative thought shifted eventually to its defence, as the focus of conservative arguments moved away from an attack on liberalism towards a critique of socialist movements. By the end of the nineteenth centurey, conservative thinkers had largely made their peace with industrialization and its dominant classes, and moved to defend their rights of property against threats posed by calls for public ownership and state planning. Indeed, except for a brief flirtation with social reformist theories of demand management in the 1950s and 1960s, conservative-inspired governments this century have normally been keen to defend the market, and to attack state planning as ineffective, inefficient, and destructive of individual freedom. This openness of modern conservative thought to liberal (and to a lesser extent, social reformist) ideas has meant that there is now no distinctly conservative way of analysing economic life; and it has given a distinctly liberal feel to the economic policies of recent Conservative governments.

If there is a considerable fusion of thought between liberalism and conservatism in their approaches to the economy, no such fusion has characterized their wider analysis of society as a whole. There, in opposition to both liberals and marxists, conservative thinkers throughout the nineteenth century insisted that any society had to be understood as more than a collection of self-interested individuals or antagonistic classes. They saw it rather as an *organic* whole, a functionally integrated set of parts, each needing to be in harmony with the rest, and each in possession of a set of *mutual* responsibilities and duties. They saw in the patterned social inequalities of previous societies the manifestation of real

---

[25]**Samuel Taylor Coleridge**: 1772–1834. Poet, critic of utilitarianism and philosopher of Romanticism. Co-author, with Wordsworth, of the *Lyrical Ballads* (1798). Wrote *On the Consitution of the Church and State* (1830).

[26]**Thomas Carlyle**: 1795–1881. Scottish essayist and historian. Critic of what he termed 'The Condition of England'. His writings include *History of the French Revolution* (1837), *Chartism* (1839) and *Heroes, Hero-Worship and the Heroic in History* (1840).

[27]**Robert Southey**: 1774–1843. One of the 'Lake poets', friend and brother-in-law to Coleridge. Author of *Letters from England* (1807) and of an immense quantity of predominantly narrative poetry. Initially sympathetic to Jacobinism, he had accommodated himself sufficiently to the existing social order by 1813 to be made poet laureate, but he remained throughout his life committed to government regulation and improvement of the social conditions created by industrialization.

differences between people's social capacities and intellectual skills, and proof that within an ordered society each individual had a particular, if unequal, place or *rank*.

This sense of society as a functionally-integrated organic whole has long been central to conservative thought. Through it, conservatives have come to see social inequality as both inevitable and necessary – indeed, even socially desirable, because it is functional to the health of the society in total. The focus of conservative concerns in social analysis has therefore been less with individuals or classes than with features of society as a whole: questions of social balance and order, social stability, the mechanisms of social integration and the maintenance of a sense of community. Conservative thought from Burke onwards has insisted that institutions and practices that have stood the test of time have a claim on our loyalty and respect for their longevity alone. The family, the monarchy, the church, private property and the nation have all attracted conservative support on this ground; and industrialization was initially resisted precisely because it threatened the sense of community inherited from the agrarian past. Coleridge's unease about industrialization, for example, rested in part in his fear that 'all traditional ties would be dissolved and . . . an impoverished mass . . . left at the mercy of the manufacturing and commercial class' (O'Sullivan, 1976, p.87). He looked to universal education and religion to reintegrate the new industrial society; and Carlyle, in similar fashion, advocated charismatic political leadership to create a new organic society in place of the one destroyed by industrial change.

Their particular solutions are now not very important – but the problem of social order and integration to which they were a response continues to preoccupy much conservative social analysis. For 'the conservative attitude demands the persistence of a civil order' (Scruton, 1980, p.27). It is not a civil order/society understood – as in liberal thought – as ultimately based on contractual relationships between autonomous and rational individuals. Society is not seen in that way by conservative thinkers. Instead, for a conservative like **Roger Scruton**[28] a society has to be understood as ultimately natural in origin, as a complex social phenomenon bound together by relationships of authority, by bonds of allegiance and, and by powerful traditions and customs. Since society exists 'objectively as it were, outside the sphere of individual choice', it – and not the individuals subject to it – becomes for conservatives the key object of study and the key concern of politics. To a man like Scruton, 'there is, to put it bluntly, something deeply self-deceiving in the [liberal] idea of a fulfilled human being whose style of life is entirely of his own devising' (Scruton, 1980, pp.37–8). Instead individuals are 'stamped permanently' by the society they inherit; and because they are, the 'customs, traditions and common culture' of that society 'become ruling conceptions' of thought and action (ibid, p.38).

[28]**Roger Scruton**: b.1944. Professor of Aesthetics at Birkbeck College, University of London. Editor of *The Salisbury Review* and author of, among other works, *Art and Imagination* (1974), *The Meaning of Conservatism* (1980), *From Descartes to Wittgenstein* (1981), *The Politics of Culture* (1981), *The Aesthetic Understanding* (1983), *Thinkers of the New Left* (1985), and *Sexual Desire* (1986).

Summary

1   Conservative attitudes to industrialization changed over time: from initial hostility to eventual advocacy of market forces. Conservatism no longer possesses any developed and distinctive economic theory of its own.

2   Conservatives recognize the inevitability of social inequality and the necessarily organic nature of all complex societies. They accordingly attach importance to leadership and to the maintenance of social order.

Power and the state

Such conservative beliefs in the frailty of human nature and the complexity of human society have prompted a particular reading of the nature of power in industrial societies. Conservative thinkers have had relatively little to say about the power relationships between men and women, and this silence is indicative of a general propensity among conservatives to see the family, and the relationships within it, as natural in origin, and as so basic to society as to require preservation in their existing forms.

Conservative thinkers have been prepared, however, to grant a role to the state which is rather different to that canvassed in any of the other traditions considered here. The conservative sense of mutual responsibilities has often sustained a concern for the provision of welfare – a Tory paternalism. Such paternalism has not derived from any developed sense of universal human rights, but has been rooted more in the belief that traditionally privileged institutions and groups have a duty to render assistance as well as leadership to less privileged strata beneath. This attitude is very visible in Coleridge's belief that the maintenance of an organic society required that the state play a more active role than liberalism allowed – to guarantee a minimum standard of living to all citizens, and extensive education to 'develop those faculties which are essential to his humanity – that is, to his rational and moral being' (O'Sullivan, 1976, p.88). Similar attitudes are evident in Disraeli's willingness to use state power to create 'One Nation', and in the willingness of more recent conservative thinkers to support the welfare state.

For conservatism has rarely opposed state action, or even state-led reform, in total. It is the pace and character of such reform which has preoccupied conservative thought. Conservative thinkers have resisted radical change as 'leaps in the dark', preferring instead either no change at all or a return to the past (among reactionary strands of conservatism), or, more normally, orderly, incremental and controlled change that did not profoundly alter the basic structures of inherited power and rank. Conservative thought has, then, given a particularly central role to *political leadership* as the orchestrator of ordered change; and has preferred to keep that leadership in the hands of those who – by birth, background and training – were decreed 'best fit to govern'.

Conservative thought has always treated the state as a key social institution and 'government as the primary need of every man subject to the discipline of social intercourse' (Scruton, 1980, p.19). Scruton at least has been prepared to argue that 'one major difference between conservatism and liberalism consists . . . in the fact that, for the conservative, the value of individual liberty is not absolute, but stands subject to another and higher value, the authority of established government' (ibid, p.19). Equally conservatives have always tended to see governing as a specific and limited activity, and have attached greater importance to the character of its activity than to its content. According to a modern conservative like Michael Oakeshott, there is a definite style of governing which is preferable to the conservative mind. It is a style appropriate to the role of government as umpire rather than as innovator. Government is not something to be used 'as an instrument of passion', Its task rather is to 'inject into the activities of already too passionate men an ingredient of moderation'. The role of government is to 'restrain, to deflate, to pacify and to reconcile; not to stoke the fires of desire but to dampen them down'. (Oakeshott, 1962, p.192).

On this view, the task of those who govern us is not 'to impose favourite projects upon their fellows'. It is to restrict themselves to 'the provision and custody of general rules of conduct . . . enabling people to pursue the activities of their own choice with the minimum of frustration'. These general rules of conduct constitute a body of law which embody 'as for a conservative it must embody, the fundamental values of the society which it aims to rule' (Scruton, 1980, p.17). It is about these rules that Oakeshott believes 'it is appropriate to be conservative' (*op. cit.* p.184).

Such a set of orientations has generated a steady if limited stream of social analysis, none of it particularly major in its innovative force, but all of it cumulatively sustaining a distinct set of analytical categories and concerns. If liberalism released into western social thought the category of the rational individual, the market and the limited state, and if marxism has given us the capitalist mode of production, classes and revolutionary change, then conservative thought has added to that repertoire notions of the organic society, of tradition and inequality, and has insisted on the importance of continuity and social order as key objects of study.

Summary

1   Conservative thinkers tend to treat the family as a natural institution, and to leave unexamined the gender relationships within them.

2   Conservative thinkers give an important role to the state as a guarantor of social order and of minimum standards. Conservatives attach central importance to the maintenance of political authority and to the rule of law. They do not look to the state for grandiose schemes of social improvement.

3   The presence of the traditions in the study of society

The individual disciplines that today constitute social science are, in the main, recent creations, products of an academic division of labour that has emerged only in the last hundred years. Their subject matter and – more importantly for our purposes – their theoretical frameworks have a much longer history: but their separate study, by individuals labelling themselves as particular kinds of social scientists (or indeed even as social scientists at all), came only with the establishment and proliferation in the nineteenth and twentieth centuries of a new generation of universities on the continent of Europe, in North America, and here in the United Kingdom. Before then – in the older universities, the dissenting colleges and among self-financing private scholars – attempts to analyse society wandered relatively freely across what later were to be discipline boundaries, with inquiries on, say, moral philosophy also stimulating observations by the same writer on history, politics, economics and psychology. Adam Smith, for example, though now canonized as an economist, was by profession a Professor of Logic and Moral Philosophy at Glasgow University, whose other major work (beyond *The Wealth of Nations*) was *The Theory of Moral Sentiments*. Equally, John Stuart Mill's major text on economics, published in 1848, actually carried the full title of *Principles of Political Economy with some of their Applications to Social Philosophy*, and he wrote widely, as we have seen, on other matters as disparate as logic and liberty.

Yet with the advantage of hindsight, it is possible to see some pattern in the tides of thought that preceded and precipitated the emergence of separate social science disciplines in the second half of the nineteenth century. Until the Renaissance re-introduced classical non-Christian thought into western culture, late medieval writings on social life operated almost exclusively within a religious framework. But with the disintegration of Catholic dominance of European thought in the Reformation, and with the parallel rise of strong nation states, a space was created for more secular reflections on the nature of human society, and on the role of government within it. That space was initially filled (in the seventeenth century) with writings that we would now see as *moral philosophy* and *political theory*, and with the first tentative explorations of the emerging *natural sciences*. By the eighteenth century, the rise of a Protestant capitalism out of a feudal and a Catholic Europe had moved Europe's intellectual centre of gravity from Italy to northern Europe; and had obliged northern political philosophers to examine a range of questions that we now recognize as distinctly *economic* in character. A century later still, the urbanization and social tensions created by that spread of capitalism had laid the agenda for the quite separate disciplines of *sociology* and *geography*. *Psychology* as a recognizably separate discipline really only flourished after 1870, its growth and application stimulated partly by the traumas of modern war, and more significantly by the consolidation − first in North America and later in Europe − of well-funded universities keen to foster high-quality discipline specialization.

So it is possible to trace the emergence of different social science disciplines in this sequential way, and to see that there is at least some connection *between* the way academic activity was reorganized and broad changes in the world it sought to understand. But the relationship between the academy and the world also coloured broad developments *within* the disciplines themselves. Each generation of practising social scientists faced a particular climate of intellectual opinion and a particular set of overriding concerns; these too affected the trajectories of their work, and the relative importance to them of the traditions of thought that we are considering here.

Much mid-nineteenth century social thought in the United Kingdom, as we have seen, was overwhelmingly liberal in its premises, and optimistic about the capacity of human reason to shape a better world. Much late-nineteenth century social thought was not: demonstrating instead that general disillusionment with the idea of progress and the nature of industrialism that touched every major form of cultural production around 1900, from art to literature and music. The roots of that disillusionment with the liberal project lay partly in the intensification of international competition, and in the growing threat of large-scale international war; but it lay too in the way that the rise of large and militant labour movements disturbed the middle class calm of the liberal intellectual world. Many leading intellectuals of the 'generation of the 1890s' − including Weber and **Freud**[29] − shared a common interest in the role of irrational forces in human personality and social history, and an apprehension about the ability of capitalism and democracy to guarantee property and peace. If the spirit of optimism remained to that generation, it became the property of the marxists, who still believed that history was a story of progress, specifically the progress of the proletariat towards a propertyless communism.

Inter-war political and social thought was then dominated by the twin concerns of irrationalism and marxism that had bedevilled the 1890s liberals: by the marxist question (recast between the wars to that of whether all industrial societies must follow the Soviet route to communism) and by the question of the irrational in politics (of whether the only alternative to communism was the abandonment of liberal democracy to the excesses of fascism). It took the defeat of fascism in World War II to re-establish the confidence of those who sought a middle way between these two extremes, a confidence which was then bolstered after 1945 by the growing evidence of the tyranny that lurked behind the mask of marxism in the Soviet bloc. In intellectual terms, the Cold War years of the 1950s were

[29]**Sigmund Freud**: 1856−1939. Austrian psychologist,the originator of psychoanalysis. Author of, among other works, *The Interpretation of Dreams* (1900), *Totem and Taboo* (1918) and *The Ego and the Id* (1927).

dominated in the West by social reformist ways of thinking: Keynesian in economics, democratic in politics, new liberal in basic values; and for a while it did genuinely appear that only the anachronistic remained marxist, only the reactionary remained conservative. But with the decay of social and political stability in the West after 1968 – with the American defeat in Vietnam, student and worker protest in Western Europe, and generalized world recession after 1973 – a revitalized marxism began to appeal once more to a new generation of intellectuals, and liberal critiques of managed capitalism became respectable again in academic circles for the first time since the war. All of which merely served to demonstrate the tenacity of our four traditions of thought within twentieth-century social science; and to make clear the way in which the importance of any one tradition rose and fell with circumstances: with the coming and going of war and peace, poverty and prosperity, consensus and conflict.

Yet even when we recognize this *general* presence of the traditions within social science, we need a sense too of their differential impact on *each* discipline. To do that, this time we will start with psychology, and then work back through the other disciplines in turn.

As we have now seen, '*psychology*, in the sense of reflection upon the nature and activities of mind, is a very ancient discipline' (Murphy, 1967, p.x). Psychology as a specialized academic discipline, however, is not. Only in the last hundred years have university departments of psychology proliferated, and recognizable spheres of applied psychology (educational, industrial, clinical, criminal) come into existence. The centre of gravity of modern psychology is experimental, not philosophical. Its contemporary concerns derive as much from its origins in the biological sciences, and from its involvement in localized research projects, as from its connections to western traditions of thought; and the scale of research activity by professional psychologists now is such as to give the discipline its own internal history and set of concerns. Yet many of those projects – particularly in the field of applied psychology – do take up the concerns of social reformism; and histories of modern psychology still tend to start, as we did, with the intellectual rediscovery of Greece and Rome in the Renaissance, and with the writings on human nature, the human mind and human knowledge of important early liberal thinkers – particularly Hobbes and Locke. For modern psychology is still exploring, among other things, a range of questions that we have met before. Is the mind a blank space to be filled by sense data, as Locke argued? Is human action driven by the power to reason, as liberal thought suggested; or do non-rational processes play a major (or even a determining) role in human thought and action? Is human nature heavily conditioned by environmental forces: by education and social circumstances, as Bentham and Mill believed; or even by the alienating experience of a class-divided society, as marxism would imply? Or do such views ignore innate, irrevocable dimensions of human personality and character that are fixed by natural forces beyond our control, as conservative modes of thought might suggest?

The concerns of social psychology stretch out to encompass questions of culture and self-definition, and on this interface to coincide with the interests of *sociology* as a discipline. Liberal thought did not place great emphasis on the role of ideas in social stability and change; but each of the other traditions has had important things to say on the origins and social consequences of ideas. Conservative thought has long recognized the importance of traditional systems of belief as guarantors of social order; and by the 1950s a conservative sociology was in place that treated societies as 'normatively integrated' – held together by shared sets of understandings and values. Intellectuals within the tradition of social reformism have been prepared to recognize that this integration could be a socially constructed one, reflective of power relationships within the society so stabilized. They have often talked of dominant value systems and of subordinate ones; and in doing so have come close to a marxist notion of ruling ideologies as instruments of class power.

More generally, the emergence of sociology as an academic discipline towards the end of the nineteenth century coincided with the emergence of social reformism as a recognizably distinct tradition of thought. The impulse to analyse social problems in order to solve them inspired early pieces of sociological research (not least on the character and causes of poverty in industrial capitalism); whilst many of the major thinkers now listed as 'founding fathers' of sociology were 'new liberal' in their politics. Conservative concerns with social order, and their emphasis on traditional institutions as guarantors of social stability, also remain a major focus for sociology as a discipline, as does the social reformist and marxist preoccuption with the character and pace of social change.

Economics as an academic discipline continues to give central importance to liberal-based interpretations of the market. Many modern economists would claim to be 'neo-classical' rather than 'classical' in their analyses of modern economies, and put *both* David Ricardo and Karl Marx into the classical camp (because of their acceptance of labour as the source of value and price). Contemporary economics prefers normally to approach the determination of the prices at which goods exchange by analysing the interplay of supply and demand, eschewing the labour theory of value in favour of theories that tie price-determination more closely to shifts in consumer preferences than 'classical' economics (of both a liberal and a marxist kind) allowed. But in spite of this, neo-classical economics remains the main bearer of liberal ideas into twentieth-century social science, where they are challenged – if at all – only by a strong current of social reformist economics associated with John Maynard Keynes. There is no distinctly 'conservative' corpus of economic theory that is distinguishable from pro-market liberalism; and though there is a definite marxist alternative to mainstream economics, it tends to be marginalized in most British and North American university departments, evident there only in the form of optional courses on radical economics.

Political science has long been shaped by the competing claims of the four traditions of thought discussed here. Much of contemporary political science is institutional in its focus, concerned with analysing the ways in which the machinery of government works: and these studies rarely trigger debate between the traditions. But political scientists are concerned too with how electorates behave, and how power is distributed in contemporary societies; and in those studies clear liberal, reformist, marxist and conservative positions can be found.

288

And of course the other face of political science, and its older one indeed, involves the study of political theory. Hobbes, Locke, Bentham, Mill, Marx and Burke all occupy important places on the syllabus of degrees in political science: and their insights on state power still fuel an important contemporary debate on the character of modern state power.

Finally, the study of *geography* also shows clear signs of the presence of the four traditions of thought. Cartography and trade grew together; and the skills of the geographer were highlighted by exploration and imperial expansion in the nineteenth century and by the needs of war in the twentieth. When geography emerged as a university discipline in the UK after 1880, the bulk of its concerns were descriptive and historical, and the theoretical frameworks that emerged in the areas of social geography were either liberal or conservative in character. They drew heavily on liberal political economy, explaining the location of communities and economic activities as the products of rational calculations of an individualist kind; and to a lesser degree they drew on conservative interpretations of Darwin's theory of evolution to explore the extent to which geographical arrangements were determined by competitive struggles and natural selection. Though the bulk of academic work within university departments of geography remains largely empirical in focus, and eschews participation in wider intellectual debate, schools of welfare geography and radical geography have emerged recently: the first working 'within the framework of the existing economic and social system', the latter more openly commited to 'both revolutionary theory and revolutionary practice' (Holt-Jenson, 1980, p.72). So social reformist and marxist ideas are represented in contemporary geography, as are ideas more obviously derived from liberal and conservative ways of thinking.

Summary

1   Contemporary disciplines in the social sciences are of recent origin, but the concerns of those disciplines are of much longer standing.

2   Social changes since the fifteenth century have shaped the agenda of social analysis in recognizable ways: stimulating the emergence of particular disciplines, and giving changing sets of concerns to successive generations of scholars, regardless of their discipline.

3   The dominance of particular traditions of thought within individual disciplines has reflected the ebb and flow of war and peace, poverty and prosperity, conflict and consensus.

4   It is possible to discern the presence of the four traditions in each of the individual disciplines in the social sciences: in psychology, sociology, economics, political science and geography.

4 The presence of the traditions in the society to be studied

We have now traced the emergence and character of four major traditions of social thought, and discussed their impact on twentieth-century social science. By way of pulling the argument together, it is worth noting in conclusion the twin presence of these bodies of thought in any social science course – not just in the categories and theories of social science which such courses use, but also in their subject matter. Since this can be a source of considerable confusion, it is worth clarifying this second 'face' of the traditions in the concluding section of this essay.

The four traditions of thought at which we have looked did more than influence the thinking of the social sciences. They also inspired political parties, influenced whole social movements, and left residues of their ways of thinking in popular culture and consciousness. Since social science now studies political parties, movements and culture, the bodies of thought therefore reappear as an *object* of study, as well as an influence on the way social objects (including themselves) are studied.

This is most obvious in the case of liberalism as a body of social thought. The new thinking of the nineteenth century – with its focus on the individual, its faith in science, its insistence on the gathering of empirical data, its association of freedom with the absence of state restraint, and its confidence in the desirability of capital and the efficiency of markets – this new thinking came to dominate every area of social life: first science, then economics, and then by 1850, in Britain at least, popular politics and culture too. By then, all other forms of social thought appeared to be in retreat before an onslaught of popular liberalism; and the liberal connections (of freedom with lack of restraint, of the market with neutrality, and so on) entered popular consciousness in a very deep way. Indeed liberal ideas became so much the common sense of the age that it became difficult to recognize them as ideas at all. They were just common sense, the terms of reference within which the vast majority of late-Victorian public figures thought and spoke. The term 'liberalism' then became uncoupled from its own ideas-system, and was appropriated instead as the possession of one particular party – that formed in the 1860s under the leadership of Gladstone. To be a Liberal thereafter (and notice the capital 'L' begins to appear) was to hold a political allegiance, and not just to subscribe to a particular way of analysing the world.

Yet in truth liberal ideas shaped the thinking of both the Conservative Party and later the Labour Party with which Gladstone's Liberals clashed. Indeed the legacy of liberal thought, as we saw, was an ambiguous and contradictory one, involving *both* a faith in property *and* a commitment to the basic equality of people.

290

In party terms, that liberal legacy split organizationally after 1916, sending many pro-property Liberals off to the Conservative Party, and the more egalitarian-minded off to Labour. We thus need to distinguish the rise and fall of the *Liberal Party* from the more general rise and dissemination of *liberal ideas* in the society as a whole. In other words, if we are to grasp the importance of liberal ways of thinking, we need to extract liberal thought from the consequences of its own success. We need to drag it back from its status as the common sense of the late-Victorian age, and from its role as the inspirer of a major political party, and see it again as a body of thought – as one among many – which has influenced and continues to influence political parties and social movements of many kinds.

The problem of maintaining a clear distinction between traditions of thought and political parties is equally evident in the cases of conservatism and social reformism. Social reformism as a body of thought emerged alongside, not just social science, but also contemporary centre and centre-left political parties in advanced industrial societies. Its theories clearly invited a kind of politics – moderate, reforming, humane – which came to dominate Western Europe for a generation after 1945. Tory 'wets', Liberals and Labourites all came to trace their politics from particular pieces of social science analysis – particularly from the wartime Beveridge Report and Keynes' *General Theory* of 1936. So there is a very intimate connection between major pieces of social reformist thinking and certain forms of state action; and that connection is evident at many points.

Conservatism is more difficult, because of the longevity of the Conservative Party in England, and because of its flexibility on doctrine over time. But even here, once we grasp that flexibility, problems fall away. The Conservative Party since 1975 has been a fusion of old conservative values (of the kind laid out under 'conservatism' as a tradition of thought above) and of a revitalized liberalism of the Adam Smith variety. Indeed it is that fusion of two bodies of thought that both gives the clue to the nature of Conservative government in recent times, and demonstrates the value of first separating bodies of thought. Just reflect for a moment on this description of the Conservative Party under Margaret Thatcher:

> Thatcherism brilliantly *combines* within a single political ideology an organic conservative emphasis on the values of tradition, family, monarchy, patriarchy, and nation with a neo-liberal emphasis on the gospel of the free market, the laws of supply and demand, the private economy, value for money, and the private sphere of the citizen against the 'creeping socialist' threats to liberty from an overweening state and an overextended state welfare system. The first, organic, half of this ideological formation draws directly on the ancient repertoire of conservatism; the second neo-liberal half derives, directly, from the free market and libertarian traditions of classical liberalism and political economy.
>
> (Hall, 1986, p.67)

What we are seeing here is that bodies of thought exist at many levels in contemporary society. They exist as *intellectual traditions*, which is how we have looked at them in this essay; and because they do, we can use them as a storehouse of ideas, categories and approaches, to be drawn upon in our own exercise of analysis. They also exist as *political ideologies*, as bodies of ideas associated with particular parties and social movements, spawning particular political and social programmes; and because they do, we can and will – where appropriate – analyse them as important forces in their own right, shaping the world in which we operate and which we are seeking to understand. But they also have a capacity to exist at the level of *popular consciousness*, to constitute key elements of what people take as axiomatic, as *common sense*; and they do this to the degree that political parties and social movements have managed, over a long period, to spread their ideologies so wide and deep in society that people almost lose their ability to see that they are subscribing to a coherent and particular body of theory at all. At this level, at the level of common sense, legacies of more than one intellectual tradition/political ideology will inevitably build up; and here too scholarship can be used, to isolate the components of dominant common sense, to trace the intellectual origins of those components, and to locate the historical processes by which this sedimentation takes place. The study of popular culture, that is, and of dominant ideologies, becomes one legitimate and important concern of social science; and to make that study, scholarship has to return to the *intellectual traditions* that underpin both culture and scholarship, to find a clear point from which to begin.

So traditions of thought need to be distinguished from the histories of the political activists who have used them; and that is nowhere more difficult for us to do – at this point in place and time – than when dealing with marxism. As with liberalism and its success, we need to recapture marxism from its past, though this time the overwhelming feature of that past that we need to recognize is the *failure* of marxism to oust liberal ways of thinking in the West. Marxism emerged in England, written in the British Museum as an analysis of predominantly English capitalism, and offered to the Western European proletariats as an indigenous and revolutionary body of thought. Many socialists were attracted to it in the generation before World War I, and they competed, as marxists, with other reformist forms of socialism, and with other non-socialist bodies of thought, for the political loyalty of the emerging industrial proletariats. By 1914, in every labour movement from the United States to Imperial Russia and from Japan to Britain, the same debates between various currents of socialist and non-socialist thought went on. Yet, in the event, only in Russia in 1917 did a marxist-inspired political party take and retain power; and elsewhere in Europe marxists were defeated, normally by more moderate forms of socialism inspired by the ideas of social reform. That pattern of success and failure has shaped our exposure to marxism ever since.

After 1917, Russian marxists claimed to have built a workers' state, and they appealed to revolutionary socialists elsewhere to give that state their prime loyalty. Marxists between the wars, organized in communist parties, did just that: building an association in the popular mind between the marxist and the *foreign*, and between marxism and *loyalty to a foreign power*, that has never gone away. In reality, the Russian revolution degenerated in its isolation from any sympathetic and equivalent revolutions in the more advanced West, and succumbed to the Stalinist terror; and marxism thus gathered an association with *authoritarian rule*, *excessive bureaucratization* and *economic backwardness* that it did not possess in the 1880s. Moreover, since the Stalinist terror did at least enable the Russian state to turn a peasant society into a major industrial one in half a century, Russia became a model for other peasant modernizers (in places as disparate as China, Vietnam, Cuba and Ethiopia). In this way marxism became the legitimating ideology of modernizing elites in Third World countries, and so acquired a *peasant connotation* at odds with the theory's original set of concerns with the industrial experience and political potentialities of working classes in the First World. Then, to complete the circle, after Soviet military successes against Nazism, and the growth of popular support in France and Italy for the communist-led resistance to Hitler, ruling groups in Western Europe and the United States recast the world on Cold War lines: to push into the popular consciousness of our generation the picture of a world divided between marxism as *the evil empire* and liberal capitalism as *the free world*.

Separating marxism as a tradition of thought out of all that history is even more difficult than separating liberalism from the Gladstonian Liberal Party. But separate we must, not least so that we can see what kind of analysis of the Soviet system marxism itself has to offer. In fact, we need to re-appropriate both liberalism and marxism from their own histories, and approach them afresh as *ours* – as strands in western culture available to us as we struggle to make sense of the world around us. For as bodies of thought, both liberalism and marxism (and also social reformism and conservatism) offer us total packages – whole *paradigms* – within which to approach the analysis of contemporary society. As we have seen, each is organized around a particular view of the human condition. Each has a sense of how analyses of contemporary situations ought to be undertaken, using which concepts, deploying which theories, looking for what sorts of evidence, and accepting which sorts of arguments as convincing. Each gives us, through all this, a particular prioritizing of causal forces, and a particular range and type of debate between scholars all operating within its basic assumptions and lines of march. Each, that is, is a whole analysis on its own, the product of many hours of reflection and enquiry by a series of fine minds over many generations.

In one sense, that means that we are extremely fortunate; we do not have to start from scratch. We inherit a social science universe already rich in scholarship, already marked by the development of paradigms of social thought, and by debates between and within them. So we can pick up, and live off, the puzzlings and endeavours of others; and we can benefit from the way in which time, and subsequent scholarship, has separated the wheat from the chaff, and directed us to those products of previous generations of scholarship with which we might most fruitfully begin our own enquiries. We do not have to work through the vast tomes of the second rate. That has been done for us, to give us an easier and more direct start.

However, by being in this position, we also gather tasks that earlier scholarship lacked. We are under a stronger obligation than they were to go through three stages in our consideration of the main traditions of thought passed down to us. (1) We have to come to know them in as much detail as we can manage. (2) We have to evaluate them, by applying their precepts to case after case, and by probing for their internal coherence and for the comprehensiveness of their coverage. (3) And ultimately we have to decide if any of them constitutes an adequate framework for our own analysis of the contemporary world. Then, if we find none of them entirely satisfactory, we have eventually to match them with a new framework of our own. This process of *theoretical discovery, application and evaluation* will occupy part of your time throughout your studies. In one sense we are all still engaged on it, even those of us privileged enough to have had the luxury of years of study. It is certainly not a journey that anyone completes in the space of one course in the social sciences. But it is a journey which you can begin here; and we just hope that it will be a journey as full of insight and excitement for you as it continues to be for us.

Summary

1   Traditions of thought have a presence in the society they exist to explain: as ideologies, as political movements and as common sense.

2   This is most obvious in the case of liberalism, which inspired a major political party in the United Kingdom and influenced the parties that replaced it. Conservatism and social reformism have also attached themselves to particular parties. Marxism has had its own chequered history: being linked to the Soviet Union, to political tyranny, to economic backwardness, and to one half of the Cold War.

3   We need to separate the traditions of thought from the history of parties and ideologies, and to examine them afresh as sources for our own analysis of contemporary social realities.

References

Arblaster, A. (1984) *The Rise and Decline of Western Liberalism*, Oxford, Blackwell.

Barry, N.P. (1979) *Hayek's Social and Economic Philosophy*, London and Basingstoke, Macmillan.

Brennan, T. and Pateman, C. (1979) 'Mere auxiliaries to the commonwealth: women and the origins of Liberalism', *Political Studies*, vol.XXVII(2), pp.183–200.

Coole, D. (1988) *Women in Political Theory*, Brighton, Harvester.

Duncan, G. (1973) *Marx and Mill*, Cambridge, Cambridge University Press.

Friedman, M. (1976) 'The line we dare not cross', *Encounter*, November, pp.8–14.

Gamble, A. (1979) 'The free economy and the strong state', in R. Miliband and J. Saville (eds) *The Socialist Register 1979*, London, Merlin, pp.1–25.

Hall, S. (1986) 'Varieties of liberalism'. In J. Donald and S. Hall (eds) *Politics and Ideology*, Milton Keynes, Open University Press.

Hayek, F.A. (1949) *Individualism and Economic Order*, London, Routledge and Kegan Paul.

Held, D. (1983) 'Central perspectives on the modern state', in D. Held *et al.* (eds) *States and Societies*, Oxford, Martin Robertson.

Holt-Jensen, A. (1980) *Geography: its history and concepts*, London, Harper and Row.

Keynes, J.M. (1936) *The General Theory of Employment, Interest and Money*, London and Basingstoke, Macmillan.

Kirk, R. (1978) *The Conservative Mind*, London, Gateway Editions.

Leigh, E. (1979) *Right Thinking*, London, Hutchinson.

Machlup, F. (1977) *Essays on Hayek*, London, Routledge and Kegan Paul.

Manning, D.J. (1976) *Liberalism*, London, Dent.

Murphy, G. (1967) *An Historical Introduction to Modern Psychology*, London, Routledge and Kegan Paul.

Nisbet, R. (1986) *Conservatism*, Milton Keynes, Open University Press.

Nozick, R. (1974) *Anarchy, State and Utopia*, Oxford, Blackwell.

O'Sullivan, N. (1976) *Conservatism*, London, Dent.

Oakeshott, M. (1962) *Rationalism in Politics: and other essays*, London, Methuen.

Pateman, C. (1988) *The Sexual Contract*, Cambridge, Polity Press.

Rosen, F. (1983) *Jeremy Bentham and Representative Democracy*, Oxford, Clarendon Press.

Scruton, R. (1980) *The Meaning of Conservatism*, Harmondsworth, Penguin.

Smith, A. (1776) *The Wealth of Nations* (reprinted by Penguin Books, 1970).

Southey, R. (1807) 'Birmingham' in *Letters from England* (published by The Cresset Press, 1951).

Thomas, W. (1985) *Mill*, New York, Oxford University Press.

Thompson, D.F. (1976) *John Stuart Mill and Representative Government*, Princeton, Princeton Universtiy Press.

Wollstonecraft, M. (1792) *A Vindication of the Rights of Woman* (published by Penguin, 1975).

Personal acknowledgements

I would like to acknowledge the help of Penny Muter, Donna Dickenson, Diana Coole and the D103 Course Team in the preparation of this chapter.

Appendix

This Reader forms an integral part of the foundation course in Social Science (**D103: Society and Social Science: A Foundation Course**) at the Open University. It is a broad, interdisciplinary course and, although it has a coherence of its own, it is also designed to give students a 'taste' of each of the diciplines of Sociology, Economics, Political Science, Psychology and Geography. It prepares students for higher-level courses in their chosen BA degree programme. Though some chapters were specially written for this Reader, most are drawn from already published sources – books and articles. This is to enable students to gain confidence in working with a variety of academic texts and to sharpen critical skills. Opinions expressed in this Reader, then, are not necessarily those of the course team or of the university.

D103 consists of seven 'blocks' of printed course material, sixteen 50-minute TV programmes, sixteen radio programmes, seven audio-cassettes, plus several items of supplementary written material. For students with disabilities, all these materials will be available in different forms (e.g. on audio tape for those with sight problems). The course begins with an investigation of the production and consumption of food both at home and abroad. It then moves on to examine the major divisions of class, gender and ethnicity in UK society, investigating how people's experiences differ depending on these divisions. The UK economy comes under the spotlight in the next block where work, both paid and unpaid, is discussed followed by a look at how markets operate and the role of governments in relation to them both nationally and internationally. The course then focuses on politics and power and poses questions about what is meant by concepts such as 'national sovereignty' and 'democracy'.

The course doesn't only address 'structural' questions around the economy and the state. It is also concerned with how people themselves shape, and are shaped by, the society in which they live. This is the subject of the fifth block entitled 'Identities and Interaction'. The sixth block discusses regional identities and investigates the interplay of local and global forces on the different regions as the UK's role in the world has changed.

Throughout the course, students will learn about theories from the various disciplines, and about the methods and procedures involved in doing social science. They will also study the four traditions discussed in Part 2 of this Reader, guided by other course material. The final block will focus on the traditions and how they are applied to contemporary society by four practising social scientists who work within each tradition.

No previous educational qualifications are required to register as an undergraduate on D103. For students returning to study after a long gap, there is specific material in the course texts designed to brush up and enhance study skills such as note-taking and essay writing. One of the set books for the course is devoted entirely to improving such skills. It is entitled *The Good Study Guide* by Andrew Northedge (published by the Open Univesity, 1990), and is available from all bookshops.

If you would like more information on D103, or any other Open University course, please write to: Central Enquiry Service, P.O. Box 625, The Open University, Walton Hall, Milton Keynes, MK1 1TY.

Index